Barry Norman's
FILM GREATS

Barry Norman's
FILM GREATS

WHSMITH
EXCLUSIVE
· BOOKS ·

All colour photographs supplied by the Kobal Collection.

The black and white photographs were supplied by:
Associated Press, p 147; BBC Hulton Picture Library, p 87; The
Bodley Head, p 24; Camera Press Ltd, pp 133, 141, 215; Columbia
Pictures, p 211; The Kobal Collection, pp 15, 19, 25, 26, 39, 83, 90,
124, 131, 136, 139 (top and bottom), 143, 149, 157, 163, 165, 167,
169, 172 (bottom), 175, 177, 183, 202, 203, 205, 206, 219, 231;
MGM, pp 29, 32, 36, 39, 43, 49, 53, 55, 57, 58, 61, 63, 97, 98, 99,
100, 102, 103, 189; The Napthine-Walsh Collections, p 129;
National Film Archives, p 226; National Telefilm Association,
p 155; The Photo Source, pp 22, 23, 227, 235; Popperfoto, pp 11,
17, 69, 71, 74, 78, 107, 123, 170, 171, 172 (top); Ronald Howard,
p 150; RKO Pictures, p 193; Rex Features, pp 199, 233; Warner
Bros., p 213.

ISBN 0 340 39450 1

This edition published 1986 by W. H. Smith & Son
By arrangement with Hodder and Stoughton Limited, Mill Road,
Dunton Green, Sevenoaks, Kent TN13 2YJ.
Hodder and Stoughton Editorial Office: 47 Bedford Square, London WC1B 3DP.

Photoset by Rowland Phototypesetting Limited, Bury St Edmunds, Suffolk.

Printed in Italy by L.E.G.O., Vicenza.

Contents

Introduction

In the Golden Age of Hollywood, said Joan Fontaine one day, the serious question that the stars would sit around discussing earnestly among themselves was: "What shall we do with all the money *this* week?" Buy a yacht perhaps, move to a bigger house, charter a plane and fly off somewhere exotic for the weekend? She thought the Golden Age lasted from about 1935 to 1945, although in fact you could stretch it a bit by adding on a few years at either end. This was the time when the stars had the security of long-term contracts at thousands of dollars a week and virtually no income tax to pay. Of course the security was by no means total: the contracts contained options that could be exercised by the studio, and only by the studio, every six or twelve months and suspension clauses, which meant that a recalcitrant star who, say, refused to play a certain part in a certain film could be placed on suspension without pay until such time as he/she begged for forgiveness or his/her guilt was thought to have been expurgated. But if all the options were taken up, which they usually were, and suspension was avoided, which was easily done if you were equipped (as most stars were) with the throat of a boa constrictor and could swallow vast lumps of pride without damage to your digestive system, the only problem that remained was: "What shall we do with all the money *this* week?"

The introduction of talking pictures, warding off the threat of radio which had begun to supplant silent movies as the most popular form of mass entertainment, heralded the start of the Golden Age; the introduction of television on a huge scale killed it. But in that interim period of twenty years or so Hollywood was a place such as had never existed before and could not possibly exist again. It was, in truth, a Dream Factory. And though its activities were, as somebody once said, akin to putting the skin on baloney it nevertheless made the American Dream come true for young actors and actresses possessed of good looks, charm, possibly talent and that indefinable commodity called "star quality"; and it created dreams on an assembly line – sometimes as many as 800 films a year – for those in the audience who lacked the imagination to dream for themselves. It could be argued that to an extent first radio and then television took over those functions but never so comprehensively and never on such a grand scale.

All the people whose lives and careers are examined in this book had some experience of the Golden Age; Chaplin indeed pre-dated it and was still around at the death. Then came the new kind of star, like Steve McQueen; he burst through to prominence and superstardom by way of television and without the aid of the studio system and its policy of careful grooming. And that raises quite an interesting point. Today when the cinema, especially in Britain, is struggling to find an audience it's common to hear people say, "Well, there aren't the stars there used to be." And that's partly true: there are not certainly as many stars but then there are not as many films being made. And there are not the studios and the long-term contracts to build a star. Therefore it could be argued that the comparative few who exist today are actually bigger stars than their predecessors because they have achieved stardom (not too difficult, given the luck of the right film at the right time) and maintained it (much harder to do) without the corporate aid of a huge organisation.

From the time I first started investigating "The Hollywood Greats" on behalf of BBC TV (and that was back in 1977) the question I've been asked most frequently is: "Ah yes, but who could you possibly find to make such documentaries about in twenty years' time?" Well, the answer is easy; right off the top of my head I can think of Brando, Newman, Redford, Eastwood, Streisand, Streep, Hoffman, de Niro, Pacino, Jane Fonda, Woody Allen – all of whom would certainly qualify. And what about Kirk Douglas, Burt Lancaster and Burt Reynolds? Or, looking slightly more to the future, Jessica Lange, Kathleen Turner, Michael Douglas and, I suspect, at least one or two of the new generation of "movie brats" whose names are not at the moment on many people's lips but will be in twenty years' time?

The fact is that it's not studios or producers or directors who make stars: it's the public, the cinema audience. Samuel Goldwyn once spent a fortune and several years trying to build a beautiful Russian-born actress named Anna Sten into a star to rival Garbo and Darryl F. Zanuck did much the same thing with such of his girl friends as Juliette Greco and Bella Darvi. But it didn't work because the public rejected these people; it knew instinctively that however beautiful they might be they didn't have star quality, "that little something extra" as Ellen Terry described it in the best definition I've yet come across.

The people in this book, however, most emphatically did have star quality. Many of their contemporaries might have amounted to nothing without the backing of their studios but these would have been stars at any time and in any place and in any circumstances. They might not necessarily have been very nice people (I doubt if Chaplin or Crawford were, for example) and they might not all have been very good actors. But in every case they had whatever it is that the public wants in its heroes and heroines and that is something that seems to transcend time or place or the fashion in looks. In this era of lean, "natural-looking" women Monroe, for instance, with her voluptuous curves, heavily dyed hair and emphatic make-up is almost archaic. And yet she is a star for any age, as great a star indeed as Hollywood ever produced. Or, come to that, will produce.

Now you may well ask why I chose the fourteen subjects here under review. Why not Garbo or Dietrich or Barbara Stanwyck, Bette Davis, Olivia de Havilland or one of the young stars I mentioned earlier? Well, quite bluntly, Garbo and the others are still alive (and long may they remain so) while my fourteen are all dead. No, hang on. Kindly remove that cynical curve from your lip. I am not in the business of literary grave-robbing or libelling the dead, who cannot answer back. The fact that the people whose lives I have looked into in my television documentaries and the books which are a more detailed extension of those documentaries are late greats is due to an historical accident. In my first TV series when I investigated the likes of Gable and Flynn my initial interest was prompted by the fact that these were people whose stardom dated back pretty well to the introduction of talking pictures. In other words, they were around at the very beginning of the Golden Age and had helped to create it. The fact that they were all dead was therefore not terribly surprising since I was looking at people who, for the most part, were already in their thirties nearly fifty years ago. But in the course of my researches and interviews for that first series I stumbled across two things, one of which *was* surprising while the other was fairly obvious. The first was that people are much franker – which is not to say salacious, sensational or spiteful – about their friends when they are dead than they would be if those friends were still alive. Biographies (even biographical sketches such as those in this book) of living people tend at best to be careful, at worst to eulogise. Thus if I had been writing about Marilyn Monroe while she was still alive any reference to her problem with drugs or her relationships with Jack and Bobby Kennedy would have had to be excluded because nobody, including Monroe, would have talked about them. Quite right, too, you might say: it was nobody's business but hers. Yet on the other hand some knowledge of all these things is crucial to any understanding of her life and death. And the prime motive behind the documentaries and the biographical essays that resulted from them was an attempt on my part to get as close as possible to the truth about and an understanding of the people involved.

Obviously I was interested in their

careers, for it was these that first attracted my attention. But much more was I curious about their personalities, their characters. How did they become stars, what did they do when they were stars, how did stardom affect them and those close to them? And that, in a way, brings us to the second, unsurprising fact that I discovered in that first TV series, namely that if you are indeed attempting to look closely at the life and career of somebody else it's only possible to achieve anything like a full picture when both life and career are over. Hence the "late greats".

I cannot claim to have known any of the people in this book, although I met some but not by any means all of them. I met Gable when I was about twenty-two and he was near the end of his life and he had just stepped off a flight from Los Angeles and shocked the young prig that I was by insisting on drinking brandy when I thought coffee would be more appropriate. I met John Wayne and enraged him by arguing politics with him. I met Crosby and Fonda and was charmed by them both in a way that, I now realise, might have astonished some people who knew them far better and more intimately. I once sat quite close to Marilyn Monroe in a London theatre and yearned for her in life even more than I did when she was on screen. In one way or another I admired all these people, for what they did if not for what they were. But – and I think it's important to point this out – I was not and never have been starstruck. It was my great good fortune to be brought up in a house where film making was the family business. My father, Leslie

Norman, produced such films as *The Cruel Sea* and *Mandy* and directed others like *The Night My Number Came Up, Dunkirk* and *The Shiralee*, which Peter Finch regarded as his favourite among all the films he made. As a result I have known actors, actresses and film technicians all my life and though sometimes I have been impressed by them I have never been overawed by them. What that means, I hope, is that I can look upon the stars – even the loftiest stars – in the knowledge that in the end they are only people and that, no matter what the publicity may have claimed, they are no more able to walk on water than you or I. So while there is no deliberate iconoclasm here, there are no eulogies either. I believe that what I have written in this book is as close to the truth as I could possibly have come.

One last thought. To quote Joan Fontaine again: "The only trouble with Hollywood is that you know you're running out of it. You go right through it and out the other end. It's not a cul-de-sac." Everyone I discuss here ran through Hollywood and out the other end and most of them emerged clutching a satisfactory bundle of loot. But most of them, too, bore the scars of the scourging and flagellations they were subjected to on the way. Stardom in the movies is largely a question of survival and nobody ever survived in Hollywood without a ration of pain and suffering. And perhaps that was necessary. For without it they may never have achieved that bizarre form of immortality that true movie stardom bestows.

Charlie Chaplin

I must begin with a confession: I have hardly ever laughed at Charlie Chaplin. I admire him enormously. I admire his grace, his ingenuity, his daring and his timing. I can sit awed and amazed at what he does on the screen. But he hardly ever makes me laugh.

Chaplin is generally regarded as a genius. Now this is a much-abused word too often applied to those whose abilities raise them fractionally above the mediocre, but in Chaplin's case it seems wholly appropriate. He *was* a genius, one of perhaps three undoubted geniuses the cinema has produced (the others being D. W. Griffith and Eisenstein). He was a genuine innovator who stretched the boundaries of what was possible in films. Almost every comic routine you ever see in pictures owes its origins to Chaplin and technically nobody has ever performed those routines better than he, although I believe others have performed them to greater comic effect.

I think it's the deliberate, carefully calculated pathos that destroys Chaplin's humour for me. He insists that you laugh at and cry for him virtually at the same time and it's too much to ask. Not that I object to pathos: there's a good deal of it in the work of Laurel and Hardy and I have been known to laugh at them so hard and for so long that people have refused to sit near me in cinemas. There is pathos in Stan's trusting simplicity and in Ollie's vast, pretentious dignity. But this is an understated pathos stemming from the fact that, come what may, this totally lovable, totally fallible odd couple are among the world's losers.

Chaplin's pathos is a colder, harder commodity. "Look at me," he says. "I'm the downtrodden Little Fellow, just like you.

Weep for me, weep for yourself." But, in fact, he's not so downtrodden; he's not just like you and me at all. Chaplin's Little Fellow has a core of steel and in the end he always wins. He may not always get the girl but getting the girl isn't necessarily the ultimate objective in life. Failure to get her and being obliged to shuffle off alone down a straight, dusty road towards a new adventure may be cause for disappointment but it's not tragedy; it's not even truly pathos, though Chaplin would have us believe it is.

Besides, before we reach the long, lonely fade-out, Chaplin has won all the really important battles. All the villains, the big, fat, nasty men who have humiliated him and knocked him about, have had their come-uppance at his hands. Like a shabby James Bond, he invariably, inevitably metes out retribution to those who deserve it. Chaplin, in fact, is a winner disguised as a loser. Therefore I see no cause to weep for him and his demand that I should do so alienates me enough to make it difficult for me to laugh at him either.

And yet the man was a genius and, as is often the way, one who sprang from a most improbable source. He was born in Walworth, South London, on April 16th, 1889. Walworth at that time was a warm, teeming, poor community, rich in humanity perhaps but by no means in worldly goods and Chaplin's parents were as hard up as anyone else.

They differed from most of their neighbours, however, in that they were both in show business, Charles Chaplin Sr. being a ballad singer and his wife, Hannah, a singer and dancer. At one time Charles Sr., who came from an anglicised French Protestant family, was reasonably well established. He had appeared often in

Charlie in 1918 and already earning 10,000 dollars a week.

Europe and once in New York but if he was good at singing he was even better at drinking and most of the family income was dedicated to this hobby. Hannah, who had once appeared in a Gilbert and Sullivan production, was of part-Irish, part-gipsy descent and at the time Charlie was born already had a four-year-old son, Sydney, by a former marriage to one Sidney Hawkes, though probably for reasons of general tidiness and family solidarity young Sydney went under the name of Sydney Chaplin.

When Charlie was a year old his father walked out on wife and children and thereafter played no significant role in their lives. Indeed, by the time he was thirty-seven he was dead of dropsy. Meanwhile, Hannah was left in fairly dire straits. Recurrent attacks of laryngitis ruined her attempts to revive her music-hall career and she was reduced to earning what she could as a part-time dressmaker and part-time nurse. At the age of four, Charlie occasionally contributed to the family income by dancing for pennies outside the local pubs.

It was Hannah who had taught him to dance and it was from Hannah that he inherited the gift of mimicry. It was also Hannah who, aspiring even in adversity to something better in life, insisted that however poor they might be, her sons' speech and manners should be those of gentlefolk. Adversity was a constant companion at that time, for Hannah's sight began to fail her too, and in 1896 she was so destitute that she and her boys ended up in the Lambeth workhouse.

Now from such appalling beginnings, which sound remarkably like the opening chapters of some Victorian melodrama, it might be assumed that young Chaplin's life could only get better. But in fact it got worse. Having left the workhouse some months before, Hannah had a mental breakdown and was committed to a lunatic asylum and Charlie was returned to the workhouse.

Undoubtedly such early hardship had a most profound effect upon him and he described it brilliantly in the first, and far more fascinating, half of his autobiography. But his son Sydney was not entirely convinced that life was quite as bad as his father had remembered it.

He talked about his childhood, said Sydney Chaplin, "all the time" and what he talked about mostly was "the poverty. That impressed him. I mean, in his work and everything that impressed him. But, of course, I found out that he was poor such a short time that it wasn't so very horrible. Most kids don't know they're poor unless they're starving; you play with a stick or a rag in the street and you have your friends – Christmas . . . he used to tell us about Christmas because he said that was a nightmare. He said, 'If I got one orange for Christmas that was a marvellous present,' and every year all of us kids we'd have to listen to that and we'd say, 'Well, next year we'll get you a box of oranges, Pa. You'll love it.' "

Whether or not Chaplin exaggerated the tribulations of his early days, they left him with a lifelong fear of poverty and insanity. And even allowing for exaggeration and the fact that poverty, like everything else, is relative and assuming that Sydney Chaplin was right and that the really hard years were comparatively few, Chaplin's childhood was by no means an easy or a conventional one.

By the age of eight he was already a professional entertainer, a member of a clog-dancing troupe called Jackson's Eight Lancashire Lads; at eleven he was peddling flowers in pubs and working as an errand boy. At about the same time his mother was committed once again to the lunatic asylum and at twelve he got his first engagement as a straight actor in the play *Sherlock Holmes*, wherein he played the page boy. He toured with this production for four years and thereafter appeared briefly in a music-hall act called Casey's Circus.

The desire to make his living on the stage was also inherited from Hannah and in her lucid moments nurtured by her. After all, it made sense: for a boy with his background and limited education the only occupation in those days that offered much chance to emerge from the ruck were prize fighting and show business and young Charlie had been on the books of a theatrical agency since his clog-dancing days.

So, too, had his half-brother Sydney and it was Sydney who made the first breakthrough. He joined Fred Karno's famous vaudeville troupe and, having established himself, introduced Charlie.

This was in 1906 when the younger Charlie was still only seventeen and Karno was not greatly impressed by him, remembering him later as "a pale, puny, sullen-looking youngster". Nevertheless, Karno swiftly recognised the boy's talent as a mime and took him on to appear in a football sketch as assistant and stooge to the troupe's star turn, Harry Wheldon. Professionally the two worked well together, although privately they didn't get along at all. According to Karno Chaplin was dour and unsociable, not very likeable and with a horror of drink that must have made him very much the outsider in a music-hall company. Furthermore he quarrelled fiercely with Wheldon who, on one notable occasion, was heard to inform him: "I have more talent in my arse than you have in your entire body."

"Yes, that's where your talent lies," said Chaplin. Future events, of course, were to prove that Wheldon's original claim was as inaccurate as Chaplin's riposte was tactless but such an exchange can hardly have made for a happy relationship. It also tends to reinforce Karno's view that Chaplin was not an easy fellow to get along with, but even so he soon became one of the company's leading comics. And when the Karno troupe went to America to appear in New York in 1910 and again in 1912 it was he who attracted most attention.

Indeed, on that second visit he was approached by Mack Sennett, who offered him a contract at 150 dollars a week to make one- and two-reel comedy films. Chaplin accepted and so he arrived in Hollywood to take up this new career in December 1913, when he was twenty-four years old.

He began with a one-reeler called *Making a Living*, which won him a cautiously approving notice in the magazine *Motion Picture World*, and then rapidly started to make a name for himself after his second film, *Kid Auto Races at Venice*, in which he improvised the tramp outfit that was to become his trademark. He assembled it in a hurry and in response to a casual instruction from Mack Sennett to "put on a comedy make-up". The final costume was a ragbag of garments borrowed from other comedians: Fatty Arbuckle's trousers, for example, Ford Sterling's boots, a cut-down version of Mack Swain's moustache. To these he added a jacket and a bowler hat that were both too small for him and a walking stick, the emblem of the man about town. The *tout ensemble* at once gave the impression of down-at-heel gentility, the image of a man reduced by circumstances to the level of a hobo but still attempting to maintain standards.

Considering that it was, or he would have claimed it was, a perfectly haphazard collection of clothes, it became a remarkably successful outfit. But King Vidor, the director, who was one of Chaplin's earliest friends in Hollywood, is not so sure that it was haphazard. Vidor had another friend, a prominent psychiatrist who wanted to meet Chaplin. Chaplin refused to see him on the grounds, Vidor believed, that "he was afraid any analysis of his character would destroy his talent, his energy and his goals and motivation."

Chaplin insisted that he didn't believe in psychiatry, psychiatrists or psycho-analysis and also maintained, "I don't have any neuroses of any sort."

Vidor reported this conversation to the psychiatrist who replied: "My God, I've never seen anybody with more neuroses. The big shoes, the big pants, the baggy crotch to the pants, the Derby hat, the moustache, the cane – they're all symbols, neurotic symbols of the poor little fellow starving to death but wanting to be a socially prominent gentleman."

How much support you give to this view depends, I suppose, on what you think of psychiatrists but Vidor believed that in this case the psychiatrist was right and that what he had said summed up "the whole basis of Chaplin's life and character".

However, armed with the Little Fellow outfit and a huge repertoire of gags and slapstick routines from his London music-hall days Chaplin quickly began to prosper. In two years he made thirty-five pictures for Keystone before leaving to join the Essanay Film Manufacturing Company, who offered him 1,250 dollars a week and the opportunity to direct. Hal Roach, another of Chaplin's early Hollywood friends, said that "his contract with Essanay laid down that if he was making a picture on location, the company – not Charlie – had to pay for the meals for the crew and the actors. So every day about eleven thirty a.m. Charlie would think of a scene to shoot outdoors because then the company would have to pay for the luncheon."

This careful attitude towards money was again, no doubt, a residue of his poverty-stricken childhood but it was also one of his abiding characteristics.

He acquired and never lost a reputation for meanness but, like many apparently tight-fisted people, he could also be quite remarkably lavish. Douglas Fairbanks Jr. said: "Charlie was famously frugal. He was said to have the first penny he ever earned. He parted with every penny as if it were his life's blood and he was a very good student of the dollar and the pound and the franc and the mark and so on and he was a very wise investor and a very shrewd businessman."

King Vidor believed that, because of his background, Chaplin was never able to convince himself that he was a rich man and thus he was never able to enjoy the delights of extravagance. "I think the house in which he lived in those early days in Hollywood was built by a studio technician and there were some things in it that were made for a film, so after a while all the plaster fell off but he never got it fixed. I remember he had a shower bath that didn't have a shower head on it, just a pipe coming out of the wall. One time, after a game of tennis, he said, 'You don't have to go home for a shower. Come and use mine.' So I got in this shower and I said, 'How do you work this thing?' and he said, 'Oh, I forgot to tell you. You take this pan and fill it from the pipe and then throw the water over yourself.' He never had it fixed, just never had it fixed."

On the same subject of money there is also the testimony of Hal Roach: "Charlie was one of the tightest guys I ever knew. I remember once we were eating in a cafeteria at lunchtime and we were going out to dinner together that night. Well, when the check came Charlie grabbed it – the first time I'd ever known him grab a check. It came to about thirty cents and he said, 'I'll pay this. You can take care of dinner.' And dinner would be about two dollars each."

Again Chaplin's son, Sydney, recalling an occasion much later in his father's life: "One night in Paris when he didn't have his glasses on he took out a 500-franc note, which was then about a hundred dollars, and gave it to the taxi driver and told him to keep the change. So the taxi driver, with a big laugh, took it and drove off. Well, my father thought he'd given him 50 francs and when he found out the truth he didn't sleep the whole night. I'll tell you, he was ill. He said, 'How could you, Christ, how could you let me do that? Couldn't you look and see what I was giving the man?' "

Around that time, too, when Chaplin was living with his fourth wife, Oona, in Switzerland, Sydney Chaplin said: "He lived like a rich man. He had a big house and a lot of servants and he denied himself nothing but he suddenly said to Oona one day, 'What are the meat prices here?' And she told him and he said, 'Well, that's it. We're not going to eat meat any more. That's ridiculous – the servants and all of us eating meat at that price. We're spending a fortune.'

"And for three days they didn't eat meat. He was always relating back to the time when he was poor. But then, after a few days of not eating meat, he said, 'Let's have a steak,' and that was that."

Generally speaking, though, his attacks of meanness occurred when he was actually required to produce cash to pay for something. Sydney Chaplin said that if his father could sign a bill and didn't have to watch his own money grasped by other hands, he would quite happily take twenty people to dinner and be a most generous host. What is more, he would invest his own capital in his films and very few actors are prepared to take such a risk as that.

Hal Roach said: "That was an amazing thing. When he built his own studio and made his own pictures with his own money – that is, when he was with United Artists – Charlie, tight as he was in some things, would arrive at the studio at nine o'clock in the morning and decide that he didn't feel like acting or directing that day. And he would dismiss the entire crew and the very large bunch of actors he had for the film and that would cost him several thousand dollars."

One implication of all this is that Chaplin regarded money chiefly as sustenance for his work, which was always of paramount importance to him. "Comedy," he once said, "is the most serious study in the world." And partly perhaps because he learned this simple, though vital, lesson more quickly and more thoroughly than his contemporaries he soon began to outstrip them in popularity.

By 1915, when he was with Essanay, spin-off industries had sprung up around him, manufacturing Charlie Chaplin statuettes and Charlie Chaplin squirt rings. At the age of twenty-six he was already becoming very rich.

At Essanay his frequent leading lady was Edna Purviance, who was to appear in thirty-five of his films from *A Night Out* in 1915 to *A Woman of Paris* in 1926. The relationship between them was far more than merely professional and it was also long-lasting. Chaplin kept her on his pay-roll until her death in 1958 and it was surprising to many of their mutual friends that they never married. Hal Roach believed this was because "she didn't want to marry Charlie. Away from the studio I imagine Charlie was pretty boring because he probably wouldn't say a word for a couple of hours if he didn't want to and then he'd talk his head off about something that was way above her, like some gag he was trying to work out for a movie."

Stan Laurel, on the other hand, was convinced that it was Chaplin who didn't wish to marry Edna Purviance because she was simply too mature and too grown-up for him. Certainly this is a point worth considering because Chaplin's taste was always for very young and very innocent girls. And this was a predilection that was to land him in trouble on several occasions throughout most of his life.

At the time he first met Edna Purviance, however, such problems still lay in the future. In 1915 he made the film that is generally regarded as the Chaplin classic, *The Tramp*, which is mostly significant for the fact that it was in this picture that he introduced the element of pathos that was to become as much his trademark as the Little Fellow costume was. By now he was in such demand that he could virtually dictate his own terms. He moved from Essanay to Mutual and from Mutual to First National and with every switch of allegiance his income soared.

There was a brief hiccup in this upward progress when America entered the First World War and letters began to pour into the studio demanding that Chaplin should enlist in the Army. In fact, he had already been turned down because he didn't meet the physical requirements, being only 5 feet 4 inches tall and weighing no more than 130 lbs. It was an unpleasant interlude for him (the receipt of white feathers through the post can hardly be an agreeable experience) but it made no appreciable difference to his box-office appeal because when he signed for First National in 1918 the contract gave him one million dollars –

to say nothing of a 15,000 dollar signing-on bonus – to make eight films. One million dollars is quite a good fee now but in 1918 it was astonishing enough to merit worldwide publicity.

But to Chaplin what was even more important than the money was the fact that he also had complete control over the production of his picture and could afford to build his own studios. So he acquired a five-acre lot just off Sunset Boulevard, put up an open-air stage, which he later roofed over, and then erected a row of mock-Tudor cottages to serve as the administration block. And there at last he set about making films the way he wanted to make them.

"Sometimes," said Douglas Fairbanks Jr., "he would film a whole day's work as a rehearsal in order to be able to look at it the next day. Then he'd film it again a second time and sometimes it would take him three or four days to do one scene.

Chaplin's first wife, Mildred Harris. She was sixteen when they married in 1918. They were divorced by the time she was twenty.

Most people couldn't afford that but he was his own boss, he had very few overheads, he paid very small wages and he had a studio which was very inexpensive. People loved working for him. They could have got better jobs elsewhere but they would rather work for him for less than for somebody else for more."

All this prosperity and success was not, however, mirrored in Chaplin's private life. In October 1918, he had acquired the first of a succession of child brides, a blonde, blue-eyed actress named Mildred Harris. He was twenty-nine and she was sixteen. More significantly, perhaps, she was also pregnant on their wedding day and a few months later gave birth to a son who died within three days. Soon after that Chaplin moved out of the conjugal home and by August 1920 the couple were divorced in an atmosphere of scandal and acrimony.

Mildred accused her husband of mental cruelty and neglect and claimed that he practised economy to such an extent that he even scrimped on funeral expenses for their child. Instead of hiring a hearse, she said, he had borrowed a car belonging to the Gish sisters. Chaplin refused to reply to what he described as "these foolish charges". This was undoubtedly the most dignified attitude to adopt but perhaps, with hindsight, it was not the most sensible, for the Mildred Harris episode was the first of several minor scandals which eventually were to help turn the American public against him.

While the divorce action was going on and Mildred Harris' lawyers were making ever more extravagant demands on behalf of their client, Chaplin was trying to finish his first full-length feature film, *The Kid*, in which he introduced the young Jackie Coogan to the screen. This became a difficult enterprise because, in order to stop the hostile lawyers from seizing such film as he had already shot, Chaplin had to keep moving from one location to another. But it was worth all the effort for, when it finally appeared, it was such a critical and popular success as to wipe away the bad taste left by the divorce action.

By then, too, Chaplin was even more securely established for in 1919 and in company with Mary Pickford, Douglas Fairbanks Sr. and D. W. Griffith he had established United Artists in order that the four of them should have greater control over the distribution of and the profits from their films, though because of his contract with First National Chaplin was unable to enjoy the complete independence offered by United Artists until 1923, when he directed Edna Purviance and Adolphe Menjou in *A Woman of Paris*, released in 1926.

One of his intentions in choosing this particular subject was that it should at last make Edna Purviance a star. But in fact it did very little for her and such stardom as it conferred went to Menjou.

Meanwhile, in 1921, Chaplin had made his first visit to England for eight years. He had been mobbed and fêted, introduced to James Barrie and H. G. Wells (and thus acquired an abiding taste for the company and friendship of distinguished writers) and been to Europe, where he met and had an affair with Pola Negri. An odd affair it must have been, too, because her English at the time was apparently limited to the somewhat enigmatic phrase, "Jazz boy, Charlie". But, despite the fact that this must have made their conversation rather stilted, they obviously got along very well because when she turned up in Hollywood a year later their engagement was announced. This, however, seems to have been much more her idea than his and the romance, if such it was, rapidly cooled down.

By this time Chaplin and his brother Sydney, who was by now his business manager, had brought their mother to America and established her in a home with a staff of her own. Mrs. Chaplin's state of mental illness had become permanent and, though Charlie continued to look after her until her death in 1930, he found it emotionally painful to spend much time with her, hence the separate homes.

He himself had moved into a house in Beverly Hills. Pola Negri had confidently expected to become the mistress of this establishment but in the event the first woman to move in on any seemingly permanent basis was Charlie's second child bride, Lita Grey, whom he married in 1924. He was thirty-five but Miss Grey, like Miss Harris before her, was only sixteen. He had first met her when she appeared as a twelve-year-old in *The Kid*. Later he put her under contract and wanted to star her in *The Gold Rush* but on location a more intimate relationship developed and they were married because, once again, Chaplin the lover had been more passionate than careful.

"This was a situation which had occurred before in Charlie's life," said Miss Grey. "Again he was in trouble with an under-age girl . . . pregnancy before marriage, and so forth. Most of the girls in Charlie's life were under age."

It was Miss Grey's family who insisted they should be married and, although he greatly resented the idea, Chaplin was obliged to agree because Lita Grey was legally below the age of consent. The wedding took place in Mexico and "he didn't want much said about it. He was pretty bitter in the beginning. On the way back in the train he was quite nasty. He made a remark that I, well, being so young and not feeling too well at the time anyway, I couldn't know whether he was serious or whether he was joking. I really couldn't tell. But he said, 'You know, it would be easy if you'd just jump.' We were standing out on the platform between two cars while the train was travelling and he said, 'We could end this whole situation if you'd just jump.' "

From this inauspicious and far from jolly start and pursued by scandal-seeking reporters the couple returned to Hollywood to await the birth of their son, Charles Chaplin Jr. It was a strange situation with the newly wed husband laying down a hard set of ground rules from the very beginning. "He said, 'I don't intend to be a husband to you. You have your mother live with us because you can't live alone all the time in your condition and I don't intend to be a husband to you.' And he wasn't because he'd stay out till all hours and when he came home we wouldn't have any meals together." Thus the young bride was left very much in the company of her mother and her grandmother, who had also moved in, and her hired tutors whom Chaplin had to provide since his wife was still of school-going age.

Even the professional contact between husband and wife quickly ceased for, as the signs of her pregnancy became increasingly evident, the new Mrs. Chaplin was withdrawn from *The Gold Rush* and Georgia Hale was signed to replace her.

Charles Chaplin Jr. was born on June 28th, 1925, according to the official records but according to both Charles Jr. and his

Wife No. 2, Lita Grey. Another child bride and mother of his sons, Sydney and Charles Junior.

mother he was actually born on May 5th. Chaplin, apparently, had the records changed (by means of a 25,000 dollar bribe) to make it appear that the child had been conceived after and not, as was the case, before marriage. But whatever the true date of the birth, the relationship between husband and wife obviously improved a little because very soon Lita Grey was pregnant again and in March 1926, another son, Sydney, was born.

"When I was pregnant with Sydney," said Miss Grey, "Charlie became quite decent. He was beginning to be very nice then." But, alas, this state of affairs didn't last very long. A little while after the birth of Sydney, Chaplin began filming *The Circus* with, as the leading lady, Merna Kennedy. Miss Kennedy and Lita Grey had been schoolfriends and it was Miss Grey who persuaded her husband to give the girl a screen test. This was rather a grave mistake on Miss Grey's part because Chaplin not only gave her the test and the role but he also gave her a diamond bracelet, a present whose significance was not lost on his wife. She, too, had been given a diamond bracelet as a prelude to seduction.

"I knew then what was going on because it was a repetition of the same kind of treatment that I got. So I think that was the thing that really ended the marriage. I just walked into his room and told him I didn't care what the result was, I was just not going to live with him any more."

As the divorce got under way Chaplin was faced by a forty-two-page document of complaint in which he was accused of threatening his wife's life, of infidelity, of mental cruelty and of all manner of other inhuman acts. The whole affair was conducted in an atmosphere of the most remarkable bitterness which, on Chaplin's part, burned so deeply and so permanently that in his autobiography he never once mentioned Lita Grey by name.

Half a century later, however, Miss Grey herself was able to look back on this brief and turbulent marriage with a far more dispassionate eye. He was not a cruel man, she said, nor particularly selfish, though he could be ruthless in defence of his career and his work. The main problem, the one that made him impossible to live with, was "enormous insecurity. Looking back, I realise how terribly insecure he was. He had trouble ordering food in a restaurant even; the waiters intimidated him. I think he never had real confidence; he never felt that anybody loved him. He said to me once, 'How can anybody love me? I'm not tall and dark and handsome and well-proportioned . . . why would anybody love me?' He never believed it was possible."

But along with the insecurity went a kind of arrogance. "One time he said to me, 'I'm the best. I'm better known than Jesus Christ' and at that age, of course, I thought, 'Oh, the vanity of this man! It's just unreal,' but as I've grown older I've come to realise that it was a pretty truthful statement. There were places in the world that knew Chaplin, where they'd probably never even heard of Jesus Christ."

The divorce finally cost Chaplin 850,000 dollars and a mild nervous collapse and caused him to delay opening *The Circus* until early 1928. Immediately after that he started work on another idea: a film about a blind girl to be called eventually *City Lights*. At this stage, however, talkies had been introduced to the cinema. How would Chaplin react to this new-fangled idea? Well, he reacted by ignoring it. In an article in the *New York Times* he maintained that silent films represented a universal art which could not and must not be ousted by the current "hysteria" for talkies. Action, he said, was more generally understood than words: pantomime was a universal language while speech as a form of communication was perforce restricted to those who could understand what was being said. In explaining this attitude to his son, Sydney, he said: "Words are cheap. The biggest thing you can say is 'elephant'."

Yet there was more to his hostility towards sound pictures than that, certainly in those days. Many of his best effects were gained by undercranking the camera and this was impossible with a sound camera which was run by a motor at a set speed of twenty-four frames a second. Just as much to the point, he also argued that English dialogue would limit, if not destroy, his enormous foreign market and when you consider that he could recover the production costs of his films from Japan alone this was clearly no small matter.

So he went ahead with *City Lights* as a silent movie and was completely vindicated when, on its appearance in 1931, it proved to be one of the most popular films of the year.

Now, until this time, his most frequent companion since his last divorce had been Georgia Hale but after *City Lights* opened in New York he went on an eight-month world tour, leaving her behind and that was more or less the end of that because soon after his return he met his next leading lady – and his third wife – Paulette Goddard. At least it is generally supposed that she became his wife (probably during 1936 when they both made a lengthy trip together to the Far East) although both she and Chaplin were reluctant to say whether they were married or not. Miss Goddard, indeed, would not even clear up the matter in 1938 when the suspicion that she was merely "living in sin" with Chaplin aroused the enmity of the American Women's Clubs and thus, since Hollywood dared not defy these baleful ladies, lost her any outside chance she might have had of landing the role of Scarlett O'Hara in *Gone with the Wind*, a role she wanted quite as desperately as every other actress in Hollywood.

When she and Chaplin met in 1932 Paulette Goddard was, by his standards, a rather elderly divorcee of twenty-one but, generously overlooking her comparative length of tooth, he took her into his home and co-starred her in his next film, *Modern Times*. That was made in 1936 when Chaplin was forty-seven years old and it was, of course, a silent picture (if you overlook the fact that Chaplin sang a song in gibberish). By that stage nobody else in his right mind would have contemplated making a silent picture but once again the public appeared to support Chaplin's belief that actions spoke louder than words because on its release *Modern Times* swiftly climbed to Number Four in the box-office top ten.

Chaplin followed this success with another satire on the contemporary scene, *The Great Dictator*, and by the time that was finished in 1940, the war in Europe was on and his relationship with Paulette Goddard was over. Unusually, considering his previous track record, it ended without acrimony and indeed with regret on both sides. They had been together for the best part of eight years and she had been a kind and attentive stepmother to Chaplin's two sons. But she was twenty-two years younger than he was and their interests were not altogether compatible.

Tim Durant, who looked after Chaplin's investment at United Artists, said: "Charlie liked his home and he liked to be looked after and she wanted to go out much more than he did."

And King Vidor said: "She used to go out on dates with other men and he'd be sitting at home, this great comedian, waiting. I thought it was quite a tragic sight."

Thus, as the 1940s opened, Chaplin, now aged fifty-one, was again alone and embarking upon the most troubled decade of his life. In a sense *The Great Dictator*, though made with the most patriotic intent, was the start of his problems. Partly because of the slight physical resemblance between him and Hitler, his films had been banned anyway in Nazi Germany but this latest picture, this obviously satirical view of the Führer, aroused the Nazis to a state of fury bordering on apoplexy. The caption under Chaplin's picture in a German propaganda book read: "This little Jewish tumbler, as disgusting as he is boring . . ." Chaplin, in fact, was not a Jew, though he never bothered to say so on the grounds that if he did he would simply be playing into the hands of the anti-Semites.

But in America in 1940 there were a good many anti-Semites and a good many Nazi sympathisers, too, and when the film opened Chaplin began to receive threatening letters from such people. Furthermore, he was attacked in the Right-wing press for insulting the German leader. The suspicion began to grow that Chaplin was a bit of a

Left-winger, a species of person always viewed with much distrust in the United States.

And when America finally entered the war this suspicion became a certainty in the minds of his adversaries for Chaplin lent his voice to the demand for a second front to be launched in Europe to take some of the pressure off the Russian armies.

In San Francisco he addressed a rally of 10,000 people, delivering a forty-minute speech that opened with the emotive word, "Comrades!" Of course, he explained, he meant nothing specific by this – "I am not a Communist, I am a human being" – but the use of the word "Comrades" along with an impassioned appeal for a second front – "Stalin wants it, Roosevelt has called for it, so let's all call for it, let's open a second front now" – led the Right-wingers to colour him, at the very least, pink. Then he followed the San Francisco rally by talking on the telephone to a mass meeting of trades unionists in Madison Square Garden, beginning with the words: "On the battlefield of Russia democracy will live or die." That may ring a little hollow now but it probably sounded quite plausible at the time, though again not to the Right-wing faction. Enmity towards Chaplin was building swiftly and his friends began to advise him to ease up on his pro-Russian speeches. Nor were they entirely wrong to do so, for he was already being ostracised in New York society.

While all this was going on the one thing that Chaplin did not need was to become involved in another sexual scandal but,

Paulette Goddard (wife No. 3) was a little mature by Chaplin's standards – comfortably into her twenties when they married somewhere in the Far East.

alas, in 1943 this is precisely what happened; a paternity suit was brought against him by an actress named Joan Barry.

The background circumstances were wearily familiar: she was a good-looking girl of twenty-two and he was fifty-four; they had first met two years earlier when Miss Barry screentested for the leading role in *Shadow and Substance*, a film Chaplin was contemplating about an Irish girl who was a kind of modern Joan of Arc.

The picture was never made but, inevitably no doubt, Chaplin and Joan Barry became lovers. Unfortunately, Miss Barry also became highly neurotic and a drinker and a nuisance. Alarmed by the lady's unpredictable behaviour, Chaplin ended the relationship, gave her money and paid her fare back to her home in New York. A few months later, however, she returned to Hollywood, broke into Chaplin's home, was charged with vagrancy, sentenced to thirty days' detention and announced that she was three months pregnant. As an afterthought she declared that Chaplin was the father, which would have been an extremely neat trick on his part because the couple had not been together for some eight months.

What complicated matters even further was that since divesting himself of Miss Barry Chaplin had met and fallen in love with Oona O'Neill, the daughter of Eugene O'Neill, the playwright. The affection he felt for her was genuine and, as it turned out, lasting, but unfortunately Miss O'Neill was only seventeen and under American law still a child. So when news of this relationship leaked out in the press Chaplin was involved in a double sexual scandal; a paternity suit being brought against him by one young woman while he was consorting with an under-age girl. There was only one solution – fortunately a solution that appealed to both of them anyway – and that was to marry Oona.

This Chaplin did at the town of Carpenteria in California in June 1943 after (a) an elopement and (b) a wild car chase in which the couple were pursued by a strong contingent of the American press. After the wedding and a brief honeymoon in Santa Barbara the couple returned to Beverly Hills, where the new bride's first task was to help her husband prepare his answer to Joan Barry's paternity case.

In fact, he had a perfect answer. The result of a blood test showed quite conclusively that Chaplin could not possibly have been the father of Miss Barry's child. This convinced everybody except the law court which refused to accept the blood test as evidence. But, in any case, the paternity suit was not now the most urgent of Chaplin's problems because he was facing criminal charges as well, having been indicted on four counts under the Mann Act, which prohibited the transportation of women (in Chaplin's case Joan Barry) from one state to another for immoral purposes. The fact that any transportation of Miss Barry had been done with her happy consent and that the most immoral purpose she had served was to sleep with Chaplin was, apparently, neither here nor there.

The legal proceedings dragged on into April 1944 at which time Chaplin was acquitted on all counts, though not before he had been comprehensively vilified in the press. Two years later the paternity case was reopened and Chaplin was found, against all the evidence, to be the father of the child and ordered to support it. The whole case, said Sydney Chaplin, was "an absolute frame-up. They proved it wasn't his child – I mean, medically proved – but they threw the proof out because the blood test wasn't accepted in California."

By the middle of the decade, then, Chaplin the great comedian had been transformed in the eyes of the American public into Chaplin the Leftie, Chaplin the satyr, Chaplin the heartless seducer and impregnator of innocent young women and finally Chaplin the apparent tax dodger, since in the past few years he had been involved in constant disputes with the Inland Revenue, though not because he was trying to cheat but because, in Chaplin's view and that of his lawyers, he was being assessed unfairly.

While the war was still on and America and Russia were allies his apparent Left-wing sympathies probably did him no great harm but his taste for young women was never likely to make him popular. For all manner of complex reasons – jealousy perhaps on the part of other older men; insecurity on the part of older women – an elderly man who consorts with young girls is by definition a dirty old man. But what exactly is a dirty old man? And was Chaplin one? If seducing young girls and making them pregnant is evidence of dirty old manhood then doubtless Chaplin qualifies for the title. But, on the other hand, in the two cases when he certainly did seduce and make pregnant a young girl he also did the honourable thing and married her. That neither marriage lasted is beside the point; far more pertinent perhaps is the fact that those who knew Chaplin well do not believe he was a dirty old man or that he was attracted to his various youthful brides and girlfriends simply on grounds of lust.

Sydney Chaplin acknowledged that his father was physically attracted to youth ("I mean, the oldest woman he married was Paulette Goddard, who was an old bag of twenty-one or something,") but insisted that what really appealed to him more was "the freshness, the non-sophistication of the young".

And Tim Durant said: "I don't think it was primarily sexual, I really don't. He wasn't one of those lascivious old men who are always pursuing women. He married all of them, remember that; and he fell in love with all of them, too. We get down to the sexual angle with everybody I suppose, but what I think he felt was that he could influence and mould these young girls. And I think he was less sure of himself with older women because they had more experience."

Hal Roach agreed with Durant that Chaplin was not essentially a womaniser: "All the time I knew him I never saw him chasing dames. And if he was doing it, why would he hide it from me? I was doing a little chasing myself."

Lita Grey who, as one of the girls Chaplin seduced and married, spoke with first-hand experience, believed that he was a romantic, a dreamer. "Throughout his whole life," she said, "he was attracted to the virginal girl. I think it was part of his creativity. He wanted to see the girl awaken; he wanted to create a person. He was intrigued, I think, by innocence. When he married Oona this was the pattern again but Charlie was a very lucky man because while the pattern may have been the same, Oona was different. She became his stability.

"Probably because of his age he'd slowed down a great deal and he needed her very badly. She was an insecure girl and I think they needed each other. She turned out to be a fabulous wife and mother and I think she brought Charlie the only real peace he'd

ever known. I don't think he'd ever been a very happy man and she brought him a measure of contentment that he'd never had before."

Chaplin himself assessed the situation in very much the same way. To Tim Durant, who had introduced him to Oona O'Neill, he said: "I've been looking for somebody like her all my life. If I'd found her before I wouldn't have had all the problems I've had in the past."

However, in 1947 Chaplin, now married once more (and, as it was to prove, permanently), supporting a child that was not his own but at least cleared of criminal charges under the Mann Act, made his first film in seven years, *Monsieur Verdoux*, a black comedy based on the career of Landru, the wife murderer. The American public disliked it but by this time they disliked Chaplin anyway, regarding his political views as dangerously liberal. At a press conference after the opening of the film he was questioned about his patriotism and his politics. And even though he insisted that he was not a Communist, had never voted in his life and indeed had no political persuasions at all, he was still accused by Right-wing publications of being "a card-carrying member of the Communist party" and a speaker in Congress demanded that he should be deported and his "loathsome pictures" be banned for fear that they might corrupt American youth.

Hollywood society now began to ostracise him in much the same way as New York society had done earlier. Living virtually in isolation, he spent the next few years planning and making his final American film, *Limelight*. By the time that was in production the very mention of his name was enough to arouse anger. Claire Bloom, the young actress who co-starred with him, said: "I used to get a taxi to the studio every morning and at first I'd say, 'I'd like to go to the Chaplin studio, please', and the taxi driver would say, 'Is that goddamn Commie still working in this country?' So finally I just gave them the name of the street and the number to avoid any wrangles. America was a fearful place at that time."

When the film was finished Chaplin and Oona decided to take a six-month holiday in Europe. Before they left he had to apply for a re-entry permit into the USA because in the forty years that he had been living

With his last wife, Oona, arriving in London in 1953. By then Chaplin had been driven out of America.

there he had never become an American citizen. This was the opportunity that the anti-Communist, anti-Chaplin faction had been looking for. The authorities stalled, refusing to grant him the permit until he had been interrogated by the immigration officials and then issuing it only reluctantly. Nor was that the end of the matter, for when the Chaplins were already on board the *Queen Elizabeth* en route for Southampton the permit was rescinded and he was informed that he would not be allowed to return to the USA unless he faced an Immigration Board of Inquiry "to answer charges of a political nature and of moral turpitude". No less an authority than the US Attorney General described him as "a person of unsavoury character".

Well, now, what was all this about? In the first place, of course, there was the suspicion of Communism, which was clearly unfounded. In a rather grandiose way Chaplin would describe himself as "a citizen of the world". It was a romantic and perhaps naïve idea but then politically he was rather naïve, tending towards the liberal (with a small 'l') though by no means a committed liberal. He was, by instinct, always far more a capitalist than a Communist.

"He pictured himself as a radical," said King Vidor, "and yet he was far from that." Vidor recalled one occasion when Chaplin ran into union difficulties while making a film and insisted that he would never have any truck with union contracts

again and that rather than do so he would stop making films altogether. "He wasn't really for the common man at all," said Vidor.

Douglas Fairbanks Jr. said: "He never stopped talking politics but you couldn't take him very seriously. His opinions would change from morning to night, sometimes from hour to hour. He would say things just to be provocative and stir up discussion." As for being a member of the Communist party, Fairbanks said: "He never belonged to any party. I can vouch for that. He was far too stingy to pay the dues to join anything."

In the political climate of the time, however, the American authorities were not to be persuaded by such arguments. They were convinced that Chaplin was a fellow-traveller if not an actual Communist and besides they were irritated by the fact that after all those years he still carried a British passport. Chaplin had never taken out American citizenship because he didn't feel it important. He was, remember, a citizen of the world and as he said to Douglas Fairbanks: "Why should I become an American? There are a lot of Americans who live in France or England or Germany and they're not asked to become Frenchmen or Englishmen or Germans. Why are Americans the only ones who say you have to become an American citizen? It's the only country in the world where they make a thing about it." That sort of attitude was hardly designed to endear him to the Attorney General's office either.

So, inspired by a crusading zeal to stamp out this dangerous radical clown in whatever way they could, the American authorities constructed a political case against him and – on a belt and braces principle – introduced allegations of moral turpitude as well. The Joan Barry paternity suit gave them a certain amount of fuel for this but in their enthusiasm they even went back to Lita Grey in an attempt to revive the sensational aspects of the divorce action a quarter of a century earlier. To her credit Miss Grey refused to dish the dirt.

Meanwhile, Chaplin, angry and bitter at the campaign against him, refused to defend himself and left America, as far as he was concerned, for good. When he arrived in Southampton he declared privately that he had "no further use for America. I wouldn't go back there if Jesus Christ was

President." Oona though did go back – to sell the family home and transfer Chaplin's fortune to Switzerland where he had decided to live.

Looking back on that time Tim Durant said: "When I first met Charlie he was the genius of Hollywood, the greatest man that ever was in motion pictures. Everybody respected him and revered him. When he left, everybody was against him. Everybody was afraid to be associated with him. They all rejected him. Well, this was the McCarthy era and there was a general fear of guilt by association."

Chaplin himself behaved with considerable dignity during the whole tawdry episode, his only public comment on the affair – and that an oblique one – being implicit in his film *A King in New York* which he made in England in 1956. It's the story of a deposed European monarch who arrives a penniless refugee in America, which he believes to be a land inspired by ideals of freedom and democracy. He is, however, rapidly disillusioned. By the time the picture was made Chaplin had broken his final ties with the USA by selling his shares in United Artists for something more than one million dollars.

In Switzerland Chaplin and Oona had four more children to add to the four who had been born in America and by the time the youngest arrived Chaplin was seventy-three years old. A few years later his eldest son, Charles Jr., died of a heart attack at the age of forty-three. He had long suffered from a drink problem and indeed his whole life had been burdened by the impossibility of living up to the name that had been imposed upon him. Without inheriting any of his father's talent, he had tried to be an actor and, not surprisingly, he had failed. Nobody could possibly blame him for that but to be called Charlie Chaplin and not to be a genius was more than he could bear and he had sought refuge, as so many sons of the famous have done, in alcohol.

It would, of course, be easy to blame the father for the fate of the son and perhaps if they had been closer things might have turned out otherwise. But Chaplin's contact with his two elder sons was necessarily limited, although he was, apparently, an affectionate enough parent. Although Lita Grey said he was not the kind to "bounce his children on his knee", Sydney remembered him as "awkward when embracing and touching and rather reserved. But he

The Chaplin family at Cap St. Ferrat in 1957.

23

had a very good heart with his kids and he was very decent." And from her observations of the Chaplins *en famille*, Claire Bloom said: "He just adored his children and that's all there is to it."

In 1966 Chaplin, then aged seventy-seven, made his last film, *A Countess from Hong Kong*. He wrote it, directed it, composed the music and played a small part as a ship's steward. The stars were Sophia Loren and Marlon Brando. With Brando he had very little rapport and it showed in the picture, which was old-fashioned and somehow listless. Critical and public reception of it was generally unfavourable and Chaplin returned to Switzerland and family life. Although he busied himself with composing music for some of his silent pictures and negotiated a very handsome fee for the re-release of nine of his feature films he had no need to work for he was an extremely rich man. In 1972 his personal fortune was estimated at more than £7,000,000.

Also in 1972, twenty years after he had been driven out of America as an unsavoury character and a dangerous Communist, he returned to the United States by special invitation and in triumph. At the Lincoln Center in New York 3,000 people gave him a standing ovation when he appeared at a gala showing of two of his films and in Los Angeles a few days later (on April 10th) he received a special Oscar in recognition of the "incalculable effect" he had had in making motion pictures "the art form of the century". It was only the second Oscar he had received, the first having been for *The Circus* as long ago as 1928.

This second, belated award was presumably America's way of saying sorry for the treatment he had received twenty years earlier and, though it can hardly have wiped away all the bitterness he must have felt, it was at least a handsome apology and Chaplin accepted it graciously, although at the same time he was undoubtedly using the occasion to serve his own ends. Sydney Chaplin said his father was not at all impressed by Oscars and that once indeed he had rejected one, informing the Academy that it was not qualified to judge his work and didn't know a good picture from a bad one. The special Oscar attracted him though because "he had just re-released all his pictures and he said, 'This is good for business.' "

Whatever he may have felt about Academy Awards, however, he certainly took considerable pride in another, and rather different investiture at Buckingham Palace three years later when Charlie the tramp, the little fellow, became Sir Charles Chaplin. But that, too, according to Sydney was an honour he had declined before.

"They offered him a knighthood years and years ago and he said then, 'It's ridiculous; I can't do it – the little fellow who is for the underdog and the average man and he's suddenly knighted. No, I can't do that. It's against my principles.' But at the end of his life I think he just felt, 'Well, it's an honour,' and he accepted."

Charlie Chaplin, Sir Charles Chaplin, who said when he received his special Oscar, "I went into this business for money and the art grew out of it," lived to enjoy that honour for nearly three years. But on Christmas Day, 1977, he died at home in his sleep. He was eighty-eight years old.

As a macabre postscript to his life and death his body was later stolen from the tiny cemetery at Corsier in Switzerland where he was buried and was not rediscovered for several months. I somehow doubt whether the old and distinguished Sir Charles Chaplin would have found that very amusing. With age and honours he had acquired a certain pomposity, as the second half of his autobiography clearly

Charlie, the Tramp, the Little Fellow, has long gone. What we have here is Sir Charles Chaplin, knight of the realm.

shows. But I like to think that the young Chaplin, the one who told Harry Wheldon that his talent lay in his arse, would have derived a considerable degree of mirth from such a bizarre happening.

He was a rare and complex man, of great arrogance and great insecurity; a man who appears to have had immense charm and a fair number of the other, less engaging qualities which often walk hand-in-hand with charm. He could be calculating, he could be ruthless in defence of himself and his work, he could be pompous and he could be cold. But then the kind of talent that he possessed is never found in men of simple good nature.

In any event whether he was lovable or not is largely immaterial. What is important is that he may well have been, in the words of the equally immortal Buster Keaton, "the greatest comedian that ever lived". What Chaplin grasped more keenly than any other comedian was the fact that farce and tragedy are very often exactly the same thing, viewed from different angles. So in his films the humour and the pathos (whatever you may have felt about the pathos) grew from the same root.

In the years since his death the inevitable process of cutting him down to size has flourished strongly. There are those who dismiss him merely as a superb mime – assuming that a superb mime is simply to be dismissed. He was not, they say, a great actor at all, nor was he a great director: he didn't even understand camera angles. Well, perhaps he didn't. But what he did understand far more than any of his critics ever did was the value of simplicity. "I remain one thing and one thing only," he said, "and that is a clown. It places me on a far higher plane than any politician." And he also said, just as pertinently: "All I need to make a comedy is a park, a policeman and a pretty girl."

For anyone less than a genius that could have been a recipe for disaster; for Chaplin it was the recipe for greatness. And if I, and perhaps others like me, find him far more admirable than funny the loss is ours and not his. In his own field Chaplin, like Jeeves, stands alone.

OPPOSITE: *Chaplin directing* A Countess *from Hong Kong.*

The classic shot from the final reel of Modern Times. *Chaplin and Paulette Goddard walk off, hand-in-hand, into the sunset.*

Jean Harlow

The story of Jean Harlow is not simply the story of a girl who, exuding sex, became the prototype for all "blonde bombshells" in talking pictures. It's also a minor tragedy and, even more than that, a kind of mystery story. Harlow died in 1937 at the age of twenty-six after a brief career, spent mostly at MGM, during which she made thirty films, seven of them merely as an extra and few of them amounting to much more than the sort of run of the mill "fix" that Hollywood peddled every week at a time when the cinema was the opiate of the people. Viewed in the context of the far longer careers of such contemporaries as Crawford and Bette Davis, or Garbo and Barbara Stanwyck, Harlow was here and gone almost before she had time to attract anybody's attention. Nevertheless, such was the impact of her unique brand of bold, good-humoured sex appeal, she is still regarded as one of the greatest stars of what was undoubtedly Hollywood's greatest period.

But what makes her particularly arresting is the mystery which, fifty years later, still surrounds her life and her death. What was her connection with such unsavoury characters as Bugsy Siegel, a notorious gangster, bootlegger and heroin pusher? Why did she marry a man who was twice her age and widely known to be impotent? And why, two months after the wedding, did her husband kill himself? Where was Harlow on the night he died? How do you explain the paradox of a professional sexpot who, on screen, never wore underwear, dyed her pubic hair platinum and rubbed her nipples with ice to make them stare unwinkingly at the camera, and the off-screen personality who, as everyone seems to agree, was not particularly interested in

sex, lived most of her life with her mother and enjoyed childlike pursuits such as visiting funfairs and playing musical chairs? What was the truth of her love affair with William Powell? Why did she die so young? Did she, as some people have even suggested, want to die?

Questions like those, many of them unanswered and by now probably unanswerable, have led to at least one scurrilous biography of her and a host of rumours which, clinging to the poor girl's reputation like bindweed, are earnestly spread by people who will tell you, with simple candour and quite undeterred by their ignorance of the facts, that she was little better than a hooker, a sexual raver who would prowl the streets and seedy hotels picking up taxi drivers and bellhops and dragging them, protesting (feebly no doubt lest she should change her mind) into her bed.

Such is the peculiarly tacky quality of manure – whether actual or verbal – that when thrown it tends to stick and when stuck it tends to harden and becomes exceedingly difficult to scrape away. Thus when my researchers and I went to Hollywood to cast a stern investigative eye on the life and times of Jean Harlow we expected to return with a tale of wild lust, a scandal of monstrous proportions. But the facts, as we discovered them, were very different though not, I think, in their own way less interesting.

To begin, however, at the beginning. Jean Harlow was born Harlean Carpentier on March 3rd, 1911, in Kansas City, Missouri, the daughter of Montclair Carpentier, a local dentist, and his wife Jean, née Harlow.

Her mother, a pretty, plumpish blonde whose head appears to have been stuffed

Harlean Carpentier in the years before she became Jean Harlow.

with a positive candyfloss of romantic dreams, concocted the bizarre name Harlean by gluing together various parts of her own two names. Not surprisingly, Harlean never really caught on and for several years the infant Carpentier was under the firm impression that she had actually been christened "Baby".

The dominant figure throughout her childhood was her maternal grandfather, one S. D. Harlow, a wealthy Kansas City property dealer, at whose insistence Harlean was sent to the right kind of school "to meet the right kind of little girl". When their daughter was nine, the Carpentiers separated, quite amicably, and were later divorced and thereafter Harlean had little further contact with her father, a fact that may have had much to do with two of her three unsuccessful marriages. After the separation mother and daughter moved in with Grandfather Harlow and lived with him for two years, at which point Mrs. Carpentier – or Mama Jean as she came to be known in Hollywood – could no longer tolerate the old man's autocratic manner and ran off to Chicago where she met, fell in love with and secretly married Marino Bello, a dark, sophisticated Italian who lived by his wits and who was summed up swiftly but not, as it turned out, inaccurately by the irate S. D. Harlow as "an Italian gangster". This was, as a matter of fact, one of the kinder descriptions applied to Bello; most of the people I met who had known him being inclined to dismiss him as "a pimp".

However, with no more blessing from her father than a grunt of rage, Mama Jean left little Harlean in her parental home and took off with Bello, who installed her in various second-rate hotels and apartments while he earned a living of sorts as a food salesman or waiter or the vendor of dubious stocks and shares.

A few years later mother and daughter were briefly reunited in Los Angeles where Harlean was sent to the Hollywood School for Girls but pretty soon Grandfather Harlow, who still wielded considerable influence on account of the fact that his money had bailed the Bellos out of trouble from time to time, had the child taken away from there and sent to a finishing school in Illinois.

Here the sixteen-year-old Harlean, unhappy and homesick, met Charles McGrew at a Saturday afternoon dance. He was twenty-one and the son of wealthy Chicago business people. Harlean wrote to her family saying she liked him better than anyone she had ever met but would give him up if she were allowed to leave school and return home. The family decided to call her bluff and discovered she wasn't bluffing at all. One Sunday in March 1927, she and McGrew eloped and were married. Now both families stepped in, the couple were promptly separated and Harlean ended up in Hollywood once more and with Mama Jean and Bello.

As a breadwinner for his wife and stepdaughter Bello proved, to say the least, inadequate and not particularly enthusiastic and so, inspired probably by wispy dreams of discovery and stardom, Mama Jean found work as an extra in silent films and took young Harlean with her. In the event, of course, it was Harlean who was discovered, initially by Hal Roach, the head of a comedy factory which turned out a succession of Harold Lloyd and Laurel and Hardy two-reelers.

An agent brought her to his studio and, as Roach recalls, "I took a good look at her and I knew that she was photogenic and there was no question that she had a good body and at twelve thirty when they left the office I had a seven-year contract with Jean Harlow." By this time she had already adopted her mother's maiden name for professional purposes.

The following week Jean Harlow started work at the Roach studios and, significantly, Mama Jean and Bello came with her, thus establishing a close liaison that was never to be broken. Later, after her divorce from Charles McGrew in 1931, Harlow was twice married again and set up homes of her own but not for long. In both cases she was back living with her mother within a matter of months.

Harlow's first role for Hal Roach was a bit part in the Laurel and Hardy comedy, *Double Whoopee*, in which Laurel slams the door as she steps out of a taxi and rips her skirt off. Before the scene was shot she was asked whether she was "under-dressed" – in other words, was she wearing flesh-coloured tights beneath her underwear. She wasn't, in fact, but being unfamiliar with this technical language and assuming merely that they wanted to be quite sure she had her knickers on, she said she was.

The result, when the skirt was pulled off, was that she was revealed to be practically naked and the excitement was such that chaos ensued on the set. Whether news of this filtered back to Kansas City and annoyed old S. D. Harlow, or whether he merely disapproved of movies in general, she appeared in Roach's office a few days later and said that her grandfather, on whom she and her mother were still dependent for the odd handout, disliked her working in pictures and would it be all right if they tore the contract up? Roach, under the impression that she was returning to Kansas City to resume married life with McGrew, agreed.

This was in 1928 when Harlow was seventeen, and whether or not she did return temporarily to McGrew is unclear. But by 1929 she was back in Hollywood, doing the rounds as an extra again with her mother. Perhaps her grandfather's disapproval had been overcome or perhaps she simply defied him. In any event, later that year she had a small part as a salesgirl in *Saturday Night Kid* and was then signed to a contract by Howard Hughes, who had just made a silent picture called *Hell's Angels* about the Royal Flying Corps. The stars were Ben Lyon and James Hall, as a couple of Oxford undergraduates who joined up in the First World War and Greta Nissen, a Norwegian actress, as the middle-class English girl who loved them both. In a silent movie the fact that Miss Nissen had an accent that was practically incomprehensible was neither here nor there but just as the film was nearing completion talkies were introduced and Hughes decided to reshoot the whole thing with sound. Now, of course, he had problems. Lyon and Hall were not all that convincing as Oxford undergraduates but Greta Nissen, as a middle-class English girl, would be, to put it mildly, unbelievable. So, for two or three months, he sought around unsuccessfully for a replacement and it was at this stage that Ben Lyon, wandering by chance on to another set at the *Hell's Angels* studio, spotted an extra named Jean Harlow. He said: "I've never seen anything like it in my life" – this, incidentally, from a man who later on was to discover Marilyn Monroe – "she had silver hair, a fabulous figure and very tight-fitting black satin gown which showed every curve in her body. I went

With Mama Jean.

over to her and said, 'How would you like to play the lead in *Hell's Angels*?' "

She responded in the wary manner of every beautiful extra believing herself threatened (or lured, according to inclination) by the casting couch. She said: "What do I have to do?" Lyon, an honourable man, explained that she merely had to meet Howard Hughes, which she did, and that night, despite Hughes' scepticism, she made a test with Ben Lyon and the next morning signed a three-year contract.

The film opened in June 1930 at Graumann's Chinese Theatre on Hollywood Boulevard and though Harlow's English accent was no closer to London than Kansas City she did at least have the advantage of sounding considerably less Norwegian than Greta Nissen. More to the point, despite the inadequacy of her acting, her obvious appeal, allied to her role as a faithless girl dallying with both leading men, brought her immediate attention as the screen's latest sex object. As one critic perceptively remarked: "She probably always will have to play these kind of roles but nobody ever starved possessing what

29

she's got." The reviews of her actual performance were less kind but even so it was quite clear that she was already on her way.

One of the more persistent rumours about Harlow concerns this period of her life, for it is said that she had some kind of affair with Howard Hughes, who was himself still in his twenties at the time. Blanche Williams, who was Harlow's maid then and indeed until her death, thinks it's unlikely that there was anything between them at all and the evidence seems to support that view. Hughes wasn't even sufficiently interested in Harlow to find film roles for her or to help her improve her decidedly shaky knowledge of the acting craft. Instead, at a large profit to himself, he lent her out to other studios and, as Hughes cashed in on her popularity as "America's new Blonde Bombshell", she appeared with Wallace Beery in *The Secret Six* at MGM; with Lew Ayres in *The Iron Man* at Universal; with James Cagney in *The Public Enemy* at Warner Bros; with Spencer Tracy in *Goldie* at Fox; with Loretta Young and Robert Williams in *Platinum Blonde* at Columbia and, again at Columbia, with Mae Clark and Walter Byron in *Three Wise Girls*, the important difference this time being that, at last, Harlow had top billing. The roles varied from gold-digger, to faithless wife, to gangster's moll and small town girl trying to make good and her reviews were not generally a great deal better than they had been for *Hell's Angels*. But who cared what the critics thought? The public had noticed her and the male section of it most certainly approved.

During the release of *Hell's Angels* she had made a series of personal appearances during which a public image, totally at variance with her private self, was manufactured for her by sharp publicity men. Thus she was credited with providing the punch-lines in such saucy exchanges as:

"Jean, how do you like to wake up in the morning?" – "I like to wake up feeling a new man."

"Are you wearing a brassiere, Miss Harlow?" – "That sounds like a near-sighted question."

"Would you steal a husband, Miss Harlow?" – "Wouldn't that be like shoplifting in a second-hand store?" And so on.

Well, all this together with her raunchy screen persona – those plucked eyebrows painted artificially into two startled but amused half-moons, those tight-fitting dresses which suggested, quite accurately, that underneath there was only Harlow – identified her as the blonde good-natured tart from the wrong side of the tracks, the easy, sleazy lay who would give a man a nice time and send him on his way with fond memories. Professionally, the picture thus created could do her little but good but privately the received impression of Jean Harlow was a burden under which she suffered for the rest of her life. She was not, by all accounts, in any way a promiscuous girl but she was inevitably treated as such. More than once she complained to her confidante, Adela Rogers St. Johns, the writer and journalist, that even her friends' husbands, mistaking the image for the reality, would make passes at her and that she grew increasingly tired of being treated "like a bitch on heat".

She also said in an interview: "Believe me, the real Jean Harlow has nothing in common with the shadow one. Sex is something which is all very well on the screen but more than a mild nuisance off it." On the other hand, if men did follow her around like randy puppies, she could hardly claim total innocence, protesting that it was nothing to do with her. She was, after all, the first actress to appear regularly in films without a brassiere or indeed any other form of underwear, and this at a time when the untrammelled bust was a startling revelation even if, as in her case, it was only suggested and not actually revealed.

She did, after all, rub her nipples with ice and she did, after all, dye her pubic hair to match the hair on her head. Admittedly, this was not done in an attempt to delude those in the privileged position of being able to compare the colour of one with the colour of the other that she was a natural platinum blonde but, more prosaically, because she nearly always wore white in her films and a tight white dress, not backed up by underwear, would reveal a distinct five o'clock shadow unless she shaved or used dye. The fact remains, however, that as far as I know, nobody ever forced her to dress that way so the virtually naked look was presumably her own idea, suggesting that somewhere in her personality there was a strong element of the tease, a desire to titillate.

And yet none of this seems to have spilled

over into her private life. Blanche Williams admits that Harlow never wore a brassiere at any time but then "she didn't need one". Apart from that unusual – for the 1930s – idiosyncrasy she dressed demurely off-screen, mostly in blouse and slacks. And, again according to Blanche Williams, she showed no personal awareness of being a particularly beautiful or desirable woman. It was almost as though Harlow herself regarded Harlow the actress as an entirely different person, or as an identity she assumed in order to earn a living but one that had little to do with her. Kay Mulvey, who handled her publicity at MGM and was a close personal friend, said she looked upon the sex image as part of the job and no more than that and that, away from the studio, she was "warm, affectionate and friendly".

"I had a little beach house and she loved to come down there and spend the night or the week or whatever. I remember one morning, very, very early, she and my young son were making mud pies and she taught him to put raw eggs in them because they stuck together better." This is not a particularly exciting anecdote perhaps, but at least it indicates a kind of knowledge you would hardly expect a dedicated sexpot to possess. Again, when she was at MGM, she would often fill in the time between takes by cutting out paper dolls, another pastime that clashes oddly with the view of Harlow as an insatiable man-eater.

Her career at MGM began in 1932 when Howard Hughes, who had presumably given up any thought of finding another film for her, sold her contract. One of his stipulations was that he would have the right to use her in two pictures over the next five years but he never bothered and that, too, seems to indicate that his interest in her was no more than slight. By the time she arrived at MGM the film *Platinum Blonde*, in which she only had third billing, had established her as *the* platinum blonde and had led to the founding of the Platinum Blonde Clubs in at least a hundred American cities. Women of all ages were beginning to imitate her dress, her make-up and her speech mannerisms. As an actress she was still finding few admirers, but as a star she had definitely arrived.

As tangible evidence of this new status she had bought a Spanish-style house in West Los Angeles where, naturally, Mama Jean and Bello installed themselves in great comfort and Bello took over the handling of his stepdaughter's money, which he proceeded to spend and invest with the foolish prodigality of one who, not having earned it, suffered no pain at its loss.

Bello was, without doubt, the most baleful influence in Jean Harlow's life and she was aware of it. She detested him and referred to him curtly in public as "Bello" but she had to tolerate him because of her mother, whom she adored. Hal Roach described the two women as being more like sisters than mother and daughter but also had the strong feeling that Mama Jean was living her own life vicariously, soaking up the limelight that she wanted but that actually fell on her daughter. Kay Mulvey said: "Mama Jean worshipped her. She was terribly, terribly proud of having such a beautiful daughter and wanted the world to see her. Her whole life was 'the Baby' and they were very, very dear friends."

But at the same time Mama Jean was besotted by Bello and remained so until their divorce shortly before Jean's death and she appears to have raised no objections when her husband tried to involve her daughter with gangsters. In the early 1930s the Mafia and other crime syndicates were thought to be trying to muscle in on Hollywood and Bello wanted a part of whatever racket was going. When Bugsy Siegel arrived in town after a no doubt lucrative career with even more obnoxious people than himself, heroin-pushing for Lucky Luciano and bootlegging for Meyer Lansky, for example, and tried to set up a protection racket, Bello was keen to get a piece of the action. But all he had to distinguish him from similar would-be racketeers clamouring for Siegel's attention was his stepdaughter.

So he used her to ingratiate himself, arranging dinner dates and the like for Siegel and his associates with Jean. There is no evidence whatsoever that she slept with any of these people, or had any kind of close association with them, but to please Bello – or more specifically her mother – she was obliged to mix with them socially and it could be that degrading experience which contributed to her embarking on the second, and quite the most disastrous, of her marriages.

By July 1932 Harlow had completed the first two films of her MGM contract, *The*

Paul Bern, Harlow's second husband, who shot himself soon after the wedding.

Beast of the City, a gangster movie with Walter Huston, and *Red Headed Woman*, in which she played a promiscuous and ambitious gold-digger opposite Chester Morris, and was embarked on her third, *Red Dust*, the first picture in which she co-starred with Clark Gable. But also that month she married Paul Bern, the right-hand man to Irving Thalberg, MGM's head of production. Why she married Bern is a question that nobody has ever been able to answer. She was twenty-one years old and he was forty-two, a physically unprepossessing little man with receding hair and a small moustache. He was known as Hollywood's "Father Confessor", the man to whom the stars, especially the women, would confide their problems. He was also widely known to be impotent and after his death he was found to be sexually underdeveloped. That he had a liking for the company of beautiful women there is no doubt but there is equally no question that he had any sort of physical relationship with them. Hal Roach recalled that, just before he married Harlow, Bern had set up another girl in a Hollywood flat and would

visit her every afternoon, the procedure being that she would take off her clothes and lie on the bed and he would read poetry to her for an hour or so. Then they would both have tea and he would leave.

Harlow first met Bern when she made *The Secret Six* while on loan to MGM in 1931 and began to go out with him regularly soon after she joined the studio the following year. Why she should have chosen him when she could have had her pick of every eligible male in a community weighed down to below the Plimsoll line with eligible males is a mystery that has never been resolved.

Several theories have been put forward, none of them wholly convincing. Kay Mulvey, for instance, believed Harlow was looking for a father substitute: "Bern was a very kind, highly intelligent man. She had immense respect for him and I think it was the father image and what he represented, his knowledge and that sort of thing, that attracted her to him." Blanche Williams thinks she married for security and to advance her career. As the wife of Irving Thalberg, Norma Shearer was given first choice of the most desirable roles at MGM. It is, therefore, possible that Harlow may have argued that as the wife of Thalberg's assistant she would at least get the pick of what Shearer left. John Lee Mayhin, the scriptwriter who wrote two of Harlow's best films, *Red Dust* and *Bombshell*, goes along with the father image theory: "She always searched for older men, I think because she missed her own father terribly." Mayhin, however, took a less complimentary view of Bern than most of the other people I talked to. "He was a man who loved to hear trouble," he said. "His attitude was 'Tell me about it, tell me about it – you're having trouble, tell me about it.' That's the kind of fella Paul was. He liked misery. I think he liked misery in himself."

What can probably be regarded as the official MGM version of the Harlow–Bern romance was advanced by Howard Strickling, the head of publicity there and the man who was privy to all the studio's secrets. According to him Bern was "a dreamer, an intellectual, gentle and cultured. He felt sorry for Jean because of her mother and Bello. He would read to her, encourage her to read and to use her brain. He built up her confidence and wooed her. He sent her little gifts and flowers, which no other man did and he introduced her to the homes of Mayer and Thalberg. She'd never been invited there before because neither man really knew her and they thought she was the kind of girl she played on screen, just a sexpot. So Bern gave her the entrée to the homes of these powerful people." But beyond all the social and professional benefits that Bern could confer upon her there were two other vital elements that may have persuaded her to marry him. First, she wanted to get away from her mother and Bello and secondly, at no time did Bern try to seduce her. Strickling said that sex never meant very much to her but, because of the way she looked men treated her as a "pushover". At this point, he believed, she had almost certainly never had an affair with another Hollywood star and her experiences with men had mostly been confined to the rough gropings of Bello's gangster friends and the scarcely more subtle approaches of young Hollywood studs whose idea of making a gentle pass was to grab whatever part of her anatomy came most conveniently to hand. Bern, by contrast, treated her like a lady, wooed her with gentle courtesy and never attempted to lay a hand on her.

The explanation of that, of course, was quite simple: he was impotent, not just psychologically impotent but incapable of having sex. But did Harlow know that? One theory is that she must have done because it was common knowledge in Hollywood. Another is that she was unaware of the fact until after the wedding. And a third, and most astonishing of all, is what one might again call the official version, once more put forward by Howard Strickling who said that Harlow was unaware of her husband's impotence until after his death – by which time they had been married for two months. Strickling claims that the day Bern's body was discovered and before making any statements to the press, he took Harlow to one side and asked her to tell him the truth about the marriage and according to him she said she had thought it strange that Bern had never attempted to make love to her but he had told her: "That will come later. For six months we will have a wonderful, spiritual romance together." She accepted this, she said, because at that time sex was repulsive to her. Picking up on that last statement there is yet another theory that Harlow

knew all along about Bern's impotence but married him nevertheless or even because of it. The most likely explanation, however, is that she made the discovery the night after the wedding, a fairly impressive ceremony attended by Thalberg, Mayer and various other Hollywood dignitaries.

Blanche Williams, who never liked Bern because she believed he was using Harlow as a front on the principle that a man with a wife as glamorous and apparently sexy as that was unlikely to be impotent, had a brief and possibly significant exchange with him on the wedding night when he came out of Harlow's bedroom and told her: "The Baby's still a virgin." Blanche said: "I knew very well she couldn't be a virgin. She'd been married before. I'm not that dumb. What I think he meant was that he'd had no sexual relations with her."

The truth of Harlow's marriage to Bern is further confused by the sordid legend that has since grown up around it. There are stories that he was so frustrated and enraged at his inability to consummate the marriage that he would beat her up and that he inflicted upon her the kidney damage that was to lead to her death five years later. There are startling tales of Harlow, bruised, bleeding and battered, fleeing to the homes of friends in the middle of the night to escape the fiend she had married. But none of this seems at all likely. As Adela Rogers St. Johns says: "She was a big, strong, healthy girl and he was a puny little man. Why should she let him beat her up?" Besides, Howard Strickling says that although all Hollywood wondered about the marriage the couple seemed happy enough, until, that is, the night of September 4th, 1932, two months after the wedding.

Once more there is a considerable mystery about the events leading up to that night – the night when Paul Bern, his naked body doused in Harlow's favourite perfume, shot himself to death in front of the mirror in the dressing-room of his home. And once more it's a question of trying to sort out what seems most likely to have happened from a veritable thicket of conflicting rumours.

According to one, Harlow was in the house when the suicide occurred and she discovered the body; according to another she had been away for the night and only learned of her husband's death when MGM and more specifically Howard Strickling called to deliver the news; according to a third, which cleverly mixes up both the foregoing, she had been away but returned and then, for some unexplained but undoubtedly sinister reason, drove off again at three o'clock in the morning and at high speed.

According to a fourth – a particularly wild one this – she had murdered Bern herself and only escaped prosecution thanks to an MGM cover-up; and according to a fifth, hardly less wild, Bern had actually been killed by a Mafia hitman fulfilling a contract put out by Marino Bello, who was naturally incensed at seeing the control of Harlow's money and business affairs passing into other hands than his own.

Sifting through these different stories, it seems most plausible that Bern had indeed sent Harlow away on the afternoon before his death. Marino Bello had gone fishing with Clark Gable and, according to Harlow's own account, as reported to Howard Strickling, Bern had instructed his wife to go and stay the night with Mama Jean, who hated to be alone. He may well have had an ulterior motive in this because it now seems likely that he wanted the house to himself so that he could have some kind of showdown with a mysterious woman called Dorothy Milette who, it later transpired, had once been his common law wife – though hardly in the full physical sense – and who had turned up, unexpectedly, in Los Angeles. There is no proof that Milette did visit him on the night of September 4th but there is circumstantial evidence that somebody was there because two – or in some versions three – glasses were found bearing the remains of drinks. They couldn't have been used by the servants because the servants had been given the night off. So perhaps Dorothy Milette did call on Bern and perhaps she put some kind of pressure on him, blackmail possibly, which in conjunction with the strain he must have been undergoing in trying to keep up the pretence of a normal marriage with a young and beautiful wife, whose disenchantment with sex was presumably not going to last for ever, caused him to commit suicide.

As to that nobody will ever know because three days after Bern's death Dorothy Milette drowned herself in the Sacramento River, leaving behind very little information about herself, save that she had been living for the previous ten years at the Algonquin Hotel in New York under the name of Mrs. Paul Bern. And Bern had lived in New York before he went to Hollywood.

What is known, or at least what is now widely accepted, is that Bern's body was discovered in the morning by his butler and beside the body was a note, addressed to Harlow, that read: "Dearest Dear, Unfortunately this is the only way to make good the frightful wrong I have done you and to wipe out my abject humiliation. I love you. Paul." And then there was a postscript: "You understand that last night was only a comedy." The butler phoned MGM and some time later MGM phoned the police.

Some people, among them Kay Mulvey, believed that Howard Strickling was the first studio representative to arrive at the house, that he found Harlow already there and immediately sent her away to her mother's with orders to insist that that was where she had been all the time. Blanche Williams, on the other hand, said that she and Harlow had in fact gone to Mama Jean's the previous day and had stayed there; that Harlow had spoken to Bern on the phone from there several times and that Bern had promised to join her later. Strickling's own story is that Harlow was never at her home, either on the night of the suicide or the following morning, that she had been notified of Bern's death by Norma Shearer, who had been told to call her by Irving Thalberg, and that in any case both Thalberg and Louis Mayer were at the Bern house by the time he, Strickling, arrived.

Furthermore, he said, he met Mayer wandering away from the place, muttering that it was a terrible business and holding the suicide note in his hand, under the curious impression that it was best kept from the police. It was only after much persuasion that Strickling was able to convince him to put it back where he'd found it. Without that note it is quite possible that the police would have taken a much deeper interest in Harlow's movements the previous night than they appear to have done. As it is, Strickling says that no official suspicion ever fell on her at all.

He also says that after the police were

called, by MGM and from Bern's house, he went to see Harlow and asked for an explanation of the note but she claimed then, and persisted in claiming later, that she had no idea what it meant, although the most prevalent belief now is that "the frightful wrong" and "my abject humiliation" referred to his impotence and that the postscript – "last night was only a comedy" – was a reference to some final, desperate and ultimately farcical attempt by him to make love to his wife.

Certainly the despair that caused him to kill himself was most probably brought about by his impotence, his realisation that he had made a fool of himself by marrying the girl and the reasonable suspicion that she was unlikely to be happy to go without sex for the rest of her life. A divorce on some trumped-up grounds would now seem to have been a less drastic and more logical solution to his predicament but a man in the mood to kill himself doesn't necessarily seek around for a logical way out.

MGM handled the newspaper coverage of the tragedy and handled it extraordinarily well. Any suggestion that the sex goddess of the screen couldn't even arouse her own husband in bed was carefully avoided and even Harlow's rapid return to work – barely a week after Bern's death – was explained as medical therapy, the only way to take her mind off her grief. She was still filming *Red Dust* and the first scene she had to do when she went back to the studio was the famous sequence in which she is taking a bath in a rain barrel and Gable turns up to ask what she thinks she's doing. Her original response to that in the script was to say: "Don't you know? I'm La Flamme, the girl that drives men mad." "When she came to that line," said John Lee Mayhin, "she looked over to me and said, 'I don't have to say that, do I?' and I said, 'I'm sure you don't' and the line was cut."

Professionally, despite Bern's suicide which, without MGM's support could have destroyed her career, Harlow continued to thrive. *Red Dust* in which her "effortless vulgarity, humour and slovenliness make a noteworthy characterisation" established her as a promising comedienne. *Hold Your Man*, another comedy with Gable, reinforced that reputation, *Bombshell*, in which she played, ironically, a film star surrounded by a parasitic family, provided further evidence of her increasing ability and *Dinner at Eight* confirmed the fact that she was now an actress of impressive, if limited, skill.

George Cukor, who directed the latter film said that she had the trick, later shared by Marilyn Monroe, of speaking her lines as though she didn't quite understand them and thus creating enormous comic effect. *Dinner at Eight* also, of course, provided one of the classic exchanges of the cinema. At the very end of the film, Harlow, playing once again a dumb *femme fatale*, tells Marie Dressler: "You know, I read a book today." Dressler, naturally incredulous, does a magnificent double-take and Harlow continues: "It says machinery is going to replace every profession," at which Dressler, staring thoughtfully at the voluptuous, tarty, satin-gowned Harlow, replies: "Oh, my dear, that's something *you* need never worry about."

Before work on *Dinner at Eight* was completed, however, Harlow had married again. She married Hal Rosson, the cameraman who had worked with her on *Bombshell*. Once again he was considerably older than herself – thirty-eight to her twenty-two – and, remarkably he bore a close physical resemblance to Paul Bern. Once again, though, nobody seemed quite sure why she had married him. Another father image perhaps, another attempt to escape from Mama Jean and Bello with whom, inevitably, she had been living since Bern's death, a desire to lead a quiet, normal married life. Howard Strickling said: "She wanted a bulwark against Bello and Hal Rosson seemed to provide it. He was a dull guy, who had never married and loved dogs. He was flattered by her attention."

Kay Mulvey believed the marriage was an escape, an attempt to establish her own identity away from her mother; she did not believe that Harlow was ever really in love with Rosson. John Lee Mayhin, who was a close friend of Rosson, says he was "a sweet, dear, gentle man but he wasn't the type of man who knew what to do with a girl like that. I don't think he ever helped her out with her emotional life."

Whatever the reasons, Harlow married Hal Rosson in September 1933, little more than a year after Bern's suicide. The couple moved to a tiny apartment on Sunset Boulevard and she wrote a novel, a love

Mama Jean, Harlow and third husband Hal Rosson, the cameraman. Behind them Harlow's stepfather Marino Bello – "the Italian gangster".

story called *Today is Tonight* about which she once said: "It deals with the contrasting difficulties that inevitably overtake most normal couples who are in love and happen to be sharing life together . . . Sex plays only the usual part in their story. I think they are like plenty of normal, happy people I see around me." The sort of people, perhaps, whose lives she envied. MGM bought the screen rights to the book without ever intending to film it. Kay Mulvey believed that they did so to provide some kind of allowance or annuity for Mama Jean.

This generosity, however, was misplaced. Within a very short time the Rossons had left their own apartment and moved in with Mama Jean and Bello in Harlow's house in Beverly Hills and soon after that Rosson moved out, never to return. The marriage, as such, lasted only eight months but even so was the longest of all Harlow's marriages. The probability is that Rosson was simply driven away by the hostility of Mama Jean and Bello, neither of whom liked him. And Harlow herself was not sufficiently in love with him to intervene on his behalf.

The fact that here she was, the world's number one sex symbol, but totally unable to hold a husband, both confused and distressed her. Around the time of the separation from Rosson she asked John Lee Mayhin, "What's lacking in me?" To which he replied, "The right man." She was eventually to find the right man but too late to do either of them any good.

The marriage to Rosson – the last of what she once described wryly as her "three marriages of inconvenience" – was Harlow's final attempt to get away from her mother and stepfather. In the end, ironically, Bello was the one who would leave, though not voluntarily. But before that happened Harlow made her first musical, *Reckless*, a story inspired by a contemporary Broadway scandal, in which she played a musical comedy star whose neurotic husband committed suicide. The film, a melodrama, did little enough for her career since she couldn't sing much and didn't dance a lot better, but it was important to her nevertheless because it introduced her to William Powell, her co-star. Adela Rogers St. Johns says that Harlow fell in love with him the moment she met him, a remark that probably owed a great deal to hindsight and Mrs. St. Johns' own romantic nature, but there is no doubt that the pair of them swiftly became very close indeed.

By 1935 when the love affair, which her friends believe was the only true love affair of Harlow's life, began Powell was forty-three and she was twenty-four. Physically he had much in common with Bern and Rosson, the dark hair swept back from the temples, the small, neat moustache, and, like Bern, he was an intelligent, sophisticated man.

Harlow's great friend at MGM was Clark Gable but they were simply friends; conventionally handsome men and those who on film were the male equivalents of herself, sex objects, seemed to hold no particular appeal for her and all her life she was attracted to the type epitomised by Powell, men of real or apparent dignity and culture, men of the world who were old enough, or almost, to be her father. Oddly enough, Marino Bello fell more or less into the same category, superficially at least, and perhaps she was repelled by him because she saw him as a counterfeit version, a crude caricature of the kind of father/lover she was seeking. Well, who knows? Harlow never explained her taste in men and indeed had the grace and good sense to reveal very little of her private life.

The affair with William Powell, who had previously been married to Carole Lombard, is another of the mysteries in Harlow's life. Blanche Williams says that he "loved her with a passion" and remembers that he once sent her an enormous box which, when it was opened and masses of tissue paper removed, was found to contain a handsome cheque with which to buy a fur coat. But Blanche also says that Harlow didn't quite return that passion. Jesse Lasky Jr., the son of one of Hollywood's founders, who had a platonic relationship with Harlow after the divorce from Rosson, says that their friendship ended when she "went back to William Powell", the clear implication being that there had been some sort of estrangement between them. Lasky further believes that the affair was "constantly on and off", possibly because Harlow was a volatile and restless character "at one moment talking to you on a deep level, searching her own soul, and the next charging around, wanting to go to the beach, to ride in a roller-coaster, to drive a car very fast or play a game".

Adela Rogers St. Johns disagrees with Blanche and says that Harlow was more in love with Powell than he was with her and says she was present when Harlow knelt beside him one day and asked why he wouldn't marry her. His reply, according to Mrs. St. Johns, was that he had already been married to one "blonde bombshell" (Lombard) and was too old to take on another.

But against that there is the testimony of Howard Strickling who believes Powell and Harlow would have married, had she lived, and "this would have been her salvation", in other words that as Mrs. Powell she could finally have cut the long, tough cord that tied her to her mother. And Kay Mulvey, who probably knew her as well as anybody and who, forty years later, could still weep at the memory of her death, maintained that Powell was "the one great love of her life. There's just no doubt about that. She was very much in love with him and he was with her. They were fantastic

for each other, they really were. Each had a terrific sense of humour and they were just great people together. It's very, very sad that she died before they were married." If that is so, and if, as Kay Mulvey said, they had been going together and spending weekends together on Ronald Colman's San Ysidro Ranch near Santa Barbara for two years before Harlow's death, why did they not marry sooner? The answer that she suggested, and it's a plausible one, is that "Jean wanted to be awfully sure not to make another mistake and I think Bill thought the same way. Also they were both working a lot and they were waiting for a time when their careers could let them be together for a while."

Powell himself, like Harlow, never talked publicly of the affair but, all things considered and bearing in mind the testimony of Blanche Williams that he had shown her the house he had had built for Harlow, the probability is that they would have married and that, as Howard Strickling said, the marriage would have been her salvation.

Meanwhile, as the relationship with Powell progressed, so did Harlow's career. In 1935 she vied, successfully, with Rosalind Russell for the favours of Clark Gable in *China Seas* and in 1936 she played a fisherman's daughter in love with Spencer Tracy in *Riffraff*, lost Clark Gable to Myrna Loy in *Wife vs Secretary*, won, lost and re-won Franchot Tone, the First World War pilot, in *Suzy* and lost William Powell (again to Myrna Loy) only to win Spencer Tracy as a consolation prize in *Libelled Lady*. The following year she co-starred with Robert Taylor in *Personal Property*. In all these films, whether the critics liked them generally or not, her own reviews were good and by now her position as the screen's sexiest, brassiest comedienne was pretty well unchallenged.

But early in 1937 there were rumours that she and William Powell had parted and she was seen in various Hollywood night spots with Donald Friede, a New York publisher who, apart from any personal interest, was hoping to bring out her novel, *Today is Tonight*. If there had been a quarrel there is one gossip writer of the period who now says, privately, that it came about because, for the first time in her relationships with men, Harlow was not the dominant personality.

In her last two marriages anyway she had been the star, "the Baby", the centre of attention. But Powell was also a star, and one whose status was equal to her own, and he was not prepared to wander along in her shadow. He was the first man to treat her as a woman and not as a glamorous celebrity and she was unsure how to react. Whether or not there was any substance to this, whatever quarrel there may have been was apparently resolved because early in May 1937, it was reported that Harlow went to the studios with a cake bearing three candles and said that Powell had sent it to her to mark the third anniversary of their first date, along with a card saying, "To my three-year-old from her daddy."

In that month, May, Harlow was completing her fifteenth film in five years at MGM, *Saratoga*, a story of love and honour and bookmakers and lost fortunes in which once again she co-starred with Clark Gable. On Saturday, May 29th, she complained of feeling ill, and after calling at the neighbouring set where William Powell was working to break the news to him, she went home and never again returned to the studio. Just over a week later, on the morning of June 7th, 1937, she died in the Good Samaritan Hospital.

What happened in the intervening eight days is unclear. She had been in bed and extremely ill with uremic poisoning, but she seems to have received no medical treatment at all. A nurse may have been called to look after her but even that is far from certain. It has been said that early in the week after she left the studio various representatives of MGM tried to visit her but were refused admission to the house by Mama Jean on the grounds that her daughter was sleeping.

What lay behind this curious behaviour was the fact that, since her divorce from Marino Bello nearly two years earlier on the grounds of his persistent adultery, Mama Jean had become a devout Christian Scientist. She did not believe in doctors, drugs or any kind of medication; she believed only in prayer and as her daughter lay dying she sought no help except from Christian Science readers. When eventually, and after much persuasion, MGM executives and Jean's friends, among them Clark Gable, were able to gain entry to the house, Harlow's condition was appalling. John Lee Mayhin said: "Clark told me that when he leant over to kiss her he could smell the urine on her breath. He said it was so shocking it was like kissing a dead person, a rotting person. He said 'It was a terrible thing to walk into . . . I hardly knew her, I hardly knew her.' "

A doctor was then summoned by Louis Mayer, overriding Mama Jean's objections, and on the Sunday night Harlow was rushed to hospital but by that time it was too late. She was given blood transfusions and placed in an oxygen tent where she died at 11.37 a.m. the following morning. William Powell and Mama Jean were beside her bed. A writer at MGM said later: "The day the Baby died there wasn't one sound in the commissary (the studio restaurant) for three hours – not one goddamned sound."

Whether Harlow could have been saved if a doctor had been called immediately she went home ill from the studio it's difficult to say. An acute infection, starting in the gall bladder, had spread throughout her system. Her kidneys were damaged and uremic poisoning rapidly set in. But what caused the infection was another matter for scandalous conjecture. It was said that she had suffered second degree burns while sunbathing, that she had been poisoned by the bleach she used on her hair, that her kidneys had been damaged by beatings she received from Paul Bern, that she had had an abortion that went wrong, that she had been killed by excessive drinking, even that she had died of syphilis. All of these can be discounted. Her death certificate in Los Angeles Coroner's Court declares that death was caused by uremic poisoning but how she contracted it nobody knows.

There is even a theory, suggested by, among others, Anita Loos, the author of *Gentlemen Prefer Blondes*, that Harlow may have wanted to die. In her book, *Kiss Hollywood Goodbye*, Miss Loos says that Powell had "walked out on Jean because he really wanted a 'little Miss Nobody' " and adds: "After Bill's rejection, Jean seemed to lose interest in everything and when stricken she refused to put up a fight. It was as if Jean took advantage of a minor ailment to escape from life." But as a theory this doesn't bear very close scrutiny. Whatever the origin of Harlow's ailment it could hardly be called minor. And William Powell's behaviour after her death seems conclusively to refute any suggestion that

the love affair between them was over and that he had rejected her.

Harlow was buried, three days after her death, at Forest Lawn, the garish and theatrical graveyard of the stars. The funeral was arranged by Mama Jean and Powell. Two hundred people were invited and in addition more than a thousand sightseers crowded round the gates to watch the funeral cortege pass by. At nine a.m. when the service began, conducted incidentally by a Christian Science reader, a one-minute silence was observed in all the studios of Hollywood. In the chapel itself Nelson Eddy and Jeannette Macdonald sang "The Indian Love Call" and "Ah, Sweet Mystery of Life", thus introducing a note of such sentimental vulgarity (for which, presumably, Mama Jean was responsible) that Carole Lombard, who was there with Clark Gable, immediately stipulated that nothing

so outlandish was to be perpetrated at her funeral. The casket was covered by 1,500 lilies of the valley and 500 gardenias, again provided by Powell and Mama Jean and it was Powell who bought the crypt, nine feet long, ten feet wide, lined with marble and costing 25,000 dollars, in which the body was interred. When the coffin was closed after the traditional lying-in-state, so beloved of Hollywood, there was a single gardenia, Harlow's favourite flower, in her hand. There are some who say it was put there by the New York publisher, Donald Friede, but Louella Parsons, the omniscient gossip columnist of the age, said that in fact it was placed there by William Powell, together with a note that said: "Goodnight, my dearest darling."

When the service was over Powell was so grief-stricken that he had to be helped by friends as he walked away and

Harlow and William Powell, probably the only man she ever really loved. But note the similarity between him, Bern, Rosson and even Marino Bello.

afterwards he abandoned the film he had been making and went to Ronald Colman's ranch for a month to recuperate. In a column written a week after Harlow's death, Louella Parsons claimed that Harlow had loved Powell more than he loved her and revealed – safely enough since the subject of the piece was no longer around to deny it – that though Harlow had said to her, "I never knew the meaning of the word love until I met Bill," Harlow herself had never really believed they would marry because Powell was shy of matrimony. But that, too, conflicts with the opinions of the friends, like Kay Mulvey, who knew both parties. As a final postscript to the affair and as an indication perhaps of the depth of feeling that had existed between Powell and Harlow, Howard Strickling said that when, a little later, he was negotiating a new contract with MGM, Powell made it a condition that the studio should pay a certain amount of money to Mama Jean.

The impact of Harlow's death was astonishing. As the English critic C. A. Lejeune wrote: "Jean Harlow died on Monday. From the time of her death until the funeral on Thursday one national paper alone, I reckon, gave her fourteen columns. That was in England where Miss Harlow had never been seen in person . . . in England where sentiment and sensation are traditionally abhorrent. Princes could scarcely have collected more space . . . It was a bizarre fact but radically sound journalism. It reflected the wishes of a multitude of readers."

As an actress Harlow died too young to have achieved very much. She was improving all the time but her range was modest and she was far better in comedy than drama. Her great accomplishment was to make sex funny and to purvey it with an appeal that transcended all social classes. She once said: "I know I'm not a great actress and except for the early part of my life in Hollywood I never believed I was. But I happen to have something that the public likes." What she had, of course, was that lusty, healthy sexuality that made men think of her as the kind of girl who would be a glorious companion in bed but also a loyal and honest friend.

As a person she seems to have been one of nature's victims: the victim of a broken home, an ambitious mother and an unscrupulous stepfather; the victim of three unhappy marriages, one of which could have destroyed her; the victim of a love affair with William Powell which, one way or the other, ended tragically for both of them. In a sense perhaps, she was the victim of her own body because she looked what she simply was not – she was a child who happened to look like a vamp. Everyone, to the end of her life, referred to her as "the Baby", not just because she was very young but because she was childlike and simple in the best sense of that word. She was also, after her death, and indeed until this day, the victim of lies and rumours and innuendos that depict her as a tart and a harlot and she was neither of those things.

William Powell, at the time of writing, was well into his eighties, living in retirement in Palm Springs and, wisely no doubt, holding his peace.* Marino Bello died, after being involved in sundry nefarious schemes with Bugsy Siegel, in 1953. Mama Jean died five years later. Jean Harlow, who herself had died so many years earlier leaving very little money and a lot of debts, thanks to the activities of her mother and her stepfather, lives on in that curious approximation to immortality achieved only by the most notable of movie stars. Her beauty, which was never classic in any case, looks dated now but her popularity lasts and the reason for that is probably quite simple; Hollywood always seems synonymous with voluptuous sexy blondes but in fact there have only been two of any real note – Harlow and Marilyn Monroe – because none of the others have shared their special qualities of naughtiness and innocence, of worldly-wisdom and human warmth, of toughness and vulnerability and, above all, of humour.

---

* William Powell died, March 1984, aged 92.

Clark Gable

One day when Clark Gable was at an age when death was something that afflicted others and would never have the effrontery to come seeking him, he was asked to suggest an epitaph for himself. The one he resolved upon was both modest and accurate: "He was lucky and he knew it."

Clark Gable was lucky and he did know it. And because neither the luck nor his awareness of it ever deserted him – except on one dreadful night when a plane crashed in flames in the mountains near Las Vegas – he became and remained for the best part of thirty years the biggest male star Hollywood had ever known. Such a statement, of course, has to be treated with some reservations, for Hollywood, after all, is a town that deals only in superlatives. The story of the forthright hireling who, after a private screening of a new film, told its producer with a regretful shake of the head that in his opinion the movie was only great is not much of an exaggeration.

Nevertheless, and scaling everything down accordingly, Gable was the biggest, although at this distance, nearly two decades after his death, it's not easy to see why. But then nothing about Gable is easy. With him, more perhaps than with any other Hollywood star, it's difficult, if not indeed well-nigh impossible, to sort the man from the myth. Hollywood has always followed the dictum of one of its finest directors, the late John Ford, who said: "If the legend is more interesting than the truth, print the legend," and with Gable that is precisely what it has done.

He stood, for instance, 6 feet 1 inch tall, a respectable height in the 1930s when people generally tended to be shorter than they are now. But there are still men about, his contemporaries, taller than he, who speak of him with awe as though he were a veritable giant, a Colossus under whose huge legs petty men walked. There are people, too, who tell of the ease and charm with which he could devastate the most sophisticated of women. Well he had his share of those as every leading man must have done (it is, after all, one of the perks of the job) but the indications are that he was more at home chatting up waitresses and messenger girls and the friendly hookers from the house of Madame Frances.

The actress Virginia Gray, who loved him and indeed loves him still despite his rather cavalier behaviour towards her, says: "He had a brain that didn't quit – it was always going." But against that Joseph L. Mankiewicz, a director and scriptwriter of exceptional ability and one of the shrewdest observers of the Hollywood scene, sums him up somewhat differently: "Not very bright. Pleasant and undemanding."

In the end, perhaps, Gable was all those things. He was whatever appeared in the eye of the beholder. Seven years after he died, Joan Crawford, with whom he had once enjoyed a brief but ardent affair, wrote without fear of contradiction: "Clark Gable was the King of an empire called Hollywood. The empire is not what it once was – but the King has not been dethroned, even after death." Indeed not. In fact what happened was that the King died and they dissolved the monarchy, an act of which, to do him justice, Gable himself might well have approved.

"The King business," he said once, with a rich but less than regal turn of phrase, "is all bullshit. I was in the right place at the right time and I had a lot of smart guys helping me – that's all."

PREVIOUS PAGE: *Gable in* Gone with the Wind *with Vivien Leigh and* OPPOSITE: *in a more relaxed pose.*

41

Bullshit or not – and oddly enough there was less bullshit involved than one is wont to find in Hollywood – Gable was the King. He was accorded the crown in 1938, at a time when Hollywood and possibly even America itself felt the need of a king of some kind and as the result of a competition in Ed Sullivan's syndicated newspaper column. "Who do you think," the readers of this column were asked, "are the King and Queen of Hollywood?" Twenty million people responded – or so it's alleged and maybe the real bullshit attaches to that figure – and Gable was overwhelmingly elected. Myrna Loy was named the Queen, a fact which, forty years later, is probably known only to the most devoted movie buff.

On Gable, though, the title sat quite easily. In those days, even before the release of *Gone with the Wind*, he was Hollywood's leading leading man. He was larger than lifesize because the cinema audience wanted him so. Already, partly through his own qualities and partly through the efforts of the publicity machine, he had become an almost mythical creature, a dream figure desired by every woman and admired by every man. And if this public Gable bore only a passing resemblance to the good-looking and competent actor of the same name who worried about whether his fame and good fortune could possibly last and who fished his false teeth out of a glass every morning, it really didn't matter.

Once again Hollywood had successfully printed the legend.

In this case the legend began in Cadiz, Ohio, on February 1st, 1901, when a son, William Clark, was born to William H. Gable, a sometime farmer and sometime itinerant oil-driller, and his wife Adeline.

Adeline Gable, a frail and epileptic woman, endured a difficult pregnancy, having already endured a brief and largely unhappy marriage and died eight months after her son was born. For a while young Clark, known in those days as Billy, was looked after by his maternal relatives, although they, being Roman Catholic, hardly won the approval of his Protestant father. But when the boy was two William Gable was married again, to Jennie Dunlap, a milliner, of whom Clark later said: "She was a wonderful woman, although I didn't realise it then. She must have loved me very much because I was certainly not what you would call well-behaved. I was rather spoiled."

Clark Gable's scholastic achievements, first at Hopedale Grade School and later at Edinburgh High School, were distinctly less than spectacular. He was a useful baseball player but his grades were indifferent and he hardly seems to have been the answer to an adolescent maiden's prayer. A girl who dated him in his high school days said later, with more brevity than charity: "He wasn't particularly good-looking. His ears were too large." This latter criticism, of course, was to be levelled at him regularly for the rest of his life.

When Clark was sixteen, the family moved from Hopedale to a farm sixty miles away at Ravenna, Ohio. The lad didn't take very kindly to farm life nor, in fact, did he and his father take very kindly to each other. Their relationship at that time and for a long time afterwards was decidedly cool but in the frequent quarrels between father and son, Jennie, the stepmother, sided invariably with the boy and thanks to her intervention he left school at sixteen and went to Akron, Ohio, to work as a labourer in a tyre factory.

It was soon after he arrived there that he visited the music hall and developed such an interest in the theatre that he took on an unpaid, part-time job as call boy with the local stock company. Within a year, however, Jennie became seriously ill and Clark returned home from Akron to be with her when she died. The funeral over, he left home again, this time for New York where he found work on Broadway as a call boy for a play called *The Jest* starring John and Lionel Barrymore.

Neither the play nor the job lasted and Clark rejoined his father, who was now oil-drilling in Oklahoma, and became an oil-field apprentice, labouring for twelve hours a day at a dollar an hour. He hated this rather more, if anything, than he had hated farming.

So when, at twenty-one, he inherited three hundred dollars from his grandfather, he decided to try the stage again, to the total horror of his father who, having only the slightest acquaintance with the theatre, was well aware that it was inhabited entirely by perverts and was adamant that acting was no job for anyone with the remotest claim to being a man. After a series of frightful rows father and son parted, not to

speak to each other again for ten years.

Clark, whose interest in the arts – such as it was – had been imparted solely by his stepmother, joined a touring company in Kansas City and, when that folded, worked in a lumberyard and then sold ties in a department store. In the summer of 1922 he signed on with another insignificant theatre company in Oregon and there, largely because there was virtually nobody else available, he began to play supporting roles of respectable size, although by all accounts he was an extraordinarily unimpressive actor. "If he had any experience," said the wife of one of his producers at that time, "it must have been restricted to putting up and taking down the tent. He could get on and off the stage but didn't even always manage that successfully." He must, come to think of it, have been a quite remarkable sight – a big, clumsy, country boy with jug ears, a mouthful of bad teeth which, though his own in those days, looked as though they'd been designed for somebody else and huge hands for which, on stage, he could never find an adequate use.

He was always conscious of his hands. Years later, in 1933, when he made two films (*The White Sister* and *Night Flight*) with Helen Hayes he told her that it was on account of his hands that he could never have become a successful stage actor since he had no idea what to do with them. "What he thought was wonderful about films," said Miss Hayes, "was that when his hands, or his bananas as he called them – his bunches of bananas – got out of control the director could always cut to a close-up and therefore he was safe on the screen. But in the theatre nobody could help."

However, back in Oregon in the early 1920s, young Gable met the second of the three older women who were to figure so importantly in his life: Josephine Dillon, a former New York stage actress turned drama coach, who was fourteen years older than he. His stepmother, Jennie Dunlap, had taught him that there was more to life than scratching around on a farm and now Josephine Dillon began to turn him into something which, on casual inspection, could be taken for an actor. She persuaded him to drop the name Billy and use the more distinguished-sounding Clark; she taught him how to act and how to move and how to lower his rather high-pitched voice to a deeper, sexier and more impressively butch level. When, in 1924, Miss Dillon disbanded her theatre troupe and went to Hollywood, Gable followed her and in December of that year they were married.

The marriage itself does not appear to have been much of a success, the relationship being more on the lines of pupil and teacher, or even perhaps mother and son, than of husband and wife. And Gable's first attempt to establish himself in Hollywood was even less successful. Mrs. Gable did manage to find her youthful husband a few jobs as an extra in silent pictures but, outside the marital home, nobody cared; nobody even noticed. The likes of John Gilbert and Gilbert Roland were the men the public fancied at the moment and alongside their elegance and sophistication the large, ham-fisted Gable must have looked like the neighbourhood thug. Trading on his brief acquaintance with Lionel Barrymore he got himself a small part in a stage revival of *The Copperhead*, in which Barrymore starred, but when the run came to an end he left Hollywood. With both his career and his marriage virtually drifting hand-in-hand towards oblivion, the town seemed to have little more to offer him. So he accepted a contract with a stock company in Houston, Texas, and there met Ria Langham.

Throughout their married life Josephine Dillon had been acutely afraid that she would lose her husband to a younger girl. As it happened she had been worrying needlessly: she actually lost him to an even older woman. Ria Langham, a wealthy, thrice-married socialite and divorcée was, in fact, seventeen years older than Gable. Clearly he had considerable impact on her for when he left Houston she followed him to New York where she accorded him her patronage and, no doubt, other things as well. If Josephine Dillon had turned the theatrical tyro into an actor, Ria Langham converted the gauche country boy into a man of the world, teaching him dress-sense and the kind of manners demanded in the café society in which she moved.

At this stage, I suppose, Gable's chief success had been, to put it cruelly, as a sort of gigolo, the plaything of a pair of older women. But now in New York in 1928 he enjoyed a small triumph on the stage in a play called *Machinal* and partly as a result of that and partly as a result of Mrs. Langham's sponsorship he landed the leading role in the touring version of *The Last Mile*. This was a play about a convict which had already provided Spencer Tracy with a short-cut to a film contract and now, when he played it in Hollywood, was to do the same for Gable.

Mervyn Leroy, who was later to direct him in *The Homecoming*, was among those who witnessed Gable's performance and he described the experience to me thus: "I was sitting in about the second row and I saw this man with his arms on the bars, you know, because it was a jail scene and I couldn't take my eyes off of him because he had such power. Doing nothing he had such power. And I knew he was a star, absolutely knew. There was no argument about it." This latter statement, of course, may owe a great deal to hindsight, but nevertheless Mr. Leroy was sufficiently impressed to arrange a screen test for Gable at Warner Brothers Studio. Mr. Leroy says he thought the result was great which, allowing for Hollywood hyperbole, means that it must have been at least adequate but unfortunately Jack Warner, the head of the studio, and Darryl F. Zanuck, his acolyte, were less moved. They thought Gable's ears were too big and for that reason turned him down.

Later on, as Mr. Leroy tartly remarked, Warners would have been delighted to have him just to photograph his ears but by then it was too late because Metro-Goldwyn-Mayer had got him. Before that happened, however, he had played his first speaking role in a Western called *The Painted Desert* in which he was shot by Hopalong Cassidy, a fate which, to judge from his performance, was no worse than he deserved and then, ironically, he went back to Warners to appear with Barbara Stanwyck in *Night Nurse*. This film was to do a great deal for Gable but, because its release was held up, he was already under contract to MGM by the time Warners realised what kind of a prospect they had allowed to escape them.

The original MGM contract came about as a result of a screen test arranged by Lionel Barrymore and was offered without much enthusiasm. One of the casting directors said that with those ears he looked "like a giant sugar bowl" and Louis B. Mayer, the studio's omnipotent little dictator, dismissed him as a passing fad – "a gigolo with brass knuckles". Nevertheless his impact on the public was immediate and by the time *Night Nurse* came out as the seventh of eight Gable pictures released in 1931, his name, despite the comparative smallness of his role, was almost as important a selling-point as that of Barbara Stanwyck.

It was in *Night Nurse* that Gable, playing the chauffeur, portrayed for the first time "the gigolo with brass knuckles". To a public which in the early years of the Depression had grown tired of, or at least needed a change from, silky Latin lovers like Valentino and Ramon Navarro, Gable was something new and different. He brought to the screen an all-American ruggedness and just a touch of the blue-collar worker. Unlike, say, the remote and gorgeous Valentino, he was the kind of man that men thought they might become and women thought they might acquire and his mildly brutish treatment of women somehow pandered to both male and female wish-fulfilment.

What he had drawn in that role in *Night Nurse* was the outline of the screen image that was to make him the King. As the director Howard Hawks, Gable's cousin-by-marriage and frequent hunting companion, put it: "What you should realise about Gable is that in all his pictures that were any good he played a heavy. He played it with a grin and people liked him and he was the first to do that."

By the end of 1931 Gable's career was securely established and he had also managed to straighten out the somewhat tangled mess of his private life. Josephine Dillon divorced him in March that year and as soon as the divorce was final he married Ria Langham. Why he was so attracted to these far more mature women – at the time of their marriage, after all, Gable was only thirty but Ria Langham was forty-seven, old enough indeed to be his mother – is not quite clear. The easy and glib answer, I suppose, is that a mother-figure was precisely what he was seeking, but perhaps that's too easy and too glib. Gable himself was never forthcoming on the subject, but there is little doubt that without the help of these two women he would not have succeeded as an actor; certainly he would not have succeeded so quickly and it's difficult to escape the conclusion that, even assuming he had

Gable with Gilbert Roland, Constance Bennett and, on his right, his second wife, Ria Langham.

been fond of or in love with both of them at one time or another, he was also consciously using them. Josephine Dillon seems to have been in no doubt about that. "Clark told me frankly," she said, "that he wished to marry Ria Langham because she could do more for him financially. He is hard to live with because his career and ambition always come first." One has to bear in mind, of course, that there spoke a woman scorned, a woman who was openly bitter about his desertion of her and what she regarded as his subsequent financial meanness towards her. Even so, it is a fact that he abandoned both her and Ria as soon as something more attractive and possibly more beneficial came along.

It's also a fact that neither of those first two marriages was distinguished by any great fidelity on his part. In that eventful year of 1931 he made two films (*Dance, Fools, Dance* and *Laughing Sinners*) with

Joan Crawford and by the time they appeared together again in *Possessed* in 1932 their relationship was a good deal more than professional and a long way removed from platonic. They were both married at the time – she to Douglas Fairbanks Jr. – although it has often been said in their defence that these marriages were already unsuccessful and heading for divorce. This, however, sounds like a typical Hollywood whitewash job, certainly in Gable's case for he had been married only a year and even during the Crawford entanglement he was also at least dallying with Loretta Young.

The Crawford romance was a clandestine affair. They would both arrive early at the studios and leave late, presumably snatching odd moments in their dressing-rooms for the serious business of the day. But, clandestine or not, it was no great secret. Also, although it was clearly based on a fierce physical attraction, it's doubtful whether it had much to do with love. Joe Mankiewicz dismissed the very suggestion by saying, a shade cynically: "No one ever had a big love affair with Joan Crawford." And the writer Adela Rogers St. Johns, who was a friend to both of them, and more than a friend to Gable, said: "It was just a volcanic explosion, nothing to do with a love affair at all. It scared everybody out of their wits because Joany was married to young Doug and Gable was married to Ria, and Irving Thalberg (the production supervisor at MGM) took the matter in hand and sent everybody off in different directions."

This was all part of the paternalism of the studio system. The big Hollywood studios would cosset their money-making stars and even protect them from prosecution if the need arose. But in return they positively forbade any action – adultery or general immorality – that could reflect on the studio image or damage the box-office take. An extra-marital relationship between Gable and Crawford could have had both those undesirable effects and thus Thalberg was swift to move in and order the affair to end.

Adela Rogers St. Johns knew Gable from his earliest days in Hollywood and in fact Thalberg asked her to look him over to see if he was suitable for the role he eventually played in one of his first films, *A Free Soul* (in which, incidentally, he did his tough image no harm at all by slapping Norma Shearer around). She remained deeply fond of him until the day he died and probably knew him as well as almost any other woman, and better, in fact, than some of the five he married. She wasn't, she says, in love with him herself although "we had an affair because it was more convenient". But the closeness of their relationship can perhaps be gauged by the following anecdote: "He always remembered my birthday and my fiftieth was coming up and he said, 'I want to give you a party.' And I said, 'Well, that's very darling of you.' He said, 'All right, let's say eight o'clock on the evening of your birthday.' So he sent a car for me and I got to his home and there wasn't a soul anywhere in sight and I said, 'Where's the party?' And he said, 'Well, look, you don't think I'm going to waste your fiftieth birthday with a lot of strange people running around here? You can always say for the rest of your life, to your grandchildren and everybody, you can always say you spent your fiftieth birthday in bed with Clark Gable.' "

With such credentials to support her views, she has perhaps a point worth considering when she dismisses Gable's first two marriages thus: "I've always put it down to the same reason that one of my sons gave when he married. He said to me, 'You know, Ma, if I could afford a good Filipino I would not have had to marry.' You've simply got to have somebody around to pick up after you and send your cleaning out and keep a pad with your engagements on it."

Whether he had married her for such ignoble reasons or the equally ignoble reason that she could help him in other, more material ways, Gable remained married to Ria Langham until 1939 in which period he established himself unquestionably as the biggest male star in the world: "Valentino in Jack Dempsey's body" as the publicity men put it with their usual understatement. By the end of 1931 – thanks largely to *Red Dust* in which he pursued the ladylike Mary Astor while he himself was pursued by the adoring but shop-soiled prostitute, played by Jean Harlow – he was in the list of the top ten box-office stars and he remained there until the war. Meanwhile, his image was being gradually refurbished. He had all his teeth taken out, some say at the behest of Louis Mayer who, according to Joe Mankiewicz, went through a bizarre medical phase during which, at his instigation, a dentist moved on to the MGM lot and started taking everybody's teeth out. Mankiewicz's personal opinion is that Gable's teeth were removed at the behest of the teeth, which were ugly and bad. Gable was not too pleased about losing them – as Mankiewicz said: "It wasn't very pleasant being the world's greatest lover on screen knowing your dentures were likely to start clacking any moment" – but in private he could make jokes about them. On hunting trips, for instance, he would poke his head out of his tent in the mornings with his false teeth in his hand and, bestowing upon his companions a wide and gummy grin, would say: "Well, fellers, here's America's sweetheart."

The hunting itself was also part of his new image. He enjoyed it anyway, but the public view of Gable the muscular hunter

At their ranch – now a
housing estate – with wife
No. 3, Carole Lombard.

was heavily promoted by the MGM publicity department and he went along with it because he was essentially the company man, biddable, undemanding and, despite his success, strangely insecure. When Helen Hayes made her two pictures with him in 1933 she found him "running scared".

"He was afraid," she said, "of his future, even of tomorrow. They were all afraid. I remember the first impression I had when I first went out there. I thought I was going to see a whole lot of actors so completely rich and secure and happy and romantic and I saw people terrified. Someone explained it to me by saying: 'Well, you're only as good as your last picture.' Clark was frightened all the time. And he was having a great battle with Metro because they were pushing him into pictures he didn't want to do. Not that he had any artistic ambitions or desire; he just didn't like the films he was being put into. And they didn't care what he liked or didn't like; he was under contract. I remember Clark playing with such ease and carelessness in a scene and being so gay and funny and then, as soon as the director called 'Cut' he would look at the camera in terror as if there were someone with a gun behind it. You know? As if he expected to be fired right on the spot."

That insecurity and the memory of his poverty during the pre-Hollywood (or, more accurately, the pre-Ria Langham) years also influenced his attitude towards money and helped to account for his reputation for meanness. The latter probably owes most to the complaints of Josephine Dillon who, for years after their divorce, maintained that he had treated her with appalling stinginess. But it was widely accepted among his friends and acquaintances that Gable had a clear idea of the value of a dollar. Where money was concerned he was cautious. Wayne Griffin, his friend and hunting companion and, at one time or another, his agent, producer and business adviser, said: "I never felt that he was tight but he had been very poor for a long time before he became successful and he didn't want to have that experience again. So he kept a lot of his wherewithal in cash funds in the bank and the safety deposit box. I tried to counsel him to get more investments but he was a little careful about that."

Jean Garceau, who became Gable's secretary when he married Carole Lombard and stayed with him until his last marriage, said: "I had an awful time getting him to invest his money – just terrible. He would run around town with maybe three thousand dollars in his pocket. He liked to have his hands on his money always. He didn't ever want to put anything into real estate because he couldn't get it out fast enough." Gable himself is alleged to have said that he never gave tips because he didn't want to buy anybody's friendship, which, if true, must have left a lot of disgruntled waiters in his wake and which would, not surprisingly, have given a strong impression of meanness. But against that all his friends have ample stories of his generosity towards them and of his willingness to pick up the bill in restaurants.

However, no matter what the cause or the symptoms of his insecurity, the insecurity itself was clearly unnecessary because, throughout the thirties, his reputation simply increased. In 1934, albeit to his own indignation, he was loaned by MGM to Columbia to make *It Happened One Night*, with Claudette Colbert. MGM did this largely to punish him because he had turned down a gigolo-type role opposite his erstwhile lover, Joan Crawford, and he was also demanding more money. Frank Capra, who directed the film, said that Louis Mayer agreed to lend Gable out because that was his way of sending people to Siberia, and added: "The first day Gable came down to the set he was dead drunk and he made it very apparent that he didn't want to be sent to Siberia."

Nevertheless, *It Happened One Night*, a simple tale of a runaway heiress and a tough newspaper reporter, won Gable his only Academy Award and, incidentally, almost ruined the American underwear industry at a stroke when it was revealed that the great man wore no vest. That film also marked the beginning of the most fruitful period of his career when he made pictures like *Mutiny on the Bounty*, *San Francisco* and *Test Pilot* and eventually *Gone with the Wind*.

At one time Errol Flynn was being considered for the role of Rhett Butler but it came to Gable virtually by public acclaim, this being the year when he was voted "the King" in the Ed Sullivan competition. It has been said that Gable didn't want the

part but the truth is that he was afraid of it, rather than unenthusiastic, and anyway thought it better suited to Ronald Colman. When David Selznick, the producer, first approached him Gable said he "didn't want the part for money, marbles or chalk". But Selznick had made a deal with MGM and Gable, now separated from Ria, heavily involved with Carole Lombard and obliged to support two homes, could not afford to be suspended by the studio. Louis Mayer, knowing this, persuaded Mrs. Gable's lawyer to keep up the financial pressure and then, offering both the carrot and the stick to his recalcitrant star, undertook to pay a 286,000 dollar divorce settlement to Ria so that Gable and Lombard could marry.

Gable finally gave in but not without the gravest reservations. He told Jean Garceau that he was going in to the film with ten million critics and he had serious doubts about his ability to satisfy any of them. Nor, when the filming began, were his fears at all allayed. Gable had never before worked with the director, George Cukor, and the two men were hardly compatible. Gable felt that Cukor was neglecting him and devoting too much time to coaching Vivien Leigh, so for five days he stayed away from the set. Selznick, faced with the choice of losing his director or his star, supported the star. Cukor was removed from the picture and Gable, given the privilege of naming the new director, chose Victor Fleming, a hunting and motor-cycling companion of his and a man whose aggressively "macho" personality and off-hand attitude towards women Gable much admired. Fleming, who was in the middle of making *The Wizard of Oz* at the time, was initially no more receptive to *GWTW* than Gable had been. But eventually he was persuaded to change his mind and so Gable made the film which, if all his other pictures were destroyed, would alone guarantee him a permanent place in any Hollywood hall of fame.

Meanwhile, he had once again settled his marital status. He and Ria were divorced in March 1939, and later the same month he married Carole Lombard, the former wife of William Powell. She was actually seven years younger than Gable, which made a nice change, a delicious and high-spirited blonde comedienne with great style and, when occasion demanded, a vocabu-

lary that could make a stoker blush. Her affair with Gable had been common knowledge for some while and though it was generally regarded with affectionate approval, it had aroused the terrible wrath of such relentlessly respectable groups as the Daughters of the American Revolution. To some extent, no doubt, it was to appease this kind of pressure group, which carried a fair bit of clout in the 1930s, that Mayer had agreed to make the divorce settlement to Ria, so enabling Lombard and Gable to marry and win a tight-lipped nod of approval from the revolutionary daughters and, just as importantly, ensuring that MGM's box-office receipts from Gable movies – not least *Gone with the Wind* – did not suffer from the fact that the star was an unashamed adulterer.

The newly wed Gable and Lombard bought themselves a twenty acre ranch in the San Fernando Valley, called each other "ma" and "pa" and somewhat unpredictably, bearing in mind their previous track records, settled down to a life of happy domesticity. It seems, by all accounts, to have been a perfectly idyllic marriage. She was more than a wife: she was a hunting companion and, being an inventive girl, introduced softer diversions during the lulls in this bloodthirsty sport. On one occasion, recalled by Howard Hawks, they were duck shooting but, as it was a foggy morning, no ducks were about. Gable said, rather sulkily, that there was nothing they could do till the fog cleared and Carole said: "Well I know something we can do," and she took him off to a nearby hide and proceeded to do it. Even Gable had to admit that this was a lot more fun than duck-shooting.

Adela Rogers St. Johns said of the marriage: "The only woman, as far as I know, that he ever was in love with was Carole. It was the finest kind of romance, man-woman thing, you ever saw in your life. They were devoted to each other." Among her many other attributes Lombard apparently had the gift of making Gable laugh (a thing most of the women who pursued him never thought to attempt) and of deflating his ego when, at times, he began to believe his own publicity.

But idyllic though it seems to have been, the marriage was also tragically brief. In January 1942, America having by now entered the war, Carole Lombard undertook a Government-sponsored tour to sell war bonds. She was supposed to travel back to Los Angeles from Indiana by train but, impatient to be home, she decided to fly instead. The plane ran into a storm and crashed in the mountains near Las Vegas, bursting immediately into flames. All the passengers, including Lombard and her mother, were killed.

When Gable learned of the accident he rushed to Las Vegas and was barely restrained from climbing the mountain himself to look for the bodies. Later, when it was certain that Carole was dead, he locked himself in a hotel room and refused to eat or talk to anybody for twenty-four hours. Then when his friends had coaxed him into returning to his home, Jean Garceau handed him a note from Carole. She had left him a series of *billets-doux*, one for every day she was away, and this was the last of them. Jean Garceau said: "That was just too much. He'd borne up very well up to that point but when he read that last note he simply went to pieces and broke down and cried and that's pretty hard to see in a big man like that."

Howard Hawks, who was Carole Lombard's cousin, believed – as did most of his friends – that Gable never really recovered from his wife's death. Hawks felt it significant that Gable's fifth and last wife was "quite a lot on the same order as Carole, not as beautiful but quite a bit like her".

In August 1942, Gable joined the American army air force. He enlisted as a private but graduated an honourable 700th in a class of 2,600 from Officers' Candidate School in Florida. He sought, and was apparently given, no special privileges. Indeed, having trained as a gunner and been promoted to captain, he joined the 351st Bomber Group in England, flying several missions over Germany as an aerial photographer and winning the Distinguished Flying Cross and the Air Medal. The Germans even put a price on his head – a reward of 5,000 dollars, instant promotion and leave for anyone who captured him alive.

Why he joined up and volunteered for combat duties when he had no need to do so is not entirely clear. He was after all forty-one when he enlisted and he could, quite reasonably, have stayed in Hollywood, as many younger actors did, making patriotic films and doing his bit for the war effort while remaining safely on the home front. Shortly before she died Carole Lombard had urged him to "get into this man's army" and he may have done so partly in deference to her wishes as well as from a sense of patriotism. Whatever his reasons his war record was distinguished by any standards and coincidentally it played an important part in strengthening and perpetuating the Gable legend.

Throughout his career he always had the good fortune to catch the mood of the age. In the Depression and post-Depression years of the thirties he epitomised a peculiarly American glamour. He was rough and tough and yet, when occasion demanded, gentle. In a matriarchal society he was one man who, on film at least, dominated his women, firmly, sometimes physically but also with charm and even courtesy. John Wayne also treated women firmly, but the difference was that he seemed to regard them as recalcitrant mustangs whose spirit had to be broken before they could be ridden with any degree of comfort. Gable, on the other hand, appeared quite happy to tolerate or even admire a high-spirited woman so long as she was finally able to accept that in a partnership of equals he was a little more equal than she was.

In the forties the image changed and was refined as Gable became a classically romantic figure; a grieving widower and a returned war hero. And in the fifties as America settled down to a period of avuncular conservatism under Eisenhower, a president whose most notable achievement in office was to lower his golf handicap, Gable was the archetypal middle-aged Establishment man. Perhaps that is why he was never deposed as King: he always gave his subjects what they wanted of him.

But the Gable who came back from the war was a greatly altered figure – a restless, disillusioned man of forty-four, bereaved, deeply affected by the action he had seen over enemy lines and out of patience with the make-believe of Hollywood. His first post-war film was a forgettable romance called *Adventure*, in which he co-starred with Greer Garson. "Gable's back and Garson's got him!" said the film publicity, to Gable's great disgust because he didn't like Greer Garson very much. Nor did the idea of appearing opposite the young actresses who had emerged during his absence appeal to him greatly. Playing love scenes with them he felt like an ageing lecher. So the first few years after his return to civilian life were unhappy ones. Much of his spare time was devoted to serious drinking and the earnest pursuit of women.

The drinking could have landed him in serious trouble in 1945 were it not for the power of MGM. Driving home drunk one night he crashed into a tree, cut himself rather badly and knocked himself out. Fortunately the man with whose tree he had collided was also in the film industry and knew the ground rules. The MGM trouble shooters were informed before either the police or a doctor. Indeed, the police were kept out of it entirely and so, quite as importantly, were the press. It was just part of the paternalistic service provided by the major studios for a property as valuable as Gable.

The women at this time posed fewer problems. He became a valued customer of Madame Frances, his friendly neighbourhood brothel-keeper, who provided him with a handy take-away service: a girl delivered to his door at night and tidily whisked away the next morning. Gable, of course, had no need to pay for his diversions: he was pursued ardently and constantly by some of the most beautiful women in Hollywood but Gable, the hunter, had no taste for being hunted himself and besides, such women made him uneasy. As Joe Mankiewicz said, they weren't really looking for Gable the man, they were looking for Rhett Butler, for Gable the King of Hollywood, Gable the great performer – in every sense, no doubt – and he felt, as any man might, that he could not rise to such expectations. To these women he would merely have been a conquest, one more notch on their suspender belts, and he was more at ease with humbler and less voracious companions. "More than anything," Mankiewicz said, "Gable believed in the one-night stand, or the easy conquest, the messenger girl or the publicity girl. He was never, remotely, the great lover."

There was, however, in these post-war years one girl who neither pursued him nor fell into the category of easy acquisition or one-night stand and that was Virginia Gray, who had appeared with him in a minor role in *Idiot's Delight*. They met again at the home of a mutual friend soon after he re- turned from the war and started going out together. "He was very, very guarded," she said. "Didn't want to get involved and said so. Spelled it out. And I thought, 'Well, who in hell do you think you are?' The women were throwing themselves at him and this he hated. The more they did it, the more he would run and he figured all women were alike. If, in a relaxed moment, he showed any emotion he'd scare himself to death and disappear for a month."

He had many fears, she said, about himself and about his career. He was not even sure whether he wanted to continue acting and the films in which he appeared – *The Hucksters*, a story about the advertising business with Deborah Kerr, *Homecoming*, in which, co-starring with Lana Turner, he played a wartime surgeon, and *Command Decision*, another war story with Walter Pidgeon – were unsatisfying. From time to time he would raise the question of marriage with Virginia Gray but immediately, petrified at the thought of any such commitment to anybody, he would turn and run.

Nevertheless, in 1949 to everyone's astonishment, not least perhaps his own, he took a fourth wife, Sylvia Ashley, a former London chorus girl, who had already been married to Douglas Fairbanks Sr. and a couple of titled Englishmen. They took the decision to marry after a party in December that year and both regretted it almost immediately. She, the famous society woman still clinging fiercely to the title of Lady Ashley to which she no longer had any right, and he, the hard-drinking outdoor man, quickly proved to be, as they had appeared, quite incompatible, although of the two it was she who tried harder to make the marriage work. She even went hunting with him, a noble effort on her part if not exactly rewarding for either of them. But Gable rapidly lost interest in the union and, after a lengthy separation, they were finally divorced in 1951. It was just before then that he returned, for the last time, to Virginia Gray.

"One day I was out in the backyard fooling around with something," she said, "and I came in through the patio and there he was, sitting in the living room, just as though nothing had happened. I thought, of all the nerve! You rip a person apart then you come in and sit with that silly grin on

your face as if it all happened yesterday and let's pick up where we left off. Well, then again, the serious discussions went on and he ran again. He was going to Reno to get a divorce but by that time I knew there was just no way for us and it hurt too much. I cared too much. And I knew, as long as I'd be around it would be this way and so, as rough as it was, I made the decision to end it. I thought, either it's going to be one way or the other. I'm not asking for marriage but I can't take this, and of course the rest is history."

And so, single again, Gable moved into the last phase of his career. Since the war he had made ten films, none of them comparable with the best of his 1930s pictures, but in 1953 he had a genuine success with *Mogambo*, a remake (directed by John Ford) of *Red Dust*, with the Mary Astor and Jean Harlow roles played respectively by Grace Kelly and Ava Gardner. It was his penultimate film for MGM because the now failing studio could no longer afford to pay him his 520,000 dollars a year salary and decided to drop his contract. When the

53

Mogambo box-office returns started to come in the studio had a change of heart and made an attempt at reconciliation but by then Gable had made up his mind to go. He had long been resentful of the fact that MGM had never offered him a percentage of the huge profits from *Gone with the Wind* and had also refused him a percentage of his subsequent films. Thus, after making *Betrayal*, another war drama, with Lana Turner, he left the studios in 1954 to become a freelance.

Ahead of him lay eight more films and one more wife, Kay Spreckles, née Williams, a former actress whom he had known for several years and whom he finally married in 1955. He was then fifty-four and somewhat surprised to find himself still in demand for romantic leads in films like *The Tall Men*, a Western, and *Teacher's Pet*, a comedy with Doris Day. The pictures he made in these last years of his life did nice business and Gable was, at last, on a percentage, though the really big money never did come his way until his last film, *The Misfits* in 1960.

Like *Gone with the Wind* this was a picture Gable did not want to make. It was a strenuous role for a man of his age and the part he was asked to play, that of a latterday cowboy rounding up wild horses for slaughter, went strongly against the Gable image. But both Arthur Miller, the writer, and John Huston, the director, were keen to sign him and the fee he was offered, 750,000 dollars, was a great deal higher than had ever come his way before. Unable to make up his mind he finally decided to raise his asking price to a million in the belief that he would be turned down.

Gable was at breakfast with Al Menasco, a wealthy businessman and his closest friend, when the producers arrived to find out whether he would play the part or not. As he went out to spring on them what he thought would be his unacceptable demand for the extra 250,000 dollars, he said to Menasco: "This won't take long. Keep my coffee warm." He was away for more than half an hour and returned, according to Menasco, with a bemused expression on his face. All he said was: "They took it."

His co-star in *The Misfits* was Marilyn Monroe and for many reasons, not least Miss Monroe's psychological problems and notorious inability to be anywhere on time, the filming was a lengthy, laborious and frustrating business. Gable did many of the roping and horse-handling scenes himself and Menasco, who was present for much of the shooting, believed that this arduous work in desert heat, combined with the on- and off-set tension caused by Monroe's disintegrating relationship with her husband, Arthur Miller, simply wore him out. "At that time Clark was nearly sixty years of age and beginning to show it and his breath was short and when he came off camera and sat down in the shade he was a pretty exhausted man."

Whether the effort of making *The Misfits* contributed to his failing health or not, Gable was dead before the film was released. John Huston has said: "Like a gentleman he made his last shot and then died a day later," but that, too, is simply part of the Gable myth. In fact he died in November 1960, a few weeks after shooting finished and as the result of a heart attack. He was three months short of his sixtieth birthday. John Gable, his only child, was born a few months later.

Gable's reviews for *The Misfits* were undoubtedly the best he had ever received, as only befitted what was perhaps the best performance he had ever given. And that, too, helped to sustain him posthumously in his pre-eminent position among Hollywood's male stars; the King had died, as the King should, at his peak.

The Hollywood that Gable knew no longer exists. Television and the record industry are more important there now than the movies. MGM which once boasted more stars than there are in heaven, has sold off most of its land and is simply a small cluster of buildings in which independent pictures are made. Gable's old ranch is an expensive middle-class housing estate and his former home, the one he bought for Carole Lombard, is occupied by two interior designers.

But if the kingdom is sleazy and run down, the King himself remains undiminished.

Gable was never a great actor; he was always Gable in another hat. But he was a serious professional, a contract star who, for most of his life, was content to follow the company line and never make waves and that gave him durability. Nobody, in a competitive business like the movies, could ever become king unless he had staying power but, equally, he could never become

king if he only had staying power. And Gable added to that a number of other qualities, none of them perhaps individually outstanding but rarely found in combination.

He knew his limitations and was careful not to step beyond them. He had an innate sense of dignity that kept his fans slightly in awe of him. Other stars, especially in the thirties, were mobbed and had their clothes ripped from their backs but it never happened to Gable. He was an actor who not only played a hero but behaved like a hero when the time came. He was a figure of glamour and a figure of tragedy. He was a sex symbol whom men could identify with: women chased him, he didn't chase them. He was, men felt, a man's man at heart, a guy who liked to take a drink and go hunt-

ing with his friends, who treated women with casual gallantry and was not above slapping them down if they got out of hand. As the *New York Times* said in its obituary of him, he was "as certain as the sunrise. He was consistently and stubbornly all man."

"The camera liked him," said Howard Hawks. "He couldn't do any wrong. When he grinned the whole audience felt better." And, of course, as he moved with as much serenity as anyone could expect in a place as fickle and mercurial as Hollywood through a thirty-year career that embraced sixty-seven films and five wives (who between them got through seventeen husbands) he had one other vital, incalculable, irreplaceable quality going for him: he was lucky and he knew it.

Gable's fifth and final wife, Kay Williams, bore him a son a few months after her husband's death. Between them his wives enjoyed (if that's the word) seventeen husbands.

55

Joan Crawford

A couple of nights before they were due to start working together on a film called *Torch Song*, Joan Crawford summoned the director, Charles Walters, to her home for drinks and a talk. It was a summons and not an invitation because Miss Crawford was much in the habit of issuing commands to her colleagues.

When he arrived Walters found her looking, as ever, as if she were about to make a public appearance, the hair and the make-up immaculate. There are those, such as Radie Harris, the Hollywood columnist, who maintain that even in her bath Crawford probably looked as if she were about to make a public appearance, just in case a crowd happened to drop by. However, on this occasion Crawford introduced a note of informality by wearing a housecoat which, once the drinks had been served and Walters was comfortably settled, she proceeded to throw open, revealing that underneath there was nothing but raw Crawford in prime condition.

Walters was simultaneously astonished, hugely flattered and somewhat embarrassed. "Well, I mean," he said, "at a time like that where do you look?" But once he had solved this not particularly difficult problem and looked his fill, the housecoat was closed and the show was over. "There was absolutely nothing sexual in what she did," he said. "It was purely professional. This was our first film together and what she was saying was, 'Okay, you'd better see what you've got to work with.' She simply wanted to show me the equipment."

Crawford was understandably proud of her equipment because she made it all herself. When she arrived in Hollywood in 1924 as Lucille Le Sueur, a name so theatrical that it could only be genuine, which it

The starlet with her first husband, Douglas Fairbanks Jr. – "the prince and Cinderella".

was, she was a plump little thing with a round face; pretty enough, certainly, but in no way outstanding. Had you thrown a stick on the back lot of MGM you would probably have hit a dozen of her.

She was a dancer then, a talented and energetic exponent of the Charleston and the Black Bottom at such fashionable night spots as the Coconut Grove where Scott Fitzgerald, surveying her no doubt through the bottom of his martini glass, was moved to describe her as "the best example of the flapper". Flattering, to be sure, but nothing more than that. To be a flapper, even the best of flappers, in Hollywood in the 1920s was nothing extraordinary, especially as the flapper in question was also by profession a dancing girl and dancing girls in Hollywood at that time were only a step or so up the social scale from hookers. Indeed, it has been suggested that Crawford herself was not, in those days, averse to a little honest hooking on the side; it has even been suggested that she appeared, cavorting lewdly, in a stag movie. But there is no evidence to substantiate either of these allegations, common though they still are in Hollywood, and it seems reasonable to attribute them to malice – and she attracted a lot of that.

Certainly it was as a dancer that MGM discovered her on Broadway and signed her to a contract and it was as a dancer that she won her first important role in *Sally, Irene and Mary* in 1925, the director Edmond Goulding having been as impressed by her exploits at the Coconut Grove as Scott Fitzgerald was. That picture was one of twenty that she made before the end of 1928 and by that time she was no longer recognisable as the Lucille Le Sueur who had come to Hollywood in 1924. She was no longer

Lucille Le Sueur for a start. The studio had decided she must have a new name and had organised a contest in a fan magazine to find one for her. For a week she went about as Joan Arden until MGM discovered they already had a Joan Arden on their books and so the alternative choice of Joan Crawford was adopted.

But her name was not all that was new. She had altered the shape of her face by having her back teeth removed to give herself cheekbones and she had changed her figure by drastic dieting or even by surgery. A popular operation among women in Hollywood at that time was to have excess fat cut away from their thighs and their calves and it has been suggested, though again without any evidence to substantiate it, that Crawford, too, had this operation. Equally to the point, the familiar Crawford look – huge, heavily-emphasised eyes, square, scarlet letter-box of a mouth and square shoulders to match – was already in evidence. And most important of all, as far as her career was concerned, she had entered Hollywood society as the fiancée of Douglas Fairbanks Jr.

Now it has been said that in Hollywood the aristocrats are those who can trace their ancestry all the way back to their own fathers. But in the 1920s a rigid social system existed there and at the top of it were Douglas Fairbanks Sr. and his wife, Mary Pickford. The height of every social climber's ambition was to be invited to their home, Pickfair, a palatial house in Beverly Hills. As a dancer and a starlet, Crawford would have been lucky to get past the gate but as "young Doug's" fiancée she was accepted, albeit with some reluctance on the part of Miss Pickford.

Crawford had met young Doug after seeing him in a play in Los Angeles. She sent him a telegram of congratulations, that telegram led to a meeting and the meeting led to their engagement, just after Christmas 1927, and eventually to their marriage in June 1929. Douglas Fairbanks Jr. maintains that his wife was accepted cordially enough by his father and stepmother but Crawford claimed that she was greeted with hostility by Mary Pickford.

She once told Charles Walters of an early meeting which, she alleged, took place in Mary Pickford's bedroom during which Miss Pickford, not looking at her directly but staring at her in a mirror, said: "If you ever dare to make me a grandmother, I'll kill you." Whether this dramatic encounter ever took place it's impossible to say but it does seem likely that Mary Pickford disapproved of Crawford, if not on social grounds then certainly on grounds of age.

At the time of the engagement, young Doug was eighteen, while Crawford could have been anywhere between nineteen and twenty-three. Most reference books give her year of birth as 1906 but this is perhaps a compromise between the birth date she claimed, March 23rd, 1908 and the more probable March 1904. Mary Pickford certainly seems to have favoured the latter and therefore believed that Crawford was too old for her stepson. Nevertheless, and whatever the differences between the two women, as the fiancée and then the bride of young Doug – "the Prince and Cinderella" they were called by the press – Crawford had found a happy short-cut into the upper echelons of Hollywood society, to which position she clung tenaciously for the next forty years.

In any event, and no matter how old she was, she had come a remarkably long way in a very short time. She was born, probably illegitimate, in San Antonio, Texas, and her parents had separated before her birth. She never knew who her father was until many years later and in fact for some time she believed herself to be the child of another of her mother's men friends, Henry Cassin. Indeed, for much of her childhood she was not even aware that her name was Lucille Le Sueur; she thought she was Billie Cassin.

At one stage during her youth she attended St. Agnes Academy in Kansas City and when Cassin, too, deserted his family, leaving them destitute, she was allowed to stay on at school only on condition that she helped to clean the rooms, make the beds and wait on other children. Vincent Sherman who, much later, was to become her friend and director, believes that she always had an innate hostility to the world because of this mortifying experience. Whether this was so or not, it was clearly a hard childhood with no father, no money to speak of and her mother working in a laundry to scrape a living.

In time, when her mother found yet another man friend, things became a little easier, but at sixteen Billie Cassin, or Lucille Le Sueur as she now knew herself to be, ran away from home to become a dancer. Eventually she found her way into the chorus of a Broadway musical where she was seen by an MGM executive and offered a film contract.

What sort of wounds such a childhood left on her it's difficult to assess. But, in retrospect, it does seem that those early experiences instilled in her an almost terrifying ambition – an ambition to make herself into something very special, no matter what the price she had to pay. And in the end the price was the complete burial of Lucille Le Sueur in a figment of the imagination called Joan Crawford.

Today, again with hindsight and admittedly without the benefit of ever having known her, it appears to me that Joan Crawford was totally unreal. Joan Crawford was a film star and that's all she was. That was all she ever wanted to be. She was the very epitome of a film star, the most durable of all the female stars in Hollywood and she played the part with relentless dedication for twenty-four hours a day, every day of her life.

She had, for instance, a fan club. Now, every star has a fan club but nobody ever had a fan club like Joan Crawford's. In 1938 when her career was on the slide – and it slid many times – the American film exhibitors described her as "box-office poison". Crawford promptly countered this deadly accusation by claiming that she had just received her 900,000th fan letter; apparently she had retained and counted them all. Other stars would keep their activities secret from their fan clubs so that they could enjoy a little privacy, but not Crawford. Wherever she went she gave her fans a complete itinerary of her movements in order that they should turn up at the hairdressers, the restaurant, the theatre or wherever to adore her. She remembered her fans' birthdays and the birthdays of their children – many of whom, inevitably, were named after her – and at Christmas she sent out anything up to 7,000 cards. When the tour buses trekked round Beverly Hills with the guides pointing out the homes of the famous for the benefit of the rubbernecks, the other stars would retire indoors and close the curtains. But Crawford would regard the arrival of the tour bus as one of the important appointments of her day and she would instal herself, immaculately turned out, of course, in some prominent place in her garden so that she could look up from her apparent task of doing a little light weeding and wave to the fans. "They made me," she said. "I owe it to them."

Such loyalty to people who were, after all, complete strangers was no doubt commendable but again a little unreal. As she grew older the fans became more important to her than the people she knew, more important even than her husbands and lovers, certainly more important than her adopted children, and at the end of her life they were all she had left.

But in the late 1920s the fan club was only in its infancy, even though the young Crawford's career was already flourishing. In 1929 she received the bizarre but much-appreciated accolade of being asked to leave her hand and footprints in wet cement outside what was then Graumann's, and is now Mann's, Chinese Theatre on Hollywood Boulevard. This is a privilege accorded only to major stars and Crawford had reached that eminence extremely fast. The same year, when she was heard singing with more enthusiasm than talent in *The Hollywood Revue of 1929*, she made the transition from silent to talking pictures without any apparent difficulty and thereafter her career soon outstripped that of her husband.

In her silent films she had mostly played bright young things, what she called "dancing daughter" roles, but in 1930 she appeared in *Paid* as a department store girl who was sent to jail, wrongly of course, and was then bent on revenge and thenceforth, either by chance or more likely by shrewd casting, she acquired a special niche for herself in the movies. Throughout the thirties and into the forties she epitomised every shop assistant's and every factory girl's dream. She was tough, hard-boiled and glamorous, a working-class girl on the make. And naturally she suffered. Suffering, sometimes relieved by a happy ending though frequently not, was the hallmark of a Crawford film. Nobody suffered as much in movies as Crawford did, though Bette Davis and Barbara Stanwyck sometimes came close, and it was the suffering that the fans enjoyed. When she was young they liked to see her suffering in poverty or similar adverse circumstances and clawing her way to the top, and when she was older they liked to see her suffering in mink while caught in an unhappy marriage or love affair. Quite often, as in *Harriet Craig*, a film in which, though she was unaware of it, she virtually played herself, the suffering was brought about by her own unreasonable actions but the fans didn't care. For them nothing in the world could beat the ecstatic pleasure of settling back in a darkened cinema with a bag of popcorn and watching Joan Crawford suffer.

There is no doubt that she tried very hard to master the craft of acting and to extend her range but she never really managed it. All her life she played that one particular kind of American woman, a dominant, irresistible woman, a born matriarch and in a matriarchal society that was enough to establish and maintain her as a star.

But the acting equipment that she took with her into each role was minimal. She could cry at will with both eyes or, if the director preferred it, with one eye at a time and she had an instinctive rapport with cameras. George Cukor, who directed her in *The Women* and *A Woman's Face*, said: "The closer the camera came the more relaxed she was, the more she showed her seductive side. She showed her heart, she showed everything to the camera and I said some place when working with her, 'You know, no lover or husband ever saw that side. In there she's more melting, more interesting than anything she ever showed in real life.' "

She had the priceless gift of touching the imagination of the audience but that was a matter of star quality and little to do with acting. Scott Fitzgerald said of her: "She can't change her emotions in the middle of a scene without going through a Jekyll and Hyde contortion of the face, so that when one wants to indicate that she is going from joy to sorrow one must cut away and then back. Also, you can never give her such a stage direction as 'telling a lie' because if you did she would practically give a representation of Benedict Arnold selling West Point to the British."

Still, in the early 1930s before this kind of detailed criticism was levelled at her, her career followed an upward graph although her private life was considerably less successful. Her marriage to Douglas Fairbanks ended in divorce in 1933, probably because what had been a very youthful romance had simply run its course. Also the fact that he was sophisticated and highly educated and she was neither of those things and that his background was wealthy while hers was poor may have made it difficult for them to achieve any lasting compatability.

Long before the divorce the two had drifted apart and she had become involved in a celebrated and passionate affair with Clark Gable, her co-star in *Laughing Sinners* and *Possessed*. As an affair it was ardent, clandestine and brief. They talked about marriage, she wrote much later on, but added in the kind of hot, breathless prose that so admirably suited her style: "I dared not ruin the dreams. I'd rather live with them unfulfilled than have them broken." In any event, the break-up with Gable and indeed with Fairbanks hardly seems to have shattered her because, even before she was divorced, she was already involved with Franchot Tone, an actor she first met in the film *Today We Live*.

Like Fairbanks, Tone came from a wealthy background, being the son of an industrial magnate and a graduate of Cornell University. He was an actor of no little talent but as "Mr. Crawford", which he became in 1935, he found his own career suffering and he had to make do with supporting roles in several films which starred his wife. She, on the other hand, had now reached perhaps the peak of her success at MGM despite the fact that the critics dismissed her as "a clothes horse de luxe".

Until 1937 indeed very little went wrong for her – professionally at least. But in that year for some reason – not necessarily to do with her work because *The Last of Mrs. Cheyney* in which she co-starred with William Powell and Robert Montgomery had done well – her popularity began to wane and, remarkably, she failed to appear in the list of the biggest money-making stars.

In 1938 an even worse fate befell her because that was the year when she was included among a list of stars declared in a full-page advertisement in the trade paper *The Hollywood Reporter* to be box-office poison by a group of distributors who announced that they were "tired of losing money on the glamour stars detested by the public". By now her box office rating had plunged from third to anywhere between twenty-fifth and sixtieth place but MGM continued to show faith in her by signing her to a new five-year contract, which at least gave her a measure of security.

Crawford herself, however, was not unnaturally worried at the turn her professional fortunes were taking and, with typical resolution, set out to re-establish her position at or near the top. "At this critical moment," she wrote, "I set my sights on the part of Chrystal, the hardboiled perfume clerk who uses every wile to catch another woman's husband in *The Women*." If she wanted the part that badly quite obviously nobody was going to stand in her way and she duly got it. According to the American critic Bosley Crowther, she hurled herself into the role of a bitch with such enthusiasm that she continued it off-screen and when sitting beside the camera to read her lines back to Norma Shearer for Shearer's close-ups she knitted distractingly all the time, never once looking up at her co-star. George Cukor says he believes this was done unthinkingly and unmaliciously but it could equally have been done out of sheer spite because Shearer, as the wife of Irving Thalberg, the production supervisor at MGM, had always been given the pick of the roles in the studio's biggest films. And in any case Crawford was not above perpetrating acts of petty malice on any actress.

When Natalie Schafer came from Broadway to appear with her in *Reunion in France* in 1942 Crawford virtually ruined her first big scene by continually moving so that her shadow always obstructed Miss Schafer's face. To this day Miss Schafer is convinced that she did it on purpose because it was

With Franchot Tone, husband No. 2, who rather wearied of being "Mr Crawford".

followed by another act of apparent spite. During the making of the same film, Miss Schafer went into Crawford's trailer dressing-room, which was at that moment empty, to look at herself in the full-length mirror. When Crawford discovered what she had done she summoned the studio policemen to guard the door and prevent her from repeating the offence.

However, *The Women* went a fair way towards re-establishing Crawford as a top box-office star and in the same year that she made the film she divested herself of Franchot Tone. The marriage had never been much of a success partly because his career had been secondary to hers and partly, perhaps, because Tone could never properly adjust himself to living with a star who could never forget that she was one. Also it was during this marriage that she had taken to alerting the fans as to her movements. (Spencer Tracy once said: "She likes to have them follow her when she goes shopping.") And Tone could never find a way to compete with this hydra-headed rival that turned up clamouring for his wife's attention whenever he appeared with her in public.

Around this time Crawford's egocentricity took her off in an unexpected direction. She decided to become a mother. Nobody knows why she had never had any children of her own. Some said that eventually she was unable to conceive because she had had several miscarriages. Others maintained that she simply couldn't bear to lose her figure for a year while she had a baby. But whether because she was unable or unwilling to have children of her own, she decided to adopt a couple – first a girl called Christina, then a boy named Christopher.

For a while she continued as a single parent, but in 1942 she met a rather obscure young actor named Philip Terry (best remembered for his role as Ray Milland's brother in *The Lost Weekend*) and six weeks later she married him for reasons which were totally obscure even to Crawford. She often said, when the marriage had come to its inevitable end, that she owed him an apology, adding: "I've never really known why I married Philip. I guess I mistook peace of mind for love and at the time believed it with all my heart."

But married again for the third time

she adopted two more children, Cathy and Cynthia, whom she described as twins, even though they came from different families and were born a month apart. Why she ever resolved to take on these unfortunate children is a matter for conjecture for, by all accounts, she was an extremely harsh mother with not the slightest aptitude for the role. Even discounting the more horrendous tales of her treatment of the brood, the discipline she imposed upon them was, to say the least, excessive.

She insisted on tidiness to such an extent that, according to Radie Harris, there was never a sign of a child in the house; never a doll or a toy to be seen. On one occasion Christopher was shut in his room all day because he had forgotten to clean his shoes. On another – and this anecdote Crawford herself recounted to Natalie Schafer with pride – he asked if he could take a chocolate from a huge box on the coffee table. Crawford said he could but he was only to have one. A little later she caught him taking another and, by way of punishment, insisted that he eat the entire boxful while she sat and watched him. When he had finished he was, not unnaturally, violently sick. "He won't do that again," said Crawford to Miss Schafer. "My children must obey me."

Gregory Bautzer, the Hollywood lawyer who was close to Crawford between her third and fourth marriages, remembers being at her home one Sunday for family dinner. Christopher was left-handed and Crawford disapproved of that and insisted that he eat with his fork in his right hand. At one point the boy forgot and used his left. Crawford immediately leaned across the table, knocked the fork and the food out of his hand and hit him across the face. "He started to cry," said Bautzer, "so I immediately went over and put my arms around him and as I was holding him – we were having a roast leg of lamb – I got it right in my face . . . There was a strictness with those children I think was probably the primary cause of the estrangement that occurred with them."

Vincent Sherman believes she wanted to be a good mother but since she appears to have shown no warmth towards the children one wonders what her definition of a good mother was. Somebody perhaps whose children reflected credit upon her. Sherman would remonstrate with her about

the rigid discipline she imposed upon them and say: "Joan, they're going to hate you when they grow up. You shouldn't do this." And then, he said, "Her jaw would get tight and she'd say, 'I'm going to raise my children to be ladies and gentlemen.' "

Christopher finally rebelled and several times ran away from home. Crawford used to complain to Radie Harris that her fourth husband, Alfred Steele, the chairman of Pepsi-Cola, had spent more than $40,000 on psychiatric treatment for the boy "trying to straighten him out". Miss Harris commented: "A lot of people thought a psychiatrist should have tried to straighten Joan out in her relationship with the children."

As they grew up the children virtually lost contact with her. Christopher married and had a family of his own whom Crawford refused to see and when Christina, who had been divorced, was married again, Crawford would not attend the ceremony.

Her third husband was Philip Terry. She felt she owed him an apology for marrying him.

In her will she disinherited the two older children, although she did leave money to "the twins".

It could be, I suppose, that something in her own childhood – a lack of discipline or an excess of it – accounted for her treatment of her adopted family. But the coolness she habitually showed towards them would suggest that, in adopting them, she was merely playing another role – Joan Crawford, mother – and that she swiftly tired of it. When she married Al Steele and moved to New York they took on an immense apartment, big enough for a very large family, but Crawford so redesigned it, knocking down walls to make several rooms into one, that there was no place for the barely-teenage twins. They had to live with a nanny in a nearby hotel and see their mother more or less by appointment. But no doubt Crawford herself regarded the adoptions as successful and certainly thought of herself as a very good mother. She even had an award to prove it, for one year – with huge but unconscious irony – an American women's organisation voted her "Mother of the Year".

But back in 1943 when the children were still young and her marriage to Philip Terry was hardly a year old, Crawford's professional life arrived at a crisis. Her contract with MGM expired and, by mutual consent, was not renewed. Her last few pictures had not done well and she was tired, she said, of the parts they offered her. "If you think I made poor films at MGM after *A Woman's Face* you should have seen the ones I went on suspension not to make." Possibly, too, injured pride entered into her decision to leave. Popular though she was, she had never been the number one female star at MGM. In the early days she had been pushed into third place by Norma Shearer and Greta Garbo and later she was kept there by Greer Garson and Lana Turner.

Ironically enough, however, on leaving MGM she immediately signed a contract – at a third of her former salary but with more script approval – with Warner Brothers where once again she found herself firmly installed at number three in the pecking order behind Bette Davis and Barbara Stanwyck. In fact for the first two years of her contract at Warners she didn't work at all but simply stayed home playing the role of Joan Crawford, housewife-

superstar, while she waited for the right part to come along.

It was a difficult period for her since Warners seemed to have little idea what to do with her. Once, she told Vincent Sherman, after she'd turned down a particular script she was summoned to the studio to discuss it. She bought a new hat and a new dress for the occasion but when she arrived she was kept waiting for twenty to thirty minutes before the producer admitted her to his presence and told her, in effect, that she'd better take what she was offered because it was hard to find work for her and nobody wanted her. She told Sherman that she went home and cried all afternoon.

But finally her patience paid off. In 1945 she gained the role of the waitress who killed for her unpleasant and undeserving daughter in *Mildred Pearce* and won the Oscar for best actress, the only Oscar she ever did win. It was after this that a new ingredient, neurosis, was added to the other characteristics of a typical Crawford role. For the rest of her time at Warners she appeared mostly as a neurotic, and of course suffering, career woman of a certain age, a woman whose affluence and apparent success barely disguised her inner discontent. It was in this sort of role that she was loaned out to Columbia in 1950 to make *Harriet Craig*, directed by Vincent Sherman. In this she played a particularly house-proud wife and Sherman introduced many of the idiosyncrasies which Crawford displayed in her own home, where everything had to be in precisely the place she had assigned for it.

By all accounts she had an obsession with cleanliness. If she stayed in a hotel, no matter how many stars it had, she would scrub the bathroom herself before using it and in at least one instance she covered all the furniture with cellophane. But then she covered all her own furniture with cellophane as well, so that she and it would look equally immaculate.

Everything in her house, according to Vincent Sherman, was "just proper". At dinner parties the table was set like an illustration from a book of etiquette. Guests who smoked would find themselves carrying ashtrays about for fear of incurring their hostess' displeasure by dropping ash on the carpets. And since the carpets were white, visitors were frequently expected to

take their shoes off before entering. Charles Walters remembers being invited for Sunday brunch and arriving to find Crawford in jeans on her hands and knees scrubbing the black and white marble floor in the hall and saying: "I'll be ready in five minutes. I've just got to clean up. I can't trust anybody any more."

Another time when he turned up to take her to a party he was summoned to her dressing-room where he discovered her in full make-up, her hair done and wearing a smart little hat with a veil, long black stockings, high-heeled shoes, bra and pants while she moved around the room constantly readjusting the curtains to make them look tidier. Vincent Sherman always felt that there was something unnatural about the orderliness and the elegance of her surroundings, as if she had no taste of her own but had learned from the advice columns what a film star's house should look like.

And yet no other film star lived quite like Joan Crawford. Her dressing-room was enormous, bigger than most people's living rooms, and the walls were lined with shelves and drawers holding her shoes and gloves and hats, hundreds of shoes and gloves and a hundred hats. Another, smaller room, just off it, housed her furs, minks and sables, perhaps seventy to eighty of them, for every possible occasion on which a fur might be worn. The total effect was less that of a woman's dressing-room than of a wardrobe department of a film studio. And Crawford knew precisely where everything was. If a friend asked for the loan of a handbag for the evening she would walk into the room in the dark and find exactly the right bag, without a moment's hesitation.

Well, none of this is at all blameworthy or risible. Clothes, after all, are a film star's vital accessories – or were in Crawford's day when the public expected their movie stars to be larger than life, more beautiful, more elegant, more ostentatiously wealthy than anyone else. And yet, as with much else in her life, there is an impression of excess, of close attention to detail magnified to obsession. What she was seeking perhaps was perfection – perfection in her surroundings, perfection in her children, perfection in her appearance. But perfection is an impossibility and the pursuit of it is chilling and inhuman.

In her career, as she sought to improve herself, the idea of perfection forced Crawford while she was shooting a film to move into her dressing-room at the studios. True, the dressing-room was positively luxurious, a kind of three-roomed apartment a great deal more splendidly appointed than the average home but a dressing-room in a studio, however grand, is no place to live. Yet Crawford would retire there each night when everyone else had gone home and, having scrubbed and cleaned and prepared herself a meal, would stay there alone, studying her script.

Increasingly, as I spoke to people who knew her, it seemed that there was little about her that was spontaneous; everything was subjugated to the needs of the role she created for herself. Whatever was left in her of Lucille Le Sueur might – or, on the other hand, of course, might not – have wanted occasionally, let us say, to let her hair down and get a little drunk. But that would not have suited the image of Joan Crawford and so it never happened. Not, at least, in public. Even when she was in love she appeared to be playing a part. Her comments on Gable, for instance – "his nearness had such impact that my knees buckled . . . a magnetic man with more sheer male magic than anyone in the world" – sound contrived and manufactured as though she were reacting according to some strict unwritten code of behaviour to which a woman in love was obliged to adhere.

When she was in love she was possessive and predatory and conducted the affair on rules established by herself. Her escort was expected to drive to her house and leave his car there while she drove them to their destination. This always worked according to plan because she had two Cadillacs, one specifically held in reserve in case the other should fail her. When they arrived at their destination, a restaurant perhaps, or a party, the ritual would always be the same: Crawford would enter first with the escort two or three paces behind and carrying her knitting bag on one arm and a small, white poodle under the other. Knitting was another of her obsessions. She would knit wherever she went, although Tallulah Bankhead once stopped her by taking the work in progress out of her hands, stuffing it back in the bag and saying: "At my parties nobody makes their own entertainment."

Mr. and Mrs. Al Steele on their wedding day.

three," he said. But was that a spontaneous display of emotion by Lucille Le Sueur or the calculated reaction of an insulted Joan Crawford?

Bautzer's relationship with her lasted more than two years and ended after a party in the home of Louis B. Mayer, who was then head of MGM. During the course of the evening Bautzer was guilty of paying rather more attention to another actress than met with Crawford's approval. Nothing was said at the time but punishment for the crime was administered on the way home at about two o'clock in the morning. As usual Crawford was driving and when she had reached a deserted spot about ten miles from anywhere, except other deserted spots, she stopped the car and said: "Darling, there's something wrong with the rear tyre. Would you be a dear and have a look at it?"

The gallant Bautzer said: "Of course, darling" and got out of the car, whereupon she promptly took off, leaving him stranded. Until then, he said, it had always been his practice after a tiff to phone her and apologise, whether or not the fault had been his. But on this occasion he was given ample opportunity to reflect on their relationship and on himself – "What the hell kind of man are you?" – as he trudged ten miles home to his hotel and he never called her again.

Clark Gable once said to Bautzer: "Don't you find something kind of masculine about Joan? Not in her looks but in her approach. She thinks like a man." She also behaved like a man, grabbing the initiative in her relationships with the opposite sex in a way that clearly pre-dated Women's Lib. In her defence Vincent Sherman said: "When you consider the kind of life that she had, where she had to fight for her own independence and struggle as she did, I think she felt that men in a certain sense were her enemies and therefore she had to fight against them." Ultimately, perhaps, she typified and even caricatured a new breed of women to which Hollywood had given birth – women who earned not only a living but a fortune; women who, in their professional lives, were as rich and as important as men; women who, in most respects, were totally independent of men.

In 1952 Crawford left Warner Brothers – again, so it was said, by mutual consent. By now, whatever her date of birth, she

When the evening was over Crawford would drive her escort back to her house where, after a goodnight embrace of such ardour as was decreed appropriate to the occasion, he would collect his car and depart. She would then allow him exactly enough time to get home and phone him, ostensibly to make sure that he had arrived safely but in fact to satisfy herself that he had indeed gone home and not perhaps to some other woman's bed. On those occasions when there was no reply to her call, for whatever innocent reason, furious retribution would be faced by that escort at their next meeting.

Greg Bautzer, the lawyer, maintains that the only scars he carries on his face were put there by Crawford in the course of physical displays of temper brought on by the fact that he hadn't returned home swiftly enough or that he had been seen having a drink with another woman. "She could throw a cocktail glass across the room and hit you in the face, two times out of was well into her forties, her third marriage had failed and her career was slipping once more. For a while she freelanced with no great success, making among other things the musical *Torch Song* at MGM, her first musical and, coincidentally, her first picture in colour. But *Torch Song* did nothing for her and neither did its successors. She was still a star and to her devoted fan club always would be but, professionally, she was at best marking time.

But on New Year's Eve, 1954, she was studying a script in her dressing-room when, at midnight, a friend called her from New York and, after wishing her a happy new year, put Alfred Steele, the chairman of Pepsi-Cola, on the line. At that time Steele was in the process of divorcing his second wife, which was convenient because, when he and Crawford met in California a little later they swiftly decided to marry and were indeed married in May 1955.

Now a new career began for her. She was, let us say for the sake of argument, around fifty and she had already extended her career as a romantic leading lady to almost indecent lengths. The kind of role for which she was suitable in that guise was becoming increasingly hard to find and so, although she did make two films during her marriage to Steele, including *The Story of Esther Costello*, her first in England, she began to detach herself from the movies. Indeed, playing a subordinate role to her husband for the first time in her varied experience as a wife, she moved to New York and became a roving ambassadress for Pepsi-Cola, travelling the world and attracting hordes of people to the opening of new factories.

The life seemed to suit her, possibly because she had simply swapped one kind of power for another while remaining as firmly as ever in the public eye. Her friends believe that the marriage to Steele was the happiest of the four, largely because he was a dominant and successful man in his own right and because he had no connection whatever with show business. Instead of moving into her life, which her other husbands had perforce been obliged to do, he moved her into his. Unfortunately, however, the happiness was short-lived. One night in 1959, Steele collapsed and died of a heart attack. Crawford reacted as typically as ever. Whatever grief she felt she kept to herself and set about organising the funeral with brisk efficiency.

"One day," said Radie Harris, "there was Joan on the phone and she said, 'The services are gonna be at St. Thomas' or wherever and the cremation is gonna be at such-and-such a place and you're gonna be in car eight and with you is gonna be blah-blah-blah . . .' like giving seats for an opening night. And I hung up the phone and I just couldn't believe it. And yet, you see, this was so typical of Joan. This was something she had to do and it had to be well organised because this is what Al would have wanted."

A week after Steele's death Crawford was offered a role in *The Best of Everything* and she accepted, probably because a return to her original career would be therapeutic at such a time of trauma, but she still retained her connections with Pepsi-Cola who, as a reward for her indefatigable efforts, gave her a lifetime appointment to the board of directors. Indeed she took this work so seriously over the next three years that she restricted her acting to guest appearances in TV shows and it was not until 1962 when she was teamed with Bette Davis in *Whatever Happened to Baby Jane?* that she made her next cinema appearance. This gothic horror story of a drunken and demented former child star (Davis) and the crippled sister (Crawford) whom she sadistically torments was to be Crawford's last film of any note at all.

Its success brought her a handful of similar roles in other, vastly inferior, horror pictures, including two, *Berserk* and *Trog*, which were made in Britain, but by 1970 her career as a movie star was finally over. For a while she continued to work for Pepsi-Cola but in the end even that was lost to her when the new management retired her, either because they wanted a younger image to promote their product or, as Vincent Sherman suggests, because she had tried to become too dominant in the company's affairs.

Losing her job with Pepsi was the ultimate indignity. Thereafter Crawford became a reclusive figure, rarely going out, rarely seeing her friends. She started to worry about money and moved to a smaller apartment, although there is no evidence to indicate that she was anything but comfortably off, to say the least.

Her friends would try to invite her out

but she would make excuses, pretending that she was about to leave town and claiming always that she was extremely busy. In a sense she was, but the work was self-imposed. She would get up at six a.m. and start dictating letters to her two secretaries, one in New York, the other in California, but these letters were nearly all to members of her fan club, the strangers who had kept faith with her through all her vicissitudes and with whom she in turn kept faith to the very end.

For the most part she would stay indoors, avidly watching soap operas and chat shows on television, eating her meals off a tray on her knees. Her public appearances became increasingly rare and in the last year or so of her life they stopped altogether. By then, although her friends were mostly unaware of it, she had developed cancer of the stomach, a long and painful illness which she suffered without complaint and for much of the time without treatment because she had become a Christian Scientist and believed that the body would cure itself. It didn't. And she died on May 10th, 1977, alone.

She appears to have been a most complex person, a mixture of insecurity and arrogance, an egotist who was yet capable of great kindness and generosity. The gifts she gave to her friends were extravagant even by Hollywood standards and the help she would offer, unsolicited and frequently anonymous, to people who were ill or down on their luck was legendary. For years she maintained two rooms at the Hollywood Presbyterian Hospital, not for herself but for people she heard about who were sick and could not afford the necessary treatment.

And yet along with this went a basic distrust of people, men and women – women because she saw them as rivals and men because she was never sure that they wanted her for herself or for the very useful kudos that could accrue from being seen around with Joan Crawford, movie star. Natalie Schafer believes that she wanted to be loved but failed "because you have to love people to be loved, really loved, and I don't think she loved anybody but Joan Crawford. It's an awful thing to say but I think that's the way she was and I think that's what made her a success – a complete feeling for herself."

That she was a success is undeniable. She lasted as a star longer than any other woman in the history of the cinema and to a great extent her career was a triumph of will over adversity, of personality over sometimes appalling material. She made more than eighty films, a great many of them indifferent at best, but often the worse the picture, the better she was, though not because she was a fine actress. She wasn't. Being an actress was not what she was good at. What she was good at was being precisely what she was – Joan Crawford, movie star. Survival as a star was her aim and her greatest achievement and everything else, husbands, lovers and adopted children were sacrificed to this ambition. She was, it seems to me, an easy woman to admire but not an easy one to like.

Whether at the end she felt it had all been worthwhile, that the creation of Joan Crawford was a sufficient monument to her life, only she could tell and she never did. Charles Walters, remembering the loneliness of the later years of her life, before the onset of cancer and after the end of her film career, and the frenetic way in which she filled her days with needless activity said: "It was almost as though Joan Crawford was trying to escape sitting down with Lucille Le Sueur and saying, 'Well, honey, where are we really and what do we want?' She kept busy enough not to face it."

Far more than Myrna Loy, who was briefly accorded the title as the result of a newspaper poll, Joan Crawford was the true Queen of Hollywood, the archetypal movie star whose like had never been seen before and will probably never be seen again.

At her death she was mourned far more deeply by her fans than by many of the people who knew her. And that seems to be at once the measure of her success and of her failure.

Errol Flynn

Errol Flynn died in Vancouver on October 14th, 1959. It was a heart attack which killed him, though such technicalities hardly matter really, since it must have been a photofinish between his heart, his liver and his kidneys as to which would put the finishing touches to him. Flynn was only fifty when he died but he could hardly be said to have been cut off in his prime because, by then, he was a quite awe-inspiring wreck, his body utterly ruined by a surfeit of drugs, a surfeit of booze, a surfeit in fact of practically everything which, taken to excess, might reasonably be expected to kill a man. At the inquest the coroner remarked that he had had the body of a tired old man, to which Flynn, had he been around to hear it, might very probably have said "Amen" and felt himself vaguely complimented. He had often said, had he not, that anyone who died with more than ten thousand dollars in his pocket must have been a failure, since he clearly had no idea how to spend his money to its best advantage. By the same token, therefore, he may well have felt that anyone who died with more than a vestige of good health left in his body could not have lived his life to the full. Flynn, dying diseased and quite likely broke – though this is not entirely certain as his financial affairs were in such a magnificent mess that they have not been sorted out to this day – was not guilty on both counts.

As evidence of the fullness with which he had led his life one has only to look at the reasons for his dying in such an improbable place as Vancouver. He had not gone there, as might have been supposed, to set up a new film. Nor had he gone there for a holiday or for the good of his health – too late for that in any event.

He had gone there, quite simply, to escape the law. Back in California the sheriff, with or without a posse, was waiting to pounce and charge him either with statutory rape (for the third time in his life) or, at the very least, with contributing to the delinquency of a minor.

The fact that the minor, a seventeen-year-old actress named Beverley Aadland, had fled with him to Vancouver and did not in any way feel herself to have been rendered delinquent by their relationship was neither here nor there. Today a liaison between a fifty-year-old man and a seventeen-year-old girl might still occasion the odd "Tut" of disapproval, but nobody goes to prison for it. In 1959, however, morality, even in Hollywood, was made of sterner stuff and Flynn, as usual, was its whipping boy. Despite all the scandal that attaches to his name, his greatest fault was this: he was born out of his time.

Of course, it's hard to say what would have been the right time for Flynn to be born: much earlier, probably, rather than later. Had he been born later his drinking and his sexual peccadilloes would have attracted little attention, though his drug addiction would have got him into trouble. Had he been born earlier, in the eighteenth century for example, the adventurer and buccaneer that he played best on screen and that he tried to be, as far as the twentieth century would allow, in his private life, might have been actively encouraged. Flynn's most attractive quality was that he lived exactly as he wished to live, without a thought for convention and, by extension perhaps, without a thought for anybody else. It's easy to say, as his admirers do, that he hurt nobody but himself but it's impossible for anyone to pursue the

The youthful Flynn – Michael Curtiz's "beautiful puppet".

ruthlessly self-centred path that Flynn pursued without leaving a number of walking wounded in his wake.

That being so, the story of Flynn's life, viewed from the point of view of a strict puritan or even from the point of view of ordinary, respectable, God-fearing people, reads like a most satisfactory cautionary tale. He had astonishing good looks, a small but highly saleable talent, a magnificent physique and such sex appeal that he seemed to walk through life on a carpet of prostrate and willing females. (He once estimated that he had spent between 12,000 and 14,000 nights making love. Since that would have meant every night for the best part of forty years it's difficult to believe, but he certainly had his share.)

Yet with all those priceless advantages he managed to finish up wrecked and virtually alone, on the skids and a fugitive from justice, a textbook example of one who, against all the odds, had managed to wrest defeat from the jaws of victory.

The saga of Flynn's journey up to the top of the hill and straight down the other side began in Hobart, Tasmania, on June 20th, 1909. Errol Leslie Thomson Flynn

71

was the son of Professor Theodore Flynn, a marine biologist and zoologist and his wife, Marelle. To the father, the wild and rather spectacular boy he had begotten was a constant source of wonder. I met Professor Flynn on two occasions in England some years after Errol's death. He was a tall, spare, gentle and scholarly man who still talked of his son with deep but bemused affection. The relationship between them had clearly been one of love and mutual admiration, although just as clearly the elder Flynn had long abandoned any attempt to understand the ways and motives of the younger.

But the relationship between Errol Flynn and his mother was very different, being based on a mutual suspicion, dislike and at times even hatred. Flynn himself made that plain enough in his autobiography, *My Wicked, Wicked Ways*, published while his mother was still alive, although he offered no real explanation for the distaste she seems to have felt for him from birth. He was her first child and he didn't have her second, a daughter, till ten years later, so perhaps his arrival was unplanned and therefore unwelcome. Perhaps, there being nothing in the rules which says a mother is obliged to love her children, she simply resented him as an interference in her way of life.

Whatever the cause of her antipathy, the amateur psychiatrist might well feel it unnecessary to look any further for an explanation of Flynn's irresponsible and self-destructive passage through life. Certainly it seems probable that his dislike for his mother, of which he never made any secret, had a profound effect on his relationship with all other women.

The young Flynn grew up and was educated, to a point, in Hobart, London and Sydney where, at the age of sixteen, he was left to fend for himself when his parents and younger sister moved to Europe. After a few shiftless months in Sydney he set off for the goldfields of New Guinea, joined the Government service as a clerk and was fired when caught in *flagrante delicto* with an official's wife. Thereafter he worked on a copra plantation, acquired part-ownership of a yacht which he hired out for documentary filming and, except for a brief spell when he returned to Sydney to be cured of gonorrhoea, made New Guinea his base for the next few years. During that time he made his acting debut as Fletcher Christian in a low-budget picture called *In the Wake of the Bounty*. It was a totally inauspicious beginning although, with hindsight, one can detect a note of prophecy in one of the lines he was called upon to deliver: "The future holds the most awful adventure of all."

The chief effect of this production was that it inspired in him an ambition to earn his living as an actor and, to this end, he went to England in 1933, advertised himself mendaciously as the star of various non-existent films, did a brief stint with the Northampton Repertory Company, appeared forgettably in two equally forgettable West End plays and made a picture at Twickenham Studios called *Murder at Monte Carlo*, the result of which was a summons to Hollywood and a successful screen test with Warner Brothers.

By then Flynn was twenty-six and, professionally, he got off to what one can only call a quiet start, playing a corpse in a film called *The Case of the Curious Bride*. Privately, his beginnings in Hollywood were much more dramatic. Within months of his arrival in 1935, he had met and married the first of his three wives, Lily Damita, a volatile French actress eight years older than himself. The marriage only lasted seven years, but he was still paying for it when he died. In fact, it lasted seven years in name only, having been considerably less than successful from the start.

When it ended in divorce in 1942, Lily, her case strengthened by the fact that she had borne him a son, Sean, extracted lavish alimony from her husband and, since she refrained from marrying again, continued to draw it until his death; not that the payments were always as regular or complete as they should have been. Flynn blamed that alimony settlement for the fact that, from the time of his divorce onwards, he was rarely solvent.

Still, in 1935 all that bitterness and indeed all the rest of Flynn's problems lay far ahead in the future. In 1935, in fact, things could hardly have been better for him. Robert Donat, who was to have played the title role in a swashbuckler called *Captain Blood*, withdrew at the last moment either through illness or a dispute over money and Warner Brothers, taking a considerable gamble, handed the active and adventurous role to the unknown

Flynn whose Hollywood career up to this point, of course, had virtually consisted of lying motionless on the floor.

The result both made and, it could be argued, destroyed Flynn. The film, directed by the Hungarian Michael Curtiz, made its leading man, in true Hollywood fashion, a star overnight and immediately typed him in the kind of role that he played so well and that he came to regard with something very close to contempt. Nobody is ever going to accuse Errol Flynn of having been a great actor, though he always thought he could have been one if only he'd been given the opportunity. But he was undeniably a superstar and although he attained that status partly because his private life was bigger, wilder, bawdier and more scandalous than any role he ever played on screen, one must also take into consideration the not insignificant fact that when you think of the great swashbucklers of the movies there's no need to think any further than Douglas Fairbanks Sr., and Errol Flynn.

It was one of the minor tragedies of Flynn's life that he never believed the ability to cut a dashing and romantic figure in costume, with a sword, on a horse or a pirate ship amounted to very much. He thought anybody could do it, but he was wrong.

That contempt stemmed perhaps from the attitude of the director, Curtiz, who had little regard for the actor and tended to describe him as "a beautiful puppet". Since the first part of that description was manifestly true and even Flynn – the least vain of men as far as his looks were concerned – must have been aware of it, it's not unreasonable to suppose that he was prepared to accept the second part as being equally true. When you add to that the fact that most of his early successes (*Captain Blood*, *The Charge of the Light Brigade*, *The Adventures of Robin Hood* and *The Sea Hawk* for example) were directed by the brilliant but disdainful puppet-master Curtiz, the result was always likely to be an actor with very little confidence in either himself or his work.

Captain Blood also set the pattern for Flynn's relationship with Warner Brothers. Halfway through the film he decided that he was being paid too little and refused to work any more until his salary was increased. With no real alternative but to agree, the studio raised his pay from 125 to 750 dollars a week, since it would have been far more expensive to scrap the film and start again with another and more biddable star. Encouraged by this success, Flynn used the same gambit again and again and, while his films were making vast fortunes for Warner Brothers, continued to get away with it.

Indeed at times it seems as though Flynn's entire career at Warners was a continuing battle against the company and in particular the head of the studio, Jack L. Warner. Vincent Sherman, who directed the actor's last major film there, *The Adventures of Don Juan* in 1947, said: "They had a kind of love-hate relationship. I'd hear them fighting terribly on the phone and then during the making of the film Warner must have called me twenty or thirty times saying, 'You tell that bastard so and so and this and that,' and finally I couldn't take any more and I said, 'Mr. Warner, I have to work with him. I can't discipline him. You pay him, you discipline him,' and he said, 'Well, don't think that I'm afraid of him.' But I think he was a little afraid, though he also had a genuine affection for him, the kind of love for an errant son almost. I was at Errol's funeral when there was a far smaller crowd than was anticipated. A lot of Flynn's so-called friends stayed away. But Warner was there."

Warner's paternal attitude towards Flynn, such as it might have been, was not returned in the same coin. Nora Eddington, Flynn's second wife, says her husband arranged for her to have a bit part, virtually her only acting experience, in *Don Juan* simply to spite the studio chief. "He said, 'If you do this little bit they won't pay you for it but I'll get Jack to buy you a new wardrobe.' He was always looking for a way to screw Jack Warner."

Flynn's and Nora's daughter, Deirdre, remembers that her father had a house in the hills looking down on the studio and she said he used it "as a place to hide from Jack Warner. He wasn't afraid of Warner and I don't think he liked him very much, although he did have a great deal of respect for him. He used to say he liked to sit up on the hill there in the house knowing he could throw rocks down on Jack Warner."

It's worth remembering, however, that both Nora Eddington and her daughter were talking about the period in the late

modern dress was never so popular at the box-office as Flynn in costume with a sword or a six-shooter in his hand.

On eight occasions during that fertile and prosperous period his co-star was Olivia de Havilland of whom Bette Davis recalled in her memoirs: "It was Olivia whom he truly adored and who evaded him successfully in the end. I really believe that he was deeply in love with her." These days Miss de Havilland herself puts it rather less passionately. There was, she says, a deep and abiding affection between them and, at one point, there was even talk of marriage, an improbable eventuality, as they both knew, since he was still securely, if not very happily, married to Lily Damita. "I suppose you could say I had fallen in love with him," she said. "It seems an inadequate sort of term, perhaps not quite accurate. I developed a very deep crush, shall we say."

She was twenty at that time and he was twenty-seven and he wooed her with some ardour, being temporarily separated from his wife. Miss de Havilland suggested that they should keep apart until he had decided what he was going to do about his marriage and, although Flynn hardly took this seriously and continued to call her and ask her out, she insisted on sticking to the arrangement until some firm decision had been made. This was wise of her, as it turned out, because within a few weeks Flynn and Damita were back together again and that was more or less the end of the matter, although Miss de Havilland admits that had he been single, "I certainly would have wanted to marry him". But whether that would have been a very good idea she is not at all sure. "He was very young. A number of pathways lay open for him in terms of a style of life. I don't know . . . he would have been a handful and I'm not sure that I was experienced enough to deal with that."

Not only was Flynn very young; he was also very immature. His method of attracting Olivia de Havilland's attention, for example, was to slip a dead snake into her knickers – not, I must add, the knickers she was actually wearing at the time but the knickers she was about to put on for her role in *The Charge of the Light Brigade*. Since they were large and roomy, nineteenth-century pantalettes rather than twentieth-century briefs, she didn't realise there was a snake in them until she had

1940s, when Flynn's association with Warner Brothers was coming to an end, a time when fashions were changing and his particular kind of swashbuckling could no longer be guaranteed to draw huge audiences. It was perhaps the time when, most of all, he felt the need for change, to break away from the parts in which he had been typecast but while he was still at Warner's the chance of doing that was remote. His few attempts to play something other than an adventurer of one sort or another had not been particularly successful and the studio was not noticeably keen for him to repeat them. As Deirdre Flynn said: "He blamed Jack Warner for a lot of his problems, careerwise, and the relationship between them was cat and dog most of the time."

In the early days, though, Flynn's attitude towards Warner was wary and grasping but not especially bitter, probably because his first seven years at the studio were quite the most successful of his life. In the period between *Captain Blood* in 1935 and *Gentleman Jim* in 1942 he made twenty films, including all those for which he is best remembered, *The Charge of the Light Brigade*, *The Adventures of Robin Hood* (quite the best picture of its kind ever made), *Elizabeth and Essex*, *The Sea Hawk*, *They Died with Their Boots On* and, of course, *Captain Blood* and *Gentleman Jim* themselves. He also made a couple of comedies, *The Perfect Specimen* and *Four's A Crowd*; a weepie, *The Green Light*; and a love story, *Another Dawn*, but, although he did well enough in all of them, Flynn in them on, whereupon, thinking the creature was alive, and acting with great presence of mind, she plunged into a deep pond in order to drown the thing. Flynn thought this was hilarious though, not surprisingly, Miss de Havilland failed to see the joke for some time and still feels it was an odd way for a grown man to declare his affection, which is what Flynn was undoubtedly trying to do. But she believes that at that time and probably until his death there was a strong element of the small boy about him and perhaps it was that, along with his remarkable good looks and more charm than was good either for him or the people on whom he used it, that explained the immediate attraction almost everybody seemed to feel for him.

Until the looks and the luck deserted him and the drugs began to take a hold, he could get away with almost anything. Hal Wallis, a senior producer at Warner Brothers, said that even when Flynn was behaving atrociously and refusing to continue with a film until his salary was raised he was "the same likeable rogue. He would make these demands, he'd disappear, he'd come back to work and he would have the top brass in the studio apologising to him for having inconvenienced him."

But inevitably it was women upon whom Flynn's combination of looks and charm had the greatest effect. Olivia de Havilland said that on first meeting him she felt "instant attraction. I thought he was the most beautiful-looking man that I'd ever seen in my life and I suppose he's still the most beautiful-looking man I have ever seen in my life." Nora Eddington, recalling her introduction to him beside the pool at his home, said: "I decided he was the most beautiful thing I'd ever seen. He had marvellous green eyes and a deep tan and his hair had lightened – it was a sort of ruddy blond. And he couldn't have been more charming."

Many years later Flynn came to England to film *Lilacs in the Spring* with Dame Anna Neagle. He was in his middle forties and the ravages of time and his own destructive way of life had left their marks, but nevertheless Dame Anna found that "he was all the things the legend had said about him. He was a marvellous-looking man, full of charm and he just knocked one sideways."

Yet, despite all that, or possibly because of it, his relationships with women were never particularly happy. He was said to be an ardent pursuer of women and perhaps he was (though more often, I think, he was the prey rather than the predator) but if he did pursue them it was noticeable that they took great care not to run so fast that he couldn't catch up. His attitude to women was always ambivalent and many people were not at all sure that deep down he even liked them very much.

Deirdre Flynn is one who thinks he did. "He'd have to," she said, "considering all the time he spent with them. Some part of him liked them anyway. But then again he wanted to spend time with his buddies, his drinking partners and he didn't feel women should be included on those occasions."

Nora Eddington, on the other hand, believes he was "really a man's man. He liked some women but he wasn't all that sexually driven that he had to seek women all the time. In fact, they sought him out – they sought after him and he'd say, 'Well, why not?'"

Against that, Vincent Sherman talked of Flynn's "constant pursuit of women" and felt it was "some unconscious desire to debase them or to reassure himself of his own manhood and vitality. He was very complex; not just an ordinary woman chaser. Errol liked men, not in a sexual sense, but he liked men much better than women. He could love a man but he couldn't love a woman. I think he was distrustful of them, maybe he was afraid of them."

Olivia de Havilland said: "He enjoyed the idea of conquest but that doesn't mean he was capable of a very deep love and of sustaining it, does it? It means the opposite if anything."

In discussing Flynn and his attitude towards women it's difficult to ignore his relations with his mother. Miss de Havilland said: "You often wonder about a man who had complex feelings about his mother, which Errol did. I think most men who have perhaps been ridiculed by their mothers are never quite sure of themselves with women." Vincent Sherman said that one day during the filming of *Don Juan* Flynn "made a remark about his mother, a very distasteful remark. He didn't like her at all: he loved his father."

What significance there may have been in this "distasteful remark" it's now impossible to say; but it is unusual to find a romantic movie star of thirty-eight or thirty-nine, twice-married and the father of three children (which was Flynn's marital and parental state at that time) discussing his mother with a film director. It's certainly unusual in the case of a heterosexual movie star and Flynn was surely that, even though it has been suggested that he had occasional homosexual relationships too. If he did they were very discreet and not, apparently, of any great importance to him.

But it does seem likely that the mutual suspicion and antipathy which existed between himself and his mother had a lot to do with his largely unhappy experiences with women in general and his tendency to treat them as sexual toys to be acquired on a whim and discarded when he was tired of them.

When they were filming *Don Juan*, Vincent Sherman said, there was "a very beautiful little girl who played one of the small roles and Errol came over to me and said, 'Why don't you tell her how much I'm interested in her and that I've persuaded you to give us close-ups and so on. That'll sort of pave the way for me.' I was absolutely shocked. It was like asking me to do a little pimping for him. But to him it seemed perfectly legitimate."

On another occasion, said Sherman, "There were two girls he called up – prostitutes. I was a little surprised. It was the first time I'd known him bring prostitutes on the set. They were sitting over in the corner waiting for us to finish the day's work and he said to me, 'What are you doing after we've finished?' I told him I was going home and he said, 'Well, I thought maybe you'd like to come up to the dressing-room afterwards.' I said, 'Errol, I don't know how you can do it. You work all day here and then go up to the dressing-room with these women . . .' He said, 'Oh, it's nothing. I just lie there reading the trade papers while they work on me.' "

Neither anecdote is much to Flynn's credit (though there is a disgraceful touch of humour in the second) and both do tend to suggest, to put it mildly, a basic disregard for women.

All this time he was still married to Nora Eddington and she was well aware of his extra-marital activities but knew there was little she could do about them. Her one stipulation was to say to him, "I know the kind of life that you like. I know what goes on at the studio and I know you can't pass a pretty face. But just don't bring it home to the dinner table and don't ever humiliate me." And with these extremely lenient rules, she said, he complied. It was probably the closest approximation to fidelity that Flynn could make. He often said that he never wanted to marry but women wouldn't let him stay single and Deirdre Flynn thinks he was probably right. "I don't think a man like that really should be married," she said. "He's just not the type."

In 1942, just before the film *Gentleman Jim* was released, Flynn had an experience with two young women that was surely calculated to leave him with a highly jaundiced view of the entire sex, even assuming that he had had an unjaundiced view previously. In November of that year he was arrested and brought to trial on two charges of statutory rape, the allegation being that he had had unlawful sexual intercourse with two girls who were under eighteen, the legal age of consent in California.

One of them accused him of having assaulted her on board his yacht. Fortunately for Flynn both girls had very dubious backgrounds and he was acquitted, but he always believed that the trial was a political manoeuvre, an attempt by the Los Angeles district attorney's office to make a public attack on the morals of Hollywood generally by using him, probably its least moral citizen, as a scapegoat.

It does seem at least possible that neither girl would have brought charges against him unless she had been encouraged to do so. One result of the trial was that Flynn gained an imperishable reputation as a satyr; the phrase "in like Flynn" took on a specific and very lewd meaning and although all the unwelcome publicity helped the box-office receipts of *Gentleman Jim* (the story of James J. Corbett, the heavyweight boxing champion) – much to Warner Brothers' surprise and gratification – it also caused Flynn to believe, bitterly, that he had come to be regarded as little more than an ambulatory phallic symbol.

What with this and the fact that, from time to time, various women whom he had never met would accuse him of being the father of their children and, by threatening to "tell all" to the press, would try to shake him down for maintenance, it's hardly surprising that henceforth such respect as he had for women was not altogether uncritical.

But the trial had one other and more pleasing result. Because of it he met Nora Eddington, who was then working in the tobacco kiosk at the Los Angeles County Court. She was only seventeen and dangerously, considering what he was charged with, Flynn arranged through an intermediary to meet her. Bearing this in mind and remembering too the taste for teenage girls that he indulged in till the end of his life, the nagging, though unfounded, suspicion arises that he possibly was guilty, technically anyway, of statutory rape despite the verdict of the jury. In any event, within a year he and Nora were married.

They actually married not because either of them thought it was a particularly good idea at the time, but because Nora was pregnant. She was a Roman Catholic, didn't even consider an abortion and wanted her child to be legitimate. She said: "When I told him, the first thing he said was, 'You know, I just don't want to get married. I care about you. I love you, but I don't want to get married.' And I said, 'Well, I can't force you to marry me but I'm going to have this child anyway and I would like it to be legal.' I said, 'Just give the child a name and you can have a divorce immediately afterwards; I'll sign any papers that you want and that'll be the end of it.' So we agreed to it. But then I couldn't get rid of him for seven years."

Flynn, who was reluctant to abandon his bachelor image and way of life, kept the marriage a secret and sent Nora to Mexico under an assumed name to have the baby. She was there for six months, during which he telephoned and visited her so often that by the time Deirdre was born the fact that he had married again was common knowledge.

Nora said: "The day after the birth I said, 'What about the divorce papers?' and he said, 'We'll talk about it later.' And he put me off and put me off and then he said, 'I don't want a divorce but I'm also not ready for marriage and a child.' And I said, 'All right, fine. What do you want me to do?' And he said, 'Well, I'll get you a separate house; whatever you want.' In other words he wanted to keep me on the side and still have his bachelor life. So I went along with it for about six months and

then I rebelled. I'd sit in that house with the baby and my parents and the nurse, and Errol wouldn't let me date anybody, although he was going out with other girls. Oh yes, certainly. He was having a ball, are you kidding? But he'd say, 'I'd rather you didn't go out right now.' And what he would do is, he'd have his weekend orgy so to speak and then he'd call me from his house and say, 'Come on up, I want to see you,' and I'd be running back and forth and between and all of a sudden I thought, I don't want this. You know? This is ridiculous, what am I doing?

"We had a lot of publicity and I met a lot of his friends and I started getting phone calls and so I began dating other men and this made him absolutely furious. So when he called to tell me to come on up I'd say, 'Well, I'm sorry, I'm not running up there at the drop of a hat. If you want to see me you'd better call me at the beginning of the week.' And when he saw it could be serious between me and someone else, he said, 'Well, I think we'd better move you up here.' So I moved in because that's what I wanted. I wanted a family, I wanted a home and I was in love with the man."

Also by the time she and Flynn settled down to a more conventional married life she was pregnant again. Her move into her husband's house in the hills was the beginning of the happiest period of their time together. He was still a big star, earning a great deal of money, and he had a wife who was tolerant of his sexual adventures so long as he was discreet about them. The only thing that really bothered him at this time was the fact that the Second World War was going on without him. He had become an American citizen and when the United States entered the war he was keen to do his bit, but his draft rating was 4F, he had an "athletic heart", suffered from recurrent malaria and also had a touch of tuberculosis and he was rejected by every branch of the armed forces.

David Niven, his friend and companion of earlier days in many a drinking and womanising bout, said: "Here was this huge man, a great boxer and a great tennis player, but he had all the things wrong for getting into the army. Here was this great hero-type fellow who was not in the war and I think it really destroyed him. I think he was lucky as hell myself, but anyway it destroyed him, poor old boy."

77

Flynn married his third wife, Patrice Wymore, in France – and promptly faced another charge of rape.

There are those who tell a different tale, who say that Flynn never had any intention of joining up but that would seem to be out of character. His early adventures in New Guinea, his love of boxing, riding, sailing and scuba diving and the fact that he had taken some brief and obscure part in the Spanish Civil War (admittedly to get away from Lily Damita and not for any particularly noble reason) indicate that, whatever his other faults, he was not a physical coward. Any impression that he might have been one stems from his own self-mockery, his habit of coming off the set of some swashbuckler mopping his brow and saying, "By God, that's the bravest I've ever been," and his suggestion in *My Wicked, Wicked Ways* that he had scampered out of Spain at the mere suggestion that he might be called upon to do a little fighting. But people who brag about their own cowardice are not usually cowards and there's no reason to suppose that Flynn was an exception.

It's most probable that David Niven was right and that rejection by the forces helped to destroy him. In the Second World War nobody sent white feathers to apparently able-bodied men who weren't in uniform but they were still subjected to a certain amount of derision. And, significantly or not, it was during this time that his drinking became heavier and he began to experiment with drugs. Nora Eddington said he had started taking them when she first met him, the time of the rape case and his rejection by the services.

"He started taking them on a low key,

you know? I was horrified by it; I'd never been around drugs. But he said that he'd never tried it and he didn't want to leave this world without trying everything. So what could I do? We were only just married. But then it got progressively worse."

In the end it was Flynn's drug-taking which caused the break-up of the marriage after seven years. Nora said: "He went from one drug to another until finally he was a mainliner. And if you've never seen anybody on narcotics, they're in another world. They go crazy, they don't know what they're doing. He whacked me around a couple of times and when he came out of it he didn't know what had happened to me or how it came about. It got progressively worse and I must have left him, I don't know, half a dozen times and then I'd go back to him because he said he wouldn't use drugs any more and he'd try to stop but that was worse. And you know you can live with it for just so long. He didn't want me to leave him and when I finally did he said he would go into a sanitorium and take the cure but by then it was too late.

"You can take just so much. I adored the man but it wears away at you and wears away and the thing that was really bad was that he drank with it and you're not supposed to do both. You know, he always said he'd never get hung up on it but he did. Those are the famous last words – 'It won't get me: I can quit when I want to' – but he couldn't. That's what killed him."

By the time Nora filed for divorce in 1948 Flynn, though still less than forty years old, was already more or less finished in Hollywood. He had worked steadily through the war years and after but his films had made little impression at the box-office and one, *Objective Burma* in which he and a handful of other Americans appeared to have won the Burma campaign without any sort of assistance from the British, caused so much outrage in London that it was withdrawn from British cinemas.

His reviews were generally less than complimentary and the criticism hurt him. He took to drinking on the set, at first secretly by squirting oranges full of vodka with a hypodermic syringe and sucking them constantly as though he were desperate for Vitamin C, and then openly, although from time to time he would try to stop. Vincent

Sherman recalled that for the first week of shooting on *Don Juan*, Flynn's behaviour was impeccable. But then the New York reviews of his previous film *Escape Me Never* were delivered to the studio. They were scathing. Flynn tried to laugh them off but the next day he began drinking again.

In October 1950, while on a trip to Europe, Flynn married the actress Patrice Wymore, then a twenty-four-year-old starlet at Warner Brothers, in the Lutheran Church at Nice and on the same day was charged yet again with rape and ordered to answer the allegations in the Town Hall at Monte Carlo. The plaintiff this time was a young French girl and once again the offence was said to have taken place on Flynn's yacht. But, just as on the previous occasion in California, the charge was decidedly flimsy and the judge had no hesitation in throwing it out of court. Once again Flynn had been proved innocent, at least of rape. But even so the Monte Carlo incident added yet another murky chapter to a life story that was beginning to read like a modern, grown-up version of *Eric, Or Little by Little*. In any event it was a pretty inauspicious start to a marriage which, like the previous two, soon began to fail.

Two years after the wedding Flynn's contract with Warner Brothers and the major part of his career in Hollywood came to an end. As a big star he was clearly finished and he was in desperate financial trouble with huge income tax demands and back-alimony suits brought against him by Lily Damita. Exactly how broke he was it is hard to tell because as Deirdre Flynn said: "He was always stashing money here and there and pleading poverty at the same time, hoping to get himself off the hook."

Certainly he must have had a fair bit tucked away – though perhaps not enough to meet his crippling obligations in America – because he put up $430,000 of his own towards an Italian co-production of a film about William Tell, for which he himself had written the script. But very soon his money ran out and so did that of his partners and the enterprise resulted in only thirty minutes of film which have never been shown. This put him into even greater financial trouble because he found himself being sued by various members of the cast and production crew of the abortive picture for $840,000 and at the same time his Hollywood business manager died leaving behind evidence of, to say the least, gross mishandling of Flynn's affairs.

Before the *William Tell* fiasco he had made a couple of swashbucklers, *The Master of Ballantrae* in Britain and *Crossed*

Flynn, face ravaged by time, drink and drugs, in his last film Cuban Rebel Girls, *with Beverley Aadland, his seventeen-year-old companion at the end of his life.*

Swords with Gina Lollobrigida in Italy, but neither of them had worked and his reputation was at an extremely low ebb when he returned to London in the mid-fifties to co-star with Anna Neagle in *Lilacs in the Spring* and *King's Rhapsody*, the first of which was not particularly successful and the second a disaster.

And so he drifted on with two more indifferent movies, until in 1957 by an irony which I don't imagine he would have appreciated (or on second thoughts perhaps he would), he began to achieve recognition as an actor when it was too late to do him much good. Even more ironically he did it by playing drunks. First he received excellent notices in an adaptation of Hemingway's *The Sun Also Rises* and then turned in a most acceptable performance in *Too Much, Too Soon* in which he played his idol John Barrymore, another actor of astonishing good looks who had ruined himself with booze. It was almost typecasting, a role for which Flynn might have been preparing all his life. The film earned mostly downbeat reviews but Flynn was good and he was good again in John Huston's *The Roots of Heaven* in which he played his third successive drunk. By then, however, the drink and drugs were destroying him fast and, as Jack Warner was to describe him later in his autobiography, he was already "one of the living dead".

The Huston film was not well received and interest in Flynn's comeback swiftly waned. In the summer of 1958 he went to Cuba to make a semi-documentary of his own, a cheap and shoddy production called *Cuban Rebel Girls*, inspired by his interest, not so much in the girls, as in the young Fidel Castro. It was Flynn's last film. As he grew old not gracefully but disgracefully his last few months were spent in the company of a seventeen-year-old film extra called Beverley Aadland. He had been introduced to her by Ronnie Shedlo, who was his secretary at the time, while he was filming *Too Much, Too Soon*. She had been working on an adjoining set and Flynn, typically, had first been attracted by her legs. It was because of his association with Miss Aadland that he fled to Vancouver to escape the law and she was with him when he died.

After his death the unfortunate girl was the victim of a great deal of snide and even vicious publicity in the American papers but her relationship with Flynn, shattered old roué though he may have appeared, was not the sordid affair that the press made it out to be. Ronnie Shedlo said: "To him, being with her was a reaffirmation of his own youth. I think he knew his life was ebbing and he hoped to recapture a youthful glow in himself. He described himself once to me as 'A bright fragment in a drab world' and I think he knew the bright fragment was slowly discolouring."

Deirdre Flynn, who was only eighteen months younger than Beverley Aadland, said: "Why does any man at that age start looking at young girls? I guess it was to reaffirm himself as a man, perhaps to boost his ego, aside from the fact that he always liked young girls anyway. I think it was a happy relationship. It certainly wasn't a rollercoaster for her. My father at that time of his life wasn't an easy man to live with but I know that she cared for him. I didn't think it was lurid or anything terrible. I liked Beverley very much. I thought the whole thing was great. Of course, now it would be nothing. I mean, people don't think twice about anything like that. Beverley was terribly maligned by the press, which I thought very unfair. She was good to my sister and me and never interfered in our relationship with our father."

When the affair with Beverley Aadland began Flynn had been separated from Patrice Wymore for some time and she and their daughter Arnella were living on his estate in Jamaica, the only piece of property he owned in those final years. Nora Eddington said: "I certainly preferred Beverley to his wife. Beverley was kind to him. She wasn't out for anything, she didn't ask for anything. She took care of him. She used to pour his drinks and she'd tell me – and I believe her because she cared about him – that she would water them down, but he was too smart for that."

By then, in any event, there was little anyone could do for him. Nora still remembers her last meeting with him a month before his death and her horror at the way he looked. She said: "Oh my God, I almost died. I started to cry. He'd told me on the phone that he'd been to two specialists and they'd given him a year to live. When I saw him at the airport I just couldn't believe it. He was like a caricature of himself, a clown. That marvellous nose that he'd had, it was, oh God, it was so huge, it was like from

here to here, you know? And his eyes were very small, you could hardly see his eyes. It was . . . it was just very sad."

Errol Flynn wanted to be buried in Jamaica but instead Patrice Wymore buried him at Forest Lawn, the graveyard of the stars and the one place in which, quite literally, he would have hated to have been found dead. Because at the end of his life he was a loser and hardly anyone in Hollywood wishes to be associated with losers, very few people attended his funeral. One of those who did was his old director and drinking companion, Raoul Walsh, and legend has it that as the body was being lowered into the grave – a grave still unmarked by any headstone – Walsh put half a dozen bottles of scotch in with it to keep his old friend well lubricated on his journey to wherever it was he finished up. Of course, it's probably an apocryphal tale but I like to believe it's true. I also like to believe that Walsh, who knew Flynn's tastes as well as anybody, would just as soon have slipped six nubile girls in there if only he could have found any willing to make the trip.

The picture which the Walsh anecdote conjures up of Flynn, indeed the general picture one receives of him, as a man who was reckless and self-indulgent, who was humorous, dashing and libidinous, who hurt others as well as himself though probably not intentionally, who was in the end his own worst enemy, may not be especially noble but it is at least more attractive than the reality of his last few years. The end of Errol Flynn was pathetic rather than tragic, the end of a man who seemed to have been bent on self-destruction. Olivia de Havilland remembers him as "unmatchable, full of warmth and charm. There was something affectionate about him, so that when he did unaffectionate things it was such a shock and so distressing because you knew he was capable of the opposite."

Deirdre Flynn remembers him as a strict but affectionate father who demanded courtesy and good manners in his daughters. He was a father who, just before his death, wrote his son Sean a letter expressing paternal concern that the boy didn't seem to have been to bed with his girl friend yet and ending with the postscript: "You needed a hundred dollars. I added an extra twenty-five for condoms and/or flowers."

Jack Warner wrote of him as "one of the most charming and tragic men I have ever met".

Flynn himself once said: "Hollywood is a lovely place to live. It's comfortable, it's warm, it's sunny but it's filled with the most unutterable bastards." He blamed those unutterable bastards for the fact that his career, in his own opinion anyway, never amounted to much, but the fault really lay within himself. He was a dreamer who was dissatisfied with what he had and always felt he might achieve greatness at something else – at archaeology, for instance, or writing. But something invariably distracted him from these lofty ambitions, the offer of another drink, perhaps, or the sight of a pretty girl passing by, and he settled for the easier options that Hollywood offered.

Deirdre Flynn believes he was not a happy man, but "I don't know that even he could say what it was exactly that made him unhappy, what drove him to do this or that, or act in such and such a way. Why the drugs? What did they do? Obviously he used them, turned to them, to escape from something within him."

Vincent Sherman said: "Something was bothering him because when you go to such extremes of drinking, when you are running from one woman to another, you're looking for something. Maybe he himself wasn't aware of what he was looking for but obviously something was bothering him to cause him to waste his life as he did."

On that last point Deirdre Flynn takes issue with Sherman. She doesn't believe her father did waste his life and she doesn't believe he would have thought so either. "I think in fact," she said, "that he probably led two lifetimes in one. It was very free, his life. And he actually did what he bloody well wanted to do. I don't see that as a waste at all."

At his peak Flynn, more than any other film star, was probably the man that every woman wanted and every other man envied. The implacable moralists among us never approved of that and no doubt derived grim pleasure from the tatty bathos of his end. But if he had an epitaph – and he hasn't because, of course, he has no headstone at Forest Lawn to engrave it upon – I suspect he might well have chosen that final statement of his daughter's: "He did what he bloody well wanted to do."

Errol Flynn sporting cravat.

81

Humphrey Bogart

When Humphrey Bogart left his hand and footprints in the wet cement outside Graumann's Chinese Theatre on Hollywood Boulevard, he wrote: "May you never die till I kill you." This message, at once tender and strangely menacing, was addressed to his fourth wife, Lauren Bacall. It was typical of a man who was always something of a paradox.

Bogart was the screen hoodlum with the rasping voice and sinister lisp who actually came from an impeccable social background. He had the hard, cold-eyed look of a professional hit man but inside the shell he was slightly softer than a three-minute egg. He was an actor of narrow range who yet became perhaps the most enduring of all Hollywood stars, a man who was snapped up by the movies in his early thirties and then took eleven years to become an overnight success.

He is revered and even idolised by the cinema-going youth of America and Europe and, at the same time, the story of his life and his career offers warm reassurance to all middle-aged men who still believe, wistfully and in defiance of the general evidence they see around them, that life can begin at forty. Bogie was the nineteenth-century baby who, somehow, grew up to be the personification on the cinema screen of mid-twentieth-century attitudes. Lauren Bacall says he always called himself "the last century boy" because he was born on Christmas Day in 1899.

"He was very old-fashioned in many ways," she said, "and he was very much a gentleman." His friend and biographer, Nathaniel Benchley, describes him as "a puritan who found himself in a business where such a thing is a rarity, so I think he very often covered up with tough talk".

Bogart was married four times, which seems excessive (though not, in Benchley's view, contradictory) for a puritan and he met Miss Bacall, his final wife and the one who could accurately be described in the language of the fan magazines as "his last and true love" on a film set. What, in Hollywood, could be neater or more appropriate than that? When you consider Bogart the screen tough guy who, as director Stanley Kramer once said (and he meant it affectionately), was just "a big sloppy bowl of mush" inside, the cynic who was truly a romantic at heart, there is little wonder that a cult has sprung up around him that is stronger than that which surrounds any other film star. In Bogart there was something for everybody.

"The last century boy" was born in New York, the son of Dr. Belmont DeForest Bogart, an eminent physician who, as Joe Hyams says, "was in the social register at a time when the social register really meant something". Hyams, incidentally, is another friend and another biographer and on balance it seems to me that Bogart had even more of the latter than of the former, which is a further indication of the appeal he has for movie buffs. His mother was an artist, Maud Humphrey, a famous illustrator in her day and a leader of the suffragette movement. One way and another the Bogarts, five in all (for along with their son they had two younger daughters, Frances and Kay) were a well-to-do, upper-class family. Young Bogie went to the best primary schools in New York and then to Phillips Academy at Andover, Massachusetts, which was possibly the best private school in America. "He grew up," said Joe Hyams, "with, if you will, a silver spoon in his mouth."

More than that, really. You might also say with a silver pusher and spoon, for when he was only one year old his face – already, it seems with hindsight, curiously sardonic and knowing for one so young – was a familiar sight in Mellins Baby Food advertisements. That Bogie was chosen for this dubious honour was due to his mother's connections and until he was eighteen it was the only thing which set him apart from other children of similar backgrounds who were clearly destined for an Ivy League education and a life of well-connected affluence in New York business circles. But when he reached the age of eighteen, the path chosen for him by his parents took a sharp deviation because he failed his examinations and could not be accepted by Yale University. His father was greatly annoyed and made no secret of the fact and young Humphrey ran away to join the navy. The war was actually over by then but nevertheless he returned with a wound about which a small legend was later to be spun.

The legend has it that the wound, which resulted in the famous scar on his lip, was acquired when he was hit by a splinter of wood while his ship was under attack by a U-boat. In fact, according to Nat Benchley, the whole affair was rather more prosaic. "Bogart was doing shore patrol duty between assignments," said Benchley, "and he was taking a prisoner to Portsmouth Naval Prison. The man was manacled and when they changed trains at Boston he asked Bogie for a cigarette. Bogie reached into his pocket to get him one and the man pounded the manacles across his face, tearing it open, and ran. Bogie just couldn't get rid of the scar. Some navy doctor, apparently a frustrated sail-maker, got to work on it and he had three plastic surgery operations, but it didn't clear up." An interesting enough anecdote in itself, though less glamorous than the legend. Bogart never actually confirmed the war wound story but, on the other hand, he never said anything publicly to deny it.

However, home again and slightly mutilated after his brief service, Bogart became friendly with the daughter of William A. Brady, a famous theatrical producer, and through her found work on the stage. It was something into which he simply drifted, largely because after trying one or two jobs on and around Wall Street he was frankly bored by the prospect of a business career.

In those early days, from 1920 onwards, Bogart said later, he would literally bound on stage shouting "Anyone for tennis?" This is probably quite untrue, since there are very few, if indeed any, plays in which anybody actually says "Anyone for tennis?" but, even though he seemed to find regular employment as a small-part actor, his was a fairly inglorious start.

Helen Hayes, who knew him at that time, said: "We were all youngsters together in New York. He was one of a vast crew of juvenile actors playing in silly comedies. We didn't think much of Bogie. He just wasn't anything very much and he was cursed with a rather plain, old-shoe face. There was nothing romantic or attractive about it. We were anxious for him. We didn't think he was worth anything."

For a long time that view, perhaps not quite so candidly expressed, was shared by Hollywood, although in fact Bogart was not even to arrive there until 1938. In the meantime, in 1926, he married an actress named Helen Mencken, who was considerably older than he. By all accounts he didn't really want to marry her at all. It was far more her idea than his but he seems to have agreed in an unguarded moment and then, not wishing to reject her, determined to see the business through. Perhaps this was where the old-fashioned gentleman came in; or again, perhaps not. Miss Mencken was a very powerful lady around Broadway and he had serious, and probably well-founded fears, that, if jilted, she could do his career a lot of harm. On the whole he probably married her partly through a misplaced sense of chivalry and partly through prudence.

Still, as it turned out, the marriage was a brief hiatus for both of them. It didn't work at all well and within two years they were divorced. A year later Bogart was married again, to another actress, Mary Phillips, whom he had first met in 1924 when they both appeared in a play called *Nerves*. Nathaniel Benchley believes that Bogart was genuinely in love with Mary Phillips, in a way that he was not with Helen Mencken, but "their various careers pulled them apart". Joe Hyams, while not disputing that, ascribes Bogart's first two marriages, and also his third, to the fact that he simply "got involved".

"It was another time and another

period," Hyams said. "People didn't live together the way they do now. He began to go with someone, he began to have an affair with her and he was a gentleman of the old school. We're talking now about the twenties and thirties and it was expected that if you slept with someone you married her and I think that's what led him into marriage."

A logical and even gallant explanation, if not particularly flattering to anyone concerned and perhaps not the whole truth anyway, because Bogart and his second wife were happy enough at first while they were both working on Broadway.

But in 1930, after a decade which had seen him achieve steady progress as an actor, though not exactly stardom, Bogart was summoned to Hollywood for a screen test by Fox, which later became Twentieth Century-Fox. His wife refused to go with him because she was working in a play and thus his first venture into the movies was also the first of several separations which, eventually, were to end the marriage.

Bogart's screen test was declared "magnificent" and he was immediately cast in supporting roles in six films, all made in rapid succession and all equally indifferent. He played a cowboy in one and a bright young socialite in a couple of others; nobody thought of him as a hard man or a gangster in those days – certainly Bogart himself didn't. And he obviously didn't impress anybody much because in 1931 the actor who was thought "magnificent" only a year before had his contract dropped by the studio and, greatly discouraged, returned to Mary and Broadway.

He did not, however, stay very long for, early in 1932, Columbia offered him a six-month contract and he headed west again to appear in three more indifferent pictures before returning, no less discouraged than before, to New York. Indeed, this time he swore he would never go back to Hollywood and for six years he kept this vow, a fairly easy thing to do because in that period Hollywood didn't approach him again.

The years of the Depression were a hard time for stage actors, just as they were for anyone else and Bogart, particularly, and Mary had much difficulty in finding work. Quite often the only way he could make a contribution to the family budget was by playing chess (at which, apparently, he was rather good) for sidestakes in New York

cafés and clubs. But among the many "downs" in his life at this time there were also a few "ups" and the greatest of these occurred in 1936 when, somewhat to his own disbelief, he was cast as the gangster Duke Mantee in the Broadway production of Robert Sherwood's play, *The Petrified Forest*. Sherwood thought the idea of Bogart, a specialist in playing rich young men about town, in that part was ridiculous and in this Bogart heartily supported him. The play and Bogart, however, were a great success and Warner Brothers promptly acquired the film rights.

Now the star of *The Petrified Forest* was the English actor, Leslie Howard, and he had sworn that when the film was made he would insist that Bogart be invited to recreate the role of Duke Mantee on screen. Such promises are frequently made by actors and seldom kept, but Howard, like Bogie, was a gentleman of the old school and was therefore as good as his word. Warner Brothers were most put out because they had earmarked Edward G. Robinson for the part, but eventually and reluctantly they acceded to Howard's stubborn demands and so Bogart went to Hollywood for the third time, never to leave again.

When the film was released Bogart was hailed as a new star by everybody except his employers, who had taken the precaution of signing him to a not very expensive contract and to whom anyway he was something of an embarrassment. What did Warner Brothers want with another heavy when they already had Cagney, Robinson and George Raft on the payroll? The studio could see very little future for him except as a kind of supporting gangster, the one that Cagney, Robinson or Raft could shoot as and when the occasion demanded, and so his career was settled for the next few years.

Indeed, in his first two years at Warners he appeared in eleven films, eight times as a gangster or some other sort of criminal, and in four of them he was killed. In fact his overall track record was even more dismal than that. "In my first thirty-four films," he said, later on, "I was shot in twelve, electrocuted or hanged in eight and was a jailbird in nine. I played more scenes writhing around on the floor than I did standing up."

It was the duration and the difficulty

of his struggle to better himself that gave Bogart a decidedly jaundiced view of the Hollywood establishment, which he later blamed for the lack of opportunity he was given during all those years as a minor heavy on the Warner Brothers lot. Jack Warner, the head of the studios, certainly had very little faith in him except as a criminal type. Indeed, the nearest thing to a compliment that Warner ever paid him was when he said: "Nothing can happen to your face that will hurt it a bit."

In an age when leading men were invariably handsome and sometimes downright pretty, Bogart was an obvious misfit, an actor doomed to play unsympathetic supporting roles. One of the very few who could see beyond that rugged and not especially prepossessing exterior to something finer and potentially more exciting was Sam Jaffe, the man who became Bogart's agent after the third coming to Hollywood and who remained his agent and his friend until Bogie's death.

Jaffe said: "When he was playing heavies and gangsters I thought he could become a leading man and many people laughed at me. I thought he could be a different kind of leading man. He wasn't a good-looking boy or as handsome as Robert Redford is today but he was a marvellous actor and I thought he had great potential as a character leading man."

At that stage, however, it was simply Jaffe and Bogart and, for a while, Mrs. Bogart (Mary had joined him from Broadway) against the rest. In the five years after *The Petrified Forest* he was constantly working, becoming increasingly familiar to cinema audiences but always, except in the odd B-picture, in secondary roles.

Meanwhile his second marriage went the way of his first. Mary Bogart was bored by Hollywood and, to her husband's resentment, went back to New York to resume her stage career. And while she was gone Bogart met and was ensnared by yet another actress, Mayo Methot, a voluptuous and alcoholic blonde with whom Bogart shared not only a love of the bottle but also a love of the sea. She moved into his apartment to keep him company while his wife was away and was discovered there by Mary on a flying visit from New York. That was the end of that marriage. Mary sued successfully for divorce and in August 1938 Bogart, trapped again, did the

honourable thing and married Miss Methot.

This marked the beginning of the booziest period in his career. He always prided himself on being a great drinker and once gave it as his considered opinion that he, Errol Flynn and Winston Churchill, three very ill-assorted bar-flies, were the biggest and finest drinkers of their time. He also insisted that the whole world was permanently three drinks below par – that if each of us took three quick belts we would be much nicer people. Somehow I don't think medical opinion would support that theory, though I dare say the distillers might. Until the day he died Bogie was partial to the odd snort (or two, or three) but during the years with Mayo Methot his alcoholic consumption must have been awe-inspiring.

Their whole marriage seems to have passed in a drunken haze, punctuated by fierce, frequent and potentially lethal fights. On one occasion she stabbed him with a carving knife and on another she threw a heavy soda-water bottle at him, missing him so narrowly and frightening him so much that he called Sam Jaffe and instructed him to take out a 100,000 dollar insurance policy on his (Bogie's) life. What he said to Jaffe was: "You see this seltzer bottle? She threw it at me but she was drunk and she missed me. If she ever connects, if she ever hits the bull's-eye, she'll kill me." So the insurance policy was taken out, with Jaffe as beneficiary, in order that he should not be the loser, after all his hard work on the actor's behalf, if Bogart should one day be murdered in a fit of drunken rage by his wife.

By all accounts Mayo Methot was a most formidable woman. When I talked to him at the "21" restaurant in New York (one of Bogart's favourite drinking haunts) Nat Benchley said: "She was a savage drunk. I've seen her throwing crockery in here just for the hell of it. Get a little scotch inside of her and she was terrible." And the barman at the same restaurant revealed that, on one occasion, Mayo created such a scene there that Bogart went and ate his lunch in the men's room, that being the one place where she couldn't get at him.

Joe Hyams said: "Mayo was very sexy, very pretty and I think he was physically attracted to her. He was drunk when he met her and they stayed drunk throughout their entire marriage. They had a tremendous drunken brawl on their wedding night and she chased him out of the house. The wedding itself was one of the classics in Hollywood history with Mischa Auer dancing nude on a table top. Bogie once said to me that Mayo got him drinking and kept him drinking because that was the only way she could hold him. They boozed a great deal and they fought a great deal and once I asked him why he enjoyed fighting with her so much and he said, 'Because the making-up was so pleasant,' which makes sense, too.''

While this was going on, while life with Mayo was punctuated by drinking bouts and quarrels, reconciliations and nights of violence when she would lock her husband out of his own house so that he had to sleep on the lawn, Bogart's career was simply marking time. He knew that most of the roles he was asked to play were worthless but, though he complained about them, he took them nevertheless. As he explained to Nat Benchley: "The only way to learn is to do it. If you're going to become an actor, then you just act. Never mind what it is, get it right, get your lines right and don't louse up the scene.''

Vincent Sherman, who directed him in 1939 in *The Return of Dr X* in which Bogart played a vampire, of all improbable things (a vampire with red lips and dark eyes and a white streak down the middle of his hair), says that nobody on the Warner's lot could with any honesty claim to have regarded Bogie at that time as star material and that Bogie knew it. "There's no question," said Sherman, "that he felt he was being wasted. He knew he wasn't held in any great esteem."

But though they could hardly have known it, the very people who treated him so dismissively were probably doing him a favour because it was this cynicism, this sardonic disbelief in the words and actions of the Establishment that became the Bogart trademark in his most notable films and appealed so strongly to the scepticism of later generations. But his immediate and most material reaction to the struggle he had to establish himself was that he began to look after his money, because he believed that only in financial security lay the freedom he wanted if his bosses should ever seriously displease him.

Thus, from what amounted to a lengthy

Mayo Methot, his third wife, who stabbed him with a knife.

and sometimes painful apprenticeship in Hollywood, there emerged the familiar Bogart character – a wary man, not easily gulled; something of a loner who despised the social conventions of Film City, the big, back-slapping parties, the ostentatious visits to fashionable night spots. He became a deflator of pomposity, a needler who, when the whim took him, would mercilessly pick upon a complete stranger for the pleasure of seeing how far he could provoke him.

Sometimes, though not very often, this led him into trouble. Bogart, after all, was a comparatively small man – less than medium height and no more than 150 pounds in weight – and he was no fighter. So, as he once explained to Joe Hyams, he devised a certain procedure to protect himself from the deserved aftermath of his verbal excesses. He said: "If you're in a club and a fight's about to start and you're going to be part of it, you throw the first punch and then run like hell to the nearest, biggest waiter and stand there and he'll break up the fight for you.''

Occasionally even this ingenious plan failed to work. "There was an agent," said

Nat Benchley, "called Paul Small. A very big man. One night Bogie needled him and Paul slapped him, right in the face. Well, they were pulled apart and people took Small into another room, calmed him down and said that needling was only Bogie's way of having fun and they told him so much that he became enraged all over again and went back and slapped him a second time."

But this waspish behaviour was simply part of a dangerous game that Bogart liked to play. After a particularly fraught scene in Romanoff's restaurant in Hollywood, Lauren Bacall told her husband: "One of these days, you're going to get your head blown off." And he replied: "You don't understand. The trick is to get a guy just to the point where he's about to slug you and then you either lie down, put on your glasses or take a drink. Just get it to that point and stop. That's the essence of the game."

To his credit, however, it wasn't only agents and other comparatively small fry that he picked on. Sam Jaffe recalls that one day he had an irate phone call from Jack Warner himself.

"Jaffe," said Warner, "your star behaved very badly last night."

"Really, J.L.?" said Jaffe, understandably anxious, for the great man was extremely cross. "What happened?"

"Well, I was at this party, everybody was dressed up and Bogart walked up to me and said, 'J.L., you know you're a creep?' "

Jaffe made the required solicitous noises. "Well, Jack, what do you want me to do about it?" he said, "I mean, I just manage his career. I don't manage his personal life. I don't have anything to do with what he says at night."

"Well," said Warner, "you ought to talk to him about it. I think it's terrible."

The next day Jaffe phoned Bogart. "Bogie," he said, "I had a call from J.L. He says you called him a creep."

"Yes," said Bogie, "I did."

"But why?"

"Well, he is a creep," said Bogie.

And that was the end of the matter, though perhaps it needs to be said that this attack on the mighty Warner was made when Bogart was a hugely established star. It was, in fact, simply a touch of revenge for the humiliations he had suffered in the past. Those humiliations were exemplified by the way he was cast in *The Return of Dr X*. Vincent Sherman said: "Warner called me up to the office and said, 'I'm going to give you this guy Bogart. For Christ's sake, see if you can get him to play something besides Duke Mantee.' "

Bogie was, in fact, forty-one years old before anything resembling stardom was visited upon him and even then the opportunity came to him quite by chance. James Cagney was offered the role of the ageing gangster brought back from prison to take part, reluctantly, in one last raid in *High Sierra* but turned it down. The part was then offered to George Raft but he didn't want it because he didn't like the idea of dying at the end of the picture. Paul Muni didn't want it either because it had previously been offered to George Raft, and Edward G. Robinson would have nothing to do with it because all those other people had been asked before him. So Bogie, the reserve heavy, got the job instead and turned in a performance of such sensitivity that at last the studio began to take him seriously.

Sam Jaffe said: "Bogart's whole career was made possible by other people turning down roles. He got the breaks because, first, there was the *High Sierra* business, and then George Raft turned down *The Maltese Falcon* because he said he wasn't going to work with an unknown director, John Huston. It was just a series of coincidences that made Bogart a star."

But even with the coincidences it wasn't easy. The role of Sam Spade in *The Maltese Falcon* was the prototype for the later Bogart roles and screen persona – the archetypal city man, tough and knowing, honourable but ruthless, brave but not foolhardy, sexual but not romantic, a natural survivor in the urban jungles. Jack Warner, however, was still not convinced about Bogart's potential. Valiantly resisting any impudent suggestion that he had been mistaken about this unlikely new star for more than a decade, he announced: "Bogart's a tough guy, not a lady's man." It was not until *Casablanca* and the odd chemistry produced by the blending of the apparently ill-assorted Bogart and Ingrid Bergman that even Warner had to admit grudgingly and no doubt only to his closest confidants, that he might have been a bit wrong.

Bogart's new-found luck – the right parts

in the right films at the right time – held firm throughout the making of *Casablanca* which, strictly speaking, should have been a disaster since the script was being written as they went along and nobody, not even the director Michael Curtiz, knew until almost the end whether Bogie or Paul Henreid would finish up with the girl.

As an example of the haphazard way in which the film was shot, there was one occasion when Curtiz told Bogart to go on to the balcony of Rick's café and nod.

"Okay," said Bogart, "but what am I nodding at? What's my attitude?"

"Don't ask so many questions," said Curtiz. "Get up there and nod and then go home."

Bogart did as he was told and didn't discover until a long time afterwards that his nod had triggered off the famous scene in which Henreid led the other clients of the café in singing the "Marseillaise" and drowning out the Germans who had been chanting aggressive Nazi war songs. Whether or not he ever quite knew what he was supposed to be doing, Bogart nearly won the Oscar for *Casablanca*, losing out in the end to Paul Lukas for *Watch on the Rhine*.

So at the age of forty-three Bogie had finally arrived. He and Mayo went to Africa to tour the Allied bases – causing German radio to announce that American morale was so low that a notorious gangster had been sent out to entertain the troops – and then, on his return to Hollywood, he starred for Howard Hawks in Hemingway's *To Have and Have Not*. His co-star was an unknown nineteen-year-old actress named Lauren Bacall.

The start of the film was less than auspicious. On the first day of shooting Bogart returned to the set after lunch slightly drunk from far too many martinis. Hawks promptly hauled him out in front of the entire crew and said: "Right, we're going to Jack Warner and see whether I get a new star or you get a new director."

Bogart said: "I don't want to do that."

"Okay," said Hawks, "what are we going to do instead?"

Bogart said: "I'm going to stop drinking at lunchtime."

And so it was resolved. In any event he soon found something far more interesting than booze to help him while away his spare time. He fell firmly in love with Lauren Bacall, despite the fact that he was twenty-five years older than she was.

This made life more than a little difficult for him because he was still married to the intensely jealous and increasingly alcoholic Mayo Methot. Inevitably there were fights when Mayo discovered what was going on. Howard Hawks recalled that one night, early in the filming, the Bogarts came to dinner at his house and started brawling. Hawks told them: "Look, first of all, whoever tries to punch the other one, I'm going to punch that person. This is my house and I don't want any fighting in it." After that, he said, they were "as nice as anybody could be . . . but I don't think it was Bacall who broke up the marriage, you know. I think it was breaking up long before that."

In the event, the divorce was surprisingly amicable for two such volatile people. It was finalised in May 1945, and afterwards Mayo went to live in Oregon with her mother. Six years later she died of an illness brought on by acute alcoholism.

Eleven days after the divorce, while they were making their second film for Howard Hawks – the classic screen version of Raymond Chandler's *The Big Sleep* – Bogart and Lauren Bacall were married. Bogie was gravely concerned about this step, feeling that a marriage between a man of forty-five and a girl of twenty could hardly last very long. It was his friend Peter Lorre who helped him make up his mind to go ahead with it, saying, philosophically: "It's better to have five good years than none at all."

Therefore, consoled if not exactly inspired by this thought, Bogart entered upon his final marriage. He was aware of the age difference, as any sensitive and intelligent man would be, but, according to Nat Benchley, he more or less solved the problem by telling his wife that "if she ever saw anyone she preferred to him, she should simply say so and Bogie would get lost." Happily, this never happened. Delmer Daves, who directed Bogart in *Dark Passage* and had known him for a long time before that, said: "Betty Bacall was a blessing after Mayo." And indeed Lauren Bacall effected, intentionally or not, a great difference in Bogart's life. The heavy drinking, which had brought him to the verge of alcoholism with Mayo, came to an end partly, in Miss Bacall's view, because he now had security, not only professional but also emotional security. He

had no need to drink heavily any more, although he never renounced the stuff completely. Towards the end of his life Nat Benchley was with him when somebody asked: "Have you ever been on the wagon?" and Bogart replied: "Yes, I have and it was the most miserable afternoon of my life."

To some extent the marital relationship was that of mentor and pupil. Miss Bacall has frequently mentioned the debt she owed to Bogie for what he taught her about acting for the cinema and about how to find her way around Hollywood. But it was also a deep and genuine love affair and what she gave him was stability – not, one would think, before time. He began to regard himself, at last, as a securely married man, and potentially a family man. For someone who had been married so often, this would seem to be a radical change in character, since a man with four wives could usually be classified with some confidence as promiscuous and a womaniser. Nat Benchley says that Bogie was neither of those things. It was the puritan streak, he says, the feeling that he should make an honest woman of the lady he had compromised that led him into his first three marriages and "he never had any action on the side, which in Hollywood is unheard of."

The desire to be a family man, which came upon him decidedly late in life, had a distressing side effect. In 1947, while he was filming *Dark Passage* with Delmer Daves he embarked upon a course of hormone pills to make him more fertile, as a result of which his hair started falling out. Daves, said: "He came down to work one morning in San Francisco and said, 'Del, have you ever found a lot of hair on your pillow when you woke in the morning? Because I did.' The next day it was worse and very soon he went quite bald. I started having pieces of wig made for him. At first he needed only a little piece and then he needed more and more. In the end he lost all his hair, although a few months after we'd finished the picture it came back again."

More accurately, it came back as it had been before he started taking the hormones, which is to say that, even when restored, his hair had receded enough to necessitate the use of a toupee, an invaluable deception for an actor but one which he regarded with scorn.

Joe Hyams said: "He hated the toupee, although I don't think he was embarrassed by the baldness. I never saw him wear the toupee except on a film set and then he'd snarl about that 'goddamn rug'."

Despite their embarrassing side effects the hormone pills must have worked because, when he was nearly fifty, Bogart became a father swapping, as it were, his hair for an heir. Sentimentally he named his son Steve, after the character he had played in *To Have and Have Not*, the film on which he met Lauren Bacall. And when, in 1952, the Bogarts had a daughter, he called her Lesley, in honour of Leslie Howard whose help and loyalty had brought him to Hollywood to make *The Petrified Forest*.

Generally speaking, however, Bogart's early reaction to parenthood was distinctly uneasy. He had never been particularly comfortable with children, as witness an anecdote retailed by Nathaniel Benchley. "He had a twelve-year-old godson in New York and one day, when Bogie was in town, the kid's mother called him up and

Bogie and Bacall. In private life he never would wear his "rug".

With fourth wife Lauren Bacall and their son, Steve.

suggested he take the boy out and give him some religious instruction, the way a godfather should. So Bogie, who couldn't think of anything else to do, took him to the '21' restaurant for lunch. Well, they sat there, making some kind of stilted conversation, and then suddenly Bogie said, 'Listen, kid, one thing you must remember – there are twelve commandments. Waiter, where the hell's my drink?' And that was the boy's religious instruction."

Initially he was no more at ease with his own children. Benchley believes that because he "came into the parenthood game late" he looked upon his offspring almost as "characters from another world. He was rather in awe of them." Nevertheless, although both of the children were still very young when their father died, Bogart had obviously got to grips with fatherhood and started to enjoy the role, because other people tell of finding him in the nursery, devotedly snarling baby talk at the infant Steve.

Meanwhile, as Bogart began to enjoy the unfamiliar fruits of a happy marriage and a thriving career that was bringing him not merely fame, which many actors enjoy, but also admiration, which is given to few, a kind of hysterical fascism, eventually to be orchestrated into mass paranoia by Senator Joe McCarthy, began to grip the American people. A grim national sport called "hunt the Reds" became more popular than baseball and a great deal nastier. In 1947 a Federal Grand Jury indicted ten Hollywood writers as alleged Communists for refusing to answer, as was after all their constitutional right, when asked if they were now, or had ever been, members of the Communist party.

In protest at this witch-hunting, John Huston gathered together a planeload of stars and other prominent members of the Hollywood community and took them to Washington to campaign in support of the so-called "Unfriendly Ten". Among these indignant and notable citizens were the Bogarts. It was a brave gesture – braver perhaps than any of them knew, when you consider that within a very short time the merest suspicion of the slightest taint of Communism would be enough to ruin a man's career and even drive people to suicide.

Bogart's participation in this act of protest did not, however, last very long. When the going became tough and public opinion started to turn against the protesters, he backed away, disassociating himself from the whole business. A lot of people, though not his friends Joe Hyams and Nat Benchley, believed that this was a cop-out, that he had lost his nerve. Hyams prefers to see it as "a re-thinking of his position and a re-estimation of what he had done". Bogart himself said later on that, initially, he had believed he was defending the Bill of Rights but then came to the conclusion that the Communist party, which was striving to make martyrs of the "Unfriendly Ten", was using him and the others.

"We went in there green and they beat our brains out," he said, in an interview with *Newsweek*. "In the shuffle we became adopted by the Communists and I ended up with my picture on the front page of the *Daily Worker*. I detest Communism just as any decent American does – the trip was ill-advised, even foolish. I am an American and very likely . . . sometimes a foolish and impetuous American."

No doubt his recantation was sincere, but it was also prudent, just as his first marriage had been prudent. When he was thinking of pulling out of his proposed wedding to Helen Mencken his brother-in-law, Stuart Rose, told him: "You're in too deep now. If you don't marry her, you'll never get another part on Broadway." And in the same way it must have been quite clear to him in 1947 that, successful though he was, any further association with alleged Communists could seriously damage his career. If, in addition, he was indeed a "decent American" who detested Communism then his withdrawal from the scene was only sensible, no matter how many people might call it a cop-out. Certainly it would be unfair to suggest that Bogart lacked moral courage. In the 1930s he appeared on the radio in support of Franklin Roosevelt, despite the fact that Jack Warner was implacably opposed to Roosevelt and had made it known that anyone at the studio who came out publicly in favour of the President would have his contract torn up and be barred from the lot.

Neither of these dire threats was carried out in Bogart's case but, at the time he made his broadcast, he had every reason to believe they might be. He was never afraid to swim against the tide as he showed in a different context in 1954.

At that time, Joan Bennett's husband, Walter Wanger the producer, shot her agent, Jennings Lang, in a car park in a fit of jealousy and in the groin. Though Lang, happily, recovered, Wanger was jailed and Miss Bennett found herself the object of scandal and professionally ostracised. "I was more or less blacklisted," she said. "I wasn't being offered any pictures. Well, the Bogarts were very close friends of ours and at that time Bogie was making *We're No Angels* and he went to the head of Paramount and said, 'I'd like Joan Bennett in the picture.' And the man said, 'Oh no, we can't have her. She's been involved in this dreadful scandal,' and Bogie said, 'If you won't have her, forget it – I won't do the picture.' So I got the part. I don't think you can have a better friend than that."

One final testimonial to Bogart's integrity and perhaps another reply to the "cop-out" school of thought, came from Adlai Stevenson, whom the Bogarts supported fervently in his presidential campaign of 1952. "Bogie," Stevenson said, "never seemed to give a damn for what people said or thought. And it was quite perilous in those days to be a Democrat, especially one partisan to me."

However, once the controversy over Bogart's aborted Washington protest had died away, he swiftly resumed the successful path he had been treading for the last few years and furthermore he now had the confidence, from time to time, to step out of the familiar Bogart character. He did so initially in *The Treasure of the Sierra Madre* which, Sam Jaffe insists, he made for the sake of Walter Huston.

Jaffe said: "Bogie came to me and said, 'Sam, there's no question that I'm going to have to support Walter Huston and I think this is the only chance Walter will ever get to do that kind of role. So I'm going to support a character actor, but a brilliant one, and I don't think it'll hurt my career.' There's no doubt that, if Bogart hadn't played in it and so guaranteed a box-office attraction, this picture might not have been made because Jack Warner wasn't that enthusiastic. But Bogie did it because he had a great admiration for Walter."

He was also quite right in his assessment of his own role. He did, in effect, play a supporting part and Walter Huston won the Academy Award.

After *Sierra Madre* Bogart returned to his more traditional character in *Key Largo* with Lauren Bacall and Edward G. Robinson and then, in 1949, disillusioned with the sort of scripts that Warner Brothers were offering him, he set up his own production company, Santana, for which he made four films, the best of them being the first, *Knock on Any Door*, in which he appeared as an attorney defending a young hoodlum played by John Derek. The Santana experiment was short-lived because the results were disappointing and most disappointing of all was Bogart's realisation that he was no better at picking roles for himself than Warners had been at picking them for him.

Nevertheless, in 1950 he ended his contract with the studio and thereafter worked as a freelance. At once he landed another, out-of-character part – probably the best of them all. One day John Huston called him and said: "I have a great story. The hero is a low-life. You're the biggest low-life in town and therefore the most suitable for the part." Wooed by these soft words Bogart went to Africa to play Charlie Allnut, the seedy, wingeing, down-at-heel skipper of *The African Queen* and so at last won an Oscar of his own.

From then on, however, his films and the roles he played were mostly routine; a newspaperman investigating a vice ring in *Deadline – USA*; an officer at a field hospital behind the lines in Korea in *Battle Circus*; William Holden's stuffy elder brother in *Sabrina Fair* and so on. There were exceptions such as *Beat the Devil*, a comedy thriller that didn't really work at all but has since attracted a small and perverse cult-following, and *The Barefoot Contessa*, wherein he appeared as a once-drunken Hollywood director.

But after *The African Queen* his most notable performance was as Captain Queeg in *The Caine Mutiny*. This, too, was not an entirely successful film ("It was crapped up with an unnecessary love story," as Bogart put it) but he himself was excellent as the mentally sick and twisted Queeg and was again nominated for an Oscar. This time he lost out to Marlon Brando in *On the Waterfront* which was, perhaps, only fair because it was Bogart's successful nomination for *The African Queen* which had almost certainly robbed Brando of the award for *A Streetcar Named Desire*.

In the last years Bogie reverted to type.

93

In *The Desperate Hours* he was virtually an older version of Duke Mantee from *The Petrified Forest* – a psychopathic hoodlum holding a family as hostage. And in his final picture, *The Harder They Fall*, he was the cynical ex-sports reporter exposing the racketeers in boxing.

This film was made in 1956 and by then Bogart was already gravely ill with throat cancer. Soon afterwards he had an operation on the oesophagus and then went home to convalesce. For more than nine months he tried to believe, or at least to convince others, that he would recover.

Sam Jaffe said: "It's hard to tell whether he was aware that he was dying. He didn't look sad, he didn't act sad. I don't know whether people who are dying of cancer ever accept the fact that they're going to die because he said to me, almost in the last stages, he said, 'What about it, bud, are there any scripts around?' I was shaken up. I couldn't believe it. His body was withering away; he must have been down to about eighty pounds then. But I said, 'Well, sure there are scripts,' and I called up the studios and said, 'You know, I think Bogart'll get well,' because I didn't want to play games and ask them to just give me a script, any kind of script. Anything I gave him I knew he'd read and if it was no good he'd know I was just playing games, pretending. So I said, 'Look, I think Bogart's going to recover,' and, of course, the studios had a lot of scripts, good ones, and I'd take them to him and he'd read them and he was very much interested. He loved life and he wasn't about to give up."

Nat Benchley, on the other hand, believes that Bogie knew he was dying. He said: "Betty (Lauren Bacall) says he didn't know but that was because he was a very good actor and he managed to hide his knowledge. He just fought it as long as he could and tried to pretend that the next week was going to be all right."

But, of all these tributes to Bogart's physical bravery, the most moving description of the end of his life comes from Joe Hyams, who was perhaps the only journalist he fully trusted and probably the only non-drinker (Hyams is teetotal by choice) ever admitted to his small and very select circle of friends.

"In the last, oh, three months of his life," Hyams said, "you could see him kind of slowly disappearing. He was just wasting away. He went from 150 to ninety pounds and he was little more than a genial skeleton after a while. But he had tremendous courage and I remember once that I went upstairs and his valet was dressing him – Bogie was lying in a big double bed – and he put Bogart's trousers on him and then he put on his smoking jacket, Bogart lying in bed all this time, and then he lifted him up gently, put him in a wheelchair, pushed the wheelchair over to the dumb waiter shaft, which was used to haul food up, put Bogart in the dumb waiter and lowered him slowly to the floor below. Then he went downstairs, carried Bogart and the wheelchair out and wheeled him through the house to the bar/sitting room where he entertained guests and propped him up in his favourite chair and put a martini in one hand and an unlit cigarette in the other.

"All this took maybe twenty-five minutes. At about five minutes to five guests started to arrive – all the people in Hollywood who were his friends and the idea was to fill him in on what was going on, give him the gossip, bring him up to date, cheer him up and in that sense it was a very social gathering and he would sit there like this for an hour or two, without really sipping because he didn't have the strength to lift the glass or light the cigarette and then, after about an hour, Betty Bacall would say it was time for everyone to go home and everyone would leave and they'd reverse the procedure – pick him up, put him back in the wheelchair, push him over to the dumb waiter shaft and take him back to bed.

"So he really had enormous courage because his doctor told me that he was going through the most agonising pain since the cancer was literally eating him up inside. But he was able, until almost a week before he died, to put on this kind of brave front – and it was never depressing. No one ever talked about the imminence of death, though it was there like a shadow in the room. Richard Burton would come, David Niven, Frank Sinatra, Spencer Tracy, Katharine Hepburn, everyone who was anyone at that time in Hollywood would be there during one of these sessions and I don't think any of us knew until almost the very end what courage it took for Bogart to get there, sit in that chair and, for an hour, try to be a host."

One Saturday night as Tracy and

Hepburn were leaving the house Bogart watched them go and, instead of saying "Goodnight" as usual, he said: "Goodbye, Spence." The next night, on January 14th, 1957, Humphrey Bogart was dead.

The funeral took place three days later at All Saints Episcopal Church in Beverly Hills. At Bogie's request the priest read the Ten Commandments – no doubt he would have read twelve if he could have found the extra two that Bogart once commended so warmly to his godson – and also Tennyson's poem, "Crossing the Bar" . . . "I hope to see my Pilot face to face when I have crossed the Bar . . ."

Afterwards the mourners returned to the family home for a drink, the sort of touch that Bogie himself would have applauded, while the body was cremated at Forest Lawn. Mythology has it that the gold whistle which he gave to Lauren Bacall after *To Have and Have Not*, the film on which he first met her and in which she said to him, "If there's anything you want, just whistle," was placed in the urn with the ashes. The story is probably apocryphal but felicitous. Bogart, the sentimental tough guy, the "big bowl of mush inside" would probably have liked to have that whistle with him.

Later on Lauren Bacall said: "Bogie is the only man I have ever known who truly and completely belonged to himself." And Richard Burton, whom Bogart befriended and introduced to the right kind of people when the young Welshman first arrived, virtually unknown, to seek his fortune in Hollywood, said: "His was the first theatrical death that deeply touched me. Hollywood has never been the same since he died."

Indeed the tributes to, and eulogies of, Bogart are endless because they continue to this day. He is the only star of the thirties and forties around whom a cult has sprung up since his death and there are many

reasons for that. In the first place he was distinctly ahead of his time. In a period when most cinema heroes were basically Establishment figures, simple, straightforward and handsome, Bogart was none of those things.

On screen he was small and slight and brave and honest – the kind of man we all feel that we might have been, or be, or become. Watch him on screen in his classic roles, being Bogart, and you wish, as you rarely wish with other actors, that you had actually known him. In his professional persona – as, I suspect, in his private life – there was about him the wary, decidedly mocking, air of one who knew that the world, and especially its ruling bodies, was full of hypocrisy. Towards rigid authority he had a sardonic and rebellious attitude that reflects far more the 1960s and the 1970s than the thirties and forties, the eras which a man born when he was might have been expected to represent.

Most of all, though, it was that sense of unwavering honesty which, in the thirty years since his death, has endeared him to new generations of young film-goers. It was an honesty that once made him suggest to his agent, Sam Jaffe, that at 250,000 dollars a picture he was being overpaid. (Jaffe countered this remarkable, if not unique, complaint by saying that Spencer Tracy received 250,000 dollars a picture and, if Tracy was worth that, then so was Bogart. Bogie, satisfied by such irrefutable logic, never raised the subject again.) So with his honesty and his toughness, his refusal to kow-tow or to be bullied he created a canon of work, a cadre of films which have often been imitated but never equalled because, at the heart of them all, was the incomparable Bogart himself, gritty, scornful, world-weary but never so cynical as to be bitter: the ideal hero or, if you prefer, anti-hero for an age of disillusionment.

Judy Garland

When you look back on the brief but eventful career of Judy Garland the overall impression is one of waste. She had talent in abundance but she never developed it to its full potential. She was certainly a great singer but perhaps she could have been a great actress, too. Admittedly, on the evidence of what, singing apart, she actually achieved on the screen, greatness is too big a word to throw at Garland the actress but her early films did at least hint at a depth of promise that was never truly fulfilled.

Well, she blamed a lot of people for that, her mother sometimes and Louis B. Mayer and MGM frequently, but in the end it was largely her own fault. Her own frailty, her own lack of discipline, her own absence of faith in herself, her own dependence on drink and drugs kept her bouncing about like a lady on a trampoline, often touching the heights and occasionally looking down on them from above, establishing new heights of her own, but never managing to stay up there. By the time she died thirty years had passed since she appeared in *The Wizard of Oz* but to most people she was still Dorothy, middle-aged and more than slightly wrecked, but nevertheless the cherished personification of the dreams and fears and vulnerability of a teenage girl. In thirty years she had accomplished nothing to surpass the performance she gave us as a girl of seventeen with caps on her teeth and her breasts strapped down to make her look younger, and with her gifts she should have done a great deal better than that.

Yet, with hindsight, it's perhaps unfair to lay the entire blame for all this profligate waste on Garland herself. She was never, in any conventional sense, permitted to be completely a child or completely a teenager.

The young Garland, before the hard living began to take its toll.

How then could she ever be expected to become a complete adult, or even as complete an adult as most of us manage, somehow, to be?

Judy Garland, or Frances Gumm to give her her proper name, or Baby Gumm as she was billed throughout her infancy, is reputed to have made her stage debut on New Year's Day, 1925, at the age of two and a half and thereafter she was, above all else, a performer. Her childhood passed in a non-stop routine of singing and dancing lessons and a series of whistle-stop tours appearing down the bill at vaudeville theatres and the like as one of the Three Gumm Sisters, the others being her older sisters, Jimmy (Virginia) and Janey. And she was barely into her teens when, in 1935, she was signed to a long-term contract by MGM. One way and another she was deprived of her childhood by the ambitions of her mother, Ethel Gumm, a frustrated singer herself, who was the inspiration, if that's the word, behind the sisters' act and she was protected from the painful, but necessary, traumas of adolescence by MGM. If anything went wrong, well, "Never mind, Judy, the studio will fix it." And the studio did. Thus she arrived at adulthood totally unprepared to deal with the ordinary problems of everyday life, never mind the extra pressure of being a superstar. If she was a psychological mess – and there's little doubt that she was – she had never had much chance of being anything else.

Judy Garland was born Frances Ethel Gumm in Grand Rapids, Michigan, on June 10th, 1922. Her father, Frank, was the manager of the local picture house and her sisters, then aged seven and five, were already veteran troupers as a singing duet,

96

The three Gumm sisters. Frances – later Judy Garland – is in the middle.

with their mother as pianist. By the time she was three Baby Gumm was a regular part of the act and, because she was so young and so tiny and already showed signs of having a remarkable voice, swiftly became the star of the outfit. In 1926 the family moved to Hollywood spending, as Garland later recalled, "three months on the road, playing one night stands in just about every city between Grand Rapids and Los Angeles" to finance the trip.

Once established in Hollywood, Ethel Gumm enrolled the girls in a dance school, arranged frequent public appearances for them and, realising that Frances was the most talented of the three, hawked her round the film studios to audition for children's roles, although never with any success. On one occasion the child was turned down for the title role in a film called *Cinderella* on account of being "too plain", exactly the sort of experience calculated to do wonders for a young girl's self-confidence. By 1934 the family trio had ceased to be the Gumm Sisters – a dispiriting business anyway because they were often wrongly announced as the Glumm, Rumm and even Dumm Sisters – and had become instead the Garland Sisters, taking the name of a well-known theatre critic of the time. And Frances, or Baby, Gumm had been further renamed Judy after the title of the song by Hoagy Carmichael.

At that time the act was well enough known to be reviewed, favourably, by the influential show business magazine *Variety*

and the *Los Angeles Herald Express*, with Judy capturing most of the attention . . . "handles ballads like a veteran . . ." ". . . the divine instinct to be herself on the stage . . ." All of which was gratifying but not much more, for this was the age of Shirley Temple, a time when potential child stars had broken out in Hollywood like chicken pox and the competition between pushy mums (some of them even pushier than Ethel Gumm) to bring their offspring to the attention of the studios was deadly. The odds against young Judy Garland being picked out of the Lilliputian horde were distinctly high but in 1935 the opportunity did come along, thanks in part to Joseph L. Mankiewicz, who was then a twenty-six-year-old screenwriter at MGM.

Mankiewicz had been taken to a concert by a mutual friend of his and the Gumms to hear the child sing. He said: "Judy was about twelve or thirteen then and she worked with her sisters. Her mother told me she wanted to bill her as 'the little girl with the leather lungs', which will give you a very quick description of her mother. But Judy's voice was something incredible even then and you knew, as you sat there, that you were in the presence of something that wasn't going to come around again for a long time. She was an ungainly, awkward little thing, but I went to MGM and said, 'Take a look at this girl.' At the time Louis Mayer was busy signing anyone with talent. His approach was very simple. He would hire anyone who looked good. It's like betting on all the horses in a race and when one of them wins you hold up the winning ticket and say, 'See, I picked it.' And that was how Louis Mayer picked his stars: he hired anyone who had any talent whatsoever.

"Anyway, he sent his secretary over to hear Judy – I don't know why that professional opinion was considered important – and she thought Judy was wonderful and Judy was signed."

There were, of course, formalities like auditions to go through and there were one or two other people plugging for her but that, in essence, is how Judy Garland's career at MGM began. Just before she signed the contract her father died of spinal meningitis. As the head of the Gumm family he had been a somewhat ineffectual man, dominated by his wife, but Judy had been very close to him and had regarded him as a staunch ally in her frequent rows with her mother. When, many years later, her daughter Liza Minnelli asked her how she felt when Frank Gumm died, Judy said: "I thought, 'Now there is nobody on my side.'"

At first it seemed as if she were quite right because there was nobody much on her side at MGM either. She attended the studio school with the likes of Mickey Rooney but there was precious little work for her to do. As Joe Mankiewicz said: "Judy went to work for MGM at the age of thirteen and became fourteen and nothing happened except that she'd sing at MGM conventions or gatherings in the executive dining-room. Deanna Durbin was also at MGM at the time and she and Judy made a short called *Every Sunday* and as a result of this Deanna Durbin was fired." (In fact, Miss Durbin was not fired. Mayer was not sure he could afford two girl singers on the payroll, even two as dissimilar as Durbin and Garland, but while he was dickering about which of them he should keep, Miss Durbin's contract ran out and she was snapped up, to his great fury, by the opposition.)

To quote Mankiewicz again: "Well, Deanna Durbin ran over to Universal and became a star with her very first film (*Three Smart Girls*) and then Mayer made a star of Judy because he'd lost the other one. He loaned her to Fox – and this is how stars are made – he loaned her to Fox to do a very inferior football picture called *Pigskin Parade* which did nothing but attract people to hear this little girl sing and Judy came back to MGM a star."

But if she was already a star to the public she was still not all that highly rated by the studio and her next, and biggest break, occurred more or less by accident. She sang a special version of "You Made Me Love You" to Clark Gable at his birthday party on the studio lot and this went down so well that she and the song were rushed into the production of *Broadway Melody of 1938*, receiving such a warm response that at last Metro began to take her seriously. She made four pictures in 1938, including *Love Finds Andy Hardy* in which she played Mickey Rooney's platonic girl friend and, in the following year, she was cast in her most memorable role of all, that of Dorothy in *The Wizard of Oz*, though even then she was faced with considerable opposition from the studio executives.

Neither Louis Mayer, who had the endearing habit of patting her on the head and calling her his "little hunchback", nor his henchmen thought she was a big enough star for the part and they wanted to borrow Shirley Temple from Fox. But the role and the songs had been written for Garland and besides, Fox weren't all that keen on lending their biggest asset to their biggest competitors, so Garland, aged seventeen but disguised to look about fourteen, got the job.

When the picture was finished some MGM executives thought it was running overlong and decided to cut one of the songs. Eventually they were persuaded to let it stay but – to demonstrate the sort of acumen that was to be found in the studio that boasted "more stars than there are in heaven" – the song these perceptive fellows wished to cut out, and probably lose for ever, was "Over the Rainbow".

The Wizard of Oz was released in 1939, became at once a classic of the cinema, won for Judy Garland a special juvenile Oscar, though God knows why they couldn't have given her a proper one, and caused MGM to realise that she was now a considerable star.

But it was at this point, with her professional problems apparently resolved, that Garland's emotional problems began

The MGM starlet and "the little girl with leather lungs".

With her first husband, David Rose.

film for the studio, and in his view, "she didn't realise how much talent she had or that she had more to offer than Lana Turner or Joan Crawford or the other clever girls around the place. She never believed that she had any strength: I mean feminine strength. She felt she was a failure in her private life; she wanted to be Lana Turner and it didn't occur to her that perhaps Lana Turner might have liked to be Judy Garland."

It was possibly because of this, because of a need to prove to herself that she was as desirable as anyone else, that she had a tendency throughout her life to chase relentlessly after the men who took her fancy. Charles Walters, the director of *Easter Parade* and *Summer Stock*, recalls that at one time she set out to seduce a very famous star for no better reason than that, being one of those rare Hollywood creatures, a happily married man, he had shown no physical interest in her. One night, at some studio celebration, she persuaded the hapless actor into her dressing-room and, encountering Walters an hour or so later, winked, gave the thumbs-up signal and said, "Got him!" It was both the beginning and the end of the affair.

However, the immediate aftermath of the Artie Shaw romance was that on the same day that she learned of the elopement, Garland also met the man who was to become her first husband. That night she appeared on the Bob Hope radio show where the orchestra leader was one David Rose, a talented musician and a kindly man who, seeing that she was unhappy, took her out after the programme. At that time he was married to Martha Raye from whom he was not divorced until May 1941. Just over a month after the divorce, on June 28th, he and Judy Garland were married. He was thirty-one and she was nineteen and Louis Mayer was furious with her because she had not sought his permission for the marriage.

As a union it was amicable but not especially successful. Apart from music they had little enough in common and temperamentally they were opposites, she being inclined to the frenetic while he was placidly easy-going. About a year after the wedding Rose was inducted into the army and in the spring of 1943 they officially separated. A year after that they were divorced.

to dominate her life. While making *The Wizard of Oz* she had fallen deeply in love with Artie Shaw, the bandleader. Although it seems most unlikely that Shaw took the affair at all seriously, there is little doubt that Garland did. Her mother disapproved of Artie Shaw, on the not unreasonable grounds that he was too seasoned a campaigner in amorous matters to be a suitable escort for a comparatively innocent girl of seventeen. Garland, however, was not at all deterred and continued to meet him clandestinely, using her fellow child-star, Jackie Cooper, as a "beard", he being her ostensible date for the evening on those occasions when she was actually meeting Shaw.

The relationship, friendly on his part, ardent on hers, lasted into 1940 when, to Garland's utter distress, Shaw suddenly eloped with Lana Turner.

What made this particularly painful was the fact that, according to Joe Pasternak the producer, Lana Turner was precisely the kind of woman that Judy Garland would have liked to be. Pasternak knew her throughout her years at MGM and worked with her on *Summer Stock*, her last

What effect drugs – uppers and downers – had on Garland's life and personality and behaviour at this time is difficult to establish. David Rose has said that during the period that he was with her he was not aware of her taking drugs at all. But it has been suggested that, as early as the age of thirteen, she was being prescribed pills containing Benzedrine and Phenobarbital, initially to help her diet. She always had a weight problem and at thirteen, when she joined MGM, she was distinctly chubby.

"There was a constant struggle," she said later, "between MGM and me – whether or not to eat, how much to eat, what to eat." At that time little was known about the dangers of the new, and apparently harmless, amphetamines, hence the pills she was given. The effect of the Benzedrine was to make her so wideawake that she needed sleeping pills at night; and the sleeping pills left her so groggy in the morning that she took Benzedrine to wake her up.

Her mother, realising that this pattern was potentially dangerous, took her off the pills but, with or without parental permission, she returned to them later, if only, to begin with, to help her cope with the long working days that were common in Hollywood then.

Garland herself always blamed the studio for her drug problem. "They'd give us pep pills to keep us on our feet long after we were exhausted," she said. "Then they'd take us to the studio hospital and knock us cold with sleeping pills, Mickey Rooney sprawled out on one bed and me on another." But this would appear to be a downright lie – certainly it's denied by Mickey Rooney. "Can you imagine," he said, "a company giving any kind of barbiturates to youngsters who were making a lot of money for them? Can you picture that? It just didn't happen." And Joseph Mankiewicz, who is not instinctively an apologist for Hollywood and least of all for Louis B. Mayer, said: "I think I should make perfectly clear that one of the most idiotic myths about Hollywood is that they fed Judy Benzedrine and Dexadrine. If Louis Mayer had heard that anyone so much as offered her a glass of sherry he'd have had the man beheaded. I mean, J. Arthur Rank was a libertine compared to Mayer in terms of behaviour of that type."

So if her mother discouraged the use of pills and MGM forbade them, the likelihood is that, after the original and innocent prescription of them, Garland found the drugs for herself. Certainly by 1943, when she and Joe Mankiewicz had a love affair, one that many people consider the most important of her life, she was thoroughly hooked.

At this point her marriage to David Rose was failing fast and her career, though satisfactory enough, was merely marking time. She had appeared in a couple more Andy Hardy pictures with Mickey Rooney and in musicals like *For Me and My Gal* with George Murphy and *Thousands Cheer* with Kathryn Grayson and Gene Kelly, in which she made a guest appearance. Garland was now twenty-one but still being treated very much as a teenager by the studio. It was a difficult and perhaps restless time for her and Mankiewicz, a witty and gifted man of thirty-four who had been around Hollywood since his teens and who was later to win Academy Awards as both director and writer (*A Letter for Three Wives* and *All About Eve*, for instance) was probably the first man in her life to treat her as a fully grown-up woman.

Recalling what Garland was like at that time, he said: "Here was a girl who had been told she was ugly, who had been locked away in closets by her mother as punishment when she did something that was supposed to be wrong; a girl who had built up a tremendous sense of inferiority, believing that nobody wanted any part of her except her voice. And her mother kept drilling that into her, day after day after day. But she was an extremely bright, witty girl somewhere under all that and I think I used to bring it out.

"She was very funny, very gay, and also she had a tremendous desire to know about things. It wasn't on any so-called intellectual level; it was simply a girl who didn't know a bloody thing about what went on anywhere and asked an awful lot of questions that I was able to answer. I think essentially I was probably the first man that Judy ever felt totally wanted with as a person. I've never known anyone as hungry for affection and later on, when she fell on hard times, emotionally, the empty times of the blues and the pills, out of nowhere there'd come that call in the middle of the night. It could be from London, it could be from anywhere and it was a call for help.

With her mother. Their relationship was not always so affectionate.

But at the same time there was a bottomless pit, a pit of emptiness and of not being wanted and you couldn't fill it for her. Nobody could.''

Still, for a while there in 1943 there were the good times, times, as Mankiewicz remembers, when "we laughed an awful lot". But also there were the pills. She was taking them, he thought, as a form of misbehaviour, to attract attention, to force people to help her. Mankiewicz, whose own wife was then in a clinic suffering from mental illness, began to worry about Garland's behaviour and habit.

"I didn't think she was mentally sick," he said, "but I was afraid that she would become so because there was no way she couldn't, considering the demands that had been put upon her, the complete obliteration of her childhood, the obliteration of love and the love/hate she'd developed for her own self. She'd been made to consider herself as nothing but a voice. I mean, even if I'd said applause is love, to Judy applause was for her vocal cords. She thought nobody really wanted her."

Mankiewicz tried to persuade her to seek psychiatric help to straighten out her emotional problems and kick the drug habit but in this he encountered the implacable opposition of her mother and Louis Mayer. "Judy's mother came to the studio to complain that I had sent her daughter to see this psychiatrist. Mayer summoned me to his office and there was a screaming fight. The mother got hysterical. Mayer got hysterical, particularly at the idea that MGM stars could be crazy. He kept asking me, how could I do this? 'This girl . . . all this girl needs is a mother's love and there's the mother. How can you deny this?' And tears were rolling down his face. He must have hated his mother. And the mother was saying, 'I know exactly what to do with her. You just lock her in a closet. What the girl needs is discipline.' And I kept saying, 'Look, the girl needs help.' Anyway, the screaming reached such a pitch that I found myself making what has become a legendary remark, I found myself looking at Louis B. Mayer and saying, 'Well obviously, L.B., this studio isn't big enough for both of us. One of us has to go.' And suddenly I realised what I'd said and looked over at Eddie Mannix, the general manager, who fell right off his chair laughing. And of course I went. I went the next week. I went to work for Fox."

After that, as Mankiewicz describes it, "explosive" meeting with Mayer both he and Garland realised that their affair was coming to an end. In a way it had to end because in those days the Hollywood studios were run like independent duchies with very little fraternisation between them and when Mankiewicz moved from the duchy of MGM to that of Fox the chances to meet became limited. By then, too, Garland had started work on *Meet Me in St. Louis* and had begun to fall in love with her director, Vincent Minnelli.

Mankiewicz said: "Our relationship never broke up abruptly or in a fight. She merely started seeing more of Vincent. He was a very kind and generous man and I think Judy found him more of a support than I was because I was more inclined to tell her some unpleasant truths. Liza (Minnelli) has told me that Judy loved me and I loved Judy at that time. I can't recall any incident over which we fought. We just became sort of long-dissolved, and Minnelli was there to offer marriage. I don't think I could have married Judy. I don't think I would have wanted to because of my instinctive fears of what was going to happen to her, what her stupid and ignorant mother had done to her. Put it this way – I was not at all surprised at Judy's decline."

That decline which, in effect, had already started before she met Mankiewicz was at least arrested during the early years with Vincent Minnelli. To begin with, Garland didn't want to make *Meet Me in St. Louis*. She was asked to play a seventeen-year-old and she thought the time had come when she should be taking more sophisticated parts. But Mayer overrode her objections and Minnelli's quiet persuasion made her believe in the role so that the finished film was her biggest success since *The Wizard of Oz*. Minnelli said: "You could tell her twenty things and you'd never know if you were getting through to her or not because people were messing with her and making her up and so forth, but by God everything would be in place. She wouldn't forget a thing."

He believed then and believes still that Garland had it in her to be a great actress. "The surface wasn't scratched with Judy at all. She could have been a Bernhardt or a Garbo. She had great potential." By the time *Meet Me in St. Louis* was finished Garland and Minnelli were firmly in love and he informed her mother, in his gentlemanly way, that his intentions were honourable and that he planned to marry her as soon as her divorce from David Rose was final.

In fact the wedding took place on July 15th, 1945, after Minnelli had directed her for the second time in *Under the Clock* in which she co-starred with Robert Walker. The start of the marriage was certainly promising.

"She was taking a lot of pills at that time," Minnelli said, "although I didn't know about it until she told me. But when we went to New York for our honeymoon she threw all the pills in the East River and said she was through with them." For a while she was true to her word but soon after they returned to Hollywood the pattern that was repeated throughout the rest of her life began to emerge. Any difficulties at the studio, any setbacks, would cause her to reach for the happy pills. Minnelli tried frequently to break her of the habit but never with lasting success, largely because she simply lacked the self-confidence to face life without some kind of prop to lean on. "At times," he said, "she knew

With Vincent Minnelli, her second husband, and Louis B. Mayer, who called her his "little hunchback".

how good she was. At times she got jubilant but mostly she was very nervous and morbid.''

As she came to depend more and more heavily on barbiturates even Mayer was converted to the idea that she needed help. Minnelli said: "He would get hold of these psychiatrists and send them up and I would wait. And they'd always come out of her room and say, 'There's nothing wrong with her, you know, she's a charming girl,' and I would say, 'Wait.' And they'd be called for again at four o'clock in the morning and they'd run away screaming.''

Yet this is not to suggest that life with Judy Garland was simply a kind of long-running nightmare. As Joe Mankiewicz put it, somewhat lyrically, "There was something about her that made you instinctively smile. Seeing Judy was like smelling a freshly-cut flower or a wonderful splash of rain.'' And Minnelli insists, too, that their marriage was a lot happier than it might sound, especially around the time when their daughter, Liza, was born in March 1946. Garland didn't work for eight months after that and for much of the time she tried hard to be a good, conventional wife and mother. But then the self-doubt and the insecurity returned and by the time she went back to the studio to start work on *The Pirate*, co-starring with Gene Kelly and directed once again by Minnelli, she was already on the verge of a nervous breakdown.

She managed to complete the film but soon afterwards, in the summer of 1947, she made an ineffectual attempt to kill herself. Minnelli believes it was merely a cry for help and to some extent help was forthcoming because MGM sent her to a sanitorium for treatment. After a few weeks she returned, apparently recovered, to begin work on *Easter Parade* with Fred Astaire. At this point, however, the psychiatrists intervened in her marriage, deciding – for reasons best known to themselves – that it would be better for Garland if Vincent Minnelli did not direct the picture. MGM agreed and he was replaced by Charles Walters. Minnelli says now, rather mildly, that he thought the whole business was "peculiar" but by then the marriage was already failing and when the filming was over Garland moved out of the marital home and into a place of her own.

Over the next couple of years her re-lations with MGM steadily deteriorated. She made a guest appearance in *Words and Music*, was dropped because of her behaviour and fluctuating weight from *The Barkleys of Broadway*, starred with Van Johnson in *In the Good Old Summertime*, and then was dropped again from *Annie Get Your Gun*. All this was punctuated by periods of ill-health and by suspensions and threats of suspension when she was too sick or too fat or too thin to do the work assigned to her. In the spring of 1949 Garland, not yet twenty-seven years old, underwent a series of electric shock treatments and in May, having been fired from *Annie Get Your Gun* because she hadn't reported to the studio on time, even though she'd already recorded the entire score for the film, she went into hospital in Boston for eleven weeks.

When she came back, once again apparently cured, she was reunited with Vincent Minnelli and Liza and agreed to appear in *Summer Stock*. But as soon as the filming began all her problems recurred. Her behaviour was as erratic as ever and she had a bitter row with her mother, the result of which was that Ethel sold her house in Hollywood and moved to Dallas to be near her eldest daughter, Jimmy. That, virtually, was the end of any closeness between the most talented of the Gumm sisters and her mother. To what extent Ethel Gumm was truly responsible for the mess that Judy Garland became is pretty well lost now in a crossfire of accusations and counter-accusations. Garland herself laid heavy blame on her mother but then she blamed practically everyone, save herself.

Joe Mankiewicz saw Ethel as stupid and ignorant; Joe Pasternak believed her to be jealous of Judy. Against that there are those who claim that Ethel was greatly maligned, a loving and caring mother who became a scapegoat for her daughter. The truth, as in most things, probably lies somewhere in between but Ethel can hardly have been blameless. Even assuming that in everything she did she genuinely believed that she was acting in Judy's best interests she must still, at least, be guilty of having driven the child too hard, of demanding too much, of being over-ambitious on her behalf. Most people are what their parents make them and Judy Garland seems to have been no exception.

However, with *Summer Stock* finished,

Garland was asked to replace the pregnant June Allyson in *Royal Wedding*. She simply failed to turn up and thus came to the end of the line. Dore Schary, who by now was the head of MGM, says that some time earlier both he and Louis Mayer had tried to persuade her to undergo a full course of treatment, had indeed assured her that the studio would be prepared to take care of her for an entire year if she would go into a clinic and make a determined effort to break herself of the drug habit. Garland refused and when the irresponsible behaviour, which by now had become only too familiar, was repeated again during the preparations for *Royal Wedding*, Schary felt the time had come to get rid of her. He said: "She complained about this, she complained about that and we had finally to make a decision. I think one of the saddest things I had to do was to tell Judy that we would no longer keep her under contract."

She reacted, he said, with anger, retorting that she could do perfectly well by herself, "and, of course, for a while she did. She did beautifully but I had a hunch she was headed down a road which was going to be rather a short one. She was heavily into drugs by that time. She was going to bed soaked with drugs and then when she got up in the morning she had to bring herself up again with more drugs. Well, you can't keep punishing yourself constantly like that."

Schary insists that MGM did their best for Garland. Vincent Minnelli is not so sure; he believes that the studio could have shown more patience with her because "she made such a terribly large amount of money for them and, when she was a star, she always came through for them."

Whatever the rights and wrongs of this argument, in September 1950, Judy Garland and MGM parted company and she set off on her own road, not always as it turned out a yellow brick road. At first she did indeed do very well. In partnership with Sid Luft, a former test pilot, producer of B movies and all-round entrepreneur, who was to become her third husband in June 1952, she went to London for a triumphant season at the Palladium and then, returning to New York, enjoyed an even greater success at the Palace Theatre. In the thirties the Palace had been New York's leading vaudeville theatre but by October 1951, it had been a cinema for fifteen years

and was growing steadily shabbier. The Garland season reopened it as a live theatre and created something of a sensation. She was booked for four weeks and stayed for nineteen. After the first night one reviewer described her act as "the most fantastic one-hour show in theatre history".

So, once more, Garland had hauled herself back to the top. As a concert artist and as a guest star on other people's radio and TV shows she was in great demand. She married Sid Luft and soon afterwards, having been pregnant on her wedding day, gave birth to another daughter, Lorna. In December of 1952 she signed a deal with Warner Brothers to co-star with James Mason in a remake of *A Star is Born*.

Inevitably, however, even this minor success story was not without its setbacks. She was still on the uppers and downers and in a fit of post-natal depression after Lorna's birth she made another attempt – at least her third – to kill herself, though, as before, the wound she inflicted on her throat was only superficial. But the most traumatic event of 1952 was the death of her mother.

Ethel had returned to Hollywood when Judy left MGM but her daughter had refused to see her. They had met, briefly, some time earlier when Ethel was in hospital after an attempted suicide of her own but there had been no real rapprochement between them. At the time of her death from a heart attack Ethel was living, to say the least, modestly, on her earnings as a clerk at the Douglas aircraft factory in Los Angeles. There is little doubt that because of the love-hate relationship she had long had with her mother, Garland had neglected Ethel over the last few years, both emotionally and financially, and there equally seems little doubt that she was afflicted with considerable guilt because of that. "I didn't want her to die," she said when she flew back from New York to help her sisters arrange the funeral.

Meanwhile the preparations for *A Star is Born* were proceeding slowly and filming didn't actually begin until the autumn of 1953. It was the first picture Garland had made for nearly four years and predictably she was stricken by nerves on the first day of shooting.

George Cukor, the director of the film, who has worked with most of the finest actresses in the cinema, found her

Garland in Summer Stock, *the last film she made with MGM. By the time they shot this number she had been off screen for two months and lost twenty pounds.*

105

"enormously gifted" but quite lacking in self-confidence. He said: "I asked her about that one day. I said, 'Why? You're so accomplished, you're so good – what the hell are you worried about?' And she said, 'Well, I'm always afraid that this is the time they're going to catch me out.' She was a very complicated creature."

Her performance in *A Star is Born* made her a hot favourite for the Oscar but in the event it went to Grace Kelly for *A Country Girl*. On the night of the Awards Garland was in hospital after the birth of her son Joey, surrounded by a TV crew ready to interview her should she win. But when the name of Grace Kelly was announced the TV men wrapped up and went away without even pointing a camera at her. Hollywood never had much time for losers.

A Star is Born was supposed to be the first in a three-picture deal with Warners but the other two films were never made, and it was another seven years before she was seen on film again. In the interim her career consisted of concerts and tours, TV and cabaret at Las Vegas. Often money was very short because, when she was working away from Los Angeles, she insisted on taking her children with her, travelling first class and putting up at the best hotels. Her living expenses were frequently greater than her earnings. And during those years in the late 1950s as she toured America and Europe, enjoying another success at the Palladium and an ovation at the Metropolitan Opera House in New York, the pattern of her life continued remorselessly – quarrels and reconciliations with her husband, a suicide attempt, an overdose, a serious illness when her liver became infected, a dependence on the uppers and downers.

In 1960 she returned to the screen in *Pepe* with Dan Dailey and the following year she was nominated as best supporting actress for her role in *Judgement at Nuremberg*. This was followed by another concert tour, including an appearance at Carnegie Hall, a separation from Sid Luft, followed by a reconciliation and another separation and a return to England where she made her last two films – *A Child is Waiting*, in which her co-star was Burt Lancaster, and *I Could Go On Singing*, opposite Dirk Bogarde in which she played a famous American singer touring Europe and much afflicted by emotional problems. Very nearly type-casting.

Back to America, another reconciliation with Sid Luft and then her own TV series, two sets of thirteen one-hour shows for CBS which, like practically everything else in her life, began on a high note and plummeted.

For twenty-six programmes she earned nearly four million dollars, enough – with even a modicum of thrift – to make her comfortably off for the rest of her life. But somehow, somewhere, the money was frittered away and, in the course of the series, her potential television career was frittered away with it. She had neither the temperament nor the self-control to knuckle down to the sheer hard graft that a TV series demands. Mel Torme, her musical director on twenty-three of the twenty-six shows, says she had "a short attention span"; if the material and the guest stars appealed to her she would work, if not, she wouldn't. So for much of the time she turned up days late for rehearsals and sometimes barely rehearsed at all. As CBS grew ever more disenchanted with the ragged quality of the show it had bought, writers, producers and directors came and went with bewildering rapidity and Garland's sense of insecurity increased.

Torme, who was arbitrarily dismissed himself in the end, remembers what he calls "the dawn patrol". Garland was separated again from Sid Luft at the time and an affair she had been having with Glenn Ford had recently finished. Time after time she would wake up, unhappy and desperately lonely, at four o'clock in the morning and then, Torme says, "our phones, any one of our phones, or in fact multiple phones would ring and Judy would say, 'Quick, I need you right now. Please come over instantly.' And you'd get over and find the house wasn't burning to the ground, nor were people breaking in with crow bars. It was just that Judy needed somebody there to talk to her until the sky got light."

Eventually, when he was fired from the series – largely because Garland, dismayed by the low ratings and the angry rumbles from head office, confused movement with action and decided that what she needed was a different musical director – Torme sued her for breach of contract. But on the day he was to make his final deposition to his lawyer, he changed his mind: "I said, 'I don't think the money's collectable anyway and I think that lady's had her very last chance of many last chances. Let's leave her alone.''

As an assessment of Garland's position and future prospects this was pretty accurate. The cinema was finished with her and so, now, had television. All that was left were the personal appearances.

Parted finally from Sid Luft she took up with an unknown young actor called Mark Herron and, accompanied by him, set off on a tour of Australia where, once again, initial triumph was swiftly followed by disaster. A brilliant success in Sydney had a calamitous aftermath in Melbourne when she turned up late and, as far as the irate and impatient audience was concerned, drunk or drugged or both.

At the end of a shambling performance she was booed off the stage and, apparently, booed all the way out of Australia. According to Herron, the crowds that turned up to see her off at the airport screamed abuse, tore up her pictures, threw things at her and advised her never to come back.

In order to recover from this distressing experience she and Herron decided to stop off for a few days in Hong Kong where almost at once they were caught in a hurricane or typhoon and Garland, feeling that even the elements had turned against her, took yet another overdose of drugs. This time the attempt at self-destruction was almost successful and for a while in hospital she was given up for dead. But, like most of the people who knew her, Herron believes she went through the motions of committing suicide without truly wanting to kill herself.

"She just wanted to ease the situation," he said. Indeed it might seem that a woman who, apparently, made repeated attempts on her own life and constantly failed could have no great conviction about it. But the reasons behind the frequent throat and wrist slashings and the overdose of pills are hard to determine. Possibly she just sought periods of oblivion in the hope that whatever problems assailed her would simply go away while she was unconscious. Possibly she was sending out silent but dramatic cries for help. Or possibly, as Joe Mankiewicz suggested, the attempted acts of suicide became eventually acts of hostility against herself. Each unsuccessful try, he said, was followed by abject, grovelling apologies for all the trouble people had

Mark Herron became her fourth husband after her triumphant/disastrous tour of Australia.

been put to and "at certain points I think Judy became aware that these demands she was making, these appeals for help, could not be met by one or two or three human beings and she was tired of having to grovel in apology and angry with herself and perhaps she said, 'Well, if that's the way it is, screw it, I'll go.'

"When she was young and made some very inept attempts at cutting her wrists, that might have been a ploy to grab attention. But later on, I think, the things she did became an attack upon herself. If you know that you're demanding more than life or any human being can give you, then maybe you decide that you're the one you should turn on."

Whatever the true cause of the overdose in Hong Kong, Garland's amazing resilience pulled her through yet again and she returned to America where, in November 1965, Mark Herron became her fourth husband. The marriage, however, did not last long. Herron wished to pursue his own career as an actor and Garland was taking work where she could find it – guest spots on other people's TV shows, another four-week season at the Palace, even an attempt at a film comeback when she at least turned up on the set at Fox to appear in *Valley of the Dolls* which, ironically, was based in part on her own story, one of the characters being a singer whose career is ruined by a dependence on uppers and downers. To nobody's great surprise she was unable to cope and was rapidly fired.

Now with Herron gone she found another man, Mickey Deans, a musician who was managing a fashionable discotheque in New York and together they went to London where she played a five-week season at the Talk of the Town and, as was now customary, was either superb or appalling depending on her health and psychological fitness, an ovation one night being followed by abuse the next. London, next to New York, had always been her favourite city and she and Deans decided to settle there. In fact, on March 15th, 1969, they were married at the Chelsea Registry Office and moved into a mews house in Kensington.

According to Mickey Deans this was a happy time for her. Somewhere, tucked away within her, there had always been a wistful dream of settling down to a life of wife and mother, to a domestic routine. Temperamentally she was quite unsuited for it and on the two occasions when she tried it, with Minnelli and later with Luft, she had signally failed. Perhaps all she really wanted, despite the nomadic character of her life, was roots and a base of her own, a common enough ambition, after all. Mickey Deans said: "One day Judy said to me, 'You know, what I'd most like to do is just have some property so I could stand on it and say, This is mine. I own this.' But in all her life she never was able to do that. At the end of her career there was no money, no capital had been put away for her, nothing. That's the terrible thing."

During the period in London Deans did his best to provide some sort of insurance for her, trying to establish a chain of Judy Garland Cinemas in America to bring her a regular and continuing income. Something of this kind was clearly necessary for she was a most inept business woman. One night, after a concert, he collected her fee in cash, some fifteen or twenty thousand dollars in hundred dollar bills and told her: "It's yours. Put it in a bank or a safety deposit box, whatever you want." Garland decided that the safest place for it was her sewing basket. With a bizarre concept of security she took it with her whenever she went out but on the other hand she also left it for three days in the unlocked boot of a friend's car. Her appreciation of the value of money was minimal. She would wonder anxiously whether she could afford to buy a glass that cost a few pence and, on the same day, would buy a plate for £200 and use it as an ashtray.

Against this haphazard background Deans struggled to bring a little order into her financial and business affairs but before he could make very much headway Judy Garland was dead. She died in their house in Kensington on June 21st, 1969, three months after their wedding. She was forty-seven years old.

She had gone to bed early the previous night with a sore throat and when Deans, who had also felt unwell, was awakened by a phone call in mid-morning he found her in the bathroom. She was in a coma and beyond anyone's help. Inevitably, predictably, she died of an overdose of drugs but, as a final irony, it's most unlikely that on this occasion she had had any desire to kill herself. She had recently returned from an enjoyable trip to New York, she was in good spirits and the probability is that she took the pills only to overcome the discomfort of her sore throat and to help her sleep.

Garland's body was flown back to America where the funeral was preceded by the customary lying-in-state, attended by thousands of grief-stricken and devoted admirers. Nor is that at all surprising. As a star she had long been fading but this hardly mattered because by then she had already transcended mere stardom and become already a legend, a legend that has grown even more powerful in the seventeen years since her death.

The reason, I believe, is that Judy Garland was quite simply special. As the critic Philip Oakes once said: "She is a great artist. She is Judy. She is the very best there is." Penelope Gilliatt called her "a harrowingly good actress"; Paul Dehn described her as "an alchemist who can turn corn golden". She was all of those things and more besides. Looked at from a material point of view her life was a disaster. She failed four times at marriage, she threw away not one career but many, she earned ten million dollars and died a million dollars in debt.

Whose fault? Who knows? Mickey Deans said: "She was beat out of money all through her life, sometimes intentionally, sometimes unintentionally." Frequently she was exploited by people who, as Mickey Rooney put it, would say to her, "You're broke. Get up there and sing." Yet in all this she was not entirely the helpless victim. Time after time she would reject the people who could and would help her and cling instead to those who wished only to use her. Though granted all the gifts that anyone could wish for she was, when you see her career in retrospect, on the skids almost from the start and, in a curious way, this was part of her appeal.

Audiences all over the world loved her not just for the enormous and unquestionable wealth of her talent but for her vulnerability, her unpredictability and her bravery. She once said: "What do I do when I'm down? I put on my lipstick, see my stockings are straight and go out there and sing 'Over the Rainbow'." But the difference between her and other stars who, in similar circumstances might have done the same sort of thing, was that with Garland it didn't matter how well the lipstick was applied and how straight the stocking seams were, you could always see she was down. She was like a battle casualty with his leg in plaster and his head swathed in bandages claiming stoutly that it was only a scratch. Garland's wounds and scars were always visible and there was something about her, an innate honesty perhaps, that made it impossible for her to hide them, no matter how hard she might try.

She was a superstar who, against all the odds, managed the considerable feat of converting herself into an underdog. She was a born winner who, by perverse acts of self-destruction, became a loser. As George Orwell said: "Any life when viewed from the inside is simply a series of defeats." Judy Garland's life was no different save in one respect – that when viewed even from the outside it was a series of defeats. She was open, transparent, brilliant and doomed. She was irresistible.

A month before her death with fifth husband Mickey Deans.

Gary Cooper

Just before Gary Cooper died the poet Carl Sandburg described him as "one of the most beloved illiterates America has ever known." On the face of it such a description seems extraordinarily apt; not all that complimentary perhaps, but certainly understandable. If, with this line of Sandburg's in mind, you think of Cooper as he appeared in his best-remembered films you can easily find yourself nodding in agreement and murmuring, "Yes, that's about right." Except, of course, that it isn't right at all or, more accurately, it's only right in part. The image of Cooper as the shy, pebble-kicking cowboy whose conversation never extended much beyond "Yup" and "Nope" and occasionally, in moments of deep thought, "Mebbe", existed only on the screen. In fact, he was an intelligent and sophisticated man, as much at home in a salon or a boudoir as he was on a horse.

It can be said of Cooper, the actor, as it can be said of all the other enduring stars of Hollywood, that he always played himself but that, too, is only part true. In his ninety-five films, most of them made for Paramount, he actually played a wide variety of roles – from Beau Geste to the sheriff in *High Noon* and the architect in *The Fountainhead*, for instance – and it would be underrating the man to maintain that in each of them he was merely playing Gary Cooper. It would be more accurate to say that he only played a certain kind of role but within that range there was scope for a good deal of variety and subtlety and Cooper was a good enough actor to provide those qualities.

He only liked to make films which, as he put it, "had something to say". One might add something positive to say, for both professionally and otherwise he took an optimistic view of mankind. And once the film he was offered had met this basic criterion he devoted a great deal of time and thought to the character and development of his particular role.

No illiterate, however beloved, would have gone to so much trouble or been clever enough, as Cooper was, to keep his deliberations and his philosophising from the public. Cinema audiences don't particularly like their heroes, their men of action, to be smart and sophisticated. They like them to be ordinary, down to earth, modest; they like them, in fact, to be "just folks" and Cooper, being smart and sophisticated, was aware of that. So the Hollywood publicity people played up his rural Montana background and he let them get on with it. Thus his admirers, Carl Sandburg among them, were left with a satisfying, though slightly distorted, picture of Cooper as the archetypal, all-American pioneer, an uncomplicated fellow whose cerebrations took him no further than recognising and accepting the difference between right and wrong.

Cooper once described himself as "Mr. Average Joe America". But in fact he was only a first-generation American. Both his parents came from England, although his father, Charles Cooper, had emigrated from Bedfordshire to the United States in the true spirit of the western pioneer, looking for land to settle and Indians to fight. In 1885, however, there was a scarcity of both and he became a lawyer instead. He had been married for some years to the former Alice Brazier, lately of Gillingham in Kent, when their second son, Frank James Cooper, was born in Helena, Montana, in 1901.

At that time Helena was still a fairly rough town, much patronised, especially at

With his mother.

weekends, by boisterous and hard-drinking cowboys and miners and by 1910 Alice Cooper had come to the conclusion that her sons needed a more civilised atmosphere in which to grow up. She therefore took them back to England where they were enrolled at Dunstable School, which their father had also attended, and stayed there until shortly before America entered the First World War.

It has been said that Frank Cooper was actually expelled for fighting and this may even be so, though it's noticeable that expulsion from school for this sort of misdemeanour figures in the official – which is to say, studio-issued – biographies of quite a number of film stars of Cooper's generation. This could be merely a coincidence, indicating that actors tend to be of an independent, rebellious and pugnacious nature, but equally it could be that, during a time when acting was widely supposed to be an unsuitable job for a real man, the studios

were anxious to establish, truthfully or otherwise, that movie stars were and always had been from childhood onwards tough and virile persons, well able to take care of themselves in a brawl.

But whether Frank was expelled or not, Mrs. Cooper and her sons returned to Helena where Charles had now acquired a ranch and had also become a justice of the Montana Supreme Court.

The elder son, Arthur, went off to join the army and so did most of the Coopers' ranchhands and it was left to Frank and his mother to look after the family spread. When the war ended young Frank spent three years at Wesleyan College, an agricultural school, and then in 1921 he went to Grinell College in Iowa to study art. By the time he had completed a three-year course there and had had some slight success drawing political cartoons with a Republican slant for various Montana newspapers, his father had resigned from the Supreme Court and returned to private law practice.

This was a decision which was to have considerable bearing on Frank's future career, for Mr. and Mrs. Cooper went to California on a business trip that took considerably longer than they had expected and, at his father's urging, their younger son travelled to Hollywood to join them.

He was now twenty-three years old, a long, lean fellow, well over six feet tall, not aimless exactly but with no clear idea of what he wanted to do with his life. He tried to find work as a newspaper cartoonist and failed. He also failed as a door-to-door salesman, trying to hustle young mothers into having their babies photographed.

So he was simply drifting from one unsatisfactory job to another when he bumped into a couple of old friends from Montana who convinced him that there was money to be made from working as an extra in the movies. They took him to Poverty Row, a ramshackle stretch of old Hollywood which, in those comparatively early days of the silent pictures, was where the makers of quickie Westerns maintained their headquarters.

By virtue of the fact that the years on the family ranch had made him an excellent horseman, Cooper was rapidly hired and through 1925 and into 1926 galloped across the screen in countless Westerns, sometimes falling off his horse as a mortally wounded cowboy in the morning and then

112

falling off a different, or even the same, horse as a mortally wounded redskin in the afternoon.

Not surprisingly, however, this somewhat painful way of life had lost much of its magic after six months or so and Cooper decided that if he were to stay in the movies it would be sensible to seek larger, more lucrative and more sedentary roles. So with the aid of an agent and a demonstration reel of film showing highlights of his work as an extra, he began to hawk himself round the studios. By now, Hollywood being for some reason tolerably well stocked with aspiring young actors named Frank Cooper, he had changed his first name to Gary after the birthplace of his agent, Gary, Indiana. As a name it seemed as good as any other and was certainly more suitable than that of his own birthplace and it appeared on screen for the first time in a film called *Lightnin' Wins*, a two-reeler in which the newly dubbed Gary Cooper provided modest support to a wonder dog.

Soon afterwards, however, a far better opportunity presented itself. The actor who was to play second male lead in *The Winning of Barbara Worth*, which starred Ronald Colman and Vilma Banky, was delayed on another film and Cooper was standing in for him in the long-shots. Eventually, the director, Henry King, decided he could wait no longer for his second lead to report for duty and handed the role to Cooper. Even though he had had no formal dramatic training of any kind, he turned in a useful enough performance to impress Paramount who offered him a contract. Cooper accepted and thus embarked on a career that was to last for thirty-five years.

Recalling those days later, he said: "When I started in pictures I think I started off something new in the way of leading men. All the leading men at that time were very, very handsome fellows. In fact I signed my big contract the year Rudolph Valentino died. Every leading man then was a real handsome son of a gun and then I sort of came along with, you know, my elbows not in the right place and I was reputed to be shy, awkward and bashful."

To some extent this rather self-deprecating assessment was reasonably accurate. He was not conventionally good-looking, though he was extremely handsome in a rugged, outdoor sort of way, and he was certainly gawky and, at first anyway, rather clumsy. But possibly because he was entirely a product of the cinema and, unlike nearly all his contemporaries, had never even set foot on the stage of a theatre, he brought to the screen a new kind of naturalism, a style of underplaying that seemed to reduce acting to total immobility and was to inspire John Barrymore to say: "This fellow is the world's greatest actor. He does without effort what the rest of us spend our lives trying to learn – namely to be natural."

This quality was summed up by Howard Hawks, who directed him in his Oscar-winning film *Sergeant York* in 1941, and who said quite simply, as he also said of Gable: "The camera liked him." This, though, is perhaps too simple because after all the camera liked a good many other stars whose styles were very different from Cooper's and indeed Hawks also said: "He worked very hard and yet he didn't seem to be working. He was a strange actor because you'd look at him during a scene and you'd think, this is never gonna do, this isn't going to be any good. But when you saw the rushes in the projection room the next day you could read in his face all the things he'd been thinking."

So in 1926 the relaxed and apparently effortless Cooper style appeared for the first time and was immediately recognised and appreciated. The following year he appeared in *It* with Clara Bow, after which she became known permanently as the "It" girl and he, briefly, as the "It" boy, thanks to a widely publicised romance between them. As an affair it was nothing very serious and probably owed a lot to the studio publicity department but at that time Cooper did have a reputation as a pretty voracious ladies' man. Howard Hawks said: "If ever I saw him with a good-looking girl and he was kind of dragging his feet over the ground and being very shy and looking down, I'd say, 'Oh-oh, the snake's gonna strike again.' He found that the little bashful boy approach was very successful."

It also appeared to produce extraordinarily fast results. After the dalliance with Clara Bow, Cooper's next and far more tumultuous affair was with the Mexican actress Lupe Velez with whom he appeared in another silent picture, *Wolf Song*, in 1929. On the first day of shooting Miss Velez

113

was driven to the location by her current paramour, Tom Mix, the cowboy actor, in two Rolls-Royces; more precisely, perhaps, Mix drove her there in one Rolls-Royce while his man followed on with the lady's luggage in another. At the end of the day Mix was obliged to return to Hollywood and the next morning Henry Hathaway, who was then an assistant, and was later to become a noted director, went round all the hotel rooms waking up the actors for their early call. Cooper was always a notoriously difficult man to rouse in the mornings and after knocking on his door several times without evoking any response, Hathaway let himself into the room with a master key and found Cooper asleep in bed with Lupe Velez asleep beside him. Bearing in mind that they had met for the first time only the previous day, the snake (as Howard Hawks would have put it) had obviously struck with enviable speed.

The affair, though to say the least tempestuous, lasted for some time, greatly no doubt to the chagrin of Mr. Mix. Delmer Daves, writer, director and friend of Cooper's, said: "Lupe excited him. She was like a wild cat and he'd never met anybody like that before. She would scratch him and bite him and do strange things but he'd laugh. She'd hit him and he'd laugh. He'd think this was the funniest thing that ever happened to a man. It's like, well you know how you get a pet dog that leaps all over you, well, Lupe would leap all over him. She was a little wild one. But when he got over that affair I don't think he ever had another one of that kind. I think you have one Lupe in your life and then you move on to calmer seas."

At this time, professionally as well as privately, Cooper was leading an extremely hectic life. Between 1927 and 1931 he appeared in twenty-five films, including his first talkie, *The Virginian* in which, confronted by a menacing Walter Huston, he delivered one of the classic (and incidentally one of the most misquoted) lines of the cinema: "If you want to call me that – smile!"

The introduction of the talkies destroyed the careers of many popular leading men but it merely enhanced Cooper's. Henry Hathaway believed that this was because Cooper was probably the first screen actor to use his own normal voice. Others, those trained in the theatre, would attempt to project their voices as they did on the stage and consequently sounded artificial. There's a saying in Hollywood that "A good voice has ruined more actors than whisky." Cooper, however, being ignorant of such technicalities as projection and hitting the back of the stalls, merely talked. As Hathaway said: "He used just his own voice. He talked as he talked normally and it sounded realistic and natural."

So he went on increasing his reputation and establishing himself as one of the leading Western stars of the cinema. He was *The Virginian*, then he was *The Texan* and after that *The Man from Wyoming*, although by way of a change he also cropped up as a foreign legionnaire opposite Marlene Dietrich in *Morocco*. But the life he had been leading, though undoubtedly full, began to affect his health. He lost weight and contracted anaemia and jaundice. His doctors ordered him to rest and so Cooper took the first of what he called his "long walks". Throughout his life at times of stress he liked to go off on his own. As his daughter Maria said: "He was a very private person. He liked being alone. He liked just being with nature. Just sitting and sorting out such problems as he had."

Normally these "walks" would last a day or so, but in 1931 something more was obviously called for and he determined to go to Europe. He went first to Paris and then to Rome where he was taken up by the Countess Dorothy di Frasso, the daughter of an American millionaire who had married into the Italian nobility and, on the strength of her inherited wealth and acquired title, had become one of the pillars of Roman café society.

Cooper's affair with Lupe Velez was more or less over by now and he was clearly ready for some new adventure. Talking later about this stage of his career, he said: "When I went to Hollywood I had no talent for acting. I had gone there full of zip and energy, ready to take on any assignment no matter how rugged. Now I was approaching thirty – not really old – but what energy I had was gone. I felt like an old man. Hollywood had burned me out and I hadn't even begun to act. I felt like throwing in the towel. I was very depressed."

The countess, however, changed all that. After some weeks in her company in Rome, Cooper's health and spirits had recovered sufficiently for him to decide to go hunting in Tanganyika and the countess went with him. And when eventually he returned to Hollywood, largely because he was practically broke, she followed close behind.

Delmer Daves believed that di Frasso had a profound effect upon Cooper, that she gave him an edge of sophistication that had hitherto been lacking in his make-up. "She tried to re-make Coop," he said. "He was still very much a Montana man when she met him and she resolved to change all that. So the Coop who returned from Italy and the African safari was quite different from the man from Montana because Dorothy had sent him to the best tailors in Rome and from then on he dressed very well. I think he felt a little grateful to her because she was so generous with him and after travelling as much as he did with Dorothy I believe he now felt he could be a citizen of the world. I think it amplified his career. When he came back to Hollywood he no longer played parts just as Gary Cooper. He started to become an actor and so I think Coop began to grow at that time as an actor."

With the Clara Bow romance and the Lupe Velez affair still quite fresh in Hollywood's memory and with the sophisticated Countess di Frasso clearly much smitten by him, Cooper the ladies' man had now acquired an awe-inspiring reputation. Helen Hayes, who co-starred with him in *A Farewell to Arms* soon after his return from Africa and Europe, approached him, she said, "in terror".

"Oddly enough," she said, "before I did the picture with Gary I became the Mother Confessor of Lupe Velez when I was working at Metro. She liked to come up into my room and unburden herself to me. She was losing Gary at that time; he was getting tired of her fiery ways and all the shenanigans and nonsense that was going on. So she wept on my shoulder a lot about that. I didn't know Gary then and that also made him a little terrifying to me. A heartbreaker, that's what he seemed to be. And then when we were doing the film together the Countess di Frasso was on the scene. She'd taken him over. She was an older woman, very worldly wise. She invaded the set because she knew the character of the picture, the passion in it, and she wasn't going to leave him loose with an actress to play that. So she kept coming around until the director closed the set."

None of which, however, is to suggest that Cooper was merely Dorothy di Frasso's creature. On the contrary, his attitude towards her was often more than a little cavalier. Henry Hathaway recalled that at one point during the relationship the countess left Hollywood to travel briefly to Europe on the *Queen Mary*. One day when Cooper was in the studio preparing to do a scene in an aeroplane suspended high up against a sky-blue backcloth a phone call came for him from the liner. Hathaway said: "It was about the first time there was a ship-to-shore telephone and, Christ, Dorothy had got through from the ship to New York, to Hollywood, to the studio and out to the stage. Cooper, between takes, was up there sleeping in the plane, so they got a ladder and climbed up and shook him and said, 'Dorothy di Frasso's on the phone; she's calling from the *Queen Mary*,' and Coop says, 'Tell her I'll call back.' "

An added complication in Cooper's life at the time of the making of *A Farewell to Arms* was that Helen Hayes had also fallen in love with him. She was married, and had been for some while, to Charles MacArthur, the playwright and scriptwriter and joint author with Ben Hecht of *The Front Page*, and she had a young child but, she said, "If Gary had crooked a finger I would have left Charlie and my child and the whole thing."

She said: "Gary was no farm boy or anything like that. He was an artist. He was a darn good artist you know and he was a very sensitive man and a very sensitive actor. Our scenes were so wonderfully enacted by him and, I hope, by me that the inevitable happened and I fell desperately in love with him, I really did. If it hadn't been that I had a very sensitive and kind and understanding and wise husband my marriage might have ended in one of those crack-ups that are so much connected in one's mind with Hollywood."

What makes this a particularly interesting confession is that Miss Hayes also starred with a number of other romantic leading men, among them Clark Gable and Ronald Colman, but never felt much passion for any of them. Yet she couldn't, she said, get through that film with Cooper without "really tearing my heart out". On reflection she thought that perhaps the highly romantic nature of the story had

Cooper and Rocky – the wife he got to know when he locked himself in the lavatory.

much to do with her infatuation but she was also attracted by the fact that he didn't make passes at her and he "wasn't a professional Lothario". There was also, perhaps, the fact that her feelings were unrequited.

"I remember once," she said, "I tried to get a little flirtatious with Gary . . . I can't even remember what it was about but I know I was getting a little over the edge there and, whatever it was, Gary just looked at me very levelly for a moment and said, 'Helen, no. Naughty.' He knew that I had a fine husband and . . . well, after that I felt twice as desirous but I got a grip on myself finally."

In such circumstances it's perhaps understandable that Helen Hayes's opinion of Dorothy di Frasso is not particularly complimentary. "A very possessive and terrifying woman," was her description. "A rough sort of woman. As for the idea that she gave him polish, I seriously resent that. He could have given her a lot of style if she'd been receptive. After the romance with Gary broke up she had a fling with a gangster in Palm Springs. Bugsy Siegel. That doesn't reflect much style and taste, does it?"

It was about this time, however, with women apparently fluttering around him like autumn leaves, that Cooper met his future wife, Veronica Balfe, the daughter of a wealthy and well-connected New York family, who had vague ambitions to be an actress and had made two screen appearances under the name of Sandra Shaw. To her friends she was known as Rocky and Cooper met her through the good offices of Howard Hawks.

Hawks said: "He called me up one day and said, 'What are you doing?' and I said, 'Going out in my boat.' He said, 'Can I go?' and I said, 'Yes. Two girls who've just come in from New York are coming out with me.' And one of them was Rocky. Well, she and Coop started to fight immediately – just the kind of argument that people get into when they like each other on sight. And then he broke that up by getting locked in the toilet and she had to help him out and so they became friends and pretty soon they decided they were going to be married."

By then, obviously, the attractions of the Countess di Frasso had started to pall because Rocky saw her off pretty briskly

116

and she and Cooper were married in New York on December 15th, 1933. He was thirty-two and she was twenty and he said afterwards, "I was delighted to be rescued from my career as a playboy. Both of us were so pleased to settle down that we did it wholesale."

Cooper did indeed settle down, not only to his marriage which, except for one brief period, seems to have been one of the steadiest and most successful in Hollywood, but also to his career. From 1936 to 1957 he was only out of the top ten list at the box-office three times and, by that criterion, may well have been the most popular movie star ever. Certainly by the end of the thirties he must have been one of the richest. Indeed in 1939–40 he was the highest-paid actor in America with an income of half a million dollars a year.

But he worked for his money. Throughout the 1930s he was turning out films at the rate of three a year and, looking back on them now, looking back in fact on his entire career, it's easy to understand why he was so popular. There was a reliability and an integrity about Cooper that was never quite shared by anyone else. Whatever role he played, whether in a Lubitsch comedy like *Design for Living*, or Henry Hathaway's drama of war and heroism on the North West frontier, *The Lives of a Bengal Lancer*, or a thoughtful Western such as de Mille's *The Plainsman*, or the social comment of Frank Capra's *Mr. Deeds Goes to Town*, Cooper always portrayed the honest man. He was never the villain; there was never the remotest touch of the heavy about him.

It could be argued – and was by men like Henry Hathaway and Delmer Daves – that it would have been a ridiculous waste to cast him as a heavy anyway and they were right because the public simply would not have accepted him in such a role. His last film, *The Naked Edge*, which he made in England in 1961 had an uneasy response because, for most of the time, the audience and his co-star Deborah Kerr were wondering whether he was a murderer. It seemed unlikely and, of course, turned out to be a totally wrong impression but just for a moment there people were worried. Gary Cooper a murderer? It was against all the laws of nature. If you couldn't rely on Cooper to be the good guy, then what on earth could you rely on?

His daughter, Maria, believes that some heroes "are up on a mountain – you can't reach them. I think though there are other heroes who somehow give you the sense that you could be that man, too, and it seems to me that my father conveyed that to the public. He wasn't remote from them. He was the average man but maybe he was the best of what the average man could hope to be."

So I suppose the essence of Cooper's acting and the reason for the success he achieved was his inherent decency. A natural sincerity shone out of him. As his friend and fellow actor Richard Arlen put it: "He was just a nice guy." And, as a result, he became on screen a sort of glorified Everyman – the fellow who always stood firmly on the side of right, never wavering, no matter what the temptations or the odds ranged against him. He had the rare ability for an actor of being able to portray goodness, a laudable but not particularly exciting quality, without ever being dull.

By 1941, just before America entered the war, Cooper had made more than fifty films. He was forty years old and at the very top of his profession except for one thing – he had never yet won an Oscar. But even that was soon to be remedied. When the war came he was rejected for military service because he was physically unfit, the result of a badly healed broken hip that he had sustained years before while riding herd on the family cows. But before either the war or his own exclusion from it, Cooper had undertaken what was to be his finest performance to date, that of the First World War hero in *Sergeant York*. It was a role that he embarked upon without much conviction and he was, in fact, talked into it by the director, his friend and hunting companion, Howard Hawks, as a favour to a mutual friend, Jesse Lasky Sr.

Lasky had been one of the founders of Hollywood but by 1941 he was badly in need of a successful film to re-establish himself and had come up with the story of Sergeant York, a devoutly religious man who had gone into the First World War as a conscientious objector, then changed his mind and ended up by capturing an entire German machine gun battalion of 132 men single-handed in the Argonne Forest.

Cooper had already turned down the role when Hawks phoned him saying: "Didn't Jesse Lasky give you your first part in pictures?" Cooper agreed that he had. Hawks said: "Well, he gave me my first job, too. I don't think it would hurt us any if we made that picture and maybe we could do him a lot of good." Cooper said: "Okay, I'll come over and see you."

When he arrived, according to Hawks, he shuffled around the place, talked of hunting for a while, asked if he could see Hawks' new rifle and generally evaded the subject at issue until the director said: "Look, Coop, we have to talk about this." And Cooper said: "What's there to talk about? You know we're going to do it." So they did. And Gary Cooper won his first Academy Award.

During the next few years he continued to make highly successful films – playing the baseball star Lou Gehrig in *The Pride of the Yankees* and Robert Jordan in *For Whom the Bell Tolls*, for example – and also undertook a 23,000 mile tour of the South West Pacific to entertain the troops. Sam Wood, who directed him in both those pictures and also in *Saratoga Trunk* in 1946, said of him: "You're positive he's going to ruin your picture. I froze in my tracks the first time I directed him. I thought something was wrong with him and I saw a million dollar production go glimmering. But I was amazed at the result on the screen. What I thought was underplaying turned out to be just the right approach. On the screen he's perfect, yet on the set you'd swear it's the worst job of acting in the history of motion pictures."

Cooper's own opinion of himself, summed up on a BBC television programme in 1959, was as follows: "I just sort of concluded the only reason I got along in pictures was because I'm an average looking fellow and I've been mistaken, coming into strange towns, for the fellow somebody knew back in Podunk or any other town . . ."

At this point one of the female panel of interviewers broke in to say wistfully: "I wish some of the average men around looked like you, I must say." Cooper accepted this interruption with becoming modesty but hastened to add: "No, I really mean that. I looked like the fellow next door or down the block and stuff. You know. There's nothing spectacular about it." It was a somewhat ingenuous claim perhaps, but at least he was consistent about it for he repeatedly maintained that

he merely represented the "average guy from the middle of the USA".

Unfortunately he rather tarnished this image in the mid-1940s when, to the disapproval of the general public, he dabbled briefly in politics, a thing any average guy from the middle of the USA is probably ill-advised to do, especially if he also happens to be an actor. He delivered, first on radio and then in the form of a newspaper advertisement, a faintly xenophobic diatribe against President Roosevelt and in support of the Republican presidential candidate, Thomas E. Dewey. The general tenor was isolationist with criticism of "the company Roosevelt has been keeping" and an expressed distaste for the idea that America should "borrow foreign notions that don't seem to work any too well where they come from". Millions of Americans, of course, agreed with him but millions of others were shocked and disillusioned, believing that this political outcry clashed oddly with the impression of Cooper received from films like *Sergeant York* and *Meet John Doe*.

Whether coincidentally or not, from this time onwards his success began to wane and perhaps it was inevitable that it should. He was now approaching his mid-forties, a difficult age for any romantic leading man, as Gable also found out. His long-term contract with Paramount had come to an end and, as an independent artist, he found it difficult to secure the right kind of part in the right kind of film. He made a pleasant enough comedy, *Casanova Brown*, again directed by Sam Wood, and then starred in and produced a Western, *Along Came Jones*, which was neither a satisfactory film nor a happy experience for Cooper and he never attempted to produce a picture again.

Throughout the second half of the 1940s he worked more sparingly, averaging perhaps a film a year, and never quite reached the pinnacles on which, hitherto, he had been wont to reside. Perhaps it was partly dissatisfaction with the way his career was progressing and partly the fact that he was approaching fifty that caused him eventually to embark upon what was, for him, a most eccentric course of action.

In 1949 he played the idealist architect, Howard Roark, in the screen version of Ayn Rand's *The Fountainhead*. It was a film that attracted little praise at the time but it improves with keeping and has since

acquired a good many admirers. However, the most significant aspect of the production was that Cooper and his co-star, the twenty-three-year-old Patricia Neal, fell deeply and obviously in love. It was a development which astonished Hollywood. Cooper and Rocky had been contentedly married for sixteen years and not a hint of scandal had attached to either of them.

True, the marriage had for some time apparently been conducted on a philosophy of live and let live, with each of them pursuing their own social interests but the relationship had nevertheless seemed to be securely based. But in 1950 Cooper asked Rocky for a separation and told the newspapermen: "I can't say we haven't had a little difficulty but I can say that it isn't serious."

The separation became legal in May 1951. There was never any question of a divorce because Rocky was a Roman Catholic and indeed it seems that Cooper did not ask for a divorce anyway. Besides, by the time the separation papers were drawn up, the affair with Patricia Neal was almost over. It was Miss Neal who brought it to an end, not without causing herself a great deal of pain and suffering. She did so because she knew that marriage between them was impossible, even though she had never asked for it, and because she had begun to realise the grief which was being caused to Cooper's family.

In an interview in New York early in 1952 with the gossip columnist Hedda Hopper she said: "I will not see him when I go back to Hollywood. I have been very much in love with him and I'm sure he has loved me. But I saw that it wouldn't work, so I stepped out. Coop is wonderful. I never knew anyone like him. We last saw each other on Christmas Eve (1951) briefly. It is, I assure you, over and ended for ever."

Speaking of that period, Maria Cooper said: "I didn't try to think too much about whether my parents would or would not come back together. As you get older what you really want most is to see the two people you love most being happy and not in pain, physical or emotional. I was lucky, I guess, in that I had a very solid sense of their love for me, whether or not my father was living under the same roof as us."

To suggest that Cooper's extra-marital romance had been prompted by what is known, loosely, as the male menopause would be insulting to Miss Neal and belittling to him. But by the time the affair came to an end he was nearly fifty-one and certainly afflicted by some form of middle-aged restlessness. His private life was in a mess and so was his career. The former he tried to straighten out, if only in his own mind, by taking the second of his "long walks" to Europe and the latter was totally restored by the film he made before he left – *High Noon*, one of the best of all Westerns.

The part of Sheriff Will Kane who, abandoned by his erstwhile friends in the town, is obliged to face four vengeful killers alone was, he said, "a part like in *Sergeant York* that took everything I had, and I gave everything I had". He even gave up much of his usual high salary to make the film, although in return he took a percentage of the profits which turned out to be an exceedingly wise move. He also, for the second time, took the Academy Award for best actor.

The trip to Europe, made before the Oscars were announced, had neither the healing effect nor the excitement of his earlier jaunt. He developed a persistent ulcer and went back to America for treatment.

The success of *High Noon* had both re-established him and to some extent typed him, for three of his next five films – *Springfield Rifle*, *Blowing Wild* and *Vera Cruz* – were Westerns. None was outstanding but they all did well enough and, with his career now settled again, he turned to the task of repairing his private life.

In 1954, wearying of the unsettled bachelor existence he had been leading for the last four years, he was reconciled with his wife. By then he was fifty-three, his health was not particularly good and no doubt he felt that it was time for him to settle down at last. Rocky had, in any event, handled the whole separation with great wisdom. She had got on briskly with her own activities and, as Maria Cooper said: "She didn't mope. I think sometimes you get strength and create the thing you want most by just going and doing what you have to do, leading your own life and not just wringing your hands over a problem. She was very determined and intelligent and she knew what she hoped for ultimately – for the family to be together."

Reunited with his wife and daughter,

Cooper settled back into the routine of making one film a year, *The Court Martial of Billy Mitchell* being followed by *Friendly Persuasion* and *Love in the Afternoon*, in the last of which he co-starred with the eighteen-year-old Audrey Hepburn. Even his most loyal admirers felt this was a mistake. A romance between a man of fifty-six and a teenage girl left the audience feeling uneasy and embarrassed. Cooper himself couldn't quite understand why people should find such a story distasteful. "Is it impossible," he asked a friend, "to believe that a young girl could fall in love with a man like me?" And, of course, it wasn't but still the cradle-snatching aspect of the film roused a good deal of indignation, not least, possibly, among other middle-aged men who didn't look like Cooper and resented the fact that, unlike him apparently, they would never again be able to fondle a nubile teenager without grave danger of ending up in court.

Perhaps as an over-sensitive reaction to all the criticism, Cooper had his face lifted in 1958, the year after *Love in the Afternoon* was released. It was an unexpectedly vain thing for him to do and maybe there was a touch of desperation in his decision to have the job done – a reluctance to face the fact that he was now too old to play romantic leads. The same year he was treated again for a stomach ulcer but he eased up neither in his work nor in his social life, which tended to be very busy both in Hollywood and New York.

The following year, somewhat to the surprise even of his own family, he was converted to Roman Catholicism. Hitherto he had been a fairly easy-going Episcopalian, not noticeably religious, and Howard Hawks, Henry Hathaway and Delmer Daves all believed that his conversion was less the result of any deep conviction than of a desire to please Rocky and Maria, who were both devout Catholics. However, Maria Cooper said: "It certainly wasn't because of any pushing or prodding from our side. He'd always been very nice and come to mass with us at Christmas and Easter, that sort of thing but generally he looked on the Church as our affair. But suddenly, one Sunday, he just sort of said: 'Hey, let me come along with you' and I guess that maybe on some of his many drives or walks or times alone in the mountains he began to feel there was something that the Catholic religion had to offer that he wanted. He didn't talk about it very much to us. Again, he was a very private man and it was his private affair but I know he did get a lot of strength and comfort from it."

In an interview soon after his conversion Cooper himself said: "I'd spent all my waking hours, year after year, doing almost exactly what I, personally, wanted to do and what I wanted to do wasn't always the most polite thing either. I've had a lot of good things in my life – maybe too many of them – fame, success, money and of course love. It's true I've had some of the other things, some disappointments, some despair, some worry. I've had some moments of swollen-headedness too, moments of horrible conceit. But on the whole it's been good for me and then this past winter I began to dwell a little more on what's been in my mind for a long time. I began thinking, 'Coop, old boy, you owe somebody something for all your good fortune.' I guess that's what started me thinking seriously about my religion." He also said: "I'll never be anything like a saint, I know. I just haven't got that kind of fortitude. The only thing I can say for me is that I'm trying to be a little better. Maybe I'll succeed."

Whether he knew it or not – and the probability is that he didn't – Cooper was already ill around the time of his conversion. That year he made a film called *The Hanging Tree*, an offbeat Western directed by Delmer Daves and for the first time in his life he found it painful to sit on a horse. The pain was in the lower part of his back and the problem was temporarily resolved when Daves had a special saddle made for him so that he could sit with his legs practically straight. During the rest of the film, Daves said, "he was never bothered by the pain again. But when he went to Europe to do his last film, in England, that hurt that he had in his back was cancer. He died of cancer of the spine."

By the time he came to London in 1960 to star with Deborah Kerr in *The Naked Edge*, Cooper had already had two operations for cancer. At that time he was not told the nature of the complaint but soon after he returned to California he knew. "He wasn't a man to be lied to," said Maria Cooper, "particularly about something like that. And he reacted as you would expect.

121

He was very accepting. He said, 'Well, I'd like it to be different but if that's God's will, that's the way it's meant to be.' He had tremendous courage. After the initial moment, when we all knew the score, we didn't talk about it. We just went on and lived our lives and did what we could. He was in a lot of pain but he went to New York and did a programme for television about the American Indians. He was always very concerned about them long before it became a fashionable banner to carry. He really wanted to do that programme. He was suffering a lot but he didn't want people to know he was ill because he thought it would just make a lot of unnecessary talk so he simply went ahead and did the show. He lived right up to the last minute. That was a marvellous thing to see because his wasn't an easy way out."

Cooper's last public appearance was at a testimonial dinner given in his honour in Hollywood in January 1961. (It was at this dinner incidentally that Carl Sandburg described him as a "beloved illiterate".) At the Academy Award presentations several weeks later he was due to be given a special Oscar for services to the movie industry but by then he was too ill to attend.

James Stewart, an old and close friend, accepted the award on his behalf and was so obviously close to tears that it became clear that the news of Cooper's terminal illness could no longer be kept secret. It was announced to the press a couple of days afterwards.

Ten days before his death he asked Henry Hathaway to come and see him. Hathaway said: "We sat down and talked and he had a hatband that was a little sliver of silver and leather with a silver buckle and I'd always admired it. I'd also asked him once where he bought a leather wallet that he had for carrying foreign money. So that last time I saw him he had the hatband and the wallet on the table and he never said, 'I'd like you to have these' or anything like that. We were sitting there and he just kept shoving the hatband and the wallet a little closer to me and a little closer and he said, 'You like these.' And he just shoved

them closer again until I took them. There was nothing sentimental in what he did and that's a real test of a man, I'll tell you."

On May 13th, 1961, six days after his sixtieth birthday, Gary Cooper died. He was buried at the Holy Cross Cemetery in Beverly Hills. His pall-bearers included James Stewart, Jack Benny and Sam Goldwyn.

Arthur Jacobs, the producer, later described him as "the greatest film star there's ever been – and that includes Gable". Maybe he was at that. Yet despite the fact that he made ninety-five films no cult or mystique has built up around him. Perhaps the roles he played were too diversified for that or perhaps what he represented was too obvious to need the constant reappraisal and theorising which go hand-in-hand with the cults that surround other movie stars. Whatever part he played he was always essentially the same character, the quiet American hero striving to remain a hero in a world growing ever more cynical and corrupt. The values he epitomised, honesty, decency, integrity, loyalty, are those which everyone professes to admire but which, nevertheless, are not so easily found in modern life.

He once said: "I looked at it this way. To get folks to like you – as a screen player, I mean – I figured you had to be sort of their ideal. I don't mean a handsome knight riding a white horse, but a feller who answered to the description of a right guy."

That certainly is what he always was on the screen and I think it inconceivable that a man could consistently play "a right guy" in ninety-five films for thirty-five years without being something of a right guy himself. I suppose if you'd suggested to Gary Cooper that his motto might have been the motto of the mythical West, that "a man's gotta do what a man's gotta do," he might quite possibly have looked down at the ground for a long time and shuffled his feet and scratched the back of his head and then, adopting the role of the beloved illiterate, have nodded bashfully and said, "Yup".

*With his daughter, Maria.
Cooper was already
seriously ill with cancer
when this picture was taken
in September, 1960.*

John Wayne

I met John Wayne only twice; on both occasions we had fierce political disagreements and the second time I believe he had it in mind to hit me.

The first meeting was in Madrid in the early 1960s when he was making an indifferent film called *Circus World* with Claudia Cardinale. Wayne in Spain – indeed Wayne anywhere – was exactly what you would expect: apparently amiable and rough-hewn but mostly huge. He was then fifty-six and beginning to run to fat, or in the rather more tactful words of a *Time* magazine film reviewer, when he walked away from you the back view of his jeans looked like two small boys wrestling in a tent.

The interview (for later publication in the London *Daily Mail*) took place in his trailer and began pleasantly enough. But after a while the conversation turned to politics and I expressed the hope that America would have enough sense not to elect Barry Goldwater to the presidency. In retrospect, of course, this was a daft thing to say to John Wayne but I was naïve at the time and unaware that he had the reputation of being so far to the right that he had never really found a politician worthy of his support since the death of Attila the Hun. Anyway, the apparent amiability vanished very suddenly and he said, drawing himself up to his full six feet four inches, in a markedly cold manner: "Senator Goldwater happens to be a very close personal friend of mine."

At this point, no doubt, I should have backtracked rapidly and returned to the safer ground of the movies but instead I blundered on and ventured a few words of criticism of the late Joseph McCarthy, the notorious Communist witch-hunter of the 1950s.

Wayne heard me out even more coldly than before and then said: "I happen to believe that Senator McCarthy was one of the finest Americans who ever lived," and after that the interview struggled for breath for a minute or two and then gently expired.

Our second encounter was in 1969 on a train travelling from Denver, Colorado, to Salt Lake City. The centenary of the meeting of America's coast-to-coast railways was to be celebrated at Promontory, in Utah, and for a reason which I have never begun to understand, the highlight of the festivities was to be the première of Wayne's most recent movie, *True Grit*, for which admittedly he later won his first and only Oscar but which on the other hand had nothing whatsoever to do with railways.

The train wandered slowly through typical Wayne country – rolling plains and snowy mountains all apparently created by God for the sole purpose of making Western movies. News of Wayne's presence on board had spread throughout the countryside and at each wayside halt hordes of people (including, at Laramie, a bunch of Red Indians in a Ford Mustang) turned up to hear him speak warmly of the virtues of being an American.

In between stops the attendant journalists on the train were split into groups of half a dozen or so and ushered into the club car where Wayne held court and granted interviews. By the time I got in there it was mid-morning and the waitress told me, with something like awe in her voice, that the great man had already consumed fifteen miniature bottles of bourbon or, as he called it, "who-hit-John".

I don't think he remembered me from Spain, which was perhaps just as well; not

"An American Legend".

125

that it mattered, really, because once more the talk turned to politics.

Wayne had just returned from exhorting the troops in Vietnam where his bicycle had been hit by a Vietcong bullet. Wayne wasn't actually within a hundred yards of the machine at the time but nevertheless the consensus among the American media was that he had had a narrow escape and this brush with death was gravely discussed by the local journalists in my group. And when the heroism of the bicycle had been firmly established I asked Wayne what he thought of the situation in Vietnam.

"Well," he said, "I'll tell you: it's easy to stop that war. All you have to do is call up Kosygin on that hot line and say, 'You send one more bullet, one more gun to Vietnam and we bomb Moscow.'"

Unfortunately, I laughed, which was a mistake because I thought he was joking and he wasn't. After that as the talk ranged over politics (in which his views certainly did not seem to have mellowed since the early 1960s) and modern youth, he appeared to take against me rather strongly.

It was a time when students were demonstrating and even rioting across America and Wayne dismissed them all as "just a buncha jerks". His philosophy, forceful if not original, was as follows: "In my day at college you got a D for being a jerk. Now you get an A. That's the difference. Look, if you're a socialist in your first year at college, okay. But if you're still a socialist when you leave you're the dumbest son of a bitch that ever drew breath." He prefaced many of his remarks with "Lemme explain sumpun to ya" and qualified them by saying, "I'm not speaking from up there on the Mount", which I took to be a biblical reference though I suppose he could have meant a horse.

In any event I bore the brunt of most of his references to "goddamn, pinko liberals" and eventually he became so irritated with me that he began to mimic my accent, thereby hoping, I suspect, to amuse and enlist the support of the American journalists present. But Americans are extremely courteous people and they were rather embarrassed by his mockery of me so they all stared out of the window and failed to laugh with him. That annoyed him even more and when I, thinking (wrongly as it turned out) to calm matters, congratulated him on his English accent – which, to tell the truth,

was really rather bad – he emitted a growl of what sounded alarmingly like rage and started lumbering out of his chair towards me. Fortunately, an alert band of film company executives interposed themselves between Wayne and me, thrust another bourbon into his hand and put him back in his seat and ushered me very swiftly out of the club car. I expect it was a coincidence but for the rest of the three-day trip I never seemed to find myself within hailing distance of him and we never met again.

I've mentioned all this in some detail largely in order to declare myself: I did not personally like John Wayne. I admired him immensely as a star and somewhat less as an actor but I did not like the man. To arrive at such a conclusion on the basis of two comparatively brief and acrimonious meetings is probably a little over-hasty and no doubt the loss is mine, because my opinion of him does not appear to be shared by the mass of the American populace.

The fact is that nearly five years after his death, John Wayne is just about the biggest and most popular movie star there has ever been. A school in Brooklyn, a cancer clinic at the University of California, Los Angeles, a tennis club and even the airport at Orange County in southern California have all been named after him. There's a nine-foot statue of him at the airport and there is planned to be a twenty-one-foot statue on Wilshire Boulevard, which though not strictly in Hollywood is in the very heart of the general area that is widely considered to represent Hollywood. Furthermore he is one of only eighty-seven Americans to have had a Congressional Medal struck in his honour.

The inscription at the foot of the statue at the John Wayne Airport in Orange County reads: "John Wayne – American legend". And that's what he is, which is really rather odd because, although he made more than 150 films few of them were very good and there have certainly been far better actors than Wayne in the movies. Yet, when you look around, you don't see any twenty-one-foot statues of them overlooking the public thoroughfares. And so it seems reasonable to wonder why all these honours and all this adulation should have been visited upon John Wayne.

The story or, if you prefer, the legend of John Wayne began on May 26th, 1907 in the small town of Winterset, Iowa, where Mary, wife of Clyde L. Morrison, the local drug-store owner was delivered of a son. The father was of Scottish and the mother of Irish descent and with a taste for alliteration and very possibly an odd sense of humour they christened their child Marion Michael. He grew up tall and brawny as any all-American boy named Marion would probably have to be. His father, the pharmacist, was however less robust and when Marion was five the family moved to California where it was believed the drier climate would be beneficial to Clyde Morrison's tuberculosis.

Mr. Morrison was a college graduate but no great shakes as a businessman. He had made very little money as a druggist and he made even less as a farmer which is what he became, as the owner of eighty acres of sagebrush in California. In the words of Michael Wayne, John's eldest son: "They had a great crop but the rabbits ate it all." Still, it was here that the young Marion learned to ride and shoot rattlesnakes, skills which were to be invaluable to him in later life.

The farming experiment rapidly proved a failure and when Marion was nine the Morrisons moved back to town, to Glendale, California, where Clyde resumed his former occupation as a pharmacist, although this time as an employee in someone else's business.

Michael Wayne said: "They were very poor and lived on tuna fish for about six months. Evidently they got a good buy on several cases of tuna fish." (The predictable result of this enforced diet was that ever afterwards John Wayne could barely bring himself to look at a piece of tuna fish.)

The Morrisons' poverty was so evident that a group of firemen took pity on young Marion and every day, as he passed the fire station on his way to school, they gave him a bottle of milk and told him to take it home for his cat, well knowing that he had no cat and was drinking it himself. It was these same firemen who gave him the nickname that was to stick to him for the rest of his life. Though lacking a cat young Marion did have a dog, a big Airedale called Duke and as the pair approached the firemen would say: "Here comes big Duke (meaning the dog) and little Duke (meaning the boy)."

On the two occasions when I met Marion, or Duke, or as I knew him John Wayne, one of the things that struck me about him was his apparently anti-intellectual attitude. If you offered him a word of more than two syllables he would sneer visibly and say: "What the hell does that mean?"

I can only assume that this was a pose, part of his carefully nurtured down-to-earth image, because in fact Marion Morrison had a pretty good education and by all accounts was something of a star pupil. At Glendale High School he was, as his son Michael said, "an achiever" and all his life, according to his friends and family, he was a voracious reader, much addicted to the works of Winston Churchill. Indeed, the director Andrew McLaglen, who probably knew him as well as anyone, said: "If you were to ask me 'Was he an intellectual or not an intellectual' I would say he *was* an intellectual, because he was an avid reader both in national and world politics and he could speak on a lot of subjects. People who looked at big John Wayne and thought he was dumb in any way, shape or form had another think coming." Perhaps then he was a closet reader, anxious to keep this unmanly vice secret from the millions of fans to whom he was the epitome of the more rugged, less cerebral masculine virtues.

On the other hand it was as an athlete, not as a scholar, that he won his place at the University of Southern California, to which he went on a football scholarship in September 1925, by which time he was armed (thanks to his father) with the three guiding principles which he tried to follow throughout his life: 1) Always keep your word; 2) A gentleman never insults anybody unintentionally; and 3) Don't go around looking for trouble. But if you ever get into a fight, make sure you win it.

He was not, however, armed with much money and was therefore obliged to work his way through college. As a member of the USC football team, the Trojans, he was one of the beneficiaries of an offer made by Tom Mix, then the Number One Western movie star and a keen football follower, of summer jobs at Fox studios. And it was there, while he was working as a general handyman and labourer, that he met the director John Ford, who was to become undoubtedly the most decisive influence on his life. Ford, who was then thirty-one, was making a film called *Mother Machree*, on which Duke Morrison was employed as a goosewrangler, which is to say that he was in charge of a herd of geese with the responsibility of pointing them in whichever direction Ford demanded.

Michael Wayne said: "I guess the geese didn't do exactly what my father or John Ford wanted them to do and Ford got onto my father a little bit about it and my father apologised. But Ford didn't let up on him and finally he said, 'You're a football man, aren't you?' and my father said 'Yes' and Ford said, 'Do you think you could block me?' Now Ford was a very physical guy, about six foot three, but I don't think physically he was a match for my father in those days, or at any time really, but he said, 'Well, get down on your three-point stance,' that's both feet on the ground and one hand out in front of you, and when my father got down, the minute he got down, Ford kicked his hand out from under him and my father went, you know, down on his face and everybody on the set got a big laugh out of it. Well, by this time my father didn't care about Hollywood or anything else; he was mad at Ford and he said, 'May I try that again?' And he got down and before Ford could kick his hand out he drove Ford over some tables and chairs and into a truck that was parked there. And the set was quiet, you know, because . . . 'Oh, my God, he's just done the most horrible thing in the world: hit this great director and really knocked him on his fanny.' But Ford got up, laughed and enjoyed the joke as much as my father did and admired him, I think; admired his spunk and the fact that he wouldn't take any crap from him."

In this violent way there began a lifelong friendship between the two men and it may not be too far-fetched to see in this incident the inception, or even the conception, of the character Wayne was to play so successfully in the movies. Once, when he was talking to me about his career, he said: "In America, I represent manhood," and that's quite true, though it was a rather primitive kind of manhood – rough and tough and boozy. In John Wayne films women were treated with gruff, backwoods courtesy and no man could ever hope to become Wayne's friend unless they had first had a quite brutal fist fight – possibly to ensure that, however close the bonds of the ensuing friendship, the audience could be confident

that there was nothing gay about Big John; but possibly, too, because the most important friendship in his own personal life had begun in just such a way.

However, after his summer job, Duke Morrison returned to USC in the autumn of 1926 but within a few months his college career was virtually over. He had suffered a severe shoulder injury in a surfing accident and it soon became clear that he would not be able to play football any more – and that, in turn, meant that he lost his scholarship.

And so he dropped out of college and in the summer of 1927, at John Ford's request, he returned to his labouring job at Fox studios. It was not much of a job but now he had the incentive of Ford's promise that one day he would be given the opportunity to act. In any event he needed work because he had fallen in love with, and intended to marry, one Josephine Saenz, whom he had met the previous November at a Thanksgiving Dance at USC.

She was the younger daughter of Dr. Jose Sainte Saenz, a Spaniard of royal descent, a wealthy businessman and the consul for the Dominican Republic. Unfortunately, neither he nor his wife approved of Wayne and since Josephine refused to commit herself to him without parental approval theirs was a tense and no doubt physically frustrating courtship. Wayne, however, was undeterred and determined that one day he would persuade the whole Saenz family to accept him.

Meanwhile he remained at Fox, essentially in the props department, for the next three years. But in that time he also appeared as an extra in crowd scenes, played an Irish peasant boy in Ford's 1928 film, *Hangman's House*, and gained his first screen credit – as Duke Morrison – the following year in *Words and Music*. More bits and pieces and extra work came his way and then he added another skill to his repertoire when he became a stuntman. The film, *Men Without Women*, directed by Ford, concerned an explosion in the engine room of a submarine and when they came to the scene in which the stars, represented naturally by stuntmen, were supposed to dive overboard the sea was so fierce that the stuntmen refused to do it. Ford thereupon turned to Wayne (who was actually employed as the props man) and said: "Show 'em up!" And his eager young acolyte obediently plunged in.

Wedding day No. 1, with his wife Josephine and Loretta Young, who lent her house for the occasion.

From then on for his first decade in pictures Wayne looked upon himself as a stuntman rather than an actor and to a large extent he was not wrong to do so, for his apprenticeship was served in Action Man Westerns and Saturday morning serials in which he was called upon to do most of his own stunts and in which anything much more than half a dozen words was regarded as a very long speech indeed and should be cut if possible lest it bore the audience to sleep.

His first break in such films came in- directly through his friend John Ford, who recommended him to Raoul Walsh as the ideal replacement for Gary Cooper (who had declined the role) in *The Big Trail*. The film was a flop – though the Cooper- substitute received good reviews – and its most important outcome was that it caused Marion Morrison (a better name, after all, for a leading lady than a leading man) to become John Wayne. As to how this actu- ally came about there is some confusion.

Michael Wayne's explanation is as fol- lows: "He had an agent and the agent's name, strange though it may seem, was also Morrison. And this guy said, 'Look, you've got to get rid of that Marion Morrison,' and

my father said, 'What shall I call myself?' and he said, 'John Wayne'." Another and just as plausible theory is that Raoul Walsh borrowed his new star's new surname from a general in the American Revolution who was known as "Mad Anthony" Wayne. That he was perhaps one of the lesser- known generals of the revolution is prob- ably due to his Christian name, since "Mad Anthony" does not, somehow, have the authentic ring of desperate heroism to it. In any case, according to this theory, Walsh was not too keen on Anthony either, con- sidering it to sound too sissy and Italian, and so on to Wayne he tacked the first name John and so it was to remain, though to his friends he continued to be known as "Duke".

Thus equipped with a new name and recognition, of a sort, as an actor the newly born John Wayne plunged confidently into two more flops (*Girls Demand Excitement* and *Three Girls Lost*), then left Fox and moved to Columbia where he developed such a dislike for the head of production, Harry Cohn, that after his brief stay he never worked for the studio again and eventually drifted to Mascot Films (where he appeared in a number of serials), before

129

moving on to Warners (where he made six films) and then signing to make sixteen five-reel Westerns with Monogram Pictures.

By now he was earning 1,500 dollars a film and was at last able to support Josephine, whom he married on June 24th, 1933 – some seven years after he first met her – in the grounds of Loretta Young's estate in Bel Air. It had been, certainly by Hollywood standards, an unusual courtship. As Michael Wayne said: "It was kind of a lengthy one. I think my mother's parents were not that anxious to have their daughter marrying an actor. My grandfather was a doctor and head of the diplomatic corps here in Los Angeles and he and my father didn't see eye to eye on anything, especially my mother. As a matter of fact, he sent my mother to Hawaii with my aunt to get her away from my father and my father stowed away on the boat, got caught, got put in jail in San Francisco and eventually got out because the local police chief was the father of a good friend of his. But, yeah, they had a really romantic courtship, you know, fraught with all sorts of obstacles but eventually they got married and went about their business."

This business included having four children – Michael, born in 1934, Antonia Maria (known as Toni) in 1936, Patrick in 1937 and Melinda in 1939. Meanwhile, the pater familias was continuing to learn his trade as the star of B-movies and serials as well as becoming, briefly, the world's first singing cowboy under the cringe-making name of "Singin' Sandy". Decently regretting this aberration he dropped both role and soubriquet to join Republic where he starred in yet another series of B-grade Westerns, directed by George Sherman and co-starring Ray Corrigan, who deeply resented his new partner.

Sherman said: "Ray was a great big guy and he was determined that he was going to be the predominant figure in the series. He wore silver belts and silver things on his hat and silver bracelets and he tried to do everything to outshine Duke. But you just couldn't, you know? Duke could walk into a room and the eye would immediately go to him. Wayne was a very graceful man, beautiful on a horse. He was poetry in motion on a horse."

It was while he was still involved in making quickies with George Sherman

that, at the age of thirty-one and after sixty-five rubbishy pictures, Wayne at last achieved stardom. The year was 1938, the film was *Stagecoach* and the director was John Ford and he, despite the protests of his producer, Walter Wanger, who was deeply unimpressed by Wayne's track record, insisted on casting him in the leading role of Ringo, the young outlaw.

His co-star was Claire Trevor, who said: "John Ford had great faith in him and had known him for many years, so he wanted to get him in this picture. But I think the higher-ups in the studio were not convinced that John Wayne could do it, so Ford asked me to make a test with him, which I did. That was the first time I met him and he was very tentative and very shy but he had a wonderful quality, I thought." Her admiration for him grew during the shooting but . . . "I didn't know – who could? – that he would be that sensational; not until I saw the picture. When I saw the finished film I was swept off my feet."

Stagecoach was an immediate success but it was more than that: it established John Wayne as a star and lent respectability to the genre of the Western which, hitherto, had been regarded as nothing more than a programme filler. Furthermore it was the first of eleven films (among them such classics as *She Wore a Yellow Ribbon*, *The Searchers* and *The Quiet Man*) that Wayne and Ford put together over a period of twenty-five years. It was a strange relationship, combining elements of father and son, master and pupil, with Ford always the dominant partner.

The style was set during the making of *Stagecoach* when, according to Claire Trevor, Ford "treated him like a child and had no regard for his dignity". In front of the whole cast he would stride up to Wayne, grab him by the head and shake it back and forth while bellowing: "You're acting with your chin. You're not supposed to act with your goddamn chin!" Miss Trevor believes that Ford's harsh behaviour was designed for Wayne's own good. "I really think Ford taught him how to act," she said. "He taught him so many great rules about acting. He taught him the principles and John Wayne took off from there."

Ford may have behaved so rudely because it was obviously in his own interests to get as good a performance as possible out of his leading man. But there is no doubt that a strongly mischievous, even sadistic, streak ran through his attitude towards Wayne. On another occasion during the filming of *Stagecoach* he took his star to see some rushes and in particular a scene in which Andy Devine was driving the stagecoach. "What do you think of that?" Ford asked. Wayne said: "Well, I think it looks kind of phoney; the reins are too loose." Ford promptly took him back to the set, confronted him with Andy Devine and said: "Tell Andy what you told me – that he looks phoney up there driving the stagecoach." The flustered Wayne tried to apologise but the damage was done and from then on there was tension between him and Devine. Many years later Ford admitted to Wayne that that had always been his intention, saying: "I wanted to juice the pair of you up a little bit. I used you."

In both those instances Ford abused and manipulated Wayne for the good of the film but on other occasions he would give him a hard time just for the hell of it. When they were filming *The Three Godfathers* in the intense heat of Death Valley Wayne arrived on set one morning with an appalling hangover, a rare occurrence because although he drank a lot he was usually quite abstemious when he was filming and certainly when he was filming with Ford.

The scene he had to shoot that day was at a dinner table with Ward Bond and Mae Marsh and Wayne was supposed to be ravenously hungry. Harry Carey Jr., who appeared in that and several other films with Wayne, said: "Ford knew Duke had a hangover. Now normally he'd do a scene in one take but this time Ford made him eat that chicken over and over and over again. He'd say, 'Duke, you're not doing it like you're starving! You're starving, remember. Now really go at it.' And Duke would just say, 'Yes, sir,' and he'd eat and eat and then he'd go and throw up. And he'd come back green. Ford rode him all that morning. He must have done the scene ten times, eating that chicken and then throwing up."

Wayne's attitude towards Ford seemed to contain a strong touch of awe and even a little fear. In public he always spoke of "Mr. Ford", never of John or Jack. Bill Clothier, the cinematographer who worked with both of them on *The Horse Soldiers*

In Stagecoach, *which brought him "overnight" stardom after eleven years.*

and *The Man Who Shot Liberty Valance*, said: "Wayne called him 'Coach' on the set – 'Okay, Coach, anything you say, Coach' – and that was the relationship. But he loved old man Ford and the old man had a way of getting things out of people that no other director had."

Harry Carey said: "Actually he had a very respectful fear of Jack Ford. It would always be 'Yes, sir' or 'No, sir'. After a film they'd go off on Duke's or Ford's yacht together and play cards and get drunk. But on the set it was healthy respect all the way. And in fact Duke was at Jack Ford's beck and call almost all the time. If Jack Ford felt like playing cards with John Wayne and John Wayne was in bed, well, he'd just have to get up and go over to Ford's house and play cards. Like, Sunday afternoon, if Duke decided he wanted to go and see one of his kids and Jack wanted to play bridge or poker, well, the minute Ford called he'd have to go over there."

According to Michael Wayne: "My father had a love for him, a respect for him and also a liking for him. The liking used to be stronger or weaker depending on the situation. One time they didn't talk for two years and my father never really knew why. He just never heard from Ford and my father would call but he never heard back. And then, out of the blue, he got a telephone call and it was as if nothing had ever happened. So it was an unusual kind of relationship but my father always loved and respected him and was always grateful to him for that opportunity in *Stagecoach*. I remember Bruce Cabot said to me one time, 'You know, Michael, I tested for that *Stagecoach* part and I did all the stuff that Ford asked me to do in the test and I jumped up and said, "Well, Pappy, how was I?" And he said, "You were great. You were great, Bruce – but Duke's got the part."'"

In the three years following *Stagecoach*, Wayne made a dozen films but was not particularly happy with any of them except the one John Ford directed – *The Long Voyage Home*, which was based on four one-act plays by Eugene O'Neill. It was more of a critical than a financial success and it was said to be O'Neill's favourite picture. At this time Wayne was regretting the fact that, unusually for a big star in that era, he was a freelance, with no attachment to any particular studio. He felt the lack of some powerful executive to keep an eye on

his career, to boost and publicise him. In the final analysis, of course, this made very little difference but it could help to explain why it took him far longer than most of his peers to reach what is now known as superstardom.

By the end of 1941, however, Wayne had made seventy-seven movies and was much in demand, though his reputation rested largely on *Stagecoach* and to some extent it still does, for it is not easy to think of a better Western. There are, however, other reasons than the quality of that first outstanding success for the special niche Wayne occupies among Western stars. In part he explained it to me thus: "I guess I was the first hero in movies ever to hit a guy with a vase or a chair." Until his advent, it seems, brawls in films had been gentlemanly affairs in which only fists were used. Wayne's claim was that he changed all that and . . . "I guess that's what made my first Westerns different from any that had gone before."

I suppose if Wayne hadn't achieved this dramatic breakthrough somebody else would have done sooner or later. Anyway, he spoke of it with bashful modesty, as if the introduction of real violence into popular entertainment was an achievement in which any man might take a certain amount of pride.

However, back at the close of 1941, America had entered the Second World War – without Wayne – and his marriage was in serious trouble. He was thirty-four and though he tried to enlist in the armed forces he was rejected because of his age and his family commitments and also because of the aftermath of the shoulder injury which had ended his football career. To do him justice he tried very hard to get into the services but even John Ford, who had become a lieutenant-commander in the navy, was unable to help him. So Wayne's war effort was, perforce, restricted to entertaining the troops near the front line and making a number of patriotic movies in which he won countless battles. Ironically, his absence, however reluctant, from the war itself and his consequent presence on so many celluloid battlefields probably did more to create the legend than active service would have done. Along with the Westerns, those war movies helped to build up the picture of Wayne as a hero for all seasons and all spheres of combat.

Meanwhile, on the domestic front Wayne and Josephine were drifting gradually apart. It was a state of affairs that had been becoming apparent for some time but in 1941 Wayne went to Mexico and there became greatly smitten by an actress named Esperanza Baur Diaz Caballos, known professionally as Esperanza Baur and to her friends by the somewhat unflattering nickname of "Chata", which in Spanish means pugnose. For some time Wayne resisted anything approaching a wholly intimate relationship but eventually he brought her to Hollywood as his "protégée". As far as Josephine was concerned that was the clincher; the couple separated and in November 1944 they were divorced, although they remained good friends until Wayne's death.

Considering the difficulties they had had to go through to get married in the first place, the time they had had to wait and the resolution they had shown, it is particularly sad that the marriage didn't last. Michael Wayne believes that the chief cause of the failure was the all-consuming nature of his father's career: "Being an actor, especially in the early stages of your career, is very demanding in terms of time. He was trying to establish himself in town; every film that he made was an outdoor adventure story, made on location, so he was gone a lot and I think that perhaps they just went their separate ways. My mother is also a very strong person and created a life for herself. So I guess they gradually grew apart. It was, of course, very disappointing to us, the kids, but we always respected both of them, loved them both, and I never heard my mother say a bad word about my father, while he always had glowing things to say about her. So it was nice to grow up with that kind of feeling and in that kind of situation."

Three weeks after the divorce became final, in January 1946, Wayne married Chata at Long Beach, California. Michael Wayne remembered his new stepmother as: "a good-looking, fiery Latin woman and I guess my father was the man to match that fire. She was really very nice to the four children and I guess she was nicer to us than she was to my father, to hear him tell it, anyway."

In any event, Wayne's second shot at matrimony was very different from his first: it was a passionate, even violent, affair

Wife No. 2, Esperanza (Chata or "Pugnose" to her friends). The marriage was brief – and turbulent.

in which vast quantities of booze were consumed by both parties. Nor was it helped by the fact that Chata's mother, herself a handy lady with a tequila bottle, lived with them for much of the time and took an active part in all the marital discord.

Chata's problem was that she had no children, had given up her own career and resented her husband's total absorption in the film business. So to get her own back for his apparent neglect, or perhaps simply to attract his attention, she had a series of casual, but strictly non-secret affairs with other men. Wayne, who was obsessed by her – possibly because to him she was often unobtainable – put up with this for quite a long time. But in the end he could stand it no more and in November 1953 they were somewhat messily divorced.

At one point she obtained a court order barring him from the marital home, in response to which he got another court order permitting him to enter the premises to visit their dog, a poodle called Pedro, which in fact he disliked intensely. In the end both parties were awarded a divorce but Chata came out of it all well ahead on points, since Wayne was ordered to pay her 150,000 dollars plus 50,000 dollars a year in alimony.

133

In fact, however, this did not prove too costly because in the winter of 1954 Chata died of a heart attack in Mexico City.

Those first two marriages – and indeed his third, which followed within hours of his divorce from Chata becoming final – throw some light on Wayne's attitude both to women and to his work.

Claire Trevor, who remained a close friend (though nothing more than that) till the end of his life, believed that he was basically not a womaniser or even a flirtatious man. "He was a romantic. He liked women but he was much more at ease with men. He was a rough, tough he-man. A lot of women found him very attractive – Marlene Dietrich for one – and sort of went on the make for him. But that made him a little shy and frightened, you know? He was a very true man, true to his marriage, to his wife at the time."

Michael Wayne said: "He was attractive to women and he was attracted by women but he was uneasy around them because he liked occasionally to use . . . I guess you'd call them 'vulgarities' . . . and so, though he was always on his best behaviour and was always a gentleman when he was around women, I think it was a little bit of a strain for him."

Along with all this, went a respect both for women and for the state of matrimony. "He was always a one-woman man," said Andrew McLaglen. "If a wife were to leave him he'd fall in love again kind of fast but he usually married the lady."

Wayne himself once told his third wife, Pilar, that he didn't understand women, a confession which hardly makes him unique but which, perhaps, helps to account for his awkwardness and shyness with them, although it doesn't explain his inability to make a marriage work and last.

The reason for that lies mostly in his devotion to his work and his career, which took priority above all else in his life. "He told me that he never wanted more than a week off," said Harry Carey Jr. "I never heard him say, 'Jesus, I'm really tired; I could use some time off.' His vacation was making movies. He *loved* to make movies."

Claire Trevor said: "He was extremely ambitious. Every successful actor I've ever known, every movie star had a dedication to his work and Duke had it, too. He wanted success; he wanted to win; he was a perfectionist."

In later years this dedication and striving for perfection made Wayne unpopular with directors of lesser calibre than John Ford, for with them he could be dictatorial. George Sherman believed that working with Ford had spoiled him: "Ford never let him utter one word of criticism about directing, because everybody was terrified of Ford. So when Duke worked with another guy, he figured: this is my opportunity to really get in there and speak out and question things."

In this, however, he was not prompted so much by egotism as by the fact that he probably knew as much about making films as anybody around. Harry Carey said: "John Wayne always knew his lines and he knew yours, too. He'd studied every aspect of the picture business. He knew about editing, he knew about camera work and when he was working with some of those younger directors, he'd say: 'No, no, no, damn it! Jesus, what have you got the camera there for?' You know? But it was because he was so conscientious and wanted to save time. If he had a fault – well, he had quite a few faults – he had a temper and he was very impatient. He couldn't tell anybody how to do something without getting excited."

By the end of the Second World War the dedicated and occasionally irascible John Wayne, aged thirty-eight and with a considerable body of work behind him, was already one of the most popular stars in America but his greatest success was still to come.

In the next few years films like *Fort Apache*, *She Wore a Yellow Ribbon* and *Rio Grande* (all directed by John Ford), along with *Red River* (Howard Hawks) and *Sands of Iwo Jima* (Allan Dwan) for which latter production Wayne received his first Academy Award nomination, boosted his career to such an extent that by 1950 he had become America's top box-office star. He was Number One again in 1951, 1952, and 1953 and from then until 1968 he was only out of the top ten once.

But by the end of the 1940s he was already something more than simply a movie star: he was becoming a kind of unofficial, self-appointed voice of America. In the latter part of the decade he had banded together with other actors and studio executives to form the Motion Picture Alliance for the Preservation of American

Ideals, an organisation that went about peering suspiciously into dark corners of Hollywood for signs of Communist infiltration. In 1949 he became the MPA's president and during his three years in office the association passed resolutions insisting that all Communists should register as such and outlined a number of elements in any film that proved it to carry surreptitious Marxist propaganda.

Wayne himself even complained to the writer Carl Foreman that the scene in *High Noon* in which Gary Cooper ripped off his marshal's badge and threw it on the ground was "like belittling a medal of honour". Against this, though, it should be pointed out that unlike many of his Hollywood contemporaries in the late 1940s and early 1950s, Wayne was not a witch-hunter and certainly never attempted to bar anyone from working on a film because of political beliefs.

True, he was a fervent and lifelong anti-Communist but above all I think he was motivated by the fact that he was a passionate and rather simple patriot. In the words of his son, Michael, he "loved being an American" and indeed in 1968 he addressed the Republican Party convention to tell them so. Frequently he observed that he thanked God for every hour he spent on American soil. "He felt," said Michael Wayne, "that this was the greatest country on the face of the earth. He told me often that in our 200-year history we've given away more to others than the rest of the world combined since the beginning of time."

Whether this expansive claim is true or not (and it would be difficult to prove one way or the other), Wayne did seem genuinely to believe that America was God's own country and gave the impression that he was only sorry that he personally hadn't discovered it, or at least pioneered it. It being rather too late for him to do either of those things he imposed upon himself the task of protecting the American way of life and what America stood for as he saw it. And all those who strayed from his line and from staunchly Republican and capitalist principles were, in his own words, "a bunch of goddamn pinko liberals" who must be regarded as so many pesky redskins attacking the stagecoach and dealt with accordingly.

As he once put it to me: "I'm just an ordinary goddamn American and I talk for all the ordinary goddamn Americans, the butchers and bakers and plumbers. I know these people; I know what they think."

In the early days of his political involvement no doubt he did know and perhaps speak for these people. But later on, towards the end of the 1960s and into the 1970s, he seemed to grow out of touch with them and was still uttering his jingoistic line when jingoism had fallen from favour. And perhaps the knowledge of that helped to account for his political anger and the bitterness of his attitude towards modern American youth during that train journey in 1969 between Denver and Salt Lake City.

Michael Wayne explained his father's involvement in the MPA thus: "It was a time in the film business when the Communist Party was making an effort to take over all of the unions. This was before television and I guess motion pictures were the medium with the largest impact on the public, so this was kind of a logical place for the Communist Party to go in and try to take over. If they had taken over the film business they could perhaps have spread their influence and philosophy across the United States and my father saw this as a great danger. As a matter of fact, I think this was the time when Ronald Reagan was president of the Screen Actors' Guild and he and my father were at the opposite end of the political spectrum. I mean, my father was a very conservative man and Reagan was a liberal Democrat at that time but he asked my father to come in and help him fight this Communist takeover, which he did and he regarded it as a real threat to the United States. I think history has proved him right."

Whether he was right or wrong there is, of course, no reason why an actor should not have political beliefs but Wayne more than any other used the popularity and fame he had achieved to propagate his, even though – as his friend and fellow actor Ben Johnson said – normally "in the picture business you don't take sides hardly. He did and he was big enough to back it up." Because of that, political pronouncements which, had they emanated from almost any other movie star, would have merited only passing interest, had the effect of sounding, in his phrase, as if they came "from up there on the Mount". And so to the rest of

135

Pilar, the third and last wife and another Latin American. Wayne was consistent, if not always constant, in his marriages.

1st, 1954, Wayne received a phone call and then turned to Pilar saying: "That was my lawyer. My divorce has become final: let's get married today."

So they did. Pilar said: "He told me I never gave him an hour's chance. He was married at breakfast, divorced at lunch and remarried at dinner. He'd always kid me about that."

This third plunge into matrimony completed Wayne's hat-trick of Latin American wives, a matter of good taste according to Pilar but a simple coincidence according to her husband. A month after the wedding he told an agency reporter that he had never been conscious of going for a particular type of woman. "They say a man follows a pattern but I haven't been aware of it myself . . . I certainly don't have anything against American women."

He remained married to Pilar for the rest of his life, though they separated in 1973, and by her he had three more children – Aissa, John Ethan and Marisa. By the strictest standards (or even by not very strict standards at all) he may have fallen some way short of being the ideal husband but he was certainly a devoted family man, co-existing with all his seven children in an atmosphere of mutual adoration.

As a father he could be strict. Michael Wayne said: "He just wanted you to do what was right. As long as you kept your nose clean you never heard from him; he wasn't constantly preaching. But the minute something went wrong the punishment was swift. You always knew where you stood. He'd just have to start to reach for his belt and we knew we were in trouble; he didn't have to hit us." He didn't have to but he would occasionally – "just a few taps, to let you know you'd done something bad."

George Sherman remembered an occasion when Wayne's eldest daughter, Toni, then a teenager, was smoking at the dinner table. "He walked up to her and said, 'Do you like to smoke?' and she said, 'Yeah, I'm enjoying it.' He said, 'Well, that's good' and he took the cigarette and shoved it right in her mouth. So that finished her smoking."

On the other hand this image of Wayne, the stern disciplinarian, is not truly representative. Claire Trevor said: "His whole family went with him everywhere. He was the most demonstrative father you could

the Wayne legend was added the picture of John Wayne, spokesman for America.

But by 1950 politics was not the only new area into which Wayne was expanding. He had also started his own company, Batjac Productions, for which he made a number of moderately successful films such as *Big Jim McClain*, *Island in the Sky* and *Hondo*. His most notable pictures in the first half of that decade though were *The Quiet Man* (another John Ford movie) and *The High and the Mighty*. Immediately after completing the latter production he went to Hawaii to film *The Sea Chase* and it was while he was on location there that he was married for the third time.

His bride on this occasion was Pilar Palette, a Peruvian actress whom he had met while on a visit to South America. They met again at a Hollywood party and began going out together. By the time Wayne went to Hawaii for *The Sea Chase* his marriage to Chata was all over and so Pilar went with him. On the morning of November imagine. He loved his children with a passion; he was always putting his arms around them and hugging and kissing them."

Marisa, the youngest of the seven junior Waynes, summed him up thus: "He was the best father I could ever have had. I loved him more than anything. He was caring and he was loving and giving and he was strict but in a good way. He disciplined me well and taught me always to be nice to everybody and to respect other people."

For Wayne the family man Christmas was the best time of the year. He would spray artificial snow all over the house, instal Christmas trees in every room and cover them with tinsel and myriads of coloured light bulbs. "You couldn't walk into our living room," Marisa said, "because there were so many presents for everybody. And he'd have reindeer up at the house." They lived then on the bay at Newport Beach and every year out on the water there was a Christmas procession of yachts. "He'd get his big megaphone out and stand there on the porch booming 'Merry Christmas!' to all the boats going round. He was just like Santa Claus."

Without wishing to detract from the obviously genuine festive spirit with which Wayne was imbued it should be pointed out that he could, of course, well afford to play Santa Claus in such a lavish style. In 1956 he announced to the press that he had become the highest paid movie star in the world with a fee of 666,666 dollars a picture, a strange sort of sum but nonetheless welcome for that. By modern standards it is not a great deal of money (Dustin Hoffman, for instance, was paid more than four million dollars for starring in *Tootsie*) but when you consider that as recently as 1953 Clark Gable had left MGM because the studio could no longer afford to pay him 520,000 dollars a *year*, Wayne's salary appears almost astronomical.

Thus the 1950s ended with Wayne on yet another pinnacle. But the movie business is such that the only thing one can predict with any certainty about it is that it will always prove unpredictable and, true to form, the 1960s began with the biggest disappointment of Wayne's career – *The Alamo*.

The Alamo incident took place in 1836 when a band of eighty-seven Texans fought an heroic but inevitably losing battle against 3,000 Mexican soldiers. In American history it stands almost as a kind of nineteenth-century Dunkirk and for all manner of reasons – among which his intense patriotism was by no means the least significant – Wayne had been planning for ten years to produce and direct a film version of it. In the event he also starred in it, as Davy Crockett, with Richard Widmark as that other legendary backwoodsman, Jim Bowie.

It turned out to be a very expensive enterprise, costing Batjac twelve million dollars and obliging Wayne himself to mortgage his home and draw on all his business interests to raise the cash. (The party after the Hollywood première alone cost 50,000 dollars.) But Wayne justified the financial risks he was taking by saying: "This is the big American story that I don't think anyone could do better than I. It's the first time in my life that I've been able to express what I feel about people." More than that, it seemed to him that the story of the Alamo summed up everything he felt about America and American values.

The film's initial reception was good; the battle scenes were much praised and the picture was nominated for a number of Academy Awards, among them best film and best supporting actor (Chill Wills). But interest in it died away fast and in the end it won only one minor award, the Oscar for best sound, despite a costly and clamorous publicity campaign to influence the Academy voters – a campaign that backfired rather badly when Wayne was sufficiently ill advised to permit a slogan suggesting that "a vote for *The Alamo* is a vote for the United States," a notion that rather turned the voters' stomachs.

Eventually *The Alamo* did recoup its money and even returned a profit but it took a long time and meanwhile Wayne was obliged to mend both his reputation, which had taken a small knock, and his bank balance, which had taken a large one. *The Man Who Shot Liberty Valance* (directed yet again by his mentor, John Ford) did much to restore the former while a constant round of work, including cameo roles in the likes of *The Longest Day* and *How the West was Won*, helped take care of the latter.

(One of his cameo roles was in *The Greatest Story Ever Told* in which, as a Roman centurion looking on at the Crucifixion he was required to utter the line: "Truly this man is the Son of God." There is a popular, though no doubt apocryphal, Hollywood story that after the first take of that scene George Stevens, the director, approached him and said: "Duke that was . . . that was great, Duke, but see, this is Christ up here on the cross. What that line needs is awe. Do you think you could do it again and this time give it just a little awe?" Wayne said: "Sure, George." So they set the scene up again and Stevens said, "Action!" and Wayne said: "Aw, truly this man is the Son of God.")

By 1964 Wayne's career and finances were once more in a flourishing state but now his health began to trouble him. He was fifty-seven years old and smoked four packets of cigarettes a day and he suffered from pains in his chest. So in September he went into the Scripps Clinic in La Jolla, California, for tests. The diagnosis was cancer of the lung. At the time this was revealed Wayne was preparing to film *The Sons of Katie Elder* for the director Henry Hathaway and he broke the news of his illness and his impending operation to Hathaway and to his son Michael in somewhat tragi-comic circumstances.

Michael Wayne said: "I remember he came into the office and said, 'Sit down, I want to tell you something.' I didn't know what he wanted to tell us but he said, 'I've got the Big C' and I think Henry thought he meant the clap, if you'll excuse the expression, because he said, 'Well, you know, they've got penicillin and things like that.' My father said, 'Look, I've got cancer, Henry, I've got cancer in my lung and I've got to have the lung removed.' Well, he was talking to the right guy because Henry Hathaway had also had cancer and Henry said, 'Well, we'll just postpone the picture for a few weeks,' and that's exactly what they did. They postponed it for maybe four weeks. My father went into hospital, had the lung removed and then Henry Hathaway had him up at 6,000 feet in Durango, Mexico, in freezing weather, jumping in and out of rivers. And my father said, 'That Henry is a mean old son of a gun but I think he really got me through this thing.' "

The four-week postponement is perhaps something of an exaggeration; Pilar Wayne said it was closer to four months, but Michael Wayne's story illustrates the apparent bravado with which his father treated his illness. He showed no fear, though he must have felt some (as Michael said, "he wasn't dumb so I know he had to be worried about it") and when he came out of hospital he made his now famous pronouncement: "I've licked the Big C."

This, it should be remembered, was before people talked so openly about cancer as they do now and for a star of Wayne's status to admit that he had had it was remarkable to say the least. For him then to add that he had "licked" it, as if it were Geronimo or some similar marauding redskin, served only to add yet another facet to the Wayne legend.

Once recovered from the operation he continued to work as hard as ever, making four films in three years before embarking on his second, and final, attempt at direction with *The Green Berets*, a story set in Vietnam and prompted, just as *The Alamo* had been, by his fervid patriotism. This was in 1967, a time when the Vietnam War was becoming increasingly unpopular in America and even the Pentagon advised him that it would be a mistake to make the picture. But Wayne went ahead anyway, largely because he conceived the film as a tribute to the troops.

Michael Wayne said: "He didn't necessarily support the Vietnam War. He supported the fact that we should be there but I don't think he supported the conduct of the war. But he did support the soldiers who were fighting there. He felt that they were the bravest and best soldiers we ever fielded and he felt that they didn't get a fair shake. So what he did in *The Green Berets* – what *we* did because I was part of it as producer – was to show them as heroes. And I guess that was the terrible thing because the criticism of the film took the form of a review of my father's politics."

Whether that was the case or not the picture received a terrible pasting when it opened in June 1968. The *New York Times* critic wrote: "It is so full of its own caricature of patriotism that it cannot even find the right things to falsify . . . No acting, no direction, no writing, no authenticity, of course." Viewed now, some fifteen years later, it doesn't seem quite that bad – no worse anyway than many another gung-ho war movie – and certainly Wayne believed until he died that it was a true and honest film.

In Big Jake *with his youngest son, Ethan, portraying quite convincingly his own father's grandson.*

In True Grit *which won him his only Academy Award for best actor.*

The way *The Green Berets* was received by the critics and his peers in the industry (though not by the public who rather enjoyed it) hurt Wayne deeply but, as ever, he swiftly bounced back. In July 1969, hardly more than a year after the disastrous opening of *The Green Berets*, he was hailed enthusiastically for his performance in *True Grit* in which, under the direction of Henry Hathaway, he played the fat, one-eyed, bellicose and elderly US marshal, Rooster Cogburn. His portrayal may well have been, as many people claimed, the best he ever gave and certainly it was good enough to win him, at last, the Academy Award for best actor. He received the Oscar in April 1970, at the age of sixty-three and after making 141 films in forty-two years.

Looking back it does seem remarkable that it should have taken him so long because among those 141 films there were several other performances – in a great many of the Ford movies alone, for example – which would not have been over-rewarded with an Oscar, especially when you consider that a number of other actors of lesser stature and not noticeably greater ability had won Academy Awards long before he did.

Michael Wayne's explanation for the fact that his father had been so long ignored is this: "He wasn't really a part of Hollywood in the strictest sense. He wasn't a part of the Bel Air circuit; he was an individual. He didn't live in Los Angeles; he lived in Newport Beach and for a long time he wasn't even a member of the Motion Picture Academy. So he wasn't really the fair-haired boy. He was quite outspoken and he had a completely different political point of view from most of the people in town."

There may well be a good deal of truth in this because, although Oscars are supposed to be awarded on a straightforward assessment of a man or woman's performance, who is to say what kind of prejudices the voters bring to bear when they make their choice?

Until 1970, however, Wayne professed not to care very much about Academy Awards, possibly because he had only once before been in the reckoning. "But when he got nominated," Michael said, "he wanted to win. He was a fierce competitor. And when he won he was a happy, happy man."

With the Oscar behind him Wayne was once again Number One at the box office in 1971 and, despite his age, as much in demand as ever. Important as his family was to him, it was never as important as his career and as a consequence his third marriage suffered much as the other two had done. In 1973 he and Pilar agreed, amicably, to separate, having discovered gradually and over a longish period of time that they had less and less in common.

When the children were younger the family was constantly together; Wayne would hire tutors for them and take them with him on location. But as John Ethan and the two girls grew older it became more difficult to take them out of school for two or three months at a time. So Wayne, busy as he was, spent lengthy periods of the year away from home and on those occasions when he did return for a few weeks between pictures it was hard to re-establish any kind of normal life. Furthermore, while he was absent Pilar quite naturally developed her own interests. "I fell madly in love with tennis," she said, "and we decided to build a tennis club. And so I was very busy and kind of doing my own thing. Maybe, too, I was searching for my own identity. I don't know . . . But I do blame myself because I think it was partly my fault that we separated."

Repeating the pattern of his first marriage and divorce, Wayne remained on friendly terms with Pilar for the rest of his life and, as before, ensured that he stayed as close to the children as possible.

Meanwhile, the films kept coming his way – more Westerns, such as *Rio Lobo*, *Cowboys*, *Cahill*, *US Marshall* and *Rooster Cogburn*, a disappointing sequel to *True Grit*, in which he co-starred with Katharine Hepburn. But by this time cops and robbers had taken over from cowboys and Indians at the box office and Wayne, fearful of being left behind by the changing times, duly played cops in *McQ* and *Brannigan*.

By then he was in his late sixties, not in the best of health and hardly needed to work any more. Once Pat Stacy, his secretary and lover, asked him why he carried on at such a frenetic pace and Wayne replied: "A man never really grows old while he's still got a project."

Pat Stacy was the last woman in his life. She joined him in June 1972, as his secretary and became his lover one year later when, with a considerable degree of macho arrogance – he, after all, was sixty-six and she was only thirty-two – he swept her away to his bed. It happened one night in Seattle where they were staying on Wayne's yacht, the *Wild Goose*, while he filmed *McQ*.

"We'd been out to the opening of a movie one night," Miss Stacy said, "and we went back to the *Wild Goose*. I started to go to my state room, other people started to go to theirs, and he put his arm around me and it just seemed the most natural thing in the world to go with him."

After that . . . "He told me I was the only woman in his life," and that's the way it remained, although those last few years with Wayne cannot have been easy for her because he was frequently ill. The trouble really began soon after he made his last film *The Shootist* in 1976. On the face of it there seems to be a considerable irony attached to that film because in it Wayne played an ageing gun-fighter dying of cancer. But the irony was more apparent than real because he had, as he claimed, "licked the Big C" and had been free of it for a dozen years.

But now his heart began to trouble him and in 1977 he went into the Massachusetts General Hospital in Boston for open-heart

surgery. The operation lasted three hours and aroused so much public interest and anxiety that, in Pat Stacy's estimation, at least 200,000 letters, gifts and get-well cards flooded into the hospital.

The operation, which involved replacing a defective heart valve with one taken from a pig, was a success and Wayne went back to his home at Newport Beach to recuperate. But the reprieve was short-lived.

Pat Stacy said: "We thought everything was going to be fine again and he was planning on making another picture. And then one morning he said, 'Pat, my stomach hurts. It's been hurting for a few days.' I really thought, 'Oh, Duke, you've become a hypochondriac; you know, you've had so many problems, you just *think* something else is wrong." But her diagnosis, though understandable, was incorrect: the pains became worse and in January 1979 Wayne was back in hospital for what was expected to be a comparatively minor gall-bladder operation. Tests, however, revealed a malignant tumour and he underwent a nine-hour operation for the removal of his stomach.

Once again the hospital was inundated with phone-calls and letters from his fans and once again Wayne bounced indomitably back.

Three months after the surgery he appeared at the Academy Awards celebrations to present the Oscar for best picture to *The Deer Hunter*, a film which he actually disliked because it showed America and the American troops in Vietnam in an unfavourable light. He looked thin and haggard (he had lost three stone in weight during his illness) but he said: "Oscar and I have something in common. Oscar first came to the Hollywood scene in 1928; so did I. We're both a little weather-beaten but we're still here and we plan to be around for a whole lot longer."

In the circumstances it was a brave and defiant statement, because by this time the cancer was spreading throughout his body. Soon after that Academy Awards night he was back in hospital where, for the first time, he was overcome by despair and seriously contemplated suicide.

Pat Stacy said: "He asked me, he ordered me, to get his gun because he wanted to kill himself. He said I'd be better off, everybody would be better off and he would be better off because he'd gotten to a point where he couldn't eat any more."

141

She disobeyed the order and . . . "He seemed resigned to the fact that he had to fight it. He told the doctors, 'We have to do what we have to do because Pat and the kids have talked me out of killing myself.' "

Early in June 1979, Ben Johnson went to visit him. "Duke says, 'Ben, I don't know if I can make it or not but I'm giving it a helluva try.' Then about four days later they called and said he was gone. But he . . . he fought it right to the last, you know."

John Wayne died on June 11th, 1979, at the age of seventy-two. Just before his death he was received into the Roman Catholic Church, at least partly, Michael Wayne thinks, to please his children, who were all Catholics. And about the same time, around his birthday on May 26th, Congress authorised the minting of a special gold medal as a tribute to him. At the urging of his friend and frequent co-star Maureen O'Hara, the inscription on it read simply: "John Wayne – American."

Wayne himself could hardly have wished to improve on that and the public, which has since bought many thousands of copies of the medal, appears to accept it as a natural and fitting description of the man. But again one wonders why John Wayne should be regarded as typifying America.

One time, between our more heated political discussions, when we were talking about his career, he said: "I found a way of selling integrity in the movies." Well, it's a moot point whether integrity, once sold, remains integrity but I think I can see what he meant. In his screen persona there was a great quality of sincerity and dependability. Wayne was the man you would like to have with you on a cattle round-up or when you hit the beaches of Normandy; the man who could be relied on to protect you from the back-shooters. He was always honourable and fair, a man of his word. Those who knew and liked him maintain that as you saw him in the films, so he was in life and Wayne lent currency to this belief with his frequent assertion that, "I've spent my whole career playing myself." This was perhaps an arrogant and, at the same time, an over-modest claim: arrogant in that it asks us to assume that the man on the screen, a man of towering moral and physical strength and exceptional courage was merely a reflection of himself; and over-modest in that it belittled his own acting ability.

He was not a particularly versatile actor – nobody, for example, could have cast him in Shakespeare or a Noël Coward comedy – but he was a great deal better than most people gave him credit for, because he had the rare gift of making acting look easy and natural. And what tended to hide this not inconsiderable talent from sight was the sheer size of the man's own personality, which was such that whether he played a rancher or a marshal, an army officer or an ex-boxer seeking his roots in Ireland, he always seemed to come out John Wayne.

Kirk Douglas, who starred with him in *Cast a Giant Shadow* and *The War Wagon*, said: "He was the type of star that doesn't really exist any more and I think he began to believe his image. He developed that one macho character and he believed in it sincerely. When I played Van Gogh in *Lust for Life*, they had a special showing of it and Wayne was there. After a few drinks he motioned me out to the terrace and we had a talk and he was furious. He said, 'Kirk, how can you play a weak character like that? Fellows like us, we're the tough guys.' He thought I was not being true to my class."

Wayne was always true to his class – or rather to the class he adopted as his own. The public knew little or nothing of his avid reading, his love of Shelley, his collection of Red Indian dolls, his interest in art and antiques or his passion for chess, for these things hardly went along with the image.

To his fans he was the common man, writ large: Everyman, if you like, but greater than that. He was Super-Everyman. All the characteristics that Americans in particular admire in a man, Wayne possessed. He liked pretty women but was never dominated by them; he played poker for fairly high stakes; he loved the sea and deep-sea fishing; he preferred the company of men and was known to enjoy settling a "friendly" dispute with a fist fight; and he drank.

His drinking indeed was legendary in itself. He was not, by all accounts, an alcoholic, but when the mood was upon him his consumption of alcohol was formidable and occasionally – not very often – he had the endearing habit of appearing in public with perhaps a slug too many of "who-hit-John" under his belt.

Michael Wayne said: "They say he drank enough to float a battleship. Well, he did. I've seen him drink a bottle of brandy after dinner – and that's after consuming maybe a bottle of tequila or a bottle of gin *before* dinner. But he would only drink when he wanted to drink. In other words, he didn't *have* to drink and he didn't drink most of the time. But if he had a weekend clear, he might drink the whole weekend."

All these qualities, along with the fact that he looked larger than life and faced his personal adversities with considerable bravery, played their part in forming the legend of John Wayne. And then, too, as Mark Rydell, his director on *Cowboys*, put it, "There was a sense of the individual in him. He felt that the group was by nature weak and that the individual was the most

important element in our society. And he felt that he represented the individual – individual thinking, individual courage."

The result of all this was that he became, in the words of his son, Michael: "The symbol of the American man. I guess it's kind of like England. There you have knighthood and chivalry; here it's cowboys and the West. He became the symbol of the cowboy and all those virtues that were ascribed to the cowboy, he had."

That America, during the last knockings of the twentieth century should still be looking for a cowboy to admire, is not quite as curious as it sounds. Harry Carey Jr. said: "He was just the perfect guy at a time of so much doubt and fear. He seemed to be the epitome of what our country should be. I don't know whether he could have

Michael (left) and Patrick, who followed Dad into the family trade as, respectively, producer and actor.

143

been elected president or anything like that but he was our hero. He was the kind of figure that our country needed."

On a similar theme Andrew McLaglen said: "He's part of the American scene, as American as apple pie. And he stood for this country – on a nationalistic level, on a personal level, on a father image level, on a hero level. He was a lot of things to a lot of people."

To a certain extent, of course, what all these men said is true – except that, whether they realised it consciously or not, they weren't really talking about John Wayne but about the *image* of John Wayne.

There is an element of make-believe, even perhaps of self-deception, in what they saw in the man and I think Wayne himself helped to foster that. In his home he had one room – a room, Claire Trevor said, that was bigger than her entire apartment in New York – full of awards and tributes and medals and God-knows-what that had been sent to him over the years. He was very proud of them all, naturally. But the danger in keeping mementoes of that kind is that, after a while, it becomes easy to convince yourself that all this adulation is for you, personally, and not for the character you have projected in the cinema.

What happens is that a movie star creates an illusion; the audience believes it and eventually the star can come to believe what the audience believes. And that, I think, is what happened with John Wayne.

The fact of the matter is that he never actually did anything heroic in his life. It's true that he faced illness and great pain with much fortitude but that's a different kind of courage; it isn't heroism.

Through no fault of his own he did not fight in the Second World War; he never won the West, rescued a damsel in distress, foiled a villain or tracked down a murderer. Well, the opportunity to do any of those things is given to very few of us.

But to the American public he *was* a hero: he was all the American heroes rolled into one. It's difficult to think of any other country in which an actor can come to represent all that is finest in his nation. Perhaps it could only happen in America where the difference between dreams and reality is often blurred around the edges and it's easy to mistake the shadow for the substance.

Wayne's shadow, cast huge on the screen, looked like the epitome of the all-American male and so the legend arose that the substance was the same. That's why they have put up all those statues – not to a man, not to an actor, but to a legend.

John Wayne would surely have approved; because in the end I think he, too, came to believe the legend.

Leslie Howard

Around midday on June 1st, 1943, a squadron of German fighter-bombers attacked and shot down a civilian airliner carrying thirteen people from Lisbon to London. The plane plunged into the sea about 180 miles off Cap Finisterre. There were no survivors.

Now why the Nazis chose to destroy this obviously neutral aircraft is one of the unsolved mysteries of the war. Many theories, none of them wholly satisfactory, have been put forward to explain what was quite simply an outrage, a callous disregard of one of the basic tenets of warfare; but it is just possible that one of the targets, one perhaps among several, was a fifty-year-old British actor, Leslie Howard, who had been lecturing in Spain and Portugal on behalf of the Ministry of Information and the British Council.

It's a romantic notion: the might of the Luftwaffe pitted against one unarmed, middle-aged Thespian and, to be fair, it is not the most popular explanation for the attack. And yet it's by no means entirely implausible. For just about three decades on stage and in the international cinema Howard had represented a version of the Englishman that was, in fact, romanticised but so skilfully projected as to appear archetypal: he was slightly vague, slightly shy, slightly – but never too obviously – intellectual and above all decidedly glamorous. To say that most Englishmen aren't really like that is merely to state the obvious; but to an international cinema audience the men of other nationalities weren't like that at all and therefore Howard served admirably as an Identikit portrait of the perfect English gentleman.

Such an image was not, of course, likely to endear him to the Nazis but on the other hand it could hardly, by itself, have enraged them sufficiently to set a whole squadron of fighter-bombers upon him. But in the early years of the war Howard was also a kind of talisman, a symbol of resistance, and his propaganda work for Britain in the form of broadcasts to America in the days when the United States was still neutral and in films like *Pimpernel Smith* and *The First of the Few* had earned him an honourable place on the Nazi hate list. So it's not altogether inconceivable that the Germans wished him dead and, given an opportunity to kill him, promptly seized it.

Whatever the reason for his death, the manner of it brought an appropriately tragic and romantic end to the life of one of the most popular and successful of all British film stars. In the words of George Cukor, who directed him both on stage and screen, he was "mysterious in a very odd way and his death was mysterious too. He sort of went off in a cloud and one never knew what happened to him. He died a kind of heroic death and that was right."

Leslie Howard wasn't really mysterious, though, except perhaps in the context of Hollywood where the stars tend to reverse the policy of the iceberg and reveal at least nine-tenths of themselves to the public gaze. In such a place Howard might easily appear mysterious because he always retained a peculiarly British obsession with privacy. His emotions and his relationships – above all his relationships with women, which were many and varied – were matters that he regarded as being of interest and importance only to himself.

In Hollywood where, generally speaking, even a movie star's most casual one-night stand is accorded a blow-by-blow account in the gossip columns, Howard

PREVIOUS PAGE: *Leslie Howard in* Berkeley Square *in fine debonair form, and* OPPOSITE, *in* Gone with the Wind, *one of his least favourite parts, with Gable, Ward Bond and Olivia de Havilland.*

145

The image of the perfect English gentleman and a truly accomplished philanderer.

Stainer, Hungarian by birth, British by adoption, who worked in a stockbroker's office in the City and his mother was Lilian Howard. The *Dictionary of National Biography*, however, had a slightly different version according to which his surname was actually Steiner and his mother's original maiden name was Blumberg. Furthermore, Leslie Howard is accorded an entry in the *Encyclopaedia Judaica*, leading to the assumption that he was, if only on his mother's side, Jewish. It's not improbable that both accounts of the family surname are correct, that on arrival in Britain Frank Steiner became Stainer and Lilian Blumberg became Lilian Howard.

What is, however, certain is that soon after the arrival of their first child, Leslie, Steiner-Stainer and his wife, the ex-Miss Blumberg-Howard, moved to Vienna with the result that their son, who was later to represent everything that was English, spent the first few years of his life speaking only German. When the family returned to London, Frank Stainer – as he now was, whatever he may have been before – again found work in the City and he and Lilian had four more children, among them a daughter, Irene, who was considerably younger than her brother Leslie.

She remembered him as "a dreamy kind of boy, thinking of everything except what he should have been thinking about, certainly in the way of schooling". This schooling took place at Dulwich College, which Leslie disliked intensely on account of his shyness and where he indulged in the most un-British habit of writing plays in Latin. "He was always thinking and dreaming of something else," Irene Howard said. "He never seemed to be quite with one. But on the other hand he was very alert, he didn't miss much really."

The dominant figure in the family was Lilian. Frank Stainer appears to have been a rather stern pater familias to whom his elder son was never very close but Lilian, a frustrated actress herself, encouraged the boy to take part in amateur dramatics in which, once he had left school, he sought relief from the drudgery of the bank where his father had found him a job. He and the bank were by no means suited to each other and there were no regrets on either side when, in 1914, Leslie volunteered for the Army and became a subaltern in the 20th Hussars.

would indeed have been an object of curiosity, because while he was alive he was regarded as an impeccable husband, practising unswerving fidelity, and it was only after his death that he was revealed as an accomplished philanderer whose track record, in the considered opinion of Humphrey Bogart, was such as to make "Errol Flynn look like a fag". (Mind you, there are those who now suggest that Errol Flynn *was* a fag to which one can only retort that if this were so he did quite an incredible job of establishing heterosexual cover for himself.)

The antecedents of Leslie Howard, the accomplished but studiedly vague philanderer, do admittedly add another small touch of mystery to the story of his life and death. The standard account of his background is that he was born Leslie Howard Stainer in Forest Hill, London, on April 3rd, 1893. His father was Frank

During an early leave at home he became engaged to a young woman whose name is now forgotten but who was known for some reason as "Buzz". At that time Leslie was not, according to Irene, at all a wordly man as far as women were concerned but clearly he had an innate ability to handle the sex because, on his return to his unit at Colchester, he struck up a friendship with Ruth Martin, a secretary in the local recruiting office and the daughter of a Regular Army officer. Such was the trust that women misguidedly placed in him that for some time he remained engaged to Buzz despite the fact that his letters to her were adorned by postscripts from Ruth, assuring the innocent fiancée that she was taking care of him.

A situation like that clearly could not last very long, even for the young Leslie Stainer, and eventually he discarded the unfortunate Buzz and became engaged instead to Ruth, whom he decided to marry at once. Irene Howard said: "There was a tremendous commotion going on because his Commanding Officer sent a telegram to my father saying, 'Your son intends to marry tomorrow.' So my poor father rushed down in a frenzy to see what it was all about. The CO, thinking he was going

to help, put Leslie on some kind of guard duty but it was too late: Leslie and Ruth had got married the day before.

"So by the time my father arrived it was all over. And when he said, 'What on earth did you do this for?' Leslie said, 'I haven't the faintest idea.' So that was his idea of marriage. I don't think he realised what he'd done or why. It seemed a good idea at that particular moment, I suppose. You see, he was very lonely; he missed my mother a lot when he went into the army and he wasn't the sort of chap who liked drinking in the mess with the boys. Ruth was very beautiful when she was young and I suppose he found her a sympathetic girl who seemed to adore him and so he could pour out all his thoughts and ambitions to her."

Fortunately for Leslie, Ruth continued to adore him and to cosset him for the rest of his life, though there were many times when it cannot have been easy for her. In the early days, Irene said, "She was great fun. I liked her very much because we went around together and she didn't seem to be bored, even though I was only a child. My mother was marvellous with her because she got on well with everybody. Ruth and my elder sister more or less ignored each

Leslie Howard and his wife Ruth, who rescued him from his extra-marital adventures and even cured his boils.

other. I don't know that they disliked each other but they certainly didn't take to each other. Perhaps there was a little jealousy there because my sister and Leslie were very much of an age and I suppose they had been fairly close."

In 1916 Howard's regiment was sent to the front line in France and a year later, having lasted much longer than most subalterns, he was invalided out of the army suffering from severe shellshock.

Frank Stainer wanted him to return to the dull security of the bank but Lilian suggested that he might try to become an actor, a far more attractive prospect, and so later in 1917 Leslie Stainer, aged twenty-four, dropped his surname and became Leslie Howard, putative actor. In 1918, he also became Leslie Howard, father, when his son Ronald was born and soon after he was an established supporting player in the West End of London in Arnold Bennett's play *The Title*. Within another year he was appearing in short comedy films written by A. A. Milne and had enhanced his stage reputation in Milne's *Mr. Pym Passes By*.

Success had come fairly swiftly and painlessly to him and, not insignificantly, considering the future pattern of his activities, had already brought him to the attention of the postwar breed of newly liberated young women. Suddenly Ruth found herself relegated to the unwelcome position of wife to a glamorous young actor while girls only a few years younger but a whole generation bolder than she began to pay court to her husband.

It was not, however, until 1920 when Howard first went to America that she can have fully realised the seriousness of her predicament. He went, initially, alone to appear in a play called *Just Suppose*, which turned out to be a highly prophetic tale about the Prince of Wales falling in love with an American girl. Both it and Howard were warmly welcomed in New York and within a few months he could afford to bring his wife and son over to join him. But by then the essential damage had been done and Howard had been discovered by American women – not a particularly difficult trick because he never exactly hid from them.

On the other hand, it doesn't appear to be true to say that Howard actually chased women; he just never seemed to have the energy, or indeed the inclination, to run from them. John Houseman, who co-directed Howard's *Hamlet* on Broadway in the mid-1930s, reckoned that like most great seducers he was a predator who disguised himself as prey. "His Don Juan operation consisted of never wanting to say 'no' and he was a man relentlessly pursued by ladies. The poor fellow was never left alone. They chased him and he would sort of demur mildly but then there came the day when he just didn't want to say 'No' any more."

The secret of this enviable appeal to women is as indefinable as the secret of star quality in an actor. Anybody who could isolate the formula for either and bottle it could become a multi-millionaire overnight. In his sister's view even Howard himself didn't really know what it was that he'd got. "He never looked upon himself as a great glamour boy at all. And he certainly didn't consider himself sexy. In fact he liked to think of himself as rather intellectual. Perhaps it was his very difference that appealed to the American women. He didn't dive at them straight away and so they thought it was up to them to do the diving."

In any event they were diving at him like kamikaze pilots by the time Ruth arrived in New York to begin tracing out what was to become the pattern of their lives. Over the next twenty years she and her husband, either together or separately, continually trekked back and forth across the Atlantic, dividing their time almost equally between Britain and America, while Howard climbed nimbly and without apparent effort to the top of his profession both in the theatre and the cinema.

And all the time Ruth had to cope with the fact that while he was unquestionably devoted to her and their children, her husband was quite incapable of resisting the temptations offered to him by other women. Like a man cheating on his own diet he was constantly nibbling chocolates between his balanced meals at home.

After the success of *Just Suppose*, Howard returned for a year or so to London but the news of his New York fame had made little impression there and in 1922 he went back again to Broadway, where he was in such demand and appeared in so many plays that one theatre critic was prompted to write: "Leslie Howard seems

148

to have been in every first night I have attended."

In 1926 he returned again to London where again the success he had enjoyed in New York capriciously eluded him and so once more he returned to America, where his performance in *Her Cardboard Lover* had the first-night audience chanting his name in an ecstasy of enthusiasm and brought unanimous agreement that he was now among the foremost actors on the English-speaking stage. He repeated the role in London to rather less acclaim, largely because his co-star there was Tallulah Bankhead, who had become the object of a cult and whose hysterical devotees screamed so loudly that most of the dialogue was inaudible. The West End production was, however, notable for the fact that Howard failed to have an affair with Miss Bankhead, though not, apparently, for want of trying on her part.

"Poor Tallulah," said Irene Howard. "She couldn't make him out at all. She tried very hard, bless her heart, but he didn't want anything to do with her. She wasn't his type."

In 1930, after further stage triumphs in *Outward Bound* and *Berkeley Square*, Howard went to Hollywood for the first time. He had made no films since those early silent comedies but now Warner Brothers offered him the lead in the screen version of *Outward Bound*. It was the first of several of his stage productions – *The Animal Kingdom*, *Berkeley Square* and *The Petrified Forest* among them – to transfer successfully to the cinema. Howard's performance in the film *Outward Bound* looks, half a century later, to be distinctly over-theatrical and indeed over the top but the picture was well received and brought him into great demand among Hollywood tycoons.

In 1931 he appeared in four American films – *Never the Twain Shall Meet*, *A Free Soul*, *Five and Ten* and *Devotion* – usually in some kind of heart-throb role, as the cinema capitalised on his stage reputation.

But Howard never really took to Hollywood and the social life of Beverly Hills. He enjoyed the climate and he enjoyed playing polo. At one time he had a string of six polo ponies and they and the sunshine were his main consolation for having to spend so much time there. Irene Howard said: "He wouldn't stay in Hollywood five

minutes longer than he had to. He felt it was all a bit phoney and he had nothing in common with most of the people there. He was a funny man. He didn't really like actors very much. He was far more interested in writers or technical people."

Given his choice – and as far as the thing was possible he made quite sure that he was given his choice – he much preferred the life of a well-heeled country gentleman with Ruth, Ronald and Leslie (his daughter who was born in 1924) at Stowe Maries, his home in Surrey. Far more than any other British star, he skilfully maintained a thriving career for himself on both sides of the Atlantic and because he planned this rather than achieved it by accident he followed his initial flurry of Hollywood films by returning home to make his first British picture, *Service for Ladies* (or *Reserved for Ladies*, as it was called in the USA), for Alexander Korda.

With his son, Ronald, at Palm Springs enjoying the only thing he really liked about California – the sunshine.

149

Howard at home in Surrey, living the life of a well-heeled country gentleman.

of the pictures he made for Warners was *The Petrified Forest* which, thanks to the teaming of himself and Humphrey Bogart, is one of only a handful of his pre-war films that is familiar to modern audiences.

It was Howard, indeed, who was responsible for Bogart being given the role of the gangster, Duke Mantee. Warners didn't want him: they wanted Edward G. Robinson instead. But Bogart had played the role on Broadway and when Howard agreed to star in the film version he did so only on condition that Bogart should be in it, too. Furthermore, he stubbornly continued to insist upon this even when Warner Brothers put pressure on him to change his mind and Bogart, who was thus given his first significant chance in films, was so grateful that he later named his daughter Lesley in Howard's honour.

It was this kind of unshakeable resolution on Howard's part that also, I suppose, helps to explain George Cukor's description of him as "mysterious". On the face of it there was nothing tough about him at all. To those who knew him only slightly he gave the impression of softness. When she first started working with him Mary Morris, his co-star in *Pimpernel Smith*, thought there was "an old-womanish quality" about him but she soon came to change her mind and in the end she said: "I don't think there was anything soft or effeminate about Leslie. I think he was a man of steel really."

That view was echoed by Michael Powell, who directed him in *49th Parallel*, and said: "He always knew what he wanted. He was a very good businessman and a very strong man. My impression of Leslie is not of the slender, rather boyish-looking man that he appeared to be. I get the impression of a man made of steel, in mind as well as in body."

It was this slenderness, the lightness of his build, that perhaps gave the illusion of weakness but his son, Ronald, remembered him as "a physical man, although he was slight. He was proud of being a fairly physical personality, a sort of butch personality in a way, although he didn't look it."

But, on the other hand, Howard was clever enough, and perhaps steely enough, to appear to be weak and ineffectual whenever it suited his purpose. For example, in order to gain attention on those occasions when the people round him appeared, quite

But at this stage he was better known and more popular in America than he was in England and when the Korda film made only a slight impression at the box office in Britain he betook himself to New York again for another great success on the stage in *The Animal Kingdom*. This in turn rekindled Hollywood's interest in him and back he went for three more films. But he always retained a remarkable degree of independence. In an era when Hollywood's object was to sign its stars to exclusive contracts that left them with only a doubtful right to the freehold of their own souls, the longest contract Howard ever signed was a three-year deal for three pictures a year with Warner Brothers. This was negotiated in 1933 and he regretted it at once, on the grounds that though it guaranteed financial security it also guaranteed boredom and bad films. This was not an entirely charitable assessment because one unreasonably, to have other things on their minds than his well-being, he would affect ill-health and indeed he was, in a small way, a practising hypochondriac.

Irene Howard said: "My mother had had a bad heart and he imagined he had a bad heart too. I remember there was one occasion when he and Ruth were having dinner in a Paris restaurant and Leslie suddenly thought he'd had a heart attack. He said he had to get out, get out of the room, get out into the air. So he fell over people's tables and stumbled outside and Ruth was in a great panic, of course, and said, 'Oh my God, Leslie's ill, Leslie's ill!' There was a friend with them, a man friend, and Ruth said, 'Oh, do go and see if Leslie's all right.' So the man rushed out through the swingdoors and Leslie was sitting on the steps in the street and the poor man fell over him and broke his ankle. And Leslie sat up and giggled at him."

But he also had in his armoury an even more potent weapon than hypochondria with which to attract attention and also to extricate himself from awkward situations, and that was a carefully-cultivated air of vagueness. It was very much a pose, a mannerism that he adopted when, for instance, he was bored. "He was very vague on things he wanted to be vague about," said Douglas Fairbanks, Jr., who was both his friend and, on two occasions, his co-star in films. "But at the same time he could appear to be vague when in fact he was very alert. You could never be really sure that he had his mind concentrated on what he was doing." It was a characteristic noted and remarked on by all those who were in any way close to him but Mary Morris was not taken in by it. "I never believed in the vagueness," she said. "He'd say, 'Mmm? Oh, yes, yes', as if he wasn't paying attention but he would always go his own way in the end. Leslie's great thing was this gentle, quiet kind of personality and maybe he found that being vague was the best method of getting his own way."

John Houseman, the writer/producer/director, who in his later years turned character actor to such good effect that he won an Academy Award for his supporting role in *The Paper Chase*, was another person who was not deceived by the pose: "He didn't strike me as a vague person at all. He was shrewd, he was very much alive and he was a very intelligent man."

In the autumn of 1936 Houseman and Howard co-directed *Hamlet* on Broadway, with Howard of course in the title role. He had never been greatly interested in the classics, although at this time he had just finished playing Romeo (after Robert Donat had declined the role) to Norma Shearer's Juliet in the lavish MGM production. Both of them – Howard, forty-three, and Shearer, thirty-six – were really too old for the parts, a thought which crossed the mind of the director, George Cukor. In the event, though, Cukor thought Howard gave an interesting performance: "He wasn't the fiery Romeo, he wasn't daring and dashing but he spoke it beautifully." At the same time Cukor was quite certain that Howard would not have made a classical actor: "He didn't have the voice, or the posture. He was a different kind of actor."

Nevertheless he was determined to play Hamlet, had spent months talking about it, had enrolled Houseman to share the directing and had even raised the money for the production himself. So, in the summer of 1936, he left Hollywood and went back to England to get ready.

"He went off," said John Houseman, "to prepare himself for this great task of performing Hamlet but when he came back to New York in the fall, ready to go into rehearsal, he really hadn't done a thing. He had done a little thinking but he hadn't learned his words even and this interested me very much because here was this man, quite arbitrarily taking on this gigantic task – it was his own money, his own operation, he didn't have to do it – and yet his indolence was such that he didn't learn the lines."

Houseman found this "terribly surprising" but, "The more I knew him the more I learned that he was this very strange mixture of great energy and great strength and of indolence. And above all he struck me as the most fatalistic man I had ever known. I had the curious feeling that he figured the whole business of his career as a miracle: he'd been born in England, lived in Vienna, became an actor and suddenly overnight had become this extraordinary matinee idol. I think he really thought, as many of us do in the theatre, you know, that he was a victim of one of those accidents that take place and that he was a man who had been favoured by destiny and that whatever happened was bound to happen anyway."

Even without the initial handicap of a Hamlet who didn't know his lines, the Howard–Houseman production was rather an ill-starred venture altogether. There were many delays while Howard got himself ready and there were a number of belated changes in the supporting cast and all these led to an ill-starred arrival on Broadway.

Houseman said: "His timing was such that his arrival in New York coincided with the arrival of John Gielgud in that great production of *Hamlet*, which simply could not fail. John had done it a dozen times before but this particularly had all the auspices: he had Lilian Gish playing Ophelia and he had Judith Anderson, I mean it was an absolute gilt-edged production. But Leslie blithely arrived in New York in competition with Gielgud. I urged him, I begged him not to do it. He could have gone on the road with *Hamlet* and made a fortune and eventually, when Gielgud was out of the way, come into New York with the reputation of his road tour behind him. But, oh no, he came into New York and into one of the biggest theatres in town; it was too big for any *Hamlet* and far too big for his. His whole performance of Hamlet was very interesting because it was beautiful but rather small, rather sinuous, very intelligent. After the try-out in Boston, where we played the Opera House, which is also a huge place, his friends came backstage and said, 'You were wonderful but you are going to make it bigger, aren't you?' So he started making it a little bigger and by the time he opened in New York he wasn't giving that original performance – he was like the frog who wants to blow himself up into an ox and so in New York he was by no means at his best."

The critical reaction was bad. Quite apart from comparing his performance unfavourably with Gielgud's, the critics thought Howard was like "a petulant schoolmaster" or "a peevish choirboy". Houseman said: "I mean, everyone was appalled at the audacity or foolishness of coming in to show himself, in competition with John who was the great Hamlet of his time."

To be fair, Howard's performance was probably not as bad as the Butchers of Broadway said it was. After a disastrous run in New York, he took the production away, dusted it off, polished it up and then went on the road tour that Houseman had advised him to undertake earlier. "By the time he reached Los Angeles five months later," Houseman said, "he was back giving a very, very interesting and quite remarkable performance."

On the face of it, Howard's determination to set himself up in competition with one of the great classical actors of this century was a gesture of pure arrogance, but if so it would have been very much out of character. Howard was a man who not only knew his limitations but also, as a rule, made a very shrewd calculation of the odds. A few years earlier he had been invited to co-star in a film with Greta Garbo, without doubt the biggest female star of her time, and to everyone's astonishment had turned her down with this explanation: "She has a peculiarly dominating personality on the screen and that is why I declined the part. I should not hesitate to play opposite the most glamorous of stage actresses because a play can be depended upon to materialise as rehearsed. A picture is different. Added to the terrific competition of her personality, which no man has equalled, the film would naturally be cut to her advantage and then where should I be?"

In view of that very balanced assessment of the probabilities, it seems likely that he knew his Hamlet would be a gamble but took the chance anyway, either out of fatalism, as Houseman suggested, or, more probably, because he planned this one, big classical performance as his farewell to the theatre, for Hamlet was indeed his last appearance on the stage and he may well have intended it to be so from the start. Unlike most actors, Howard didn't really like acting. To both Douglas Fairbanks and his sister Irene he confessed that it embarrassed him, that he felt it was no way for a grown man to be earning a living.

Undoubtedly he enjoyed the material rewards that came with it and certainly nobody ever forced him to be an actor or to continue acting as long as he did. But the role of actor, and especially the role of matinee idol and star, made him uneasy. "I think he felt it was all right to start with," said Irene Howard, "when he was young and just getting going. But it didn't satisfy him later."

Stage acting in particular began to lose its attraction for him by the middle of the

1930s. His son, Ronald, believed that by then the constant repetition, night after night, of the same role bored him and drained him of physical energy. "The really physical actor enjoys it. He enjoys putting on the make-up, he enjoys the adrenalin charge he gets when the curtain goes up. But I think Leslie never quite recharged his batteries and after he'd been about six weeks in a production he'd explored all he could do with it, whereas in films there wasn't this repetition and boredom; every day brought a different set-up."

As time went by, even acting in films became less and less satisfying and his interest began to turn towards directing and producing. In 1939 he took his first step along that path by co-directing (with Anthony Asquith) Gabriel Pascal's film version of *Pygmalion*, in which he played Professor Higgins.

The picture was an enormous success (and is still absorbing to watch even today) despite the fact that Howard and the author, George Bernard Shaw, had serious disagreements about it. Irene Howard said: "Leslie tried to say that Higgins was obviously in love with Eliza but Shaw wouldn't have it. 'Oh, no, no,' he said, 'nonsense. He's just interested in her as an academic proposition,' and Leslie said, 'You don't realise what you've written. The man's in love with her. Couldn't we suggest this in one line at the end somewhere?' But Shaw still wouldn't agree. So Leslie had to suggest what he felt in the way he played the part and managed to get it over."

Shaw, much disgruntled by the way things had turned out, wrote when the film appeared: "It is amazing how hopelessly wrong Leslie is. However, the public will like him and probably want him to marry Eliza, which is just what I don't want." He was right about one thing at least: the public did like Howard. They also liked the film, though without Howard they might not have done. Wendy Hiller, who played Eliza, said: "It wouldn't have had a world market if Leslie hadn't played it. He was the only possible person at that time to do it. If you were criticising you could wonder whether, in the purely Shavian sense, he was entirely successful. But he *was* entirely successful for the film."

Pygmalion, however, did far more for Howard than merely confirm his status as a top-ranking romantic actor and open the

way for a new career as a director. Indeed it had the most dramatic effect upon his life because during the course of it he fell in love. Up to this point – and with only one exception – Howard's extra-marital adventures had, broadly speaking and in the words of his son, Ronald, taken the form of "a sort of high-wire act with various attractive ladies. He had a kind of ethereal quality, there was always something held back, something intangible and I think women found this particularly fascinating. And he was very sensitive to admiration from women but I don't think he was too carried away. He always kept the thing in perspective and he was very discreet."

The only time he had come close to falling off the high-wire was in his affair with Merle Oberon. This probably started around 1934 when they made *The Scarlet Pimpernel* together, smouldered on for some while and then burst into leaping flames the following year when Howard was appearing on Broadway in *The Petrified Forest*.

He was then so taken with the lady that he left the family home in New York and moved into an hotel to be with her. This, in itself, was unusual. In the past when he was involved in one of his dalliances Howard might not have come home until dawn but at least he had come home. Now, however, he had broken away from wife and children and for the first and only time Ruth seriously considered divorce. She left New York for Los Angeles to give herself time for thought before she made any irrevocable decision and in the meantime the Oberon affair fizzled out.

It ended in most unromantic circumstances when Howard was afflicted with an attack of boils with which he coped far less philosophically than Job had done, though admittedly in rather different circumstances. Miss Oberon apparently was perfectly prepared to provide comfort and solace but Howard decided that in these dire straits there was only one woman who could really help him and that woman was Ruth. So he took himself and his boils back to her.

But it had, for a while, been quite a famous affair and, unusually, news of it had reached the press. A reporter, approaching Howard on the subject, asked if there was any truth in the rumours of a possible divorce and Howard, bristling with

153

self-righteousness, replied: "Certainly not. No man would throw away the sort of family life I enjoy. My wife and children are essential to my existence."

And indeed this was true. Howard was passionately fond of his children and, in his own way, of Ruth. But if they were essential to him so were his extra-curricular adventures. The accepted explanation for his conduct is that when a woman made him an offer he couldn't refuse he was too weak even to contemplate refusing it. But unless he suffered from satyriasis, which is possible but unlikely, there must have been some deeper psychological reason for his multitudinous affairs. Perhaps this endless parade of casual women scratched some philanderer's itch that otherwise he couldn't reach.

In any event he needed his family and he needed his women but, with the exception of the Oberon escapade, he kept his emotions, if not his appetites, under control until he made *Pygmalion* and fell in love with a young French woman named Violette Cunnington. She was the secretary and assistant to the producer of the film, Gabriel Pascal, and she was about twenty years younger than Howard, who was then forty-five, a dangerous age for a man to fall in love – or at least as dangerous as any other age.

By the end of the film Violette had become Howard's personal secretary and travelled with him to Hollywood where he was to make *Gone with the Wind*. Later, to avoid scandal and to kill off the rumours that were beginning to surround them, Howard brought Ruth and Leslie out to Hollywood and established them in a house in Beverly Hills, the only house he ever owned in California. But at the same time he set up Violette in another house only a few streets away and spent at least half his time living there with her.

About that relationship with Violette Cunnington, Ronald Howard said: "It was the most serious affair in his life, without any question. She was the most charming girl, most attractive. In fact I fell for her myself. At that time [during the making of *Pygmalion*] I didn't realise how serious the affair was. I just thought that he was rather lucky at his advanced age to have such an attractive young secretary. I thought no more about it than that."

In those early days, first in London then in Hollywood, the affair was still comparatively discreet and probably accepted by Ruth as just another passing fancy on her husband's part. Howard, in any case, was much involved with playing Ashley Wilkes in *Gone with the Wind*. This is perhaps his most famous role but it is also the one that in a certain respect has done his reputation the greatest harm. He disliked the part intensely and resisted offers to play it for some time, arguing that "I haven't the slightest intention of playing a weak, watery character such as Ashley." In the end the producer, David O. Selznick, overcame his resistance by offering him, as a quid pro quo, the leading role (opposite the young Ingrid Bergman) in *Intermezzo* and – this was the clincher – agreeing to let him co-produce that picture.

That Selznick knew what he was about is proved by the success of *Gone with the Wind* and the excellence of Howard's performance in it. But that Howard, too, knew the dangers is equally proved by the fact that he is now largely remembered as Ashley, a fact that does a gross disservice to his memory. Those who have only seen him in *Gone with the Wind* – and they must be counted in millions – will for ever think of him as "a weak, watery character" and will probably never realise that it's an immense tribute to his ability that, though he was not in the least weak and watery, he could project such an image so memorably.

While *Gone with the Wind* and *Intermezzo* were being made, Howard continued to lead his double life in Beverly Hills but by now it was the summer of 1939 and war in Europe was clearly inescapable. So together with his family – and Violette – he returned to England for good. He was planning to go there anyway to make a film (which never in the end got off the ground) called *The Man Who Lost Himself*. But his agent, not exactly an unbiased witness after all, capitalised on his client's move by extolling his "typically English, blind, unswerving loyalty to King and country" and indeed this was not entirely hyperbole. Howard by then was forty-six years old and he could easily have sat out the war in America. Many other British actors did so, after all.

But both Ronald Howard and Michael Powell believe firmly that in this time of national peril England was where Howard wanted to be. And so, inspired by patriotism as much as anything else, he returned to Britain and again set up two separate homes for himself: one in Surrey, where he deposited Ruth and his children, and the other in Denham, Buckinghamshire, where Violette was installed.

Ronald Howard said he knew then, for the first time, that the affair was serious. "He began to divide himself into two parts, as it were. He lived most of the week in Denham and came home to us at weekends."

Now at this point it may be wondered how Ruth reacted to this state of affairs and indeed how she had reacted over the years to all the other states of affairs in which Howard had involved himself. At times she seems to have been, quite understandably, extremely jealous of her husband's casual lovers.

But she always had, and must have known she had, an exceptionally strong hold on him. Marc Connelly, a member of the famous literary Algonquin set in New York, to which Howard had been an occasional visitor, once said: "Leslie is always afraid Ruth will go out in the morning before he's awake and forget to put the manacles on."

This is not, however, to suggest that Howard was at all henpecked; no husband who lived the way he did could possibly be so described. Rather did he use Ruth as a shield and a means of escape from difficult situations. The fact that until he met Violette he had never been inextricably involved with any other woman is probably due to his having allowed, or even encouraged, his wife to rescue him from entanglements that he didn't really want in the first place. Thus he was quite content to give the impression, to men as well as to women, that he was manacled to her.

"I think," Irene Howard said, "that she just sort of looked after him, mothered him, saw that he had everything that he wanted and of course he worshipped his children. He never would have broken up his home, of that I'm absolutely sure. And she would never really have gone off and divorced Leslie under any circumstances. Besides which, he was very discreet always. He didn't embarrass her." But he did use her; she was his excuse for his failure to do things he had never wanted or intended to do; she was the "heavy". If Howard let anybody down Ruth was always given the blame.

Douglas Fairbanks remembered her as the controller of the family finances. "I don't believe Leslie could sign a cheque by himself. He and I had a bet on something relatively trivial and he lost and he had an awful time paying me back. I didn't mind whether he paid me at all but his sense of honour required that he should. Nevertheless it took him about six or eight months to get around Ruth and explain what he wanted the money for. I think he was just allowed pocket money. Ruth took care of everything for him and paid the bills on his behalf. I think he was very dependent on her. I don't mean in a maternal sense, though he did seem to inspire the maternal instinct in women all over the world. They wanted to protect him and he didn't need any protection at all. But I think Ruth made herself over in such a way that he really would be dependent on her. I don't think she allowed him to be independent and I don't think he wanted to be either. He might have been frightened of her sometimes but on the other hand they did get along well and the marriage lasted a long time, so it was a good arrangement."

Violette Cunnington in
Pimpernel Smith.
Howard's relationship with her was "the most serious love affair of his life".

To John Houseman, Ruth was the stabilising influence in the marriage. She didn't, he thought, like her husband's philandering at all but she adjusted to it and as far as possible dealt with it. When the cast of *Hamlet* included "the most extraordinary collection of beautiful women", Ruth "simply didn't encourage the young ladies to moon around Leslie's dressing-room".

George Cukor, too, had the impression that occasionally Ruth fought off the women on Howard's behalf. "She was a very understanding lady but she didn't sit still all the time. There were some eruptions now and then, there must have been. To be married to a fascinating actor who has a roving eye is very difficult."

But if things had been difficult before they must have seemed well-nigh impossible when Howard fell genuinely in love with Violette Cunnington. That the matter was resolved without divorce, scandal or even bloodshed seems to be due entirely to the extreme tolerance and reasonableness of the two women. Of his mother Ronald Howard said: "She was a marvellous person. It's not all jam, you know, being the wife of a film star; you have to compensate for this butterfly you're married to and she compensated by being a very positive personality in her own right. She was very tolerant and understanding and I don't think Leslie would ever consciously have hurt her in any way. When we were young it was a very good marriage. It had its ups and downs with Leslie's flirtations and liaisons with various actresses but I don't think you can take that sort of theatrical relationship very seriously. Besides, he was successful in using his family as a sort of retreat, as an escape apparatus. Whatever happened he was always trying to get home to Ruth. That was his sanity really."

In the Violette Cunnington affair, however, matters were for once taken out of Ruth's hands and the compromise that was agreed upon was of Violette's devising. Ronald Howard said: "It was, let's say, a sort of French solution. Violette said, 'I will not break up your marriage, Leslie. We will do this in the French manner.' In France a man can have a mistress but he has to be married first and this was the case here." Violette accepted that Howard was firmly married and would not leave Ruth and so reconciled herself to the role of "other woman".

Ronald Howard said: "The protocol, the relationship between Ruth and herself was very good. They never clashed." Howard would return to his family at weekends and Violette encouraged him to do so. During the week he would live with his mistress. "On the surface everything went on perfectly equably. But of course underneath I presume Ruth was again very deeply hurt."

In the early war years, then, Howard divided himself neatly between two homes and otherwise devoted himself to helping his country in whichever way he could. He joined the "ideas committee" at the Ministry of Information and produced a document called "Notes on American Propaganda" in which he outlined his proposals for documentary films: "The first of these films should concern itself with placing the war guilt irrefutably upon the Nazis . . ."

He then put this theory into practice by co-writing, directing and starring in *Pimpernel Smith*, in which he played an English intellectual, a university professor, rescuing other intellectuals from Germany. The Germans hated this film, particularly Francis L. Sullivan's parody of Goering, and Howard was immediately placed on the Nazi blacklist.

While *Pimpernel Smith* was being made Howard had already started his series of "Britain Speaks", regular broadcasts to the United States whose object was to put the Allied case to the neutral Americans and enlist their sympathy and support.

That he was successful in this enterprise is evidenced by the fact that he earned the hatred of the German propaganda minister, Joseph Goebbels, and was denounced by the British traitor William Joyce, Lord Haw-Haw, who declared in his own broadcasts that once Britain was conquered Howard would be among the first people to be shot.

Undeterred by such threats Howard continued making films whose aim was at once to entertain, to raise morale and to plead Britain's cause to the non-aligned nations. *Pimpernel Smith* was followed by *49th Parallel*, directed by Michael Powell, and then by *The First of the Few*, which Howard directed and in which he played R. J. Mitchell, the inventor of the Spitfire. A critic later described it as "Leslie Howard's masterpiece and his monument".

When the film was completed he made

what was to be his final public appearance, in the role of Lord Nelson, in a pageant entitled *In Praise of Britain* which was held on the steps of St. Paul's Cathedral and soon afterwards began work on producing and directing (though not acting in) *The Gentle Sex*, a tribute to the women's army, the ATS. But while that was in production Violette Cunnington became seriously ill.

It was the autumn of 1942 and she and Howard were now living in a cottage at Stoke Poges. The illness began with a small and apparently insignificant swelling on her nose. The swelling gradually became worse and more painful and finally she was taken to hospital where, after two days, she died of cerebral meningitis.

"Leslie was heartbroken, really heartbroken," Irene Howard said. "It was such a shock, you see, to everybody – we were all very fond of her and her death was the last thing anybody expected. She was quite young and seemed very healthy and Leslie was completely shattered."

At this dreadful time once again Howard's dependence upon Ruth and her own remarkable qualities of sympathy and understanding came into evidence. As soon as she heard that Violette was seriously ill in hospital, Ruth went to London to comfort her husband. And when Violette died and he was so distraught that he had to be tranquillised, Ruth took him back to Surrey and nursed him for two weeks. At the end of that time when the sharpest agony of his grief had been somewhat blunted Howard announced his intention of returning to the cottage he had shared with Violette.

By then *The Gentle Sex* had been completed by Maurice Elvey and Howard, anxious to get back to the studios and give himself something else to think about, began work on the production of *The Lamp Still Burns*, a hospital drama starring Stewart Granger. Howard approached Wendy Hiller to appear in it and, she said: "I noticed an enormous change in him; physically he'd aged and looked very frail. Later somebody who was closer to him mentioned that after Violette's death the poor man had taken to spiritualism and was earnestly and hopefully trying to get in touch with her. It sounded so tragic, as though he couldn't face up to her loss. So she must have had a great impact on his life."

Violette Cunnington was originally buried in the Mortlake cemetery, near the hospital where she died. But later Howard had her body moved to the churchyard at Stoke Poges – the churchyard of Gray's *Elegy* – because that was close to the cottage where they had lived together, the cottage which, he told Ronald, was "absolutely haunted. He kept hearing her voice and felt she was walking behind him through the rooms."

He had still not recovered from the loss of Violette when, in April 1943, he was invited to undertake a lecture tour – a propaganda tour, in effect – of Spain and Portugal on behalf of the British Council. He was reluctant to go on the grounds that lecturing was not his forte and agreed to do so only after the direct intervention of Anthony Eden who, after Winston Churchill, was the most senior member of the Government.

He was accompanied on the trip – an extremely successful one – by his accountant, Alfred Chenhalls, a burly man who somewhat resembled Churchill himself. Both in Spain and Portugal Howard was accorded a film star's reception wherever he appeared to lecture on *Hamlet* and to show *The First of the Few*.

The two men's travel arrangements were vague and right up to the eve of their eventual departure for home they had made no plans to return. It was only on that night that Chenhalls declared he could stay away no longer and made the reservation on Flight 777 from Lisbon to London.

There were, in fact, no vacancies available but Howard had flight priority – indeed he was the only person on the plane with that privilege and thus the only person who, once he had made his reservation, could be quite sure of a place aboard. And he and Chenhalls were given their seats only after two other passengers were taken off to wait for a later flight.

The following day, on June 1st, Flight 777 took off for London and three hours later was attacked and destroyed by the German squadron. Among the many theories that have been suggested to explain this action the most widely held is that the Nazis believed Alfred Chenhalls was indeed Winston Churchill. Churchill himself subscribed to it but there is no evidence to support it. And it does seem wildly improbable: what would Churchill have been doing in a totally unprotected aeroplane in the middle of the war?

The Germans put forward a number of contradictory reasons for the attack. First they said that Flight 777 was an armed plane, then that it was a fighter, then that it was escorted by bombers and finally that the whole thing was an error by unbriefed pilots. But none of them is plausible. With so many aircraft involved and in broad daylight there was no possibility of a mistake: the attack had been deliberate.

Ronald Howard, who did extensive research into the matter after the war, said: "I don't think they were only after Leslie. That was perhaps a plus for them, I don't know. But they were certainly after three other men who, I feel, were probably more important than Leslie."

One of these men was the head of the petroleum company, Shell, and was also rumoured to be the head of the British Secret Service in Lisbon; another was the head of the London branch of the Jewish Agency for Palestine and had been involved in helping many Jews to escape from Europe; and the third was an important executive of the British steel industry.

Certainly the death of any of these three would have been more important to the Nazis than the death of a mere actor and it probably is too far-fetched to suggest that the plane was attacked on Howard's account alone. It's much more likely that he was merely one of a whole job lot of people whom the Germans preferred dead but, nevertheless, he was by no means an insignificant target. In 1945 the *British Film Year Book* described his wartime presence in England as "one of the most valuable facets of British propaganda" and propaganda, as the Nazis would have been the first to appreciate, was a vitally important weapon.

In Britain Howard's popularity was immense and his death was mourned more widely and more deeply than perhaps that of any other British star. In a dark and perilous time for the nation he had been a glitteringly romantic figurehead but he was also far more than that. Even without his wartime activities he would still have occupied a prominent place in any history of the British cinema, for he was a brilliant and versatile actor – not a heavyweight perhaps, but at the very least an outstanding middleweight.

He had great comic timing, a superb lightness of touch and innate humour, all of which made him ideal for sophisticated comedy. But he also had, or could assume, an air of gravity which made him equally at home in drama or tragedy. And there was, too, as his son said, that ethereal quality, an apparent detachment that meant that when he was on screen he was the one you watched, no matter who else was with him. To think of him only as Ashley Wilkes is to ignore the greater part of his ability.

In the international sense he was not perhaps a great star, rather he was, as Douglas Fairbanks put it, "a very fine co-star. When he made *Secrets* with my stepmother, Mary Pickford, it was considered a great coup for her to get him because of the prestige of his name, not because of his drawing power. He was not himself a great star but those who were great stars looked upon him with the highest respect and awe."

That he was not a great star in the cinema – though he had certainly been one in the theatre – was entirely a matter of his own choice. The kind of superstardom that, in the 1930s, could be conferred only by the backing of a big studio which, in exchange for the exclusive use of his services, would have built him up and sustained him in the public eye by constant and careful exposure, was his for the taking. But it was not something he wanted. He refused to settle permanently in America, he refused to sign a long-term contract with any Hollywood company and in fact he only appeared in twenty-five films.

Always he preferred independence, the freedom to pick the roles he wanted and the wider enjoyment to be derived from pursuing his career on both sides of the Atlantic and in the theatre, until he grew bored with it, as well as the cinema.

Nevertheless, despite the comparative rarity of his screen appearances – it's interesting to note, for example, that while Howard was making his twenty-five films Clark Gable was appearing in forty-five – he occupies a special niche of his own. Just as Gable was thought in his time to epitomise America, so Howard with his grace and style, his wit and charm was firmly believed to epitomise England and though he may not have been the greatest movie star Britain has ever produced he was, in his own way, without equal.

Marilyn Monroe

I only ever saw Marilyn Monroe once. She and I were in the audience at a Sunday night performance at the Royal Court Theatre in London in 1956 when she was in England to film *The Prince and the Showgirl*. God knows what play they were doing that night: I only remember Marilyn – white-blonde hair like vanilla-flavoured candyfloss and an oddly timid expression, as if she were afraid of something. The audience perhaps, people like me who just stared at her. It's a very un-English activity to stare at complete strangers but you couldn't help staring at Monroe. She simply sat there in the stalls, doing absolutely nothing to attract attention and yet arousing so much interest that the play itself was a mere diversion in the background, performed valiantly and no doubt excellently but more or less unnoticed.

She was married then to Arthur Miller and him I met twice. The first time was at the gates of the house in Surrey where they were living and where she had been taken ill. He came out courteously enough to tell me and other members of the press that he had nothing very much to say.

Our second meeting was in Ireland some years later when Miller was visiting John Huston to discuss the forthcoming production of his screenplay *The Misfits*, Monroe's last completed film. I arrived at the house a few minutes behind Miller, just in time to see the butler, a young Irishman in a white coat, accost him on the doorstep.

"Yes? What do you want?" asked this butler.

Miller said: "My name is Arthur Miller. I have an appointment with Mr. Huston."

"Just wait a minute," the butler said and then, glancing back over his shoulder into the house he called, in the formal manner of Irish butlers, "Mr. Huston, there's a feller here to see yez."

On such flimsy evidence it is, I know, quite unfair to say that I was not much impressed by Arthur Miller, but I was overwhelmed by Monroe. I admired Miller, of course, as a writer but sitting there in the house with him and Huston I wondered what Monroe had ever seen in him. No doubt Miller's friends, especially later when she was dead and ever more scurrilous memoirs of her were coming out virtually every hour on the hour, must have asked themselves the same question in reverse. But that's how it always was with Monroe: either you were for her or against her; there was no intermediate course, no room for indifference.

Norman Mailer once described her as "every man's love affair with America" and at her peak she was certainly that: an object both of lust and adoration, the most marvellous symbol of sheer femininity in the history of the cinema, the ultimate Sex Goddess proudly presented to the world by the United States of America in general and Twentieth Century-Fox in particular. There were other sex goddesses around at the time, not least Sophia Loren and Brigitte Bardot, but they stood on pedestals slightly lower than Monroe's. Loren was totally a woman, sophisticated and ungirlish; Bardot was a petulant, dangerous child and Monroe was a devastating combination of the two.

It was America who created her, set her up way on high (the better no doubt to stare up her skirt) and it was America who tore her down again. I wonder why. When you look at the books and the magazine articles that have been written about her and are still being written about her, two

decades after her death, it almost seems as if there was a national need to believe that this woman, who once had been idolised, was not only no better than but in fact a great deal worse than anybody else. Perhaps it's something in the egalitarian American soul that denies anybody the right to be different, to be "special". All right, the argument seems to run, so Monroe was sexy. So what? She was also a slut and a whore; she was a no-talent; she was neurotic and megalomaniac; she was undependable; she was a drug addict. Columns of personal reminiscences, ghost-written on behalf of people who barely knew her, make these points again and again and are eagerly devoured by a public that says, "See? I told you so."

What on earth had she done to deserve such treatment? Whom, apart from herself, had she ever really hurt? Well, it's true that she often made life extremely difficult for film directors and producers but these are big, strong men (or, if you prefer, since men of power in the film industry are often of diminutive stature, small, strong men) well equipped and handsomely paid to deal with temperamental actresses. It's also true that she had three marriages and none of them worked out but at least one of her three discarded husbands continued to love her until the day she died and indeed he probably loves her still.

I find it hard to believe, in fact I refuse to believe, that she was the monster posterity has decreed her to be. I believe rather that she was a victim, a sexual Wizard of Oz, a confused and bewildered creature who used the remarkable physical gifts with which nature had endowed her to keep at bay a world that, on the whole, simply frightened her.

Heaven knows she started off with the kind of background, the kind of handicaps, that were most likely to set her off in any direction other than upwards – into delinquency, perhaps, into crime, into prostitution. She was born on June 1st, 1926, in Los Angeles and was registered as Norma Jean Mortensen. She was registered thus because Mortensen happened to be her mother's married name but whether her father was Mortensen himself or another fellow entirely, named C. Stanley Gifford, is very much open to question. Not that it really matters a great deal because Mortensen, a baker, and Gifford, an employee

of a firm called Consolidated Film Industries and her mother's more or less casual lover, had disappeared from the scene before Norma Jean put in her appearance. Thus she was either the legitimate daughter of a vanished husband or the illegitimate daughter of a vanished boyfriend, neither of which is a particularly desirable start in life. In any event she was certainly the child of a one-parent family.

This, of course, is not necessarily an insuperable obstacle to a happy life but Norma Jean's mother was a considerable handicap in herself. She had been born Gladys Pearl Monroe, later – on her first marriage – became Gladys Baker, then Gladys Mortensen and, at the time her daughter was born, she was working as a negative cutter in the film industry. But she was also mentally ill and came from a family with a long history of mental illness. She suffered from paranoid schizophrenia and spent lengthy periods in various asylums, clinics and mental hospitals.

So, in effect, Norma Jean grew up without a father and, for much of the time, without a mother, too. Because of Gladys' mental condition she was shunted about from one foster home to another and in 1935, when she was only nine, she was placed in the care of the Los Angeles Orphans' Home in Hollywood. There she stayed for nearly two years, a traumatic experience because she knew all along that she was not an orphan. She kept telling people so but nobody took any notice. Once she tried to run away but was found again and taken back. In later years she told positively Dickensian stories of the way she was treated in the orphanage, alleging that she was made to wash up and scrub floors all day long. These tales were, at best, exaggerated. Life in the orphanage cannot have been easy but it certainly wasn't brutal. Norma Jean's memories of it probably reflect her mental, rather than her physical, wretchedness at the time.

In June 1937, however, she was rescued from this place by Grace Goddard, a friend of her mother, who first placed her briefly with foster parents and then took her into her own home. That time with Grace and Erwin Goddard was the happiest period of Norma Jean's childhood. Grace was perhaps the closest approximation to a mother of her own that she ever had and Grace's aunt, Ana Lower, was also a considerable influence on her, introducing her into the local Christian Science Church (Gladys, incidentally, was also a Christian Scientist) and giving her a religious belief to which she clung devoutly at least until she was in her twenties.

The Goddards lived in the town of Van Nuys, California, and Norma Jean attended the high school there from September 1941, until March 1942. She was then nearly sixteen, 5 feet 6 inches tall and already capable of doing wondrous things to the shape of a sweater. It was at this point that she met James Dougherty, who was around twenty-one, had a good job at the Lockheed aircraft plant and had been something of a celebrity in his day at the Van Nuys High School; an easy-going, athletic young fellow who, at the time Norma Jean entered his life, was much involved with another girl who had attained the lofty title of "Queen of the Santa Barbara Festival".

Dougherty had long been aware of Norma Jean as just another kid around the neighbourhood, nice looking certainly, but not to be compared with a Queen of the Santa Barbara Festival. It was only when Grace Goddard asked him to take the kid to a local dance that he realised that what he held in his arms was not a kid at all but a very nubile young woman and matters, he said, progressed from there in a way that was not necessarily in the best interests of the Queen of the Santa Barbara Festival.

Indeed, they progressed so rapidly that on June 18th, 1942, Norma Jean became Mrs. James Dougherty. To some extent the match was arranged by Grace Goddard, who believed that marriage was the best and most convenient way to get Norma Jean settled down. But Dougherty was at least willing and Norma Jean was enthusiastic since her groom was a good-looking young man, much sought-after by the neighbourhood girls and thus an excellent catch for her.

The bride herself was hardly more than two weeks past her sixteenth birthday, straight out of school and a virgin. This latter piece of information is not as impertinent or as irrelevant as it might sound because later on as Marilyn Monroe's tales of her childhood became ever more lurid and unreliable one of the claims she would most frequently make was that she had been raped by a lodger at one of her foster homes when she was only nine. Another claim was that she had had an illegitimate child when she was fifteen. Dougherty, however, would lend no credence whatsoever to either of those stories. "I was the first," he said. "Believe me; I know. There's no way she could have had a child and there's no way she could have been raped."

To begin with the marriage was happy and carefree enough. Dougherty taught his bride to shoot, fish and skin rabbits and she in return taught herself to be a neat and efficient housewife and an original cook who planned her dishes according to the colours of the ingredients. Peas and carrots featured prominently on the Dougherty menu because she thought they looked pretty nestling side by side on a plate.

Dougherty's memory of his first wife, nearly forty years later, was of a bright, warm, attractive girl with few friends of her own (mainly, he thought, because other women regarded her as a potential threat), who then – as later – was in urgent need of love, recognition and attention. "I imagine," he said, "that I was kind of like a father and a brother as well as a husband to her." But she needed to love as well as to be loved and so, early in the marriage, she wanted to start a family. Dougherty, however, dissuaded her. "I felt she was too young emotionally to begin raising children. I wanted her to wait at least until the war was over. She begged me to let her have a baby but I said, 'No, not yet, not yet. Wait until you're a little older.' "

Generally speaking this was the only point of disagreement between them although there was, he recalled, another occasion when he upset her rather badly. "She wanted to bring a cow into the house one time because it was raining and the cow was getting wet and was mooing and I told her, I said, 'You can't do that. That's crazy.' She felt very bad, you know, because I mentioned the word 'crazy'." From then on he was careful not to repeat the error because even the most jocular accusation of craziness would "make her become pensive and worried", and this was due to the family background of mental illness. Of that she was reminded during the early days of her marriage when she was reunited with her mother. "When they first met," said Dougherty, "it was almost like strangers because Norma Jean hadn't seen her since she was a small child."

162

Gladys was then spending one of her increasingly brief periods out of hospital but, as Dougherty said, she was never really cured and even at that time was showing signs of the religious mania that later was to dominate her personality and that was to confine her to an institution where she was supported by her daughter.

The idyllic part of the Dougherty marriage ended when Jim was inducted into the Merchant Marine and was sent overseas. There was little he could do about that, America being at war at the time, but nevertheless Norma Jean regarded his leaving her as a form of rejection. Dougherty argued, reasonably, that it wasn't anything of the kind and that he was hardly a free agent in the matter but she was not to be convinced. "I think one of the worst things her childhood left her with was a sense of rejection," he said. "So many times she was transferred from one foster home to another and each time to her it was a rejection. When I went overseas she saw it as another rejection and I think that was one of the things that started the beginning of the end for us."

When her husband was away, Norma Jean's security went, too. She was obliged to give up her own home and move in with Ana Lower, Aunt Ana as she called her, and fond as she was of Aunt Ana she was lonely without Dougherty. To counteract this her mother-in-law found her a job at the Radio Plane factory. It was a fairly humble, manual job but one day an army photographer called in to take propaganda pictures on behalf of the war effort and decided to use Norma Jean as a model. She revealed a natural talent for the work and the photographer recommended her to a modelling agency in Los Angeles.

From that moment she was embarked upon a new career: the agency signed her up and soon her photographs began to appear in a large number of magazines. Dougherty had no objection to the modelling work but gradually, as she developed the ambition to become an actress, he began to grow worried. "I knew that if she got into the movies she was going to run into problems. It's a dog-eat-dog world with a lot of phonies in it and I knew she wouldn't be able to handle that."

Norma Jean, on the other hand, believed she could handle it. The modelling work became more and more important to her

and by the time her husband came home on his second leave from the Merchant Navy she was on the covers of twelve different magazines. On that occasion she was an hour late meeting him off the train. He didn't think it too significant at the time because punctuality was never one of her virtues but, as he learned later, her failure to be at the station waiting for him was due to the fact that she had been taking a film test. "She never told me," he said, "because she knew I wouldn't approve." More accurately she didn't tell him then; she waited until he had returned to his ship in Shanghai and then revealed all in the "Dear John" letter that is dreaded by every serviceman abroad.

"She wanted a divorce," he said. "Of course, she couldn't divorce me while I was overseas because I wouldn't sign the papers until I could get home and talk to her. Then she told me she was going to be an actress and said they wouldn't even consider her until she was divorced, because they didn't want her having babies once they'd spent the money to bring her from a starlet to a star. She said, 'Even though we're divorced it doesn't keep us from being together. You can come and see me, take me out.' I said, 'No, thanks,' and that was it."

At first Dougherty rejected the idea of a divorce altogether, but by now Norma Jean was sharing a tiny apartment and indeed a bed with her mother and when, on his next

Monroe the starlet, aged twenty-two, and just another plump, near-blonde around Hollywood.

leave, her husband arrived at three o'clock in the morning there was nowhere for him to sleep. The following day they met to discuss their future and: "It was very emotional. We both cried and she said, 'I've got to go this way. This is my chance,' and I said, 'Well, that's it,' so I signed the papers."

If all this appears to be ruthlessly self-centred behaviour on Norma Jean's part, it's perhaps worth remembering that she had, rightly or wrongly, felt rejected by her husband's absence abroad and that in the modelling and cinema worlds she was for the first time in her life being treated as an individual in her own right, as somebody of importance. She was at last being given recognition and attention and these can be highly seductive to someone who has been totally deprived of them.

The divorce from Dougherty became final in September 1946, and by then Norma Jean was twenty, although she wasn't to remain Norma Jean for very long. Three months earlier she had been to see Ben Lyon, the head of casting at Twentieth Century-Fox, who was sufficiently impressed to offer her a contract at 75 dollars a week. He also decided that she should change her name. Henceforth she was to be Marilyn, after the musical star Marilyn Miller whom Lyon very much admired, and Monroe because that was the maiden name of Norma Jean's mother.

The name was not the only thing that was changed. Some time after she had signed the contract she talked on the telephone to Dougherty who asked her, with some concern: "What's the matter, you got a cold or something? Your voice sounds so low, so different."

"Oh," she said, "I had to lower my voice because they told me it was more sexy."

But what kind of person was this newly created Marilyn Monroe with the low, sexy voice and the tight clothes that caused her to wiggle so devastatingly when she moved? It has been suggested that at this time she was busy working her way to the top on the casting couches of Hollywood. But if so this would seem to indicate that she had changed her personality as drastically as she had changed her name because Dougherty was convinced that she had been faithful to him, despite his absence abroad, until the marriage ended.

And Ben Lyon, too, refused to believe the stories of her early promiscuity. When I talked to him a few months before he died he remembered her as a very nice girl, a rather lonely girl who lived modestly and – on her small salary – quite often in debt at the Studio Club, a sort of YWCA for young actresses. Once she was so broke that she asked him to lend her a few dollars, an occasion he recalled vividly because, he said, she was the only person in Hollywood who ever borrowed money from him and insisted on paying it back.

At the same time he didn't exactly deny that the opportunity to advance her career prostrate on a casting couch was absolutely denied to her. Quite often, he said, producers at the studio would call him up and remark casually, "That new blonde you've got, what's her name, Monroe, is it? Well, I may be able to offer her something. Send her up to my office at six o'clock." Both Lyon and Monroe were perfectly aware that anything that was likely to be offered to her in a producer's office at six o'clock in the evening would have very little to do with films and he didn't believe she ever accepted any of these invitations. The circumstantial evidence at least suggests that he was probably right, for had she been more sexually compliant her career at Fox would surely have prospered far more than it in fact did. During her brief initial spell at the studio she appeared only in two minuscule parts in very negligible films and after a year her contract was dropped. In the first, *Scudda Hoo! Scudda Hay!* a romantic comedy starring June Haver, she was virtually an unidentifiable figure in the background in a boating sequence and in the second, *Dangerous Years*, a story of juvenile delinquency, she was seen for about two minutes.

Had she been promiscuous the most significant thing that happened to her at Fox might have been the fact that she attracted the attention of Joseph M. Schenk, an executive producer at the studio, who was already about seventy years old. He was a prominent figure in Hollywood who had been married to Norma Talmadge and at one time or another had been chairman of Universal Artists, founder of 20th Century Productions and head of Twentieth Century-Fox. On a less fragrant note he had also been involved with union racketeers and, during the early 1940s, served a prison sentence for tax evasion.

If she had offered such a man more than friendship, the studio would hardly have treated her in so cavalier a manner as it did. But Schenk, who had set himself up as the young starlet's protector, failed to intercede on her behalf – or certainly failed to intercede effectively – when Fox decided not to take up its option on her services, though he did persuade Harry Cohn of Columbia to put her under contract and it was at that studio that she played her first significant role in *Ladies of the Chorus*.

It was there, too, that she acquired her first drama coach, Natasha Lytess, who, from then on, was always on the set when Monroe was working. (Always, that is, until her pupil discarded her some years later in favour of Paula Strasberg.)

In Monroe's early days at Columbia there was talk of giving her a screen test for a certain role and John Huston, the director, overhearing this talk came to the conclusion, no doubt accurately, that what the test in fact amounted to was an elaborate trap to get her into somebody's bed. Rather nobly and without even knowing her Huston sprang to the damsel's rescue by volunteering to direct the test himself in colour and with John Garfield playing opposite her, thus making the proposition so expensive that it was reluctantly dropped by its proponent. Huston claimed that by his action he had "warded off a fate worse than death for Marilyn Monroe". Whether he did or not, the episode casts an interesting light both on her character and her relationship with Joe Schenk. In the first place it seems unlikely that anyone would go to such lengths to bed her if she were, as has been alleged, already a willing occupant of casting couches. And in the second place if Schenk, still a powerful man around Hollywood, was, as has also been alleged, more than just a protective grandfather figure it seems equally unlikely that some studio producer or director would risk incurring his wrath by trying to seduce his girlfriend. There was, after all, no noticeable shortage of pretty blondes around, most of whom could safely be lured to a casting couch without upsetting anybody. The blondes themselves might be upset, of course, when having given their all they found themselves discarded but they were hardly important and certainly not in the way that the likes of Joe Schenk were important.

Around this time, too, there was another small but significant event: one day, while she was filming *Ladies of the Chorus*, Monroe failed to report for work. An emissary was sent to enquire the reason for this absence and found her in her room at the Studio Club quite ill with hunger. Her salary was small, her debts – for clothes and rent – were large and she had simply been unable to afford the money to eat. Once again the strong implication seems to be that, no matter what might be claimed to the contrary, she was not Schenk's mistress; or if she was his mistress it was clearly a role she played for love and not for money.

With the completion of *Ladies of the Chorus* Columbia, like Fox, decided she had no future to speak of and dropped her contract. Once more Joe Schenk appears to have been of very little help. So in the autumn of 1948, aged twenty-two, she was again a free agent. She appeared briefly, though quite memorably, in *Love Happy* when she wiggled outrageously into the office of private detective Groucho Marx and said: "Some men are following me," and just as briefly and far less memorably in *A Ticket to Tomahawk*, but by the summer of 1949 she was so hard up that when the photographer Tom Kelly asked her to pose in the nude for a calendar picture and offered her fifty dollars to do so, she agreed.

These days when it's comparatively rare for even the most serious young actress to be allowed to keep her knickers on in a film for more than about ten minutes, posing nude for a calendar is hardly sensational.

In her first film, Scudda Hoo! Scudda Hay! *Monroe's role, minuscule to begin with, was deleted entirely in the cutting room.*

165

But in 1949 it was considered that only tarts went in for that kind of thing and it's a measure of Monroe's desperation that she agreed to Kelley's suggestion. From that low point, however, her fortunes began to improve. After a promotion tour for *Love Happy* she returned to Hollywood and met the second, and by far the more important, of her elderly protectors, Johnny Hyde, executive vice-president of the William Morris Agency. Hyde had been born in Russia and had come to America as a child acrobat with his parents' vaudeville act. When he grew too big to be hurled about with any degree of safety either to himself or the fellow acrobat responsible for catching him he became an agent and swiftly rose to the upper echelons of agency by discovering Betty Hutton and bringing Rita Hayworth to prominence. By the time he met Monroe he was fifty-three, suffering from a heart complaint and separated from his wife.

According to Rupert Allan, who was to become Monroe's press agent, Hyde was "brilliant and very successful, a very wealthy man. He was small and unattractive-looking, no physical presence to speak of, but he was devoted to Marilyn and she was very fond of him." He was in fact so devoted to her that he bought her contract from her original agent and set about making her a star, an aim in which he was somewhat hampered by the fact that Monroe was only the latest in a swiftly changing line of blondes in whom Hyde had interested himself.

It took some while before the rest of Hollywood began to realise that this time it was different, that this time he was really serious both in his love for and his belief in the girl. Hollywood woke up to this fact about the same time as Hyde's wife did. Producers reacted by looking at Monroe with new interest and Mrs. Hyde reacted by suing for divorce.

Hyde's promotion of Monroe was simple: he took her to every important function, restaurant and party in Hollywood and he talked about her to everyone he met. The first man of influence to succumb to this bombardment was John Huston who, on Hyde's insistence, let her read for the part of the dumb blonde in *The Asphalt Jungle*, which she did effectively enough for him to give her the role. When filming began Monroe reported for duty with her drama coach, Natasha Lytess, who had given up her job at Columbia to devote herself to her young protégée.

Huston said he didn't object to this attendance though he was surprised by it since it was "unique in my experience" for a supporting actress to turn up with her own individual drama coach. Whether the presence on set of Miss Lytess actually did any good he wasn't sure but on the other hand it didn't do any harm.

Johnny Hyde's next move on Monroe's behalf was to persuade Joseph L. Mankiewicz to give her the small but eye-catching role of Miss Caswell, another dumb blonde, in *All About Eve*.

Mankiewicz, who had been quite impressed by her work in *The Asphalt Jungle*, agreed to take her on and found that all went well as long as "I pointed her in the right direction and said, 'Repeat after me' every now and then, because she didn't know much about acting, she didn't know what to do with a line."

She seemed to him a lonely girl. When, at the end of a day's shooting, Mankiewicz and others would go out for a drink before dinner, "We'd find Marilyn having a drink by herself and we'd ask her to join us, which she would. But the next evening we'd again find her alone. She would never assume that we wanted her to join us or that she was indeed a part of our group."

Mankiewicz said this struck him as rather sad and added: "I also found it sad when one day she came on the set carrying a book under her arm. I thought it was a little odd for her and I said, 'Marilyn, let me see what you've got there.' It was *Letters to a Young Poet* by Rainer Maria Rilke, which was even more astonishing, because she had no idea who Rilke was. She said, 'I just go into the bookshop on Hollywood Boulevard and I pick up a book and open it at random and if what I'm reading interests me, I buy it. Is that wrong?'" Mankiewicz told her it wasn't wrong, but an excellent way to go about reading. What saddened him about the incident was the reflection it cast on her desperate need to improve herself. Together with her dependence on her coach, the carrying about of books which she might, or might not, actually have read all the way through indicates that even at that early stage in her career she was not content merely to be the dumb blonde that all of Hollywood assumed her to be.

All of Hollywood, that is to say, except Johnny Hyde, who doggedly continued pleading her cause in the offices of the mighty. In 1950 she was seen in six films and four of them, including of course both *The Asphalt Jungle* and *All About Eve* – the most significant of the six – had been set up for her by Hyde. That same year he also negotiated a seven-year contract for her with Twentieth Century-Fox. But apart from providing plastic surgery to remove a minuscule bump on her nose, this was virtually the last thing he was to do for her. At the end of 1950 Johnny Hyde died of a heart attack. By then Monroe was living with him at his home in Beverly Hills, having moved in to recuperate after her nose operation.

Almost from the first time they met Hyde had been eager to marry her but she always refused on the grounds that, fond though she was of him, she didn't love him enough for marriage. And she turned him down again when he proposed to her for the last time when literally on his death bed. His reason for doing so then was to safeguard her future, for as his widow she would inherit his very considerable estate and be financially secure for life. But the idea of marrying a dying man just for his money appalled her.

With Hyde gone, however, life became more difficult. Twentieth Century-Fox did little to promote her career because the head of the studio, Darryl F. Zanuck, had scant regard for her acting ability and thought of her merely as a marketable commodity, which indeed she was because the public swiftly took to her.

And that was just as well, for in 1952 there came the potentially destructive revelation that she had posed in the nude for Tom Kelley's calendar. "What did you have on, Marilyn?" the reporters asked her. "Just the radio," she said. In the circumstances this was the perfect answer since it apparently showed her to be precisely the delicious but empty-headed blonde that she played in most of her films and the public can forgive a delicious but empty-headed blonde almost anything. Far from destroying her career, the calendar revelation gave an enormous boost to the box-office receipts of her current film, *Clash by Night*.

At this point Monroe was constantly working. In three years, from 1950 to 1952,

she appeared in seventeen films but despite that, despite her increasing popularity, she was unhappy about the way her career was progressing. Neither her work with Natasha Lytess nor her enrolment in the acting classes run by Michael Chekov, a disciple of Stanislavski, could convince Zanuck that she was a serious and gifted actress. Furthermore, since the death of Johnny Hyde she had been living a more or less solitary life. True, in 1951 she had met, been greatly attracted by and begun an affectionate correspondence with the playwright, Arthur Miller. But he was married and living in New York and it was not until April 1952, when some friends invited her to make up a foursome at an Italian restaurant on Sunset Strip, that she formed any lasting romantic attachment. On that occasion her dinner partner was Joe diMaggio, a recently retired baseball player so revered as to be a national institution. Monroe had no interest whatsoever in baseball but even she had heard of diMaggio and the attraction between them was instant.

Inez Melson, who was Monroe's business manager from 1951 onwards, said: "I'm quite sure she loved Joe but one of the attractions was that he belonged to a big family. Every weekend, before they were married, Marilyn flew up to San Francisco to be with his family and I think she liked the idea of being part of it. I know she would have liked a family of her own. The thing she wanted most in the world was to be a mother."

In many ways 1953 was Monroe's best year. DiMaggio was a constant, devoted presence in her life, eager to marry her, and suddenly her career began to blossom. *Photoplay* magazine selected her as "the best newcomer of the year", thus proving that it takes many years to become a newcomer in Hollywood. Her eighteenth film, *Niagara*, in which she played an unfaithful wife plotting to kill her husband, established her at last as a star and she followed this with two delightful comedies, *Gentlemen Prefer Blondes* and *How to Marry a Millionaire*. On the debit side there were, as ever, differences of opinion with her directors, partly because she would only put her trust in Natasha Lytess. Never mind whether the director was satisfied with a particular take, if Lytess gave it the thumbs down Monroe would insist on doing it again. And again. And again. Still, by and large, the only event that seriously marred her onward progress that year was the furore that attended the gala evening at which she picked up her *Photoplay* award.

Monroe chose for this occasion a dress so revealing that diMaggio refused to escort her and even Joan Crawford, hardly the most demure of women, was moved to attack her in print for "flaunting her sex". Monroe was deeply distressed and yet later in the year, when she and Jane Russell were jointly granted the accolade of being asked to leave their hand and footprints in the cement outside Graumann's Chinese Theatre on Hollywood Boulevard, she suggested that being who they were they should perhaps leave the imprints of their breasts and buttocks as well.

It was the kind of impish remark which, taken together with her lapse of sartorial taste at the *Photoplay* award, underlined the contradiction in her character which she was never really to resolve. On the one hand there were the acting lessons, the drama coaches, the desire to be taken seriously; and on the other her almost narcissistic pleasure in and display of her magnificent body. (A few years later when she was making a film for George Cukor it became so apparent that she wasn't wearing any underwear at all that the continuity girl approached Cukor and said: "We've just got to do something about that five o'clock shadow.")

Such incidents merely lent ammunition to those who mocked her longing to be taken seriously. How could she hope for respect, they argued, how could she expect her ambition to make a film of *The Brothers Karamazov* to be greeted with anything much better than ribald mirth, when she flaunted herself like that?

The answer quite possibly is that Monroe was an innocent who saw no connection between the way she looked and her acting ability and if that were so she at least had an arguable point. There's nothing in the rules that says actresses who wish to play in films based on classic novels must be built on the general lines of broom handles; equally there's nothing in the rules that says a woman as superbly constructed as Monroe should not take pride and pleasure in her body and, by transmitting her own pleasure, enable countless millions of cinema goers to enjoy it too.

In January 1954, Monroe and Joe diMaggio were married. It was a curious match because, apart from the fact that by then they were both national institutions, they would appear to have had very little in common. He was a shy and reticent fellow who disliked and distrusted Hollywood and was perfectly happy to sit around watching television of an evening; and she was, well, she was simply Monroe. What diMaggio offered her, though, was love and the part of her that was still Norma Jean was always in search of that.

As it turned out, however, love alone was not enough. As part of their honeymoon Mr. and Mrs. diMaggio went to Japan, where he was to promote baseball, and to Korea, where she did no end of good for the morale of the American troops by waving her hips at them.

By 1953 everyone, not just Monroe, had discovered that Gentlemen Prefer Blondes. *For her stardom started here.*

169

Her second husband Joe di-Maggio, the baseball star. It was the marriage of the all-American hero and the all-American heroine and, perhaps not surprisingly, it didn't last.

In both countries there is no doubt that Monroe was the greater attraction and diMaggio began rapidly to understand that he had acquired more than a wife: he had acquired the world's Number One sexpot, an object of adoration and lust. Another movie star might have been able to accept that; a retired baseball player could not so easily do so.

Thus the problems that were to end the marriage were already starting to reveal themselves. Eight months after the wedding Monroe was beginning to drink too much and was going to a psychiatrist. This was not diMaggio's fault; true he was possessive and, understandably, a little jealous since no husband could take much pleasure in watching other men openly leering at his wife. But the main problem was that Mr. and Mrs. diMaggio were simply incompatible, no matter how much fondness existed between them.

And so when Monroe set off for New York to film *The Seven Year Itch* diMaggio did not accompany her. He did join her later but, in retrospect, it might have been better had he stayed at home because he arrived just in time to watch the filming of that famous scene when Monroe stands over a grating and the breeze from below blows her skirt up around her neck.

Billy Wilder, the director, described the occasion thus: "Two things happened which amused me greatly: (a) there were 20,000 people watching, held back by police and barricades and (b) there were fourteen electricians killing each other over

who was going down under that subway grid and working the fan that was to blow her skirt up. Well, it all got so out of hand that we couldn't shoot the scene there on Madison Avenue. The crowd and the electricians got unruly. So we went back to Fox and dug a hole there and twelve more electricians fought for the job."

Meanwhile, on that night in Madison Avenue, diMaggio was standing on the sidelines, shocked and embarrassed.

Wilder said: "I'd have been upset, you know, if there were 20,000 people watching my wife's skirt blow over her head. (She did wear panties, mind you. Please.) But there was take after take and, well, you know New Yorkers. There were various little comments being shouted from the sidelines and diMaggio didn't like it very much."

Not surprising, really. In the mid-1950s a glimpse of lady's knickers, be they ever so chaste, was a rare sight and not one which any husband would wish to share with 20,000 cheering strangers. Questioned by a reporter, diMaggio refused to comment on what he had just witnessed and the following day he returned to California. A few weeks later, in mid-September 1954, Monroe consulted a lawyer and soon afterwards the press was formally told that the diMaggios were separated. Billy Wilder said: "It was always a kind of strange marriage to me, the kind you invent for an MGM picture – you know, the Lady and the Boxer, with Max Baer and Myrna Loy. Only in the picture they would never be married."

The break with diMaggio also coincided with Monroe's first temporary break from Hollywood. Soon after she completed *The Seven Year Itch* in November 1954, her previous film *No Business Like Show Business* was released and her notices were dreadful. If that were not bad enough Fox, unimaginatively, offered her yet another sex comedy entitled *How to Be Very, Very Popular*. In *No Business Like Show Business* she had performed a highly erotic dance number called "Heat Wave" in which she had worn very brief black panties and the effect, to the casual and prurient observer, was that she wasn't wearing pants at all but was, in fact, flashing her pubic hair. The prurient Ed Sullivan, a powerful columnist, described the scene as "frankly dirty". Embittered by this attack and the latest rubbish offered to her by her studio, Monroe declared that she no longer felt contractually bound to Fox and flew to New York to launch her own company, Marilyn Monroe Productions, which she had formed with the photographer, Milton Greene.

In New York Arthur Miller came back into her life, she began to study under Lee Strasberg at the famous Actors' Studio, *The Seven Year Itch* opened and was an immediate box-office success and she and Joe diMaggio were divorced. At the Actors' Studio (where a fellow student Eli Wallach found himself "amazed at her desire, her eagerness to learn") Natasha Lytess was replaced as her resident coach and guru by Strasberg's wife, Paula.

And on the advice of Milton Greene, and no doubt of Paula Strasberg too, Monroe renegotiated her contract with Fox on terms more advantageous to herself. She signed a new seven-year contract under which she would make only four films for Fox and would be free to do outside productions.

The first picture she made under this revised deal was *Bus Stop* in which, playing opposite Don Murray and directed by Joshua Logan, she gave what is still generally considered to be the best performance of her career. It's a minor tragedy that she was rarely allowed to play roles of such weight again, in this case the role of a pretty but shop-soiled singer in a tawdry night club who appears, to the young and innocent cowboy portrayed by Don Murray, as a sort of angel. With a few more films of that calibre in her record her reputation would have stood even higher than it now does. As it is – and in the words of Billy Wilder, one of the shrewdest and most percipient of Hollywood directors – "She made her name playing trivia, absolute, total trivia and to make it playing trivia is much tougher than playing Ibsen."

The film with which she followed *Bus Stop* was not exactly trivia but even so it was something of a disappointment. In 1956 Monroe now aged thirty went to England to co-star with Laurence Olivier in the screen version of Terence Rattigan's *The Prince and the Showgirl*.

On the face of it this should have been quite a sensational pairing: the greatest English-speaking actor in the world and the sexiest woman in the world. But in the event – and for reasons that were totally beyond the control of Olivier, the director as well as the co-star – it was no better than mediocre.

Before she left for England Monroe had finally married Arthur Miller. The old friendship between them, rekindled by her arrival in New York in late 1954, had swiftly developed into something deeper and more passionate than that. Miller had left his wife and obtained a divorce in Nevada. But at the same time he was under investigation by the House Un-American Activities Committee on suspicion of harbouring Communist sympathies. It was an extremely awkward time for him but the pressure was greatly relieved by his public announcement that he was going to marry Monroe. At once the HUAC lost interest in him on the grounds, no doubt, that anybody who was about to marry the national sex symbol could not possibly be a Commie.

It was an odd time and they were odd circumstances in which to reveal an impending marriage and there are those among Monroe's staunchest friends who feel that Miller's behaviour was not entirely selfless. Rupert Allan, her press agent, said: "She thoroughly admired him. She thought he was a father figure and she thought he was a great talent and a great writer and a great intellect, all of which he was not. The way he announced their engagement was rather bizarre. He announced it to the press in Washington when he was up there for the HUAC, then he

Husband No. 3, the playwright Arthur Miller. The Body and the Egghead. This didn't last either.

The notorious – but by today's standards curiously innocent – nude calendar. "What did you have on, Marilyn?" she was asked. "Just the radio," she said.

Posing in England during the making of The Prince and the Showgirl. *The cheesecake shots were better than the film.*

telephoned her in New York and told her what he had done."

How did she react to that?

"She was surprised, she told me, but she was very happy."

Did she blame him for his action?

"No, no. She went out and campaigned for him. It was good for him, you see, to marry the All-American Girl image."

Leaving aside that parenthetical dismissal of Miller's professional ability, what he had done would certainly seem to be pragmatic, though not necessarily as cold-blooded as Mr. Allan makes it seem. There was no doubt that bride and groom were equally attracted to each other. Eli Wallach, a friend of them both, said: "I think they were very much in love. I found them a place to spend their honeymoon on Long Island and they were very happy together."

Yet Wallach, too, said he thought Miller was "very smart" to make his announcement at the time he did and it certainly helped him to get back the passport that had been confiscated from him in 1954. Even so: "I think he saw in her a vulnerable lady whom he could protect against all hostile forces and she saw in him a father, a man with knowledge, a creative person and that's what she wanted. I'm sure she entered the marriage with the idea that she was going to make a go of it this time, with the feeling that 'this is going to work'. I think both Marilyn and Arthur Miller were determined to make a go of their marriage, to prove to all the scoffers, to the press and all the intellectuals who said, 'How could you do this – Beauty and the Beast, the Brain and the Body – how could you do that?' that it could come true."

The couple were married in June 1956, and almost immediately left for England and the filming of *The Prince and the Showgirl*. For newly-weds this should have been an idyllic interlude; instead it was an unhappy time for all concerned. Monroe was insecure at the thought of acting with a man of Olivier's stature and insecurity meant that she was perpetually late on set. Paula Strasberg constantly interfered, over-riding Olivier's direction and making Monroe insist on countless retakes. In turn, Olivier became quite naturally irritated by the pair of them. By now Monroe was taking uppers and downers as a matter of habit and even her new husband was growing a little disillusioned.

Norman Rosten, the poet, who, along with his wife, had befriended Monroe during her spell in New York, said: "She was a difficult woman, you know. We liked her and we say the nicest things about her and she deserved them: she was a very gallant person. But she was trouble and she brought that whole baggage of emotional difficulties of her childhood with her. She was very insecure and she had psychiatrists in attendance, if not every day then a number of times a week."

One of the reasons for her emotional problems was the fact that she desperately wanted but was unable to have a child. Soon after she and Miller returned to America she did in fact become pregnant but it was tubular and had to be aborted. The inability to have children caused her deep depression – it was as though she were merely some kind of sexual toy and not a complete woman at all.

Whitey Snyder, her favourite make-up man in Hollywood, believed that "If she could right away have had a child – because she loved children so much – if she could have had one of her own to take care of I'm sure it would have helped her immensely."

But that, alas, was not then possible; nor was it ever possible. What she had, instead, was the bitter disappointment of an obligatory abortion. For a year afterwards she was away from the cameras, recovering from this personal tragedy and doggedly studying acting. Her partnership with Milton Greene was dissolved; she and Miller moved into a farm and then to an apartment on New York's East Side and it was August 1958, before she returned to the film studios to star with Jack Lemmon and Tony Curtis in Billy Wilder's *Some Like It Hot*.

By now her working pattern was fully established: as always she arrived on set with her drama coach (still Paula Strasberg) but now the entourage had grown to include her personal hairdresser, make-up man, press representative and various others whose titles and duties were unspecified.

A great deal has been made of the fact that at about this time Monroe was notoriously unreliable, that she was either late reporting for work or that she didn't turn up at all. The implication is that she was carried away by delusions of grandeur, believing herself to be so important that it didn't matter if she kept others waiting.

But against that it must be remembered that she had *always* been late, even when she was a mere starlet and a moment's lateness could have led to her dismissal. To attribute her apparently selfish and careless behaviour to conceit is to miss the point. Monroe's inability to be anywhere on time stemmed from her basic insecurity: it was not a lack of belief in herself but a lack of confidence in herself and these are by no means the same thing. You can, as she said, believe you have the ability to do a thing well but at the same time you can lack the confidence to go out there and do it. So even at the peak of her success there was an anxiety about her, a desire to please that spilled over into her performances and could be quite heartbreaking, invoking in both men and women a powerful urge to protect her. That insecurity stayed with her throughout her life and in her later years she tried to deaden it with drink and barbiturates. One of its manifestations was the fact that despite her status in Hollywood her friends were not other stars or directors or producers or executives but men and women in rather humbler walks of life: make-up men like Whitey Snyder, publicity men like Rupert Allan and theatrical gurus like Natasha Lytess and Paula Strasberg.

And another of its manifestations was her amazing inability to be anywhere on time, a trait noticed by Jim Dougherty in the days before she was even a model.

Now the psychological explanations for chronic lateness for appointments are too numerous to list but Monroe's own explanation is worth considering. Whenever she had an important date, she once said, she would lie for hours in a bath and quite forget the time. The bath was a treat not for Marilyn Monroe but for Norma Jean who, she claimed, as a child had invariably been obliged to bath in water already used by other people. And the subsequent lateness was a form of punishment, a rebuke – again not to the people who were waiting for Marilyn Monroe but to all those who had never waited for and never had time for and never paid attention to Norma Jean.

But touching and even true though this plea might have been it would have brought very little comfort to Billy Wilder, to Tony Curtis and to Jack Lemmon as they waited, hour after hour, for their tardy colleague to arrive.

173

Wilder said: "I wanted to strangle her because she was never on time and she never knew the lines. What I think it comes to is that she had no sense of time. She had a superb sense of timing, which is a totally different thing. She could be just extraordinary – she could be sweet, she could be warm, she could be trying very hard and then again she could be miserable, she could be offensive, she could be rude, she could be unapproachable and, worst of all, she just wouldn't show up, she wouldn't be around.

"I treated her every which way I could imagine to kind of help her along but it was very difficult. We were working at Fox – now she'd worked there for six or seven years and we'd have like 300 extras and she'd show up at two in the afternoon. I'd say, 'What happened?' and she'd say, 'I lost my way.' Now she was living at the same house, the studio wasn't moved overnight and yet she'd lost her way."

As a possible explanation for such conduct it might be worth pointing out that at this time Monroe was pregnant again. "One day," said Wilder, "Arthur Miller took me to one side. He said, 'Look, do me a favour, please. We've just found out that Marilyn is pregnant and we don't want anything to happen to the baby. So why don't you let her go home at four in the afternoon? Don't keep her here till six.' I said, 'Arthur, you know what time she turns up here?' He says, 'Well, she leaves the house at seven in the morning.' I says, 'She may leave the house at seven in the morning but she shows up here at eleven thirty and if I can get one shot by two thirty or two shots by four I'm very lucky. If she came on time she could go home for lunch and stay there.' "

If the lateness were not enough to complicate Wilder's life there was also the presence of Paula Strasberg and Monroe's occasional and in a way magnificent inability to remember her lines. Of the drama coaches and their importance to her, Wilder said: "I guess she was kind of like somebody who's not too steady walking and hangs on to a railing or a piece of furniture."

(There were others who said the drama coaches simply confused her and that she would have been a better and easier actress without them. But Rupert Allan believed they were psychologically important to her because "acting wasn't easy for her. It was a torment. She worried. She was filled with anxiety and apprehension.")

Of the inability to remember her words Wilder said: "For a good part of the picture she never fluffed a line but when she fluffed, boy, did she fluff. I remember a scene when the two boys [Lemmon and Curtis] were in a room disguised as girls and she was to knock on the door and say, 'It's me. Sugar.' [That was her name.] And she was to come in and since she was having problems in the love story she was depressed and she wanted to have some whisky. So they brought some whisky along and put it in the dresser and she was to ask 'Where's the whisky?' and she was to go to the dresser and find it. Well, we ran like forty-seven takes – and that was just outside the door. She would knock, the boys would say, 'Who is it?' and she would say, like, 'Sugar, it's me,' and we'd do it again. So finally, since she was outside the room we printed it up and pinned it on the door – 'It's me. Period. Sugar. Period.' Well, when she got that and actually got into the room she couldn't remember 'Where's the whisky?' So we went into every drawer in that dam dresser; no matter which one she opened there it was in huge letters, 'Where's the whisky?' She couldn't miss it but by now we're on take sixty-three and the boys, you know, they've been standing there since six-thirty in the morning in high-heeled shoes and they're crying with pain.

"So I say, 'All right, let's take ten minutes,' and I took Marilyn aside and I said, 'Marilyn, don't worry,' and she looked at me and said, 'Worry about what?' It just meant nothing to her."

This, alas, was not an isolated incident. There were several other occasions when they ran into thirty or forty takes and before the film was over Tony Curtis had developed such a passionate hatred for her that when he was asked one day what it was like kissing her, he replied that he'd rather kiss Hitler, which is a fairly considerable admission from one who had started his life as Bernie Schwarz in the Jewish sector of New York. No doubt he would withdraw that statement today but there's little doubt that he meant it at the time. And clearly the fact that she caused so much aggravation helped to account for the popular image of her around Hollywood as a temperamental monster.

174

Jack Lemmon, however, did not believe that the fluffing of lines or the lateness had anything at all to do with temperament. In particular the lateness, he said, "must have gone all the way back to her childhood. There were a number of things, I'm sure, that caused her to be unable, literally unable, to face something until psychologically she could do it. Nobody could say, 'Look, this is a professional commitment. You must do it.' She couldn't face it until she herself was ready. It was the same thing during takes. Very seldom do I remember Billy Wilder saying, 'Cut.' Marilyn would stop, because if she thought the scene wasn't going well, even though I did or Billy did or Tony did, she would suddenly stop in the middle and wring her hands and say, 'I'm sorry' and walk off for a minute. She had a built-in alarm clock and it just went off when things weren't going well for her."

Now that would appear to be an exceedingly self-centred attitude but Lemmon was convinced that there was far more to it than that.

"She wasn't just the giddy blonde, you know. She had a certain intelligence about her work and she was a gifted comedienne. There's no question about that. She understood comedy and she developed herself. Nobody gave her those marvellous mannerisms – that thin, high voice, the funny look, whatever it was that was Marilyn and that people imitate and never come up to. That was all her. She developed that character and most of the time she bent the part to her. She didn't try to be totally different as a character actor; she was smart enough not to do that. Ultimately I think she used what talent she had more fully than maybe any other actor I've ever known. Olivier, for example, probably uses eighty to eighty-five per cent of his talent and the rest of us use about the same: you try but you can't get it all. But I think Marilyn came close to using a hundred per cent of her talents. They weren't that big but, damn, she used them all. That's why she would stop in the middle of a scene – it may seem selfish and it is but it wasn't meant that way. It was the only way she could work. She knew her limits and she went to those limits. It wasn't easy for her: she was fighting all the time, struggling to achieve what she could, trying as hard as she could. She didn't have the talents of

some other actors, there's no question, but she was using more of what she had. It fascinated me to watch her work."

Whatever trouble she caused and whatever her reasons for causing it, *Some Like It Hot* was financially Monroe's most successful film. Professionally she had arrived at another peak but her life was once again in a mess. In November 1958, she had a miscarriage and the following year, still intent on having a child, she went into hospital for corrective surgery, although by then her relationship with Arthur Miller was under constant strain.

Her use of sleeping pills and wake-up pills had led on more than one occasion to an accidental overdose but the usage was in itself only a reflection of the fact – noted by Jack Lemmon during the filming of *Some Like It Hot* – that she was essentially unhappy. No doubt Arthur Miller was unhappy, too, and this shared state of wretchedness was only enhanced when early in 1960, while filming *Let's Make Love*, she had a celebrated love affair with her co-star, Yves Montand.

Montand himself was married to Simone Signoret and it seems fairly clear that neither he nor his wife took the dalliance

With Yves Montand during the filming of Let's Make Love *which, misguidedly perhaps, is what they did.*

with Monroe too seriously. Monroe, however, did.

During the preparations for the picture both couples, the Millers and the Montands, lived in adjoining bungalows at the Beverly Hills Hotel. They became friends, though nothing more than that until Simone Signoret had to return to Paris and Miller to Connecticut to get on with his writing. "And that," said Rupert Allan, "left the two alone, working together very closely and both physically attractive. What happened was inevitable I would have thought."

Inevitable or not, it wouldn't necessarily have been too damaging if the affair had remained secret. In any event it would have passed soon enough because Montand had no intention of wrecking his marriage on Monroe's account. Unfortunately it didn't remain a secret. "It was Yves," said Rupert Allan, "who let the cat out of the bag. He let Hedda Hopper, the columnist, come to interview him. He didn't know English that well and he admitted they were having an affair. Marilyn was unhappy that it came out in the open, I'm sure, because first of all it had to hurt Arthur Miller – in fact it enraged him – and she also didn't want to hurt Simone Signoret, of whom she was very fond."

The liaison continued throughout the making of the film but not for a great deal longer and Monroe, according to Rupert Allan, was "very much upset" when it ended with Montand's departure for France and a return to the conjugal home. It was a far deeper affair for her than it ever had been for him.

What is more it virtually ended Monroe's marriage, although both husband and wife agreed not to announce their decision to divorce until after the filming of *The Misfits*, the picture which Miller had written especially for her.

The shooting, directed by John Huston who had earlier saved her from that fate worse than death and then given her her first real chance in *The Asphalt Jungle*, took place in Reno. Clark Gable was the co-star and others in the cast included Montgomery Clift and Eli Wallach. Miller and Monroe, maintaining the pretence that all was well in their private life, lived in the same hotel, though she spent little time with him off-set, preferring the company of her entourage of six.

Eli Wallach said: "What was happening away from the film was infinitely more dramatic. He was in one suite, she was in another. They'd get together for a press conference but there was a coldness and a hardness in their relationship. And yet on the set in the film she had to be this lovely lady falling in love with this cowboy, Clark Gable. There was a turmoil in her that, I think, was making her ill."

And indeed she was ill. John Huston said: "The girl that did *The Asphalt Jungle* was tremulous, young, aspiring, ambitious and obviously glowing. The one that was in *The Misfits* was not tremulous but trembling, an addict, hooked. She'd dived off the high board and the swimming pool was empty."

By this time, he said, she had become quite dependent on drugs to put herself to sleep. "I think she was afraid of not being herself the next day, of not being her most beautiful. That's the way it started and she became so hooked that she had to take drugs to wake up. Sometimes she would take overdoses and they'd have a hell of a time to get her to wake up at all."

Eli Wallach believed that Huston was "a genius" in dealing with Monroe on that film. "He handled her with great delicacy, never pressured her, never blamed her for anything, always made her welcome and comfortable off the set." Nevertheless the drug problem and her consequent lateness on or even absence from the set created numerous difficulties. In the middle of the production they had to abandon shooting for two weeks while Monroe was sent back to California to a hospital to be weaned off the pills.

Huston said: "She was a very sick girl, sick like an addict is sick. They took her to a hospital in Los Angeles and she was put under the care of psychiatrists to get her off the drugs." When she returned she seemed quite recovered but "it was only a few days before I discovered she was back into the drugs again".

And yet *The Misfits* is generally regarded as one of Monroe's very best films, one whose acclaim has increased over the years. Of Monroe's contribution to it Huston – not a man lightly to give praise – said: "I thought it was beautiful. I liked it very much. What I saw on the screen erased the anxieties and the pains that went into getting the performance."

It was her last completed film and I asked Huston, who had directed her at both ends of her career, how he thought she had developed since *The Asphalt Jungle*. He said: "Well, she wasn't an actress in the sense of the English, Shakespearian-trained actor who does a variety of roles and has virtuosity. She was herself and she could present herself very well. She wasn't an actress in the legitimate stage sense but in the motion picture sense she was a very fine actress indeed."

Even so he could not imagine her carrying on, as an actress, into middle or old age. "I think she would have gone on for a few years and then, as her beauty faded, she would have retired."

Did he, I asked, mean that, unlike other actresses who were also beautiful in their time but managed to weather the inevitable fading of their looks and moved on into playing character roles, Monroe was entirely dependent on her beauty?

"No, not beauty alone," he said. "But beauty was part of her fascination. It contributed largely to it because it was unique. There was an article in a magazine once in which her masseuse was quoted as saying that Marilyn's flesh was different from other flesh. Well, there was something honeyed about her, something fetching. But as time went on her beauty would have coarsened and that fragile, tremulous, lovely thing that we all witnessed would have been gone and then she would have lost her appeal because her appeal was largely physical."

Perhaps Monroe, too, was aware of that and perhaps that's why her drug addiction was more noticeable and caused more concern on *The Misfits* than it had on any of her previous films. By the time it was finished she was already thirty-five and her body, though still superb, was no longer that of a young girl. Facially, too, she was not quite so pretty as she had been and, unlike actresses such as Garbo, Dietrich and Katharine Hepburn, whose beauty is based not so much on prettiness and youthful sexuality as on delicate bone structure, her looks – as Huston said – would probably have coarsened with age.

It could well be, therefore, that she was beginning to feel a certain panic about her future. She had very little money – indeed, by the standards of other stars both of her time and since – she had never really earned

vast amounts of money. And if her main assets were beginning to decline what would become of her in three, five or ten years' time?

Whether such thoughts bothered her or not, she was in a very bad mental and emotional state by the time *The Misfits* was completed in November 1960. With the film over she officially announced her separation from Arthur Miller and once again left Hollywood and took an apartment near the East River in New York, where she was continually hounded by the press who were anxious to find traces of another man in her life.

In the midst of all that she learned, to her great distress, that her co-star Clark Gable, whom she had very much admired, had died of a heart attack. So by the time she went to Mexico in January 1962 for her divorce from Miller she was already in a state of near-nervous exhaustion and it was really no great surprise that on her return to New York she collapsed under the combined burden of emotional stress and far too many barbiturates.

In The Misfits, *Monroe's – and Clark Gable's – last film and for each of them one of their best.*

177

Nor was that the end of her problems because, for some unaccountable reason, she was taken to a hospital for the mentally disordered where, to nobody's astonishment, far from improving, her condition continued to decline. From this awful place she was rescued by the faithful Joe diMaggio, to whom she had turned not as a lover but as a friend when it was obvious that her marriage to Miller was breaking up. DiMaggio took her to a much less frightening hospital where she stayed for three weeks and later that year, after she had recuperated, she went back to California.

By then she was dependent both on her pills and the regular ministrations of a psychiatrist but nevertheless she made an attempt to restore some kind of order to her life. With the help of the ever-faithful diMaggio, whose devotion to her extended throughout her life and beyond it, she bought a fairly modest house, the first she had ever owned, in Hollywood. And then, in April 1962, she returned to Fox to make a film called *Something's Got to Give*, an ironic title because finally it was Monroe who gave.

She signed for the film because contractually she was obliged to do so but Whitey Snyder was convinced that she never wanted to make it. "She kept putting it off and putting it off and finally the studio forced her to start." The plot involved her in a nude bathing scene and she was willing, perhaps eager to do it, possibly because she had been getting herself back into trim, physical shape and was anxious to prove to any doubters who might be around that the famous body was still in good nick.

But, Snyder said, "She was never healthy. I don't think that her body was very strong. She was physically sick lots of times. I think that was because of the pills and not eating right. Some days she just couldn't show up and finally they dropped her after five or six weeks of off and on, hit or miss situation. The studio dropped her; they shut the picture down."

Snyder, who worked with Monroe for years, watched the pill habit developing. She would go straight home after a day's shooting, he said, and take a sleeping pill because "she wanted to look good in the morning; she wanted to get to sleep right away. But then," he said, "she'd probably wake up at nine thirty at night or something and take a couple more pills. Well, they'd put her down again for a while but after midnight she'd wake up again and take some more. It's like a drunk – you don't know when to stop. I'd say to her, 'Marilyn, you're going to kill yourself, you're going to mess up,' and she'd say 'I know,' but she'd go right on doing it. A lot of times she'd come to work and you couldn't get her awake for an hour and a half."

In view of the way she died this testimony is rather significant but, on the other hand, if the drugs were making her too ill to report for work on time or even report for work at all, it becomes easier to understand the apparent callousness of Fox in dismissing her from the film, though it would have been hard to persuade Monroe of that.

When she was finally given her cards she was, according to her housekeeper, Mrs. Eunice Blackmer, "deeply hurt" but it's difficult to sympathise with her too much because one weekend in May, while she was apparently too ill to work, she flew to New York at the invitation of Peter Lawford to sing "Happy Birthday" to President John F. Kennedy at a massive celebration of said birthday at Madison Square Garden. She looked superb and sang prettily and the studio, which had already incurred excess costs of around one million dollars on the film because of her erratic behaviour, was furious with her.

She was able to work on about six more days during the next two weeks and on June 1st, her thirty-sixth birthday, the crew gave her a party. But a few days later she was fired. Lee Remick was signed to replace her but when Dean Martin walked off the film on the grounds that he had agreed to co-star with Monroe and only Monroe, the whole enterprise was dropped with writs fluttering about like confetti. In a statement issued through her secretary Monroe said: "It's time some of the studio heads realised what they're doing. If there's anything wrong with Hollywood it starts at the top. It seems to me it's time they stopped knocking their assets around."

And she did have a point. If her own behaviour had been less than admirable, Fox could hardly claim that they had been surprised by it. From the start they had known what they were taking on because by then her emotional and psychiatric problems and her drug addiction were no secret in Hollywood. Besides which, they were not exactly granting any favours by way of salary, for her fee for the picture was only 100,000 dollars – less than £50,000 – which, considering her stature, was truly a pittance.

Although there was talk around the end of June of the studio reinstating her and an alternative film project was discussed, nothing ever came of it. The few scenes she shot for *Something's Got to Give* were the last in which she ever appeared on film.

On the night of Saturday, August 4th, 1962, Marilyn Monroe was found dead at her home. How she died and what precisely had happened to her between her dismissal from the picture and her death have since become the subject of so much speculation that the truth is impossible to determine.

It has been suggested that at this time she was having an affair with the US Attorney-General, Robert Kennedy, the brother of the President. It has also been alleged that, as a result of this, she went into hospital in July to have an abortion; that the affair on his part was merely casual and on her part so serious that she believed he would leave his wife and marry her.

There is, however, no real evidence either to support or refute any of these claims. Frederick Guiles, author of *Norma Jean*, the best and least sensational of her biographies, sets out both the affair and the abortion as facts; Norman Mailer, whose copiously illustrated biography *Marilyn* appeared much later, is not so sure.

There's no doubt, though, that she knew both Jack and Robert Kennedy well. Whitey Snyder remembered driving her to a party at Peter Lawford's house for dinner one night when both men were there and Eunice Murray Blackmer was present on one occasion when Robert Kennedy visited Monroe at home. "I think she appreciated having him as one of her admirers," said Mrs. Blackmer, "but I don't know more than that."

The strongest evidence to support Guiles' theory that an affair took place between Monroe and Bobby Kennedy – evidence, as a matter of fact, to which Guiles was not privy – came from Inez Melson, Monroe's business manager. What she told me, she said, was something she had never publicly revealed before, although she would have revealed it if Bobby Kennedy had been nominated for President.

"Naturally," she said, "I felt very badly when he was assassinated but I didn't want him to be President, because I felt that a man who was father to ten or eleven children didn't have any right to be fooling around.

"Now I didn't know that he was [fooling around] excepting for the fact that going through Marilyn's possessions after her death I found a letter that Kennedy's sister, Jean Smith, had written to her in response to a letter Marilyn had written extending her sympathy over the old man's [Joseph Kennedy's] stroke. In this Jean Smith said, 'We understand that you and Bobby are an item and we hope that when he comes back you will come with him.' Well, I just didn't think that was nice, you know. I was really angry about that because I could understand why Marilyn would be attracted to somebody who was a great personality and you don't criticise somebody for having admiration but I just didn't feel the family should approve of it . . . I didn't like the idea that 'We understand you and Bobby are an item'. It's just like she was a sort of concubine."

Unfortunately the letter from Jean Smith no longer exists. Mrs. Melson destroyed it just as, in her capacity as executrix of Monroe's will, she destroyed most of the papers she found in Monroe's house after her death, including letters from Arthur Miller – all of them, incidentally, signed "Pa".

She destroyed those papers, she said, to avert any danger of them falling into the wrong hands – the hands, for instance, of the press, who were making sensation enough out of the sex goddess's demise – and she also destroyed the drugs she found in the house. There were "bottles and bottles and bottles of them and we emptied them all down the toilet".

Why had she done that?

"I don't know. What would you do with a lot of sleeping tablets? What motivated me at the time is that I knew there would be reporters and photographers around there and I didn't want them to see all those pills."

And that brings us to the second mystery of Monroe's last days: the mystery of how she died. Again the stories about that night are legion. Certainly her psychiatrist had visited her during the day and it has been rumoured that Bobby Kennedy did, too, and that she had dinner with him. But Mrs. Blackmer, who was with her all day, who was the last person to see her alive and who, indeed, discovered her body, denied that.

"I didn't really see much of her that day," she said. "She was in her robe and very much in her room and just wandering around in the garden. It was a quiet day." At one point Monroe's press agent, Pat Newcombe, arrived. "Marilyn came into the room where we were talking and joined us but she seemed a little distracted." Then later, after Newcombe had gone, "Marilyn came to me and asked if we had any liquid oxygen in the house and I didn't know what she was talking about and she turned and walked away." At this point Mrs. Blackmer, slightly disturbed but not too much so for Monroe's behaviour was never predictable, called the psychiatrist, a frequent visitor to the house in any event, and he arrived about 4 p.m. and talked to Marilyn in her room. He did not, however, stay very long and when he left Monroe and Mrs. Blackmer were alone in the house.

"Marilyn went to her room and then there was a telephone call from Joe diMaggio's son – he was one of those she would talk to at any time; she was very fond of him – and she talked to him in a loud, happy, gay, wonderful voice."

Up to this point then it had been a fairly normal day by Monroe's standards. She had been a little restless and there was, apparently, a certain amount of tension between her and Pat Newcombe but none of this was unusual. The psychiatrist, Mrs. Blackmer learned later, had suggested to Monroe that she should go for a drive in the evening to relax her but after the phonecall she returned to her room and "She stood at the doorway and said, 'Well, we won't go for that ride after all,' and then she said 'Goodnight' and closed the door."

That was the last time Mrs. Blackmer saw her alive. What happened after that not even she knows but it seems likely that at some time during the early part of the night Monroe either made or received a phone call, although nobody has ever come forward to admit having talked to her.

Mrs. Blackmer awoke, for no particular reason that she could think of, around midnight. "I opened my bedroom door, which was right next to hers, and I was aware of the telephone cord going into her room. And this was the alarm for me because she never slept with the telephone in her room because it might waken her if she had got to sleep. So I immediately called the doctor."

In normal circumstances that might seem a curious thing to do. If she were concerned, why call the doctor? Why not knock on Monroe's door and see if she was all right? The circumstances in Monroe's house, however, were not what other people might call normal. Mrs. Blackmer's reasoning was that if Monroe was asleep it would be a shame to waken her. But because she was concerned and needed reassurance from somebody she felt the doctor – by which she meant the psychiatrist – was as good as anyone: he, after all, was in fairly constant attendance on Monroe.

On his advice Mrs. Blackmer went outside the house and peered through the bedroom window. "The light was on and Marilyn was lying, without any covers, on her bed. So, of course, I ran back to the telephone and the rest is history."

In fact, everything happened in a considerable rush thereafter. Monroe's medical doctor was summoned and so, for some inscrutable reason, was the fire brigade. The press arrived fairly swiftly, too – no doubt tipped off by the firemen. While chaos ensued outside, Mrs. Blackmer and various doctors went into Monroe's bedroom.

"The phone was under her. She was lying on her face and the phone was right there, caught in her arm and her hand." She was naked except for her brassière but this again was not unusual. Monroe never wore a nightdress and the only time she wore a bra was in bed, her argument being that she needed the uplift more at night than during the day.

It was some time before the police were called and a sinister interpretation has been put upon this but again, bearing in mind the total confusion of the situation, it is perhaps understandable. What with the press and the baffling presence of the fire brigade and the necessity to keep photographers out of the bedroom it would not be altogether surprising if the idea of summoning the police only occurred as an afterthought.

But as a result of the confused events of that night all manner of theories have sprung up around Monroe's death. The first, which I think can be swiftly discounted, is that she was murdered either in an attempt to extricate the Kennedy family from a scandal (Monroe, the argument goes, was about to announce her love affair with Bobby) or, conversely, to implicate them in a scandal. (The reasoning behind the latter is a bit hard to fathom.) But either way no evidence of, and no really plausible motive for, murder has ever come to light and Mrs. Blackmer, who said she was accused by innuendo of being one of the murderers, treated the whole suggestion with scorn.

The second theory is that Monroe deliberately killed herself and indeed the coroner's report attributed her death to "probable suicide". But this is based on circumstantial, rather than irrefutable, evidence, the circumstances being that she had certainly taken a massive overdose of sleeping pills. But what motive would she have had for that?

No suicide note was ever found and when I asked whether Monroe had, that previous day, been in the mood of someone who might even possibly be contemplating taking her own life, Mrs. Blackmer said: "I doubt that very much. She had told me – one of the very first things she warned me about – that if she took sedation, which was every night, she was apt to forget and would take a second dose too soon. This was what she had to be careful about, so the first thing I was concerned about after she died was that this was what had probably happened."

What compounds the mystery, of course, is the unexplained presence of the telephone in her room. This has been used to reinforce the suicide theory, the argument running that Monroe, realising that Bobby Kennedy had no intention of destroying his marriage and ruining his political career in order to marry her, had deliberately taken an overdose of drugs and then, regretting it or possibly wanting him to know what she had done and why, had phoned to tell him so. The only fact available to back up this theory is that Kennedy was indeed in town that night. (In fact, he flew off the next day in a great hurry as soon as her death was announced. But that action on his part was not necessarily sinister. Whether he had had an affair with her or not – and I'm strongly inclined to believe he had – he had certainly been seen in her company and his rapid disappearance from

the scene was probably due to the natural, though perhaps ignoble, self-protective urge of an aspiring politician to put as much distance as possible between himself and a potential source of embarrassment and scandal.)

The third theory is that Monroe died of accidental overdose and this is the one that is held by her closest friends. All of them had warned her at one time or another that she was taking far too many pills, and that one day she would forget how many she had taken and swallow one dose too many. Rupert Allan, for example, had spoken to her about this when "I caught her opening up the capsules and putting the contents in water to get the action faster". Whitey Snyder had talked to her about it; Monroe herself had warned Mrs. Blackmer that she was aware of the dangers of overdosing.

So the possibility of accidental death is very strong and it is supported by her friends with arguments that are perhaps not as trivial as they may seem. Inez Melson, for instance, refuses to believe that she committed suicide because "she wouldn't hurt people. She wouldn't hurt a fly," and she knew that by killing herself she would bring pain to "millions of people who adored her".

Rupert Allan said: "I'm positive she didn't kill herself on purpose. People who saw her body afterwards said that her hair needed a dye job very badly. She also needed a pedicure. Marilyn would never have gone out and let people see her when she didn't look great, her best. Never. No way."

Both lines of reasoning seem odd but who knows? If it was not her character to hurt people or to allow herself to be seen except at her best would she step out of character when she prepared to kill herself?

Or is suicide out of character anyway for anyone? And does a suicide really care whether her hair needs attention and her toenails are not at their prettiest? The argument simply goes round and round although, perhaps significantly, Rupert Allan recalled that Monroe had once contemplated suicide by jumping from a high building. When telling him about it she said she had changed her mind because there was a woman standing right below and she was frightened of landing on that woman and killing her, too. But what she had also told him was that she had been wearing a green tweed suit on that occasion and the story would seem to indicate (a) that she didn't wish to hurt others and (b) that she was conscious of her dress and grooming on what was intended to be her positively last appearance.

One other person who believes firmly that Monroe's death was simply a tragic accident is Jim Dougherty, her first husband. He said: "If Marilyn, or Norma Jean, had intended to commit suicide she would have written a note to someone; she would have told them why. She loved to write letters. There's no doubt in my mind that it was an accident."

Again, of course, this is merely a personal conviction but it's not unimportant that, at the time of Monroe's death, Dougherty was a member of the Los Angeles Police Department.

True, he was not personally involved in the enquiry into the circumstances of her death but as far as the murder theory is concerned he said: "The finest police department in the world investigated it and they came up with nothing and that's enough for me." And on the suicide theory he said: "I asked the man who investigated it what he thought happened and he said, 'Well, she just took an overdose,' and that was it. She was taking them to go to sleep and she was taking them to wake up and she just took too many."

I believe – perhaps because I want to believe, perhaps simply because it's kinder to believe – that Dougherty was right: that she took sleeping pills before she went to bed and that she woke up – once, twice, who can tell? – and in her fuddled state took more pills, too many more pills.

Marilyn Monroe was buried in Westwood Village Cemetery, just off Wilshire Boulevard. Her crypt is modest and only a few yards away from the din of constant traffic. But upon it each week without fail are placed four red roses. They are put there on the instructions of Joe diMaggio, whose love for her was so constant that, greatly eligible though he is, he has remained single since their divorce.

Both diMaggio and Miller seem strange partners for her but though, in most ways, the two men were very different they also had quite a lot in common.

They were both, in their own fields, the best: diMaggio the best baseball player, Miller in his time the best American play-wright. And they were both highly moral and rather solemn men, a great deal older than Monroe. They were more surrogate fathers perhaps than husbands and that's an uneasy role to fill, especially when you are married to a woman who needs a father *and* a husband, a lover *and* a friend, who needs constant reassurance and respect and, above all, unswerving affection. Monroe sought these things from all manner of people, including her theatrical gurus, and never really found them.

It has been said that Hollywood killed her but that's too glib and too simple. Hollywood didn't kill her: it just failed to understand her, to understand the pain and the effort it took her to be what she was and to be as good as she was. In Hollywood she was often treated as something of a joke, a walking fantasy figure. It was acceptable to like her but not to admire her because "for Chrissake, she's just a dumb blonde, you know what I mean?"

What Hollywood quite overlooked, because such qualities are rare in the film business, is that there was about her an innocence and a sweetness that no other actress ever shared. During her association with Robert Kennedy she asked an educated friend to draw up a list of topics that she might discuss with him and a list of questions she might ask him. Hollywood would have pointed to this as evidence of her stupidity but in fact it was evidence of her sensitivity. She admired the man greatly, she was probably in love with him and she simply didn't want to bore him.

The irony of her death is that it was both tragic and, in an awful way, timely. She was thirty-six – not by any means old by normal standards but dangerously old for a sex goddess. Norman Rosten, the poet and her friend, said: "Where would she have gone from there? I mean, she couldn't continue to play the girl with the figure for ever and she knew it."

Billy Wilder said: "I knew it wasn't going to be a simple third act curtain for her. I just could not visualise Monroe in a rocking chair or in the Motion Picture Relief Home or married to somebody who was a pilot for United Airlines."

And, perhaps most brutally, but also most honestly, Joe Mankiewicz said: "Marilyn's death, coming at the time it did, was probably the very easiest and best and gentlest thing that could have happened to her. What everyone forgets is that Marilyn's career was finished: she wasn't about to get another film; she didn't have much money; the studio didn't want her and the men who wanted her were going to get increasingly lower in level. She was thirty-six and I put it to you, as a Queen's Counsel might say, imagine Marilyn alive today – very fat, boozing it up. I think she'd have been a painful, dreadful mess and nobody would be able to remember what they do remember, which is this incredible, offbeat, zany, wonderful, dizzy blonde. That's the way we should remember her and her death was the best thing that could have happened to her."

As an actress she was consistently underrated and sometimes cordially hated by her directors. After each of the two films he made with her Billy Wilder swore he would never work with her again. But nearly two decades after her death he told me that "never a week passes when I don't wish she was still around".

In an even higher tribute Joshua Logan described her as being "as close to genius as any actress I've ever known". That may be pitching it a little high but Logan's opinion is at least to be respected. What she certainly was, and what she proved herself to be time and again, was a most wonderfully gifted comedienne, a woman whose combination of abundant physical charms – a positive cornucopia of femininity – and wistful shyness made you at once want to laugh at her and yearn for her and protect her. Nobody since has come even remotely close to matching her. She was confused, yes; she was insecure, yes; she was demanding of more love and devotion and loyalty than any one person could reasonably be expected to give, yes. But when you look at her background none of this is surprising. She had a surfeit of all those warm and desirable qualities which myth and the movies instruct us that all American blondes ought to have – but only she had them. And yet, when you stand back and examine her life, she was doomed from the start: there's a dreadful, ruthless logic to the way she lived and the way she died.

If only, you think, if only someone had given her a great big hug when she was still a little girl and said, "Hey, listen, I love you," then maybe everything would have been different. But in that case she prob-

One of Monroe's last publicity shots, taken just before she was fired from Something's Got To Give. *Within a week or two she was dead.*

ably would never have become Marilyn Monroe and the world would have been the poorer for it because Marilyn Monroe was something rather special.

As Billy Wilder said: "She had no handle on life but, by God, she had some other things that if you knew what they were you could sell the patent to DuPont and they'd manufacture it. You would think that it's not difficult to make another Monroe; it should be easy – a blonde, a small girl with a sweet face, my God there should be thousands of them, they should come from all over the world."

But they don't. You can take every possible identifiable ingredient that she had and put them together and multiply them and add in the date and the number you first thought of and at the end of it all you've got is a blonde, small girl with a sweet face and a remarkably voluptuous body. But you still haven't got another Marilyn Monroe.

It's now six or seven years since that brief appraisal of Marilyn Monroe was written and since then a good deal of new information has come to light, most of it to be found in Anthony Summers' excellent book *Goddess: The Secret Lives of Marilyn Monroe*. In particular her love affairs (if love can be said to have entered into it, except on her side) with both Jack and Bobby Kennedy are now common knowledge. In 1979/80 these things were known and talked about by her close friends but only off the record.

Where Anthony Summers' research has been most revealing, however, is in piecing together the events of the night of Monroe's death. If I may paraphrase his findings, it now seems likely that she was found comatose and close to death some time before midnight; that a remarkable number of people (not including the police) were called to her house; that among them were Peter Lawford, the President's brother-in-law, and perhaps Bobby Kennedy; that an ambulance may have been summoned to take her to hospital in Santa Monica and that she died either in the ambulance or, unrecognised and unidentified, at the hospital and that her body was returned to her home before the police were notified; that papers, including a note or letter she had been writing that night, were removed from the house (probably by Peter Lawford) before the authorities were called in.

Furthermore, the records of her phone calls were removed by the Secret Service from the local telephone company and various organs of her body were destroyed before they could be properly analysed. It is this latter fact which has lent weight to the murder theory, the argument being that the organs were disposed of because they proved that the fatal dose of barbiturates had not been voluntarily ingested by her but had been administered by someone else. (Against that, of course, a proper scrutiny – especially of the smaller intestine – might just as well have proved that she had indeed taken the drugs orally and without coercion.)

My own instinct – and that, I think, of Anthony Summers – is to reject the murder theory despite the new evidence. I believe that (a) if the Kennedys had wanted her dead they could have found a far more efficient way of doing it, (b) nobody – and nobody connected with anyone – whose interests would have been served by her death would have taken the trouble to summon an ambulance in an attempt to save her and (c) if she had in fact been murdered it would have needed the complicity of a

Laughton in 1934.

large (too large) number of members of the Los Angeles Police Department and the coroner's office to cover it up. If you accept those presumptions, then the disappearance of the telephone records is not particularly sinister: it's reasonable to assume that they were removed in order to hide the fact that Monroe had made several phone calls to Bobby Kennedy in Washington.

I don't think either of the Kennedy brothers emerges from this with very much credit at all. They seem to have behaved in the self-seeking, self-protecting way that you would expect of politicians.

So then, what of the suicide theory? Again I was interested and encouraged to discover that Anthony Summers doesn't believe that either. His conclusion is that the mass of papers removed from the house were those which would have proved an amorous association with Bobby Kennedy and that, whatever it was Monroe had been writing before she died, it was not a suicide note but more likely a despairing letter to Bobby Kennedy. It was this, I think, that Peter Lawford removed and destroyed.

The most likely eventuality is that after a phone call, or series of phone calls, that night with Peter Lawford – and very possibly Bobby Kennedy himself – the most spectacular sex symbol/love goddess in the history of the cinema had finally realised that the Attorney-General of the United States had no intention of sacrificing everything for her; that she had taken sleeping pills, as she always did, to ease her pain; that she had started to write a letter of recrimination to Kennedy and that she had either taken too many pills or, in a befuddled state, had forgotten that she had swallowed any at all and had taken more.

I believe now, as I believed before, that Marilyn Monroe's death was an accident. But more and more I have come to agree with Joe Mankiewicz's assessment that, heartless though it might seem, it was the best thing that could have happened to her. Because she died so young Monroe has attained a kind of immortality as the epitome of what is desirable and adorable in woman. A Monroe still alive today, in her sixties, gross and hooked on drugs and alcohol would have destroyed everything that she had earlier created. She was a butterfly and nature takes care to ensure that butterflies never outlive their welcome or their beauty.

Charles Laughton

Charles Laughton was a large, fat, "ugly" man as, in his moments of fear and insecurity (and he had his share of those) he himself would have been the first to admit. Indeed "ugly" was his own description of himself; nobody else applied it to him because nobody else believed it. He was also a homosexual, which except to other homosexuals and a few very close friends he would never have admitted at all. But in addition to being large, fat, "ugly" and homosexual, he was quite possibly the finest screen actor there has ever been, an actor of true greatness which, in his more arrogant moments (and he had his share of those, too) he would not only have admitted but would have been swift to point out lest the fact had momentarily escaped your attention.

In the varied opinions of his friends and relatives, Laughton was lovable, hateful, kind, cruel, insecure, vain, a genius and a monster. But above all he was a great actor. Billy Wilder, the eminent director, has no doubt whatsoever where Laughton stands in the league table of greatness. "My God," says Wilder, "who was there better than Laughton?" The question is rhetorical but he answers it anyway. "Nobody," he says. "There has never been anybody that even came close."

The larger question concerning the extent to which the ugliness, the homosexuality and the greatness were connected is more difficult to answer. Would he have been as great had he not been "ugly" and a homosexual? Paul Gregory, Laughton's friend, manager, producer and the man who rescued him from a professional decline that was not only premature but was beginning to look positively humiliating, believes the "ugliness" – or more accu-

rately, Laughton's belief in his own ugliness – was vital.

Gregory is convinced that an obviously handsome Laughton would have been a different man, possibly a happier man but undoubtedly a less successful one; that he was impelled by a determination to prove that however grotesque he believed himself to be he still had as much talent as, and possibly more than, any other actor anybody cared to name. Laughton's own view was different. He believed that the key to his ability was his homosexuality and once told Gregory so, putting forward the theory that being a homosexual gave him a talent of a finer grain than not being a homosexual. Gregory denied this, arguing not unreasonably that it wasn't actually necessary to be homosexual to be talented, but Laughton was unconvinced.

As a homosexual Laughton was at once bold and guilt-ridden and suffered under what his friend Christopher Isherwood called "the heterosexual dictatorship", as Isherwood himself had done. It was perhaps because of this that Isherwood says of him: "He was very, very insecure." He also believes that insecurity led Laughton to worry incessantly about his work "and rightly. I mean, as an artist one should keep testing the thing again and again, hammering it to see if it rings true or not." If, then, insecurity is a vital ingredient in the composition of an artist, Laughton came to his destiny extremely well-equipped.

He was born in Scarborough on July 1st, 1899, the eldest son of Robert and Eliza Laughton who owned a small hotel, the Victoria, nearly opposite the railway station. The hotel thrived and so did the Laughtons. They had two more sons, Tom

Laughton in his last film, Advise and Consent.

and Frank, and eventually moved from the Victoria to a much grander establishment across the road.

Because hotel keeping is a demanding business the children saw little of their parents and were mostly brought up by the staff and various nannies. The dominant personality in the household appears to have been Eliza, a somewhat matriarchal figure who had the ambition and the head for business that her husband lacked. According to Tom Laughton Eliza's name was evoked by the staff or the nannies as the ultimate deterrent if the children threatened to get out of hand: "If you don't behave we'll bring your mother to you."

Nevertheless in Tom's recollection it was a happy childhood, involving visits to theatres, of which Scarborough as a fashionable seaside resort had several, and Pierrot and Punch and Judy shows on the beach. But Charles, the homely fat boy, had other memories. Years later he told Paul Gregory how other children would jeer and throw stones at him in the street.

Eliza Laughton was a staunch Roman Catholic who brought her children to heel not by beating them but by making it clear that she was going to pray for them, a much more subtle and altogether nastier and more effective punishment. By her decision the three boys were educated first at a convent of French nuns and then at Stonyhurst, the Jesuit College, where Charles was deeply unhappy. This is not, of course, surprising because in the entire history of the world no fat boy has ever been happy at an English public school and a fat boy who was hopeless at games and interested in art, literature and wild flowers was clearly doomed to years of utter misery.

The passion for wild flowers and also for art stemmed from his Aunt Mary, his father's eldest sister, who lived in a cottage just outside Scarborough. She was an ardent collector of pictures and other works of artistic merit and a devoted gardener and she shared these enthusiasms with her nephews. From an early age Charles would insist on people accompanying him for apparently endless hikes across the countryside to look at a special kind of violet or some rare wild flower.

Anyone with that kind of sensitive nature was most unlikely to find a sympathetic audience at a school like Stonyhurst and Laughton, not surprisingly, hated the place. He arrived there as an obedient Roman Catholic and left it as, at best, an agnostic with a deep suspicion and dislike of all forms of authority. Almost immediately he was exposed to another kind of authority – the army which, though probably no sterner than an English public school, would hardly have been more palatable to him.

It was 1918 and he enlisted as a private in the Royal Huntingdonshire Regiment, resisting all his mother's attempts to make him take a commission, on the grounds that the company was better in the ranks. Apart from the fact that he was sent to France, fought at Vimy Ridge, took part in a bayonet attack and was gassed, very little is known of Laughton's wartime experiences. He had cultivated the habit of secrecy at Stonyhurst and for ever after was inclined to keep his deepest and most painful feelings to himself.

When the war was over, he was sent to Claridges in London to be trained in the hotel business for which he had no particular taste. He spent most of his spare time and nearly all his money on cheap seats at the theatre and would talk of little else when finally he returned to Scarborough to take his rightful place, as the eldest son, in the family hotel.

He stayed there for some time, although by now he was making it quite clear that what he wanted to be was an actor and, as Tom Laughton recalls, making it equally clear that he had no gift at all for the hotel business. "He looked upon the hotel as a production, which of course it should be," said Tom. "He transformed the decor and he introduced music but he didn't like the chores. He didn't like getting up in the morning and he wouldn't do the shopping. As for the guests, he found them fascinating as a study but I don't think he was very good at looking after them." Eventually he was able to persuade even his mother that Charles Laughton, hotelier, was a nonstarter and was allowed to return to London to study at the Royal Academy of Dramatic Art.

By now he was twenty-four and success attended him immediately. At RADA he won the gold medal as best actor of his year and, on leaving the Academy, had no difficulty in finding continuous employment in the professional theatre. He appeared in Gogol (*The Government Inspector*),

Ibsen (*The Pillars of Society*) and Chekhov (*The Three Sisters* and *The Cherry Orchard*) and by the middle of 1927 had earned such a reputation that he was offered the title role in Arnold Bennett's *Mr. Prohack*. This play assumed enormous significance in his life not simply because it introduced him as a leading man, despite the handicap of his unusual and far from handsome appearance, but because it also introduced him to Elsa Lanchester, a young actress who played the part of Prohack's secretary.

Her initial response to him was not exactly favourable. "A rehearsal is a very icy thing," she said. "You know, there's a working light hanging in the middle and everybody looks grey. He looked greyer than anybody. He was plump, well, fat really, and pale. I think I said that he reminded me of a baker's boy who has just come out of the bakery and was covered in flour." But despite this unflattering first impression she found herself attracted to him, largely because they had a mutual interest in art, antiques and the countryside. By coincidence, Elsa too had an Aunt Mary who was devoted to art and wild flowers and who, like Laughton's Aunt Mary, had also passed on her enthusiasm to her niece. In the early days of their acquaintance Elsa and Laughton would often go by train into the countryside, especially to Sussex, just to look at the flowers and the gardens.

Elsa herself was small, lively, and although attractive, by no means conventionally pretty and she was not deterred by Laughton's appearance or his own opinion of his appearance. "He was really better-looking," she said, "than a lot of good-looking people who are so good-looking you could throw up." In any case, the attraction was obviously mutual for, by the time *Mr. Prohack* closed they were living together and on February 9th, 1929, prompted by Laughton's mother who, in Elsa's version anyway, had a middle-class respect for the conventions, they were married at a registry office in London.

For the first two years their marriage appeared to be happy and normal enough. But then when Charles was rehearsing the role of the murderer in the stage adaptation of C. S. Forester's *Payment Deferred*, with Elsa again in the cast, there occurred what was perhaps the single most traumatic event in their lives.

A boy, a male prostitute, arrived at the Laughtons' flat in London insisting that Laughton had picked him up in the street and had refused to pay him. He created such a disturbance that the police were called and both the boy and Laughton were notified to appear in court.

According to his biographer, Charles Higham, Laughton immediately told Elsa what had happened. His confession was both tearful and complete. He told her that he had had several affairs with boys and young men, most of them prostitutes, and that much of their activities had taken place on the sofa in the flat. Elsa, to whom this knowledge of her husband's homosexuality was a most horrifying revelation, responded first and rather touchingly by ordering him to get rid of the sofa and secondly by being stricken with a temporary deafness that was quite obviously psychosomatic. Elsa herself says now: "I hadn't thought about homosexuality, ever, in connection with him," and doesn't recall any immediate sensation of shock. "I said: 'That's quite all right, don't think any more about it. It's all right, it's perfectly all right,' but of course a thing like that, since I didn't know, since he didn't tell me, the feeling that you've been deceived I think starts to eat in . . . it boomeranged years later." The most dramatic effect of this boomerang was her determination never to have children. "I gradually felt, I think as every woman probably feels, that the father of children should be the right father for children and . . . I gradually knew I didn't want to have children." In later years when Laughton talked dreamily and unrealistically of adopting his protégée, Maureen O'Hara, or expressed his regret at never having had a son, he would accuse Elsa of having refused to have children for selfish reasons that were nothing to do with him, but she insists that in fact her resolution was formed on the night he made his original confession.

The result of the court case that ensued from the disturbance caused by the boy prostitute was extremely fortunate for Laughton. The magistrate, a man presumably of the most amazing naïvety, merely warned Laughton about his "misguided generosity" towards the boy, as though all that had taken place had simply been a gesture of philanthropy on the actor's part, and the case was dismissed. Had matters gone otherwise, had Laughton been convicted, as he might well have been, of homosexuality, his entire career could well have ended there in court. He would most probably have been ruined in England and certainly he would have had no chance of an international career. As Charles Higham said: "I very much doubt if he would ever have come to Hollywood because the attitude here was then, as it is now, enormously anti-homosexual. The idea of Louis B. Mayer or Cecil B. de Mille, who abhorred and despised homosexuals more than anything else, hiring such a person would have been unthinkable." And yet, ironically, both de Mille and Mayer were to be extremely important in helping to further Laughton's international career.

Elsa Lanchester says, surprisingly perhaps, that the incident with the boy prostitute made no great initial difference to her marriage. She had been brought up in a free-thinking and socialist household in which the only doctrine was the doctrine of tolerance so that when she said: "It's all right, it's perfectly all right," she genuinely thought it was. For his part Laughton started going to an analyst, Ernest Jones, whether in the hope of purging himself of homosexual desires or merely of the guilt they instilled in him neither Elsa nor probably Laughton himself was entirely clear.

In any event, he soon lost interest in analysis. "After he'd been three times," said Elsa, "the nurse called up and said: 'Well, where's Charles Laughton? He's not here.' When I asked Charles about it he said that Ernest Jones had told him that he, Charles, knew more about himself than Ernest Jones could ever tell him. This was a kind of vanity, the actor's 'I know' character – 'I know people and no one can tell me by plunging into my past what I am.' I'm sorry he didn't stick to it."

Gradually, however, and inevitably once Laughton's homosexuality was accepted, the relationship between them changed, becoming in the end a strong but platonic friendship. "It sort of separated us a little bit," she said, "but we never talked about it. I wish we had. If he'd gone on with Ernest Jones we probably would have done. I'd have liked to talk but he wouldn't. He wasn't capable of talking, he just couldn't." She believes that this inability to discuss what must, after all, be a colossal problem in any marriage where

it occurs, was due to guilt of some kind but guilt about what she is not sure even now. She doesn't think he felt guilty about marrying her and not telling her about himself, but perhaps he did about not being a "normal" man and not wanting to be "normal" at a time when homosexuality was a criminal offence. His secretiveness about the matter extended even to his own family. His younger brother, Frank, was also a homosexual and had admitted the fact openly to his mother and brothers, all of whom were as supportive as a fairly close family might be expected to be. It is possible that Charles had confided to Frank about his own homosexuality but he did not confide in the others.

The middle brother, Tom, said: "I was never aware of it in any shape or form until Elsa told me and I was just astounded. I never saw the least sign that he was but maybe he was. I don't know and I don't care."

However, the run of *Payment Deferred* which, had the court case gone another way, could have ended disastrously for Laughton instead ended in triumph. It was such a success that the production was taken to Broadway where, again, it opened to good reviews, although it ran only three weeks. Laughton then directed a Broadway version of *Alibi*, adapted from an Agatha Christie story – once more to good notices – and at the end of his stay in New York he signed a three-year contract with Paramount.

Before then he had made a few modest pictures, two-reelers mostly, in London but his film career really began in Hollywood in 1931 with a series of films like *The Old Dark House*, based on J. B. Priestley's *Benighted*; *The Devil and the Deep*, with Gary Cooper; *Payment Deferred*, *The Sign of the Cross* (in which, despite the strong disapproval of the director, Cecil B. de Mille, he played Nero as an effeminate homosexual) and *If I Had a Million*, the Ernst Lubitsch comedy in which Laughton, as the clerk who has unexpectedly inherited a million dollars from a total stranger, takes a long, deliberate walk through the office building where he works to blow a farewell raspberry at the boss. By and large the films were not greatly impressive but Laughton was and he was beginning to gain recognition as a character actor when Alexander Korda brought him back to London in 1933 to play the title role in *The Private Life of Henry VIII*. This was a picture which, despite its early difficulties, turned out to have the most far-reaching consequences. It established the British film industry on an international basis, it established Korda at the head of that industry and it established Laughton as an actor of exceptional ability.

In the light of all that, it seems incredible that at first Korda had the utmost difficulty in persuading anyone to distribute it. Indeed, it sat on the shelf for six months until United Artists agreed to take it on, whereupon it was an immediate success. Laughton's huge, bravura performance won him the Academy Award for best actor, to say nothing of ecstatic reviews.

The acclaim that was thrust upon him would have been enough to satisfy most actors but Laughton, being Laughton, regarded his success with deep suspicion. In his own opinion he had missed some vital element in Henry's character and so, no matter what anyone else said, the portrayal as far as he was concerned was a failure. To make matters even worse the international celebrity that he had now acquired made him a widely recognised and widely imitated personality; every mimic and impressionist added Charles Laughton to his repertoire. Well, again most people would have taken this as something of a compliment but to a man who hated his own appearance and suspected his own gifts that kind of recognition was intensely painful.

Laughton's repugnance for his own appearance and his dissatisfaction with his acting simply increased along with his fame and success. "As an actor," said Elsa Lanchester, "he didn't have any particular method but he did try to be a real person, to get into the character and he always started off a film in desperate unhappiness because he didn't feel that he was anywhere near what he was aiming to be. In fact it's absolutely true that in every film he did he said, 'I can't go on with this unless you shoot the first three days again.' And the directors had to say 'Yes, Charles, we'll shoot it again,' but then the film went on, it would be cut and we'd see the rushes and he could never find those first three days. Even so, he was never satisfied."

Yet beneath the agonising and the self-doubt, neither of which ever left him, there was also, as there had to be, a belief in

With his wife, Elsa Lanchester, in their Hollywood garden.

himself as an artist. Christopher Isherwood says that Laughton was not a vain man but "he liked himself", he realised fundamentally how good he was. Paul Gregory says: "He had greatness, no two ways about it. He was the only genius I've ever known. I think he thought he was great, too, and was sort of comforted by that thought and wanted people to think he was even greater." But, with it all, Gregory says, he was "one of the most frightened human beings I've ever known, frightened of himself. I think his being so unattractive as he was gave him an enormous complex and there would be times when he wouldn't want to be seen. And yet I've seen him when he was absolutely, radiantly beautiful and I told him that one time. He had done a show and he'd been hateful before, absolutely hateful, and he'd gone on stage and really I've never seen anything so beautiful as Laughton was in that performance. Afterwards we were riding in the car and I said: 'Charles, I can't help but tell you that you were absolutely beautiful on that stage tonight,' and he turned round and looked at me and said: 'You rotten son of a bitch, why do you tell me that?' and he burst into tears and it was just terrible, you know? It was like Niagara Falls because he didn't even cry lightly."

With Henry VIII serving as the foundation stone of his career as a leading man Laughton now entered on the most fruitful phase of his time in Hollywood. His portrayal of the Victorian father in *The Barretts of Wimpole Street* dominated the whole film, quite overwhelming Norma

Shearer and Frederic March as the romantic lovers. MGM and Louis B. Mayer (happily ignorant of Laughton's sexual proclivities) asked him to stay on and play Mr. Micawber in *David Copperfield*. It seemed a splendid piece of casting to everyone except Laughton. George Cukor, the director, recalls that "he looked marvellous, just like the illustrations, but he was not comfortable. He didn't feel that he had the geniality or the innocence and he was quite right. It was too bad but he simply didn't have the innocence to play Micawber. I believe he was generally unhappy about everything. He doubted himself all the time. He said, 'I am not good, not good.' He was a most accomplished actor – a very intelligent man – but I feel he was tormented and because of that he tormented other people I should think." After three or four days of this torment and self-doubt Laughton left the cast and was replaced, very probably at his own suggestion, by W. C. Fields.

But this was a brief and ultimately insignificant setback for he swiftly went on to appear in *Ruggles of Red Gap*, his own favourite picture, in which he played the English butler in the wild west. Then, as if deliberately showing off the kind of virtuosity which few other film actors could match, he appeared as Javert in *Les Miserables*, as Captain Bligh – his most famous and most imitated performance – in *Mutiny on the Bounty* and, returning to England to work for Korda again, took the title role in *Rembrandt*.

All this in the space of two years and accompanied, inevitably, by the usual agonising, especially when he played opposite Clark Gable in *Mutiny on the Bounty*. The two men did not get on well, each thinking the other was trying to steal the picture, an absurd delusion on Laughton's part since Gable was never in the same league, let alone the same division, as an actor. But what added to Laughton's worries, according to Charles Higham, was Gable's sheer physical presence. Here was a big, handsome man "a 100 per cent man, a masculine man", the very antithesis of Laughton and "the knowledge made him suffer horribly". Higham believes that with Laughton, more than with most other actors, the playing of great and significant characters like Henry VIII, Bligh and Rembrandt was a way in which he himself could feel significant and important. "He could become somebody greater than himself and lose himself but I don't think it led him to any deeper understanding of himself. In fact, in a way, it increased his sense of inferiority because after he cast off the robes and the costumes he had to go home and be an ugly, unappetising, unhappy man pursuing other men. I mean, what a contrast – from all the magnificence and glamour to this furtive, horrible life he was leading."

Nevertheless and whatever Laughton's own state of mind his reputation was now reaching a peak. His films were making money and in the opinion of one critic, Mark van Doren, his performance as Bligh "fixes him in my mind at any rate as by far the best of living actors". And when *Rembrandt* was revived in London in 1949, thirteen years after it was made, the *Daily Telegraph* critic said of it: "Laughton never again did anything so good."

So, in 1937, apparently secure at the top of his profession, Laughton again came to London to play in the screen adaptation of Robert Graves' *I, Claudius* for Alexander Korda. Nearly thirty years later what was made of this film became the centre of a BBC TV documentary called *The Epic that Never Was*. For Laughton the entire enterprise was a horrendous experience.

The intolerant and dictatorial attitude of the director, Josef Von Sternberg, drove him literally to tears. He was confused by the constant changes in the script and for a long time he was unable to find a key to the character of Claudius. Then, when at last he did begin to feel his way into the part, inspired thanks to God knows what actor's alchemy by the abdication speech of King Edward VIII, the filming was abruptly cancelled. Merle Oberon, who was playing Messalina, was badly injured in a car crash. Shooting was suspended while she recovered and was not resumed. The reasons for this were never explained by any of those concerned, but the generally unhappy feeling on the set, together with rapidly mounting costs, probably had a lot to do with it. In any event, Laughton greeted the cancellation of the picture with great relief and refused ever to speak to Von Sternberg again. The irony of the whole affair is that, had it been finished, it might have been Laughton's greatest accomplishment. As to what he would have been like as Micawber one can only speculate; but on the evidence of what exists of *I, Claudius* there is no doubt that a quite superb performance was in the making.

The aftermath of the Claudian fiasco was another, though different, fiasco. Laughton decided to set up his own company, Mayflower Productions, so that he could have complete control of his work. In three years (from 1937 to 1939) Mayflower made three pictures, *Vessels of Wrath*, adapted from a Maugham short story about a missionary (Elsa Lanchester) and a beachcomber (Laughton); *St. Martin's Lane*, a tale of London buskers with Vivien Leigh grossly miscast as a Cockney and Daphne du Maurier's *Jamaica Inn*, one of the least satisfactory films Alfred Hitchcock ever directed. None of the pictures was particularly good and none of them made money, so the company was a failure both artistically and financially. Tom Laughton says, with hindsight, that the whole idea was doomed to disaster from the start. "It was utterly wrong. Charles was an actor. He turned out to be quite a good director on the one film he did direct but he was essentially an actor. He wasn't fit to have financial responsibility and he couldn't stand it. It took him all his time to worry about his performances and that's as much as he could do. He wasn't a businessman."

Mayflower Productions was wound up in 1939 and Laughton returned to Hollywood to play Quasimodo in *The Hunchback of Notre Dame* – his last great performance of the 1930s and indeed his last for many years. During the making of the film, while in fact he was shooting the famous bells sequence, war was declared in Europe and he thought seriously about flying back to England to offer his services, though the idea was clearly preposterous. He was already forty, grossly overweight and he still suffered from the side effects of the gassing he had received in the First World War. Eventually he decided to stay in America – for which action he was much criticised by the British press – and did his bit for the Allied cause by selling War Bonds.

It was at this point, during the war years, that his career began to go into decline. He worked consistently through the 1940s but not to any great effect, almost as though he were living on the credit he had stored up with his handful of superb performances in the previous decade. Admittedly when viewed now, forty years later, even some of his most famous pictures – *Henry VIII* for instance, *Les Miserables* and *Hunchback* – look quaint and dated but the same could never be said of Laughton's performance in them.

In the forties, however, not only the films but even Laughton himself seemed below standard, although inevitably there were exceptions to that general condemnation: there was *This Land is Mine*, a wartime propaganda effort about the French Resistance directed by Jean Renoir, in which Laughton was highly effective as a mild schoolteacher; there was *The Canterville Ghost*, adapted from the story by Oscar Wilde, which elicited from him a clever and witty performance; there was *The Suspect*, with Laughton as a meek Edwardian driven to murder, and later there was *The Big Clock*, a thriller which once again saw him being larger and more splendid than life. But set against these were the potboilers, such as the children's picture *Captain Kidd* and the Deanna Durbin comedy *Because of Him*, which one can only assume he made simply for the money. Laughton was never above prostituting his own enormous talent in exchange for a quick fee, not out of greed or acquisitiveness but usually in order to buy a painting. As early as 1935 he had used his entire savings, at that time rather less than £10,000, to buy Renoir's *The Judgement of Paris* and ever afterwards he was inclined to invest whatever spare cash he had lying around in works of art; although invest is not the correct word. Laughton valued his collection not for its resale value but for its own beauty.

When he bought the Renoir, Elsa Lanchester said: "He called me and said, 'I've seen a painting I can barely live without. It's a great picture and the most important thing that's ever happened in my life. Do you mind if I spend our savings on it?' So we acquired the Renoir and over the years we acquired other pictures and works of art as well and every time it was something he was passionately fond of. It was a great passion. A lot of people say they have that passion, like Edward G. Robinson may or may not have had it. But everything he bought he knew he could sell for more. Charles didn't give a thought to whether he could sell a picture for more, not ever. There was a time when he was getting sort of low because the films weren't too hot

for him, when we had to sell some of his collection and we sold the Renoir. But even then it wasn't because of what we could get for it. It was because he'd read somewhere that Gertrude Stein had said: 'Don't keep a picture when it's gone into the wall,' and Charles looked at the Renoir one day and said: 'It's gone into the wall,' and he sold it. But after that he started collecting all over again.''

Professionally perhaps the most important event in his career during the 1940s was that he had begun to give readings and recitals in public. Originally he did this merely as part of his war effort, to entertain the troops and with no thought of making a career of it but within a few years these readings were to become a significant part of his repertoire. Also, as his films failed to make money and the Hollywood moguls, who always loved money better than any actor, began to talk of him ominously as "a commercial liability" he returned briefly to the stage, appearing in Los Angeles and New York in Bertolt Brecht's version of *Galileo*. The New York reviews were not particularly enthusiastic but the play did well during its limited run. One other development in Laughton's life that occurred around the same time was that he started holding acting classes at his home. Shelley Winters was a regular attender, Robert Mitchum, Robert Ryan, Paulette Goddard and Peter Ustinov turned up occasionally.

It's difficult now to judge precisely what these classes achieved. Shelley Winters says: "You worked six days a week from seven or eight p.m. until eleven. He demanded that your sights be very high for yourself. He made you understand you weren't just in business to make money and in those days when the studios told me I was a hunk of meat, a blonde bombshell, he made me understand I was an artist and a human being and I could demand respect and dignity.''

Paul Gregory's view is altogether more jaundiced. "It was just an ego trip for Laughton. He fancied himself with people following him around adoring him.''

Laughton's partnership with Gregory began in 1950, the year in which he and Elsa moved into what was to become their final Hollywood home, a large, rambling house with a tropical garden that looks like a miniature jungle, and in which they both became American citizens. Given Laughton's love of America and its comparatively classless society, together with the fact that he had never been accepted – and had never tried to be accepted – by the English community in Hollywood, this was a logical step.

But the most far-reaching event of 1950 was the meeting in New York with Paul Gregory, an agent turned impresario, who heard him recite from the Bible on the Ed Sullivan TV Show and was immediately struck with the idea of taking him on a reading tour of the country. Laughton's initial response to this suggestion was fairly cool but Gregory managed to attract his attention by talking about the potential fortune that such an enterprise could mean to them both.

"I think the persuasion was purely money,'' Gregory said. "When I told him that I thought we could make between eight and ten thousand dollars a week, it was pretty much the factor that convinced him.'' Laughton wasn't exactly hard up at the time but, as he confessed to Gregory later, his career was no longer on the peak that it had once reached and "he told me, and I like this statement, that he was down to his last 50,000 dollars.'' Furthermore, his film career had plunged to such depths that he had signed a contract, for a mere 25,000 dollars, to appear in a frightful movie called *Abbot and Costello Meet Captain Kidd*. The one thing to be said about that was that from there the only way was up.

The partnership lasted six years, and, financially and artistically, was a phenomenal success. The reading tours, consisting largely of passages from the Bible and Dickens were followed by more ambitious, though similar, productions in which Laughton toured with Cedric Hardwicke, Agnes Moorehead and Charles Boyer in readings of Shaw's *Don Juan in Hell*, and with Tyrone Power, Raymond Massey and Judith Anderson in Stephen Vincent Benet's *John Brown's Body*. Laughton, the reader, also made records and appeared on radio and TV and won himself a whole new audience of admirers in the United States and Canada.

The association culminated in 1955 when, again thanks largely to Gregory's help, Laughton turned film director for the only time in his life to make *The Night of the Hunter*, a strange, almost terrifying story, scripted by James Agee, about the pursuit by a psychopathic lay preacher (Robert Mitchum) of two children who could tell him the whereabouts of their dead father's money. Before starting work on it Laughton ran all D. W. Griffith's films in a private cinema to capture the mood he wanted and the result of this one essay as a director is a picture that is both lyrical and nightmarish, one that was grossly underrated in its day, being dismissed by the critics as "too arty" but that is now regarded as a classic of the American cinema.

The making of the film, however, was fraught with hazards as indeed was the entire partnership with Paul Gregory. Laughton's cavalier attitude to costs meant the picture was over budget from the first week of shooting and besides he was ruthless in his attitude to James Agee. Gregory said: "Charles Laughton could eat people up. Agee came to me one day – and he was drunk all the time – and he said, 'Laughton is driving me to drink, he's killing me.' Laughton would keep him in the house, working with him, till two or three in the morning and he didn't know, he never knew, if it was for the work or just for the company and Agee died from this treatment. He died the next spring."

No doubt the drink helped a little too, and Laughton could hardly be given all the blame for that. But nevertheless Gregory is convinced that Laughton's attitude to Agee

left him a broken man, in spirit if not in health.

Gregory said: "The name Charles Laughton to me conjures up immediately about fifty or sixty different emotional reactions. He was at once wonderful, at once impossible and destructive."

Even on the reading tours, perhaps especially on the reading tours, Laughton's behaviour was often eccentric. "He did naughty things," Gregory recalled, "like going into a hospital in Salt Lake City for fourteen days when he wasn't sick – he was in there eating chocolates. He did it just to get even, with whom I don't know. With me, I guess. I don't think he enjoyed the reading tours as such. He loved it when I'd call him and say, 'Charlie, we've got 250,000 dollars worth of bookings,' but as the time neared he would think of all kinds of reasons not to have to go on this tour and postpone the first week and it would be like pulling a tooth to finally arrive at

Laughton showed immense talent as a director with The Night of the Hunter. *But he was never encouraged to direct again.*

the time when that car headed out across country to meet those commitments and all the time he'd be griping about this and that . . . Have you ever tried to push an elephant? Because that's what it was like."

In addition he would wilfully, and on some mischievous impulse, ruin deals that Gregory had worked hard to pull off. Once they had a conference with a Methodist Church group as the result of which it was agreed that Laughton should record a series of Bible readings that would have brought in millions of dollars. All that remained was for the contracts to be signed when Laughton turned casually to the leader of the Methodist contingent and remarked: "Well, old boy, you know the Bible is full of shit?" The churchman, to whom this revelation came as a considerable surprise, immediately called off the entire deal.

The partnership with Gregory ended soon after the completion of *The Night of the Hunter*, partly because their joint attempt at filming Norman Mailer's *The Naked and the Dead*, with Laughton again directing, ended in disaster. "I raised five million dollars for it," Gregory said. "We had a special budget for the script and, my lord, within six months he spent the entire amount. He was sending people all over the world like he was J. Arthur Rank or somebody. So, of course, the people who were putting up the money called me in and said, 'What's the meaning of this – 500,000 dollars spent and the camera hasn't even begun to turn over?' And I'd say to Charlie, 'Look, what *is* happening?' and he'd disappear and wouldn't talk to me when I called. Well, you can't work with somebody like that. And when the deal fell apart he couldn't stand up to it and fled and left me with it." Gregory finally produced what he admits is an "inferior film" of *The Naked and the Dead* but at least the backers got a return on their money. Laughton, on the other hand, was never again asked to direct.

But, possibly by way of compensation, his acting career began to thrive once more. He returned to England to star in David Lean's screen version of *Hobson's Choice* and, in 1957, when he and Elsa Lanchester appeared in Billy Wilder's adaptation of the Agatha Christie story, *Witness for the Prosecution*, both were nominated for Oscars.

Wilder's total admiration for Laughton,

the artist, stems from that picture. "He had audacity," Wilder said. "He went to the very brink of the ridiculous but he stopped there. You know, when we had finished the principal photography there was only one thing left to do and that was to shoot the reactions of the jury to all the stuff that had happened during the trial.

"Laughton came by the studio one day and asked what I was doing and I told him. He said 'How do you do that?' I said, 'Well, I'd have various shots of the jury from this side and that and they'd have to react to Tyrone Power, Marlene Dietrich, to the judge, to you and blah, blah, blah.' He said, 'Well, who's reading the lines off-stage?' I said, 'I don't know. Maybe the script girl or somebody.' He said, 'Let me do it.' I said, 'Charles, this is wearisome. This is a chore.' He said, 'I must do it,' and there he was in a Hawaian shirt and unshaven – you could still see his breakfast on his shirt – and he played all the parts and it was one of the most stunning displays of a universal talent. He played Dietrich better than Dietrich ever was, he played Ty Power better than Ty Power, he was just fabulous, absolutely fabulous. I was enthralled. This was like a one-man football team. He played the goalkeeper and the striker and the referee too. It was fantastic what he did . . . Laughton was a personal friend of mine, you understand, but I found him at times petulant, at times sloppy, at times grouchy and then he wouldn't talk for three days. But my God this was an actor who brought with him a great big bag of stuff. He would discuss a scene with me and he would say, 'I could do it this way,' and I'd say, 'That's good.' Then he'd say, 'Or I could do it this way,' and I'd say, 'That's better.' And then came twenty more versions and I'd say, 'That's it, that's it,' and the next morning he would arrive and say, 'I thought of something last night. There's one other way,' and that would be absolutely stupendous too."

In 1959, and two years after *Witness for the Prosecution*, Laughton went to Stratford-upon-Avon to play King Lear and Bottom in *A Midsummer Night's Dream*. To play Lear, a character with whom he felt a great affinity, a shared sense of having been persecuted by others of smaller stature than himself, had been a lifelong ambition, almost an obsession. He worked on his interpretation of the part for a full year at his home in Hollywood, often with Christopher Isherwood acting as adviser, critic and audience. These impromptu rehearsals took place in what Laughton called "the school room" at his house. Isherwood said: "I used to sit in that little room and watch and when I see the scene now, sort of impressionistically, it's like sitting all alone in the front row of a gigantic movie theatre where a vast face, dozens of times larger than life, is hanging right over you and saying things like, 'When we are born we cry but we come to this great stage of fools' and this kind of thing and I just wept, you know, and I was transfixed."

But, unhappily, despite all this devoted and careful work Laughton's Lear was not well received. His brother, Tom Laughton, believes Charles was already ill, with the beginnings of the cancer that was soon to kill him, when the Stratford season started and that, as a result, he was both disappointing and disappointed with the critical reception he received. Isherwood, who saw the stage performance, remembers being "tremendously impressed" but adds: "Of course, you know, nothing could be the same as those private auditions. They were something that one might have perhaps once in a lifetime."

So Laughton went back again to Hollywood, for the last time, feeling rejected by Britain or at least by the British critics, although their condemnation of his King Lear was mitigated, in part, by their enthusiastic reception of his performance in the West End production of Jane Arden's play *The Party*, in which he played a hard-drinking solicitor with incestuous feelings for his daughter. Not a cheery role but a successful one for Laughton.

At this point, towards the end of 1959, his health was deteriorating fast and he made only three more films – *Spartacus*, in which he played the Roman Senate leader opposed to the powerful Crassus, played by Laurence Olivier; a war film set in Italy, *Under Two Flags* wherein he appeared as an admiral and, finally, *Advise and Consent*, in which he gave a superb and memorable performance as a corrupt Southern Senator whose bigotry and hatred of homosexuality represented just about everything that Laughton himself detested. By making the character a soft, persuasive monster he cleverly exposed all the bigotry and intolerance. But by the time the film was made

Possibly the finest screen actor Britain has ever produced.

in 1962 Laughton was dying, although he would not admit it even to himself.

His friends, however, knew the truth. Billy Wilder was planning to film *Irma La Douce* and wanted Laughton to play Moustache but, knowing of the actor's grave illness, was preparing to recast when one day he received a summons to Laughton's home . . .

"He said, 'Don't listen to whatever they tell you, it's not true. I'll prove it – come and see me at my house.' I went that lunchtime . . . he had had his male nurse dress him up, comb his hair, shave him, maybe even put a little make-up on him, and he was sitting in a chair at the swimming pool. He said, 'Now look at me. Do I look like somebody that's going to die?' And he got himself out of the chair and he walked around the pool. He must have been in tremendous pain but he just wanted to say to me, 'Wait.' This was one of the finest performances I tell you. I was very touched . . . I wiped my eyes as I walked out of the house, knowing full well that I would never see him alive again."

During all this time and despite the fact that each led a separate and private existence Laughton and Lanchester had stayed together and they did so until the end. Mostly she would keep away from the house when he was entertaining a boyfriend, although she got to know some of them quite well. "When he was with one in particular," she said, "I used to go to

195

the market every day and get two peach pies for them. I didn't mind. I don't mind a bit of peach pie myself." In any event she had, understandably, friends and relationships of her own. The interests she shared with her husband were not sexual but domestic – they had their house, their paintings, their garden. Towards the end of his life, at the beginning of his final illness, Laughton said to her: "I wish this whole sex thing would finish, just disappear."

By then a gentler kind of homosexual friendship seems to have replaced the more active homosexual passions in his life. "I was very glad," Elsa said, "that in later life he got fond of people, which is a very different story, you know. That was safer and nicer." The marriage itself, she said, was not simply a front "though you could call it that if you wanted to. We were very, very attached and we wanted people to see that we were happy, so we showed the happy side. It wasn't a particularly easy life but we were both on tour quite a bit and afterwards we always came home as soon as possible and if you'd seen us at the airport you'd have thought we were Romeo and Juliet. We had, in a way, to be apart in order to become attached."

Charles Higham, the biographer, believes the marriage worked because they both decided to take second best rather than nothing at all. "In other words, if she'd said, 'No, I can't tolerate living with a man who's having affairs with men,' she would have lost Charles and he would have lost her but they meant an enormous amount to each other because they enjoyed the same things – they had gardening in common, love of flowers, love of woodlands, love of England, deep affection for the Californian countryside and a tremendously similar taste in art."

Paul Gregory said: "Elsa gave Charles a fixture in life that he needed and as much as he spat and clawed and kicked at it, he still needed it. That was the one thing of respectability he liked – he liked having a Mrs. Laughton. He would like it even today. He wouldn't just come right out and say, 'This is my boyfriend.' He was always very deep with all that."

Perhaps because of the reticence he learned at Stonyhurst he was always secretive about his homosexuality even with his closest friends, those he could have trusted to understand and lend encouragement.

Soon after meeting and becoming friendly with Christopher Isherwood in 1959 he bought a house at Malibu, next door to Isherwood's because, he said to Elsa, he wanted to be "near his own kind". Even so Isherwood was only peripherally aware of Laughton's homosexual activities . . . "I really had, as a matter of fact, amazingly little contact with him, with his friendships with boys or contacts of any kind with boys. That was all rather kept a little bit aside." But from what he did know of Laughton's private life he felt that there was "a great deal of a father and son thing in those relationships, an element of instruction and being proud of the one who is instructed."

Laughton's affairs with other men need to be emphasised if only because of the historical context in which they occurred. Today it may not matter much whether an actor is homosexual or not but in Laughton's time the conditions were very different. Homosexuality was socially unacceptable and indeed against the law. Thus a homosexual who was in the public eye could not help but lead a furtive and even a guilt-ridden life, with the fear of being found out ever close to his thoughts. And a homosexual like Laughton who went in for casual affairs with highly inappropriate people rather than for a steady and settled relationship with one man must presumably have suffered more than most.

Because of the closeness of their professional relationship over six years Paul Gregory probably observed more of Laughton's private life than anyone except Elsa Lanchester. "Charles was aggressive as a homosexual," he said. "He wasn't a little worm in the wood. There were always people popping up whom he'd brought along, who were following on in the bus behind you. And he made it more difficult for himself, too, because he wasn't content to have just one, he'd have a ménage of them. Some of them would end up in prison and you'd get calls from wardens and letters threatening him. He had set himself up as a target."

They were not then, these men and boyfriends, Laughton's intellectual equals in any way? "Of course not," Gregory said. "They were the dregs, low class kind of people. He had a sort of Higgins complex about being able to make them into something. He'd say, 'I've got this young man who has star quality,' and it would be some wretch he'd met along the way and he'd have no star quality at all, except to Charles. They weren't physically similar but they were all young, very young. On a college campus or someplace Laughton would encounter someone to whom he would give a "scholarship" and he'd call me and say, 'Put 500 dollars in such and such an account,' and then I'd join him later and say, 'Well, where's the scholarship boy?' and he'd say, 'Oh, I got rid of him in Palm Beach or somewhere.' They'd come and go. I didn't have too much to do with all that except to write the cheques for him and hide them from Elsa and his accountants."

With all this going on it's not at all surprising that Laughton was, by general agreement, a tormented man. To what extent that particular torment helped his development as an artist perhaps he alone could tell. But whatever the contributory factors – and homosexuality and his conviction of his own physical ugliness were undoubtedly among them – his artistry is undeniable. He was an actor of remarkable range, intelligence and sensitivity. If his performances often looked to be over the top, that was because of an unkind twist of fate: his very appearance was over the top. As Peter Ustinov said, even when he was sitting perfectly still and in repose he was already doing too much but if you look beyond that huge, remarkable face Laughton's acting was full of subtlety and wit. His film career was a thing of ups and downs, mostly consisting of splendid performances in unworthy vehicles, but at its best his work was superb by any standards.

Laughton died, of bone cancer, in the school room of his home in Hollywood on December 15th, 1962. He was sixty-three years old and he was still trying to convince himself and everybody else that one day he would be well enough to work again. Before he died, thanks to the efforts of his two brothers, he had been received once more into the Roman Catholic faith.

Thinking back, a decade and a half later, on the man he had known, Christopher Isherwood said: "It was possible to love him. I think many people quite misunderstood him, you know, or didn't see that side of him." Then, after a long pause . . .

"I rather loved him, yes. But again I was fully aware of how difficult he could be with other people."

Elsa Lanchester said: "I know that I've become a more live, complete person since he died. But if I'd died first I would say that Charles would be a more tortured man because we all think of what we might have done but didn't and I know he would suffer deeply because of what he might have done."

Tom Laughton remembers a perfectionist who was difficult to work with, a man who could be ruthless when it involved his work but also a brother who was a "kind, gentle, marvellous man".

Billy Wilder talks of "this universal, interested, fascinating man – the complete Renaissance man, one who could talk engrossingly and knowledgeably about Impressionist painting and Burgundy wine, who could phone at eleven thirty at night and say 'You must come over straightaway. I have a plant which will open at midnight and it opens only once a year and you must see it.' " Wilder says: "There was no way of saying 'Who the hell cares? I've seen plants open and close, no big deal.' Oh no, I had to be there."

I asked Paul Gregory whether, given the opportunity, he would go through his years of business partnership with Laughton again and he said: "I don't know. What I didn't know at that time was his disposition. He was cruel and I don't think we have a right to be cruel to anybody and he was cruel not only to me but to other people. There was a cruelty there that was frightening – in his rudeness, in his talk with you sometimes, the things he would say to you, the way he would attack you in areas where you weren't able to respond."

And then, summing the man up, he said: "Charles had to have turmoil all the time. Whatever the situation he'd pit somebody against somebody else. He just couldn't help it. He had to do this. But out of this garbage he'd created, he would grow a rose, a rose of extraordinary blossom would come and then it was so beautiful you would weep for the beauty and weep for the injury . . . And that was Charlie. He could embrace you out of your life. It was all enormous."

Henry Fonda

One day, when he was on his honeymoon, Henry Fonda took his new bride to the beach: the sort of thing husbands often do in such circumstances as Fonda would have known better than most because he was already on his third honeymoon, one for each wife so far. Susan, the latest Mrs. Fonda, only twenty-two years old and naturally anxious to please her man, took his watch and laid it carefully on a piece of driftwood so that sand wouldn't get into the works.

"It was quite a rare watch for that time," she said. "It showed the hour, the day, the month, what time the moon came up and went down and it did everything but dance." Having performed this thoughtful uxorial duty Susan joined her husband in the sea, emerging some time later to find that the tide had come in and the driftwood had vanished and so had the watch.

"I was devastated," she said. "I ran up the beach and said, 'I've lost your watch,' and I burst into tears and I just felt terrible."

And Fonda eyed her coldly and said: "Don't cry. Crying is disgusting."

At which point . . . "I turned round and cried some more. He didn't like displays of emotion. Boy, did he ever marry the wrong party."

Well, he was good at marrying the wrong party; he had a positive gift for it. By the time he had finished his experiments in matrimony he had been on five honeymoons and it was only with his fifth and final bride that he found a lasting contentment and happiness. That the other marriages failed was, in at least three cases out of four and as he would readily have pointed out himself, largely his own fault. For it was a curious paradox of his nature

that while he was a man of immense charm, a most honourable and decent man capable of arousing abiding affection in others, he found it virtually impossible to display any kind of deep emotion, especially love. That he could feel love there is no doubt; but a love, however passionate, that is never allowed to reveal itself is something of a handicap to a successful marriage.

Fonda was aware of this shortcoming but unable to understand it himself. Or, at least, he said he was unable to understand it but since he hardly ever seems to have shared his innermost thoughts with anybody I suppose it's quite possible that he had in fact worked it all out but chose not to disclose his findings. James Stewart, who was probably his closest friend for more than fifty years, claimed that in all that time they never discussed either marriage or politics which, if true, is remarkable.

Oddly enough there was nothing in Fonda's early background to explain his emotional reticence, although there was certainly one incident that helps to account for the staunch and humane liberalism that he practised all his life. He was born (on May 16th, 1905) and brought up in Nebraska, the heartland of America, his birthplace being Grand Island, although he only lived there for six months before his parents, William and Herberta, moved to Omaha, where Fonda Sr. became a printer. There, too, Henry – or Hank, as he was known to his intimates – was joined by two sisters, Harriet and Jayne.

The Fondas, originally of Italian descent, were Christian Scientists, not particularly well-off but not poor either: a solid, sober, hard-working, affectionate and caring family. The affection was probably implicit rather than overtly explicit

With Susan (wife No. 3), who was told that tears are disgusting . . .

198

but the caring, in a general, social sense anyway, was given practical demonstration by William when in September 1919, he took his son, then aged fourteen, to watch a lynching.

This event, which the local law was presumably unable or unwilling to prevent, must have been reasonably well publicised because the Fondas, father and son, made a special journey downtown to watch it. The victim was a young black man who had been accused of raping a white woman. He had not actually been found guilty of this crime but legal niceties mean little to a lynch mob. On this occasion they dragged the terrified youth out of the courthouse and strung him up from a lamp post. William Fonda's motive in taking his young son to watch this appalling act had nothing at all to do with morbid curiosity: he simply wanted the boy to understand, graphically and unforgettably, what hatred and intolerance could lead to. And Hank never did forget.

This dramatic and horrifying episode apart, however, the young Fonda's upbringing appears to have been placid and unexceptional. He was unusually shy, perhaps, but otherwise much like any other youthful middle-class Nebraskan. At the age of eighteen he went to the University of Minnesota in Minneapolis to study journalism but exhausted himself by doing various odd jobs to work his way through college. As a result he did badly in his exams, dropped out of university, returned home – and by accident became an actor.

A friend of his mother's, one Dorothy Brando – the mother at that time of a year-old son called Marlon, later to become something of an actor himself – was running an amateur theatrical group called the Omaha Community Playhouse and she asked Hank if he would join the company.

John Houseman, who was later to direct Fonda on stage in a triumphant portrayal of Clarence Darrow, the legendary American lawyer, said: "The reason he found acting such an enormous satisfaction and joy was that he was a very timid, diffident and slightly insecure young man who suddenly discovered that the minute he went out there, even in a not very big part, he was somebody else. When he went through that door on to the stage he became somebody else; he didn't have any of the problems of his own life to deal with; he dealt with the problems of the character he was playing. I suppose all actors are like this to some extent but I've never known anyone else for whom it was so totally, completely true."

Fonda's own explanation was, typically, more laconic: "I liked the feeling of being up there after I realised that all eyes were not on me all the time. I lost most of my self-consciousness and began to relax."

Initially William Fonda was less than enthusiastic about his son's new interest, arguing that he should be out pursuing a career instead of frittering away his time on amateur theatricals. But after Henry won unanimous applause in the title role of *Merton of the Movies* (playing a grocery clerk who prayed each night that God would make him a film star) even the elder Fonda gave his support and Hank began to seek and find jobs with various small theatrical companies.

But it was not until 1928, when he was twenty-three years old, that the next significant opportunity came his way. He was taken to see the University Players – a bunch of Ivy League graduates and undergraduates from Harvard, Yale, Princeton and the like – in a production of *The Torch Bearer* by George Kelly. He was immediately enchanted by them all and by none more than Joshua Logan, who was playing a comic character called Huxley Hossefrosse.

Logan said: "I stepped onto the stage and said, 'Anybody here, David?', which was my first line and I heard a howl of laughter out in the audience. It sounded like somebody sobbing in a high voice and being strangled at the same time. It was a terrible sound but so funny that the whole audience laughed at it and after that every time I said a word this funny howl came and the audience roared with laughter. At the end I got a tremendous hand and I was a huge success but only because of this terrible thing that was happening and I didn't know who it was. I went backstage and was taking my make-up off in our communal dressing room and the orchestra leader came in and said, 'I'd like you to meet somebody, a friend of mine from Omaha. His name is Henry Fonda,' and this funny, long-legged, long drink of water came in. He had this cherubic face – perfect, handsome, beautiful almost – and a funny, long, wiggly body. I can't explain it: he caved in at the chest and came out at

the pelvis and he wore black stockings and . . . well, in those days plus fours were the big thing but his were more like minus twos. He really was an odd-looking man with this beautiful face and he looked around the room and said, 'Were you Huxley Hossefrosse?', pointing at me, and I said, 'Yes' and he let out this terrible yell, this appalling laugh and I knew immediately who he was and I've loved him ever since."

The affection was mutual and Fonda at once began a four-year association with the University Players which was to prove significant in all manner of ways. First, it gave him experience and exposure in a variety of roles; secondly it led to lifelong friendships with both Logan and James Stewart who, in fact, replaced Fonda in the company when he left; and thirdly it led indirectly to his first meeting with a beautiful and gifted young actress named Margaret Sullavan. In April 1929, and in between University Players' seasons he appeared in a musical at Harvard. Margaret Sullavan was also in the cast and she and Fonda promptly fell in love. It was by no means an easy relationship for Miss Sullavan was a volatile and high-spirited character who appeared to be attached to a remarkably short fuse. Nevertheless, the romance flourished and on Christmas Day 1931 they were married at the Kernan Hotel in Baltimore. She was twenty and he was twenty-six and Joshua Logan was at the wedding.

"They got married in the big old dining room where the whole company ate. It sounds grand but it was the saddest big dining room you've ever seen in your life. We sort of ate like people in the army – we went by with our plates and they slopped the food on. I would say it was the most pitiful little marriage ceremony ever. Then they went off on their honeymoon but they didn't stay on it at all. They got quite lonely that night without the rest of us and they came back the next day."

The marriage itself was almost as brief as the honeymoon. Temperamental differences, squabbles, tantrums and shouting matches became so frequent that within four months they had parted. Joshua Logan said he was not surprised that the marriage came so swiftly to an end: "I was surprised that it took place at all. You ask if they were at all suited to each other. Well, I don't know that either of them was

suited to anyone. They were very special people. On stage they were magic together but they had their own ideas and though they seemed to get along very well together the moment they were married there were difficulties. I never knew exactly what but mostly I'm sure they were intellectual difficulties."

And yet there was more to it than that. In his biography – *Fonda: My Life*, written by Howard Teichmann – Fonda told how he had heard that his wife was having an affair with a producer named Jed Harris. Many nights after that he would stand watching their apartment, knowing the lovers were in there together and waiting for Harris to leave. But all that would happen was that the bedroom lights were turned out . . .

Teichmann quotes Fonda as saying: "I couldn't believe my wife and that son-of-a-bitch were in bed together. But I knew they were. And that just destroyed me. Never in my life have I felt so betrayed, so rejected, so alone."

Afdera Franchetti, the aristocratic Italian socialite who was later to become Fonda's fourth wife, believed that that was the most destructive and in many ways the most telling experience in Fonda's life, leaving him with emotional wounds that would take thirty-odd years and four more wives to heal.

"Somehow, I think, he never got over that," she said. "That marriage had an enormous effect on him – more than any of the others. It conditioned him for life, so that he couldn't show his emotions and was always a little bit afraid of being hurt again. I don't think she played around with other *men* but she was a very young and bewitching woman and she did play around with the one other man and in a very cruel way. And Fonda was also young and sensitive and not very sophisticated and it scarred him for life."

Soon after his separation from Margaret Sullavan Fonda left the University Players and worked for a while, mostly as a backstage odd-job man, with a theatre company in Maine. But in the autumn of 1932 he went to New York and moved into an apartment with Joshua Logan and two other actors, James Stewart and Myron McCormick, where they set up a kind of small-scale commune. According to James Stewart, "The fellow who was working sort

In his final film On Golden Pond *with Katharine Hepburn, for which, at last, he won the Oscar he had deserved so often.*

201

Margaret Sullavan, the first wife, whose less than benign influence may have helped spoil his next three marriages.

of bore the financial burden and then, when we were all working, we'd put money into a general fund to take care of expenses when we all got fired."

Memories of who did most of the working at that time differ rather sharply. Stewart remembered Fonda as being "the busiest of us all. He had parts in summer stock, in small theatres in New Jersey and in small, try-out theatres." By contrast, Joshua Logan remembers him best as the communal cook but thought that, as an actor, "he certainly should have been losing confidence because everybody else worked except Fonda. James Stewart worked every minute of the time and so did Myron McCormick and so did I – as a company manager or a box-office manager, whatever job I could get. But Fonda couldn't get anything."

Obviously, though, he did manage to find the occasional job but nothing that amounted to very much until in March 1934, he did a comedy sketch with Imogene Coca in a show called *New Faces*. The agent

Leland Hayward was sufficiently impressed to arrange a 1,000 dollar a week film contract for him with producer Walter Wanger. The only slight snag in this deal was that there weren't actually any films for him to appear in so he stayed on Broadway where, at last, the long-awaited big break came his way. He was given the leading role in Marc Connolly's play, *The Farmer Takes a Wife*. It was an immediate success (as, too, was Fonda) and Twentieth Century-Fox swiftly acquired the film rights, seeing it as an ideal vehicle for Janet Gaynor. They did not, at the time, have any plans for Fonda. Instead they offered his role to Gary Cooper and then Joel McCrea but as neither of them was available they decided that the man who had created the part on stage might just as well do it on screen, too, and so they borrowed him from Walter Wanger. Thus in March 1935, two months short of his thirtieth birthday, Henry Fonda went to Hollywood, assuring everyone that it was just for a short time and that he would be back on Broadway very soon. But in that he was wrong.

Fonda's performance in *The Farmer Takes a Wife* still looks a little overblown, a touch stagey, but it would have been much further over the top had it not been for the director, Victor Fleming, who, early in the shooting, took his new young star to one side and pointed out that in the movies there was no need to hit the back row of the gallery. A different kind of acting, a more relaxed and realistic kind of acting, was needed for the cinema and Fonda learned the lesson quickly. He was to improve with each succeeding film but even in that first one and despite his tendency to overplay it's possible to see clearly the beginnings of the Fonda style, a kind of acting that is so subtle and natural as not to seem to be acting at all. Hollywood, the critics and the audiences were all duly impressed and Fonda's return to New York and Broadway was indefinitely delayed.

It was, said James Stewart, simply a part of the "tremendous creative talent" of the man that he adapted so swiftly to the demands of the cinema. "His career just took off. It really happened pretty quick and in a year or so he was recognised as a very important leading man in pictures." Certainly he was busy enough: Fonda made three films in 1935, another three in 1936 and four in 1937.

Around this time, too, James Stewart also received the call to Hollywood where he and Fonda shared a house, double-dated with Lucille Ball and Ginger Rogers, built model aeroplanes and for a while entertained a scheme to dig a tunnel from their garden into that of their next-door neighbour, a certain Greta Garbo who, even in those early days, insisted that she wanted to be alone and thus presented a challenge to the red-blooded and probably randy young men in the adjacent house. Stewart maintained that, in his recollection, they did actually start digging the tunnel but had to abandon it when they encountered some such obstacle as a gas main or a sewage pipe.

But this bachelor existence did not last long, at least not for Fonda. One of the films he made in 1936 was *Wings of the Morning*, a romantic tale in which he co-starred with the French singer and actress, Annabella. It was made in England (the first Technicolor picture to be shot here, in fact) and it soon became evident that Fonda's interest in Annabella was more than merely professional. She, naturally, was flattered and to some extent anyway, pleased, rather to the displeasure of her husband. Rumours, greatly exaggerated but nevertheless confusing, began to drift across the Atlantic about the alleged romance that was taking place on and off the set. Joshua Logan was among those who heard the rumours and took note. What he did not hear, however, was that Fonda's amorous interests had changed direction.

He had met and fallen in love with a twenty-seven-year-old American widow, Frances Seymour Brokaw, whose multi-millionaire husband, George, had died earlier that year, leaving her with a daughter.

The Seymours (Seymour being Frances' maiden name) were a socially and politically prominent New York family, supposedly descended from Lady Jane Seymour. Frances and Fonda travelled through Europe together on an extended courtship. He proposed marriage in Budapest; she accepted in Paris and they returned to New York together to get married. Joshua Logan was to be the best man, although until the couple actually arrived he was by no means sure who the bride was to be.

"I think Fonda was still slightly in love with Annabella," he said, "and I couldn't

Fonda as the romantic leading man, before he became the conscience of America.

quite work out whether it was Annabella he was talking about when he said he was going to be married."

The wedding – the big social event of the season in New York – took place at Christ Church on Park Avenue on September 17th, 1936. The marriage lasted some thirteen years and produced Fonda's two famous children, Jane and Peter, but as with Fonda's first venture into matrimony Joshua Logan could never understand why it happened at all.

"Frances became his wife and the mother of his children. She was a beautiful girl but I never believed they ever had anything to do with each other. Well, it's apparent they did because of the children. But she never talked the same language as he did: she always talked about houses and dresses and jewels and money and sex and various things that he would never mention. She never saw plays or movies and I couldn't quite see why they were so close together. They built a beautiful house and had a wonderful life and wonderful kids but I

203

just never saw them having fun together."

Since the marriage did last a considerable time (certainly by Hollywood standards) it seems reasonable to suppose that the couple, especially in the early days, enjoyed a fair amount of fun together. After the wedding they moved back to California and rented a house off Sunset Boulevard while they planned to build a home of their own. (In those early days their closest neighbours included Fonda's agent, Leland Hayward, who was now married to Fonda's first wife, Margaret Sullavan. This is not altogether an amazing coincidence. The upper levels of Hollywood society consist of a comparatively small number of people. Everyone knows everyone else and sometimes it's possible to imagine that, sooner or later, everyone marries everyone else.)

In those upper levels of society, the Fondas were swiftly accepted, not so much because he was a promising young star but because she, being a millionairess in her own right and very well connected, was recognised as having class, a commodity always in short supply and therefore much prized in the film community.

And so with his social success assured, Fonda swiftly began to increase his reputation as an actor, first showing his versatility by stepping out of character to play a killer in Fritz Lang's *You Only Live Once*, then moving on to co-star with Bette Davis in *That Certain Woman* before returning to the theatre – always the medium in which he felt happiest – to play the title role in *The Virginian* at the Westchester Playhouse. Encouraged by the play's reception he returned to Broadway in *Blow Ye Winds* but the experience was not a happy one because the production closed after only thirty-six performances and Fonda was obliged to return to Hollywood where, in 1938, he appeared in five films, opposite such notable leading ladies as Bette Davis again (in *Jezebel*), Joan Bennett and Barbara Stanwyck.

Although by this time he had made fifteen films and was already thirty-three years old he was not yet considered big enough to carry an important picture on his own, perhaps because he worked for a variety of studios who used him as a foil for their own contract stars. But in 1939 his status improved immeasurably when John Ford cast him in the title role of *The Young Mr. Lincoln*. Initially, he was reluctant to take the part, feeling that Abraham Lincoln, who had always been his hero, was simply too big a character for him to portray. Ford, however, talked him into it, largely by pointing out that as far as the film was concerned Lincoln was not the great emancipator of America but merely a smart, though unassuming, young country lawyer. Thus reassured Fonda gave one of the finest performances of his career.

The picture opened in February 1940, in which month Fonda became a father for the second time, now having a son – Peter – to join his daughter, Jane, who had been born on December 21st, 1937, and who, in honour of her supposed ancestor, was known as Lady Jane for the first few years of her life.

According to Joshua Logan, Fonda's reaction to fatherhood was one of delight. "I remember he was certainly terribly happy when the children were born," he said. Logan was not asked to be godfather to either of the Fonda offspring, though he had served in that office for the children of Leland Hayward and Margaret Sullavan who, when the Fondas moved into their new home, had also moved nearby. There was consequently a certain amount of to-ing and fro-ing between the two families but, Logan said, "the Fonda children were always a little bit distant towards us compared with the others. They were beautiful and fine and well cared for but we never got very chummy with them."

A possible explanation for this apparent aloofness is that Jane and Peter had inherited their father's shyness, although Afdera Franchetti suggested that it may also have been due to the fact that they were already somewhat self-contained children, having little to do with their own parents. She said: "Henry was very busy and according to him so was his wife. She was a very domineering, intelligent career woman. So she looked after the business matters and he looked after his career and the children were cared for by nannies."

At this point, however, the Fondas appeared to be an exceptionally happy and settled family and Hank's career was advancing rapidly. After *The Young Mr. Lincoln* he had made *Drums Along the Mohawk*, a John Ford Western that did his reputation no harm, and then in 1940 he starred, once more with Ford directing, in what is probably his best-remembered film, the adaptation of John Steinbeck's *The Grapes of Wrath*. It was Fonda's performance as Tom Joad that established firmly and indelibly his screen image as the epitome of the honest, liberal American, the caring idealist. It also won him his first Academy Award nomination as best actor although, surprisingly, the Oscar went to his friend James Stewart for his performance in *The Philadelphia Story*. It says much for the power of Fonda's portrayal that Stewart himself actually voted for him. And Joshua Logan, remembering the film more than forty years later, said simply: "Fonda was superb in *The Grapes of Wrath*. That last scene was his signature – Fonda at his very best as a young man."

So at last, as an Oscar nominee, Fonda was accepted as a real star, one whose name above the title was guaranteed to draw at least a respectable audience and capitalising on this he made thirteen films between 1940 and 1942, the last of which was *The Ox-Bow Incident*. At this time, he was under long-term contract to Twentieth Century-Fox and it is a reflection of Fonda's prestige that *The Ox-Bow Incident* was made despite the studio's reluctance and misgivings. No doubt Fox could see little future in a story in which a cowboy (Fonda) was unable to prevent the killing of three men by a lynch mob. Fonda, who never really got along with Fox and actively disliked Darryl Zanuck, the studio head, insisted on it being made anyway, his enthusiasm for what was certainly a grim movie no doubt stemming from the hatred of mob violence that had been kindled in him more than twenty years before when he and his father watched the black man being lynched in Nebraska.

In the event *The Ox-Bow Incident* was his last film for three years. By the time it was released in 1943 he was in the American navy, which service he had joined in August 1942, on the grounds that he had no desire to fight the Second World War on a back lot but wished to be where the action was. He was trained as a signalman, commissioned as an officer, and by 1944 was assigned to the staff of Vice-Admiral Hoover on active service in the Pacific. Towards the end of the war, when his ship, the *Curtis*, shot down a Japanese plane, Fonda and another officer swam out to the aircraft to retrieve its map and flight plans

One of Fonda's best and most memorable roles, as Tom Joad in The Grapes of Wrath.

205

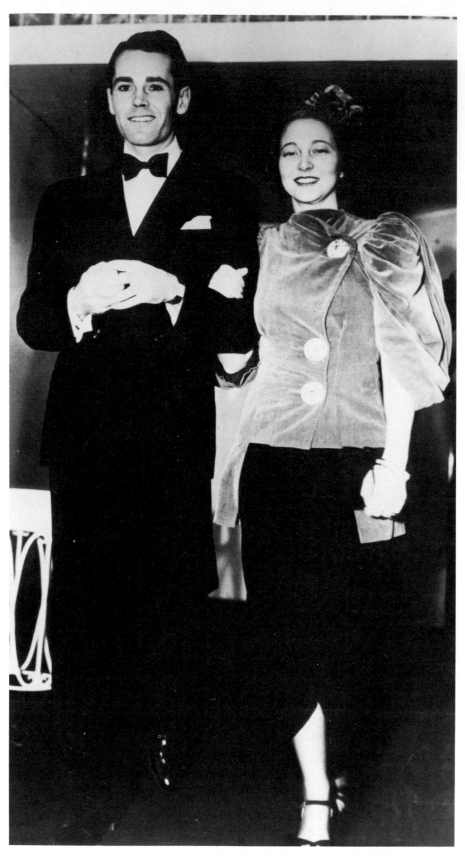

With Frances, his second wife and the mother of Jane and Peter.

and for this action, and for his work in plotting the course of Japanese submarines, he was awarded a Presidential Citation and the Bronze Star. Altogether his was a most respectable war record, and in 1945 he was given an honourable discharge and returned to Hollywood and family life.

But the family he rejoined at the age of forty was by no means as settled as it had appeared before he joined the navy. In the first place, Peter, who was only two when his father went to war, hardly recognised him. And in the second place Frances, reacting as many a wife did in wartime, had eased her own loneliness by indulging in the occasional affair. She was now thirty-six and worried about ageing and losing her looks. At the same time, Fonda himself had changed during those years apart; he had become if anything even more introspective than he had been before and was now prone to outbursts of rage that stemmed perhaps from the tensions and frustrations that he felt at home. Although he and Frances stayed together, the marriage was decidedly shaky.

But for him, as always when his private life was beset by problems, there was the consolation of work. He picked up his film career pretty much where he had left it and between 1946 and 1948 he made seven films, none of them of the quality of *The Grapes of Wrath* but at least two of them – *The Fugitive* and *Fort Apache*, both directed by John Ford – of better than average quality.

This spate of activity culminated, to Fonda's great relief, in the end of his contract with Twentieth Century-Fox, which took him out of the clutches of the detested Darryl Zanuck and left him free to consider a proposition put to him by his old friend, Joshua Logan.

Together with Tom Heggen, Logan had written a play called *Mister Roberts*, based on Heggen's short stories about naval life in the Pacific during the war. Fonda, an old navy man himself, asked if he could hear it. His interest in the project was fairly dispassionate because he was virtually committed to making another film but Logan read it to him all the same and, when he had finished, asked: "What do you think of it, Hank?" Fonda replied: "I'm going to do it, I'm going to play it."

Logan pointed out that there was, by way of a snag, this movie that Fonda had also said he would do, to which Fonda replied: "I've got the toughest agent in the world and if he's any good at all, he'll just talk me out of it. If he doesn't, I'll leave him."

The agent proved to be quite as tough as his client had predicted and in February 1948, Fonda opened on Broadway to ecstatic reviews in what proved to be the biggest stage success of his life and one that was mainly responsible for keeping him away from the cinema for seven years.

The part of Mister Roberts was ideal for him because it demanded all the characteristics of integrity, decency and honesty with which he was already associated in the public mind. But even so it was not staged without difficulty. As Joshua Logan said: "Roberts was the hero that everyone followed." But as he also said . . .

"At first Hank was suspicious of me; he didn't realise that I'd had as much experience in my field, the theatre, as he'd had in his. He thought I was still a member of the University Players or the Princeton Triangle Club or something and he kept saying, 'Are you really sure you mean that, Josh? This is Broadway, you know.' "

This kind of remark is practically guaranteed to irritate a Broadway stage director but Joshua bore it stoically until one day, during rehearsals, Fonda asked: "Do you understand Roberts?"

Logan, who could take no more, replied: "Understand him, you arsehole? I *wrote* him! You come to my house tonight and I'll tell you all I know about Mister Roberts and then you can decide whether I understand him." Fonda accepted the invitation, Logan harangued him deep into the night and at the end . . . "Hank got up, didn't say a word except 'Thank you very much', shook my hand and left. But after that he never gave me another moment's worry. He listened to everything I said from then on."

Fonda was often difficult and argumentative in the early stages of rehearsal, especially in the theatre. But his attitude and his suspicions were caused by his constant search for a kind of perfection rather than big star temperament. "He was arrogant," Logan said, "but he was arrogant the way he was when I first met him. He was always arrogant."

The success of *Mister Roberts* and the clear signs that the play was destined for a long run led to considerable domestic upheaval. The Fondas sold their home in California and moved to Greenwich, Connecticut, but there family life deteriorated even further. The rift between Fonda and Frances became even wider and he found increasing difficulty in communicating with his children. Jane has told of "long car rides in which not a word would be spoken. I would be so nervous that my palms would be sweaty from riding in absolute silence with my own father." And the writer, Radie Harris, recalled a night at the circus when she sat next to Henry, Jane and Peter, and again no word was spoken. "He didn't buy them hot dogs, candy or souvenirs. When the performance was over they simply stood up and walked out. I felt so sorry for all three of them."

Worse still, Frances was now showing signs of mental illness. She had begun to live virtually as a recluse in her own home, staying in her room endlessly checking business accounts and not even joining her family for meals. By August of 1948 she had entered a hospital in Massachusetts to undergo treatment and though she was released after eight weeks she returned there again early in the new year and from that time onwards, as the clinical depression from which she suffered worsened, she was almost a permanent resident.

It was against this background that, early in 1949, Fonda met and fell in love with Susan Blanchard, stepdaughter of the lyricist Oscar Hammerstein II. Fonda was then forty-four and she was twenty-one, but the age difference, according to Susan, meant little. "He was a very nice, shy, simple man. In a sense I think he was less sophisticated than I was. He was a product of the American mid-West – very honest, very straight and honourable and, at least at that time, I think rather naïve. An American Gothic."

True to those mid-Western principles Fonda decided that he was not going to indulge in some clandestine affair with Susan Blanchard; instead he went to Frances, who was then enjoying a remission of her mental illness, told her he was in love with someone else and wanted a divorce, a request which she agreed to calmly enough and in October she started the legal proceedings. But the following month she suffered a relapse and returned to hospital.

Her health had declined to such an extent that it was feared she might become suicidal, which diagnosis proved only too accurate, for in April 1950, in a sanatorium in New York she killed herself by cutting her throat with a razor blade.

On the face of it Fonda's reaction to his wife's death was astonishing: that same night he simply went on stage as usual in *Mister Roberts* and, as usual, gave an immaculate performance. Joshua Logan said: "Frances' death was a shock to all of us and a terrible blow to Hank. And yet he went on and played and played very well. I'll never understand how he was able to do it."

Fonda's own explanation was that plunging himself back into work was the only way he could have got through the night. And Susan Blanchard said: "I think he didn't know what else to do. He was not a man to break down in public, ever – and not really in private either." Nor, during the time that Frances was ill, had he ever discussed her condition with Susan. "I never knew what his thoughts were. I knew that she was ill but he simply didn't talk about it. He was not a man given to revealing his innermost thoughts." Therefore when he insisted that the show must go on within hours of learning that his wife was dead . . . "It was very much in character. He was a person who always did what was expected of him. He never let anybody down and he was extremely professional. Also I think he was emotionally numb at that time and the only way for him, let us say, to survive was to work."

When Frances' will was read it was discovered that she had cut her husband out of it altogether and had left the bulk of her estate to her three children – a daughter by her first marriage, Jane and Peter.

Barely nine months after the suicide, just before the new year, Fonda and Susan were married in New York. Their honeymoon in the Virgin Islands was marred first of all by the episode of the watch and then, far more seriously, by the news that Peter Fonda had been involved in a shooting accident. He and another boy had borrowed a shotgun and, according to Susan, "Peter had the gun right against his gut and was trying to force a bullet into it when it went off and shot him in the stomach. He was very lucky because the bullet missed all the vital organs."

The incident, which terrified Henry Fonda, did not, however, serve to bring him any closer to either of his children. His relationship with them, Susan said, "was very good towards the end of his life. I think they resolved a lot of the problems they'd had between them." But at the time of her marriage to their father . . . "they'd rebelled, like any children do, and it was more difficult for them because he wasn't the kind of man who could talk easily. I don't think they were in awe of him. I think they desperately wanted to please him but because he wasn't demonstrative there was great frustration for them. There was mutual love between them all, very much so, but I think he felt a lot of things that he couldn't verbalise. He wasn't the sort of father who would come into a room and throw his arms around his children. I don't know . . . I often wonder what his own childhood was like in terms of his relationship with his parents. You know – whether they were very authoritarian. I was always trying to find out but he said he didn't remember a lot. I'm not sure whether that was so. Perhaps he didn't want to remember."

Fortunately, however, the relationship between Susan and the Fonda children became and has remained close. Because she was not very much older than Jane, or even Peter, she was able to serve in the capacity of friend, rather than stepmother. And so, while his new young wife concerned herself with family and domestic matters, Fonda felt free to immerse himself as deeply as ever in his work, which in Susan's opinion was "the most important thing in his life".

When *Mister Roberts* finished its Broadway run, he went on tour with the play; and when the tour ended he returned to New York to star in *Point of No Return*, another hit which ran for 364 performances in 1952 and 1953 and when that, too, was over he found himself in his third consecutive stage success, playing the reluctant defence lawyer in Herman Wouk's *The Caine Mutiny Court Martial*.

By then he had also become, legally if not physically, a father for the third time. He and Susan had adopted a girl, Amy, to whom – possibly because he was older now than when his first family had been born – he showed, for him, remarkable tenderness. "I used to have one day off a week," Susan said, "and then he would take care of Amy and feed her and bath her and dress her. He was very sweet with her. I think he was very good with small children. When they grew older and got minds of their own, when they could talk back – that's when the difficulties started."

Fonda stayed with *The Caine Mutiny Court Martial* until May 1954, at which point he was asked to play his original role in the film version of *Mister Roberts* and because the play had become very special, very personal, to him he accepted immediately. But the filming proved to be far less congenial than the stage production had been, essentially because Joshua Logan had been replaced, as director of the movie, by John Ford. Hitherto, Fonda's professional relationship with Ford had been nothing but beneficial to both of them. By 1954, however, Ford was pretty far gone in alcoholism and his views on how the play was to be filmed were, to say the least, eccentric. He changed the impetus of the story, developed minor characters to the detriment of the others and added an unnecessary amount of broad physical comedy to the action.

As Joshua Logan put it – and it must be remembered that Logan spoke with a certain amount of bitterness because he always regarded *Mister Roberts* as *his* play, the one *he* should have directed on screen: "I could have done a better job with my left hand than Ford did. I must tell you that, because that's the way I feel. He took the play and threw it away and started over again."

And clearly Fonda, too, felt the same way for early in the filming there was, literally, a fight between him and Ford. What actually happened in this fight is open to doubt: I, personally, have heard three different versions of what took place. According to Logan, after one particular day in which the director had introduced all manner of elements which appeared to have nothing to do with the original story, Ford said: "Well, Fonda, how do you think it went?" Fonda replied: "It was shit." At which point, "Ford poked him in the jaw and knocked him across the room. Then they were grabbed by everybody in the place and pulled apart so the fight couldn't go any further. But Fonda never spoke to him again as long as they lived."

Fonda's version, fairly similar, ran as follows: "Pappy (Ford) turned to me and said, 'Okay, what's the matter? I know something's eating you.' And I said, 'Pappy, everyone knows you're the best director in the business but I have to be honest and tell you you're making some big mistakes.' Then I told him what they were and suddenly he rose up out of his chair and threw a big haymaker and hit me right on the jaw. It knocked me over backwards. I was more embarrassed than hurt. I just walked out of the room. Half an hour afterwards Pappy came to apologise. But from then on our relationship was never what it had been."

The most graphic description, however, came from Jack Lemmon, then a comparatively unknown actor who had been cast as Ensign Pulver (for which role, incidentally, he won the Academy Award as best supporting actor). In Lemmon's submission the original script of *Mister Roberts* was to Fonda tantamount to the Bible and people tampered with it at their peril. Ford tampered with it quite recklessly and Fonda began to seethe, to ask of his fellow actors what the hell was going on. The climax came, in the Lemmon version, at about two o'clock one morning. Lights were on, the sound of upraised voices was coming from Ford's room and "naturally little ol' Pulver's got to see what's going on. So I sneak down and look in there, through the crack in the door and they're really going at it. John Ford was about 100 at that time; I don't know but he sure wasn't young. Hank, who was very tall, had got his hand out, holding Ford back. Now Ford is trying to hit him but he can't reach him – he's about six inches short and Hank's holding him off and very calmly but very loudly telling him, 'Don't do it, don't fool around. We did the play for years and we think we know what works and what doesn't work.' And Ford's saying, 'You can't tell me how to make a film.' It was hysterical. And then finally Hank just gave Pappy a push and he went backwards onto the bed and that ended it."

Well, you pays your money and you takes your choice but, however the sordid little scuffle resolved itself, Ford left the picture to be treated for his alcoholism and Mervyn Leroy took over the direction, throwing out Ford's innovations and reverting to the script as written. Later still Joshua Logan was asked to reshoot a few scenes but the result was, in Logan's words, "a mish-mash. It was nowhere near the film it could have been. It could have been one of the greatest pictures of all time, I think. But Fonda was never as good in the film as he was on the stage. He really was in such a dark mood that he didn't play it well, comparatively."

Nevertheless, the screen adaptation of *Mister Roberts* marked the end of Fonda's Broadway interlude and his return to Hollywood. In 1955 he went to Rome to play Pierre in Dino de Laurentiis' film of *War and Peace* and it was there that his third marriage came to an end.

"I think the main problem," Susan said, "was a difference in personalities. Although we thought alike in many areas we had very different characters. I tried to save the marriage; he did, too, and I don't know that it wouldn't have lasted longer if I'd been more mature and he'd been more able to talk. I tried to get outside help; I went to a therapist to talk about it and I was very concerned because I'd grown very close to the children and loved them very much. It's hard for me to remember now exactly what triggered the end. I really couldn't break it down and analyse it for you. I think we simply weren't emotionally suited to each other. I loved him very much and I know he loved me but it was as if we were sort of passing each other on different levels, not really connecting. He was a very self-sufficient person in terms of his work and the fact that he was a good painter and also did wood carving. He could get lost in these occupations. I needed more human contact than he did and I was lonely. It was like living alone."

So, around August 1955, after five years of marriage, she left her husband in Rome and returned with Jane, Peter and Amy to New York. Many years later Susan said of Fonda: "I think there's a scream inside Hank that's never been screamed, a laugh that's never been laughed." And to me she explained that remark by saying: "He found it almost impossible to really let go. When he was playing a part he could accomplish any kind of emotion; as himself he was very restrained and buried and I think there were a lot of emotions that cover a whole range of feelings – happiness, misery, rage, whatever – that were simply not released."

Did she never find out why? "I was just a young wife," she said, "not an analyst."

Occasionally, very occasionally, she had seen Fonda lose his temper and then it was "terrifying. But he was not given to emotional outbursts at all. It's my personal theory that he had a lot of rage in him but he didn't let it out very much."

Thinking back on a marriage that had ended more than a quarter of a century ago she said: "I was afraid of him. It may not have been justified but that's what I felt. I felt that he was judging my behaviour and I always had to sort of watch my step. I always felt that if I was too free and behaved the way I would like to behave and be very open I would not get his approbation and that somehow I would be punished emotionally." If this made Fonda sound Victorian and puritanical well, she said, maybe that's the way he was. "But I think you have to look at it in the context of the kind of upbringing he had, where there were rules and regulations. I think he was very uncomfortable breaking any kind of rules or doing anything that rocked the boat in any way. He was very moved by many things in his life and he certainly had strong emotional responses. But translating these emotions into action in any form was something else again. I mean, many times in his relationship with the children I think he would have longed to be able to talk to them but he couldn't. It wasn't that he was deliberately withdrawn; he simply couldn't cope with heavy emotional *Sturm und Drang*."

Fonda wept when Susan informed him that she wanted a divorce, but by then it was too late for tears. "I didn't think he would change or I would change. We were both very sad and bewildered. It was really awful."

So she left him. But before the filming of *War and Peace* was finished, before he left Rome, Fonda had already discovered the woman who was to be his fourth wife, Afdera Franchetti, a beautiful Italian aristocrat even younger than Susan. When they met, Afdera was aware that Fonda was married and separated but typically, "He didn't talk very much about her; he just said that she had gone." What she liked immediately about him, she said, was his shyness, his reserve, the fact that he didn't behave in any way as a famous film star might have been expected to behave. They courted one another fairly surreptitiously at first because Susan's divorce did not

210

come through until May 1956 and it was ten months later before Fonda and Afdera were married at his home in Manhattan. By then he was fifty-two and she was only twenty-three but the age difference she said (as Susan had said before her) made no difference at all. "Being Italian I had a certain sophistication and he had this young, naïve thing about him, like a student. No, I never felt the difference in age, not even at the end of the marriage."

It was not a marriage that lasted long but it was certainly eventful. On the eve of the wedding Afdera was stricken with terrible doubts, partly because what had been a deliciously clandestine romance was now about to become open, formal and official and she spent the entire night weeping and declaring that she wanted to go home. The result of all these tears was that her eyes were so swollen at the ceremony and afterwards that she cut them out of all her wedding photographs. For an introverted man Fonda coped with this Latin emotion very well, proving to be a loving and indulgent husband. He never actually said he loved her – Afdera soon realised that such a declaration would be too much to hope for – but he showed it in the way he spoilt her. Once, for example, thinking to please her and make her feel at home, he hired an artist to paint Venetian murals in their home. "At the time," she said, "it irritated me enormously but now I think, my God, I was so lucky." Another time she had "nagged him, casually, since September" about a fur coat she wanted for Christmas. But when Christmas came there was no coat; instead there were dozens of other costly presents and, the *pièce de résistance*, a Canaletto hanging over the mantelpiece. When no coat was forthcoming, Afdera said, she began to sulk and was ashamed of herself later. But a very young and over-indulged wife, especially one married to a man who is firmly established at the top of his profession, is almost certain to have a distorted sense of values.

And Fonda, of course, was very much at the top of his profession. On his return from Rome he had filmed *The Wrong Man* for Alfred Hitchcock, played an ex-sheriff turned bounty-hunter in *The Tin Star* and then co-produced and starred in the movie version of a successful TV play called *Twelve Angry Men*, a courtroom drama in which once again he played the unbiased,

uncorrupted and incorruptible American. The director Fonda had chosen was the then unknown Sidney Lumet, who remembered him as a nervous, fussy producer who disliked the job so much that he decided never to try it again.

But as an actor, Lumet said, "He was perfect. He didn't know how to do anything false; you couldn't even beat him into it. Hank always had the best of American liberalism about him; the whole idea of a man fighting for justice was enormously appealing to him. So his performance was heroic without him ever having to play the hero."

Twelve Angry Men was a critical success but a box-office failure, though it has since developed something of a cult following. For Lumet it won an Oscar nomination for best director and caused him to form a lifelong friendship and admiration for Fonda whom he regarded as equal with Spencer Tracy as the very best of all American screen actors. During the making of

. . . And Afdera (wife No. 4), who couldn't think of a single good reason to divorce him.

the picture Fonda invited him home to dinner and to meet Afdera, which experience remained vivid in Lumet's memory.

Afdera, he said, was "enchanting, very, very fond of him and very, very scatterbrained". The dinner party itself, however, was bizarre. "It was a sit-down dinner for thirty or so. There were four tables of eight. Dessert came and there was a sort of *soupe anglaise*, I guess, and there was some sauce in there. The centre pieces on the tables were gardenias and Afdera's Italian friends thought of picking out these gardenias and dipping them into the *soupe anglaise* and throwing them from table to table and pretty soon they were all doing that. And I looked over at Hank and from the expression on his face I knew this wasn't going to work out. His sense of order had been rather violently disrupted."

Afdera dismissed this incident with Latin insouciance. "Once only it happened," she said. "It was one friend of mine, who was in a very bad mood and she did throw an ice cream. That became snowballed in history for ever." A reflective pause and then . . . "The room had just been painted. But it only happened once."

Nevertheless, Sidney Lumet's prediction that "this wasn't going to work out" swiftly became true. By 1961 Fonda and Afdera were divorced. If it was an attraction of opposites that had led to the marriage it was also, ironically, the fact that they were opposites that ended it. Afdera knew that he loved her – "I never had a second's doubt about that" – but felt that the marriage had begun on the wrong footing. They had had no period of struggling together because Fonda was able to offer her everything she could have wanted, so she had no chance to mature, to become a proper wife. She had no need to cook because they had servants; she had no need to watch the pennies when she was shopping because Fonda was already rich. And she had no real rapport with Jane and Peter, who had become less close to their father after his divorce from Susan.

"I think I wasn't unhappy enough before I married him," she said. "Therefore I took for granted all those wonderful things he did for me. If it had been maybe ten years later I might have understood more and tried to work things out better and do what he wanted me to do."

It was Afdera who decided she wanted the divorce. Fonda tried to dissuade her – "because he didn't want another failure. I just wanted to be free. In fact, when I went to Mexico for the divorce I couldn't think of a thing to say against him." In the end the judge and the lawyers settled for the time-honoured compromise in such matters of "incompatibility". As part of the divorce settlement Afdera kept the Canaletto, which she had been given so disappointingly instead of the fur coat. "I was very glad of it," she said. "Eventually I sold the picture and lived on the money for several years."

Her memories of Fonda, she said, were mostly good ones and her only regret, after the divorce, was that they did not remain close friends. There was no animosity; they merely had few opportunities to see one another. Her feelings for him were of admiration. "His weakness, I think, is that he was perfect, if that is a weakness. Whatever he did, he did well." On the other hand he could be a cruel enemy. For instance, there were several people he instructed her to avoid because of his own antipathy towards them, among them Darryl Zanuck, with whom he had had many a bitter run-in during his years with Fox, and the actor Ward Bond, whose extreme right-wing political views were anathema to the liberal Fonda. "He could be quite ruthless. He scared people a lot, I think. He had this kind of aloof look. I think maybe he intimidated me also. Perhaps he was self-centred but when you're a big star you become self-centred, no? But he was a good man and he had a helluva life."

With four wives down and one to go Fonda thrust aside personal problems, as he invariably did, by plunging ever more deeply into his work. At the age of fifty-six he was in as much demand as ever, not always for leading roles perhaps – in many of the twenty-one films he made in the next ten years he played cameo parts – but even so, possibly because he was such a constant presence on the screen, he was listed among America's twenty top box-office attractions in 1967.

His relationship with his children, however, was still cool. Joshua Logan remembered directing Jane in her first film, *Tall Story* and . . . "Fonda came over to the set and they were photographed together. But I always had the feeling he came as a fan and not out of great fatherly love. I'm sure

212

there was some there; I'm sure that Jane and Peter both felt something towards their father but it wasn't very demonstrative. Hank talked about Jane as though she were another person, quite removed from him. But he considered her the greatest actress in the world."

Meanwhile, Fonda himself was adding to his screen reputation as the quiet man of integrity, appearing variously as the president of the United States, the secretary of state designate, a candidate for the presidency, several high-ranking army and navy officers and an attorney. He had also become deeply immersed in his painting, mostly examples of still life executed with minute, painstaking attention to detail. A lot of actors paint – or anyway purport to paint – but it's generally conceded that Fonda had genuine talent and today his pictures are collectors' items that would fetch highly respectable prices on the open market and not simply for their curiosity value either.

So work and painting and the occasional date with a variety of young women filled his time and, as far as he was concerned, would continue to do so, for after the divorce from Afdera he had vowed never to marry again. His inability thus far to make any marriage work understandably disturbed and puzzled him. Once, looking back on his marital record, he said: "I'm goddamned ashamed of myself." Why then did he marry so often? John Houseman, the stage director, believed it was because "he was a loner and he was very uxorious. He had to have a woman and it had to be a wife. He was not given to promiscuous sleeping around. When he fell for a woman he had to marry her."

Susan Blanchard agreed with that. "I think he was very uncomfortable when breaking the rules. He was not a womaniser, he was not a playboy and I think the reason he married so many times was because he was so conventional. Where he came from one got married and did one's duty and that's the way it was. If he had a relationship with a woman he felt he had to marry her."

Nevertheless, noble though his motives may have been in getting married in the first place, he did seem to show a deplorable lack of commitment to matrimony once the ceremony was over. It's not enough merely to marry a woman; she has a right to expect

a certain amount of loving care and attention afterwards and it was in this area that Fonda was a noted failure.

"He was – and he was the first one to say it – a lousy husband," said Jack Lemmon. "And in his opinion, though not necessarily his children's, he was a lousy father, too. For a long time it was something he couldn't cope with. I think that without necessarily being selfish he was a very driven and consumed man about his career and the way he wanted to conduct it. And very often the scales tip over and something has to give – either your profession or your personal life."

Or, as Susan Blanchard put it: "His career always came first."

But all that was to change with the advent into his life of one Shirlee Mae Adams, an airline hostess and occasional fashion model, who was introduced to Fonda one night over dinner in a Hollywood restaurant. Fonda was immediately smitten but this time the courtship was slower. He and Shirlee had known each other a considerable time before they were married

With Shirlee, his fifth and final wife. With her, he said, he had at last "hit a home run".

213

in New York on December 3rd, 1965. Fonda was then sixty, Shirlee was thirty-three – another notable age difference which again was of no concern to either husband or wife.

Fonda's own comment on this, his fifth and as it was to turn out, his final marriage as reported by his biographer Howard Teichmann in *Fonda: My Life* was: "After stepping up to bat five times I finally hit a home run." So in the baseball game of love and marriage he had at last made a winning score. He had, on his own admission, mellowed – not before time perhaps at the age of sixty – and besides by the unanimous accord of his friends and even his former wives, Shirlee was the ideal mate for him . . .

Jack Lemmon: "He was devoted to Shirlee and she to him. A lovely, lovely lady. He eventually found a great peace in that relationship."

Sidney Lumet: "She was totally open and direct. She made him feel good and I'm glad they found each other."

John Houseman: "It was an extraordinary marriage that couldn't have been more successful."

Joshua Logan: "She gave him great pleasure and she was very careful of his life. I think she cared more for him than anyone did."

Susan Blanchard: "I think she was a wonderful wife, I really do, and she took such care of him when he was ill – above and beyond the call of duty."

Afdera Franchetti: "In his way he believed in marriage. He was always a one-woman man and it showed when the right woman appeared. I think we were all right in a way but our timing was wrong. With Shirlee the timing and everything was right."

And finally Fonda himself, as quoted by Howard Teichmann: "And we lived happily ever after . . . Every day I wake up and take a look at Shirlee and think, 'This is it. She was worth the wait. I really feel she's the only wife I ever had.' "

So with his personal life now settled, Fonda moved into the 1970s as a hugely respected senior citizen of American show business. There were movies – sixteen of them during that decade – starring roles on television and acclaim on Broadway, notably for his performance as Clarence Darrow in a one-man show that dealt with seven cases conducted and won by that great lawyer, crusader, liberal and humanitarian, a man very much after Fonda's own heart. John Houseman directed it, though not without problems. In the early stages there were occasional tantrums from Fonda as he strove, as usual, for the perfection that in the end, despite all his efforts, escaped him as it escapes everyone else. Even so his performance was magnificent for unlike most movie stars he had the ability to make the transition from film studio to stage with great ease, possibly because the theatre always had the greater appeal for him.

Houseman said: "I think he was completely miserable if, every eighteen months or so, he didn't get back to the theatre. In order to do that he would even appear in summer stock somewhere because he felt the need constantly to renew his contact with live audiences."

Fonda opened in New York as Clarence Darrow in March 1975, and it was during the run of the show that the ill health that was to beset him for the rest of his life first became evident. "When we opened in Chicago," John Houseman said, "he began to lose his voice. Then we opened in New York and he got it back but again he started to lose it." The problem, however, was not caused by his throat or his larynx but by heart trouble. He had an operation for the insertion of a pacemaker and, remarkably soon for a man of seventy, he was back on stage playing not only on Broadway but also in Los Angeles and London.

Houseman said: "That was the beginning of his bad health. After that he went through hell. It was discovered that he had a huge tumour in his pancreas and that was removed, then later he had further complications and his courage in going on working, being in and out of hospital, was absolutely extraordinary."

Fonda's last appearance on Broadway was in 1978, playing a Supreme Court judge in *First Monday in October*. He also went on tour with the play as far as Chicago where he had to drop out because of a hip ailment that was later diagnosed as cancer.

At this point he could, if he had wished, have looked back with justifiable pride on a quite remarkable career. Not one of his contemporaries, or even those in the generation behind him, came close to matching the record of success that he had achieved

Fonda, Jane and Peter in what, at one time in their relationship, would have been an extremely rare moment of fond togetherness.

on both stage and screen. He had made eighty-three films, not all of them good but each of them distinguished by his presence, and he had appeared, usually in the leading role, in seventeen Broadway plays, many of them box-office hits and nearly all of them critical successes. And yet, amazingly, he had not won a single important award. Oscar nominations, yes – he had won those; but the Academy Award itself, never. To other, lesser, actors the Oscars sometimes seemed to have been handed out like gift vouchers on a detergent packet but for forty-five years Fonda had been consistently overlooked. For this neglect his friends offered various explanations. Sidney Lumet, for example, said: "His work was so good for so long that it became expected and also, in the nature of the work, it was never spectacular. He never played the drunk running down Third Avenue, he never played the lunatic in the asylum, he never played the Hunchback of

Notre Dame. The parts were calm, the performances were calm and they needed a little bit of looking at. Another factor is that Hank was never among the biggest money-makers. In the past how a picture did commercially had a great deal to do with the Academy Awards. Very often they went to the four or five biggest financial hits of the year and Hank didn't have many of those."

Jack Lemmon said: "People were never surprised that Hank was nominated or gave a great performance. There was a simplicity in his playing, almost at times as if he wasn't acting at all. There were no great histrionics going on: he wasn't climbing the walls and pouring tears and that. I think the Academy voters just took him for granted and very often some flashier performance would grab them and they'd vote for that."

And so Fonda, the consummate craftsman who often declared that if an audience

215

could detect the seams in his performance he wasn't doing it right, lost out time after time to less able performers who believed that an actor should be seen to be acting.

But as the 1970s came to an end and Fonda himself approached seventy-five, a man in ill health whose mortality was becoming increasingly evident, there was a universal change of heart. The awards and honours that had hitherto eluded him came suddenly in abundance: the American Film Institute saluted his "lifetime contribution to the cinema"; he was given a special Tony for his "outstanding contribution to the theatre"; and he was one of five Americans honoured for their achievements at a special ceremony at the Kennedy Centre in Washington. Furthermore in 1981 the American Academy presented him with a special Oscar in recognition of his "enduring contribution to the art of motion pictures". Well, that's the one they give to almost everybody who manages to live a long time without committing the unpardonable sin of becoming poor or out of work. But the real award, the one every screen actor covets, the Oscar for the finest performance in any one year, had still escaped him. Even that, however, was to come his way.

The circumstances that were to bring him the trophy that crowned his career were in themselves like the ingredients of a film script.

As the 1980s began he was on much easier terms with Jane and Peter, but still not as close as any of them would have wished. But all of this changed with Fonda's last film, *On Golden Pond*.

Mark Rydell, the director of the picture, said: "It was true that, aside from political differences – which, by the way, were resolved long before this film – Henry and Jane had numerous personal difficulties. Henry was a very private man; he was very self-absorbed, a consummate artist deeply interested in his work. I probably would categorise him as less than the greatest father because he was a committed man. And I think that led to resentment and bitterness and feelings of exclusion. I'm not trying to justify or attack him in any way but these things existed and I know that Jane was deeply hungry to resolve these problems with her father."

The way she achieved this was to acquire the screen rights to the Broadway play *On Golden Pond* and offer the film as a starring vehicle for Fonda and Katharine Hepburn. She could hardly have chosen anything more apposite for the story concerned an elderly couple, returning to their holiday home by a lake for what, the audience assumes, will probably be their last summer together. And it is during this period that the father and his daughter, played by Jane Fonda, finally resolve the differences between them that have undermined their relationship for years. As it happened in the film, so it happened in fact.

This, as Mark Rydell saw it, is what took place during the shooting . . .

"Jane was sick to her stomach, literally, every day before she had to play a scene with Henry, because she was so in awe of him and so hungry for his affection, for the father she really needed. He, on the other hand, very careful, very modest with his feelings, was finally indeed overwhelmed by her candour and her need for him. It was just inescapable. They had a quite remarkable psycho-drama that went on every day on the set."

Towards the end of the film there is a particularly touching moment when the daughter pours out the emotion, the love, she feels for her father. And, said Rydell . . . "It was absolutely genuine. I had to cut out great portions of his response. He sobbed, which was not in character for Norman (the role Henry Fonda played). His response was absolutely . . . torrential. He sobbed helplessly when she reached out and touched his arm and said, 'I want to be your friend.' We had to stop shooting; I mean, he was just overcome. And he was very careful with his emotions, very much in control of himself; but this overwhelmed him. And she was a basket case – you know, asking her own father for the affection and consideration that she had longed for for so many years."

Later, when the film was finished, Rydell also had an opportunity to observe Peter Fonda's attitude to his father. "I was invited to the Utah Film Festival to present an award, the John Ford Medallion, to Henry, who by this time had become ill. Jane was working on another picture so they invited Peter to accept the award. It was rather a large occasion, with thousands of people and the press and TV, and it seemed only proper as I got up to talk about Henry that I should say something about Peter and Jane. I said I thought it was wonderful, a testimonial to the strength of the family, that they had been able to overcome the obstacle of having to follow a father who had become a monument, a symbol of America, and had carved out their own lives. And I glanced down, about to introduce Peter, and he was sobbing helplessly. I really had to stall for a few moments until he could pull himself together and when he came up on the stand he took the medallion, his eyes swollen with crying, and he said, 'I'm not going to give this to my father.' I thought, 'My God, what *are* you gonna do?' And he said: 'I'm going to take it home to my ranch in Montana and maybe then he'll come to visit me.' So there was a deep hurt in these children. It's hard really to evaluate but I know that there was injury."

There was one other curiosity about the filming of *On Golden Pond*. Not only was it the first time Fonda and Hepburn had appeared together: it was the first time they had ever met, though each had been in or around Hollywood for the best part of fifty years. When Rydell introduced them, Hepburn said: "Well, it's about time." Later on, as a material token of her esteem, she presented Fonda with a hat that had been worn by Spencer Tracy, with whom she had conducted a very long love affair. Fonda wore it throughout the picture.

The film opened to excellent reviews and even better business. In February 1982 Fonda won the Golden Globe Award for best actor but by then he was too ill to attend the ceremony and Jane collected the trophy on his behalf. A month later he was, at last, named best actor at the Academy Awards celebration and again he was too ill to receive the Oscar himself and Jane stepped up to take it in his stead.

By this time everyone knew that Fonda was dying and I suppose it could have been argued, cynically, that this award – which, whatever you may think of it and of the absurdity of comparing a number of disparate and unrelated performances and declaring that one is better than the rest, is still unchallenged as the most important prize the movie business can bestow – was a farewell present from a grateful industry. But such an attitude would be insulting to Fonda. His performance was indeed superb; true, in the past he had given others equally as good and gone unrewarded but no matter. As Mark Rydell said: "It was not a sentimental award, it wasn't a gift award. He deserved it: he *won* it. And I know that it moved him very much."

Some four months after winning the Oscar, Henry Fonda died in hospital in Los Angeles, with all his family around him. He was seventy-seven years old and he had made eighty-five films in a career that lasted more than four and a half decades. But it was never the bulk of his work that counted; it was the quality. To James Stewart he was, "the finest actor of his generation"; to Sidney Lumet he was "an absolute barometer of truth. His style was totally naturalistic and yet heroes of epic proportions would always come out"; to Mark Rydell he was "the absolute dean of American actors". And Jack Lemmon said of him: "Nobody could make me more proud to be a member of the same profession."

But he was more than just a great screen actor. He was, as Mark Rydell had put it, a monument, a symbol. If John Wayne represented, to the cinema audience, the pioneering courage of America, Fonda represented the nation's conscience. The characters he played were fierce opponents of ignorance, oppression, intolerance and prejudice and they reflected the man himself. It is certainly true that in his private life he was a great deal less successful – except in his last few years – than he was in his career but he was never less than an honourable (and, in my own brief knowledge of him, immensely charming) man and it could well be that all the difficulties he encountered with his first four wives and with his children were due to a crippling and by no means rare inability to express his emotions.

Perhaps, as John Houseman suggested, it was only when he was on stage or on screen that he was able to throw off his inhibitions and, paradoxically, reveal himself. Great artists are rarely simple men and Henry Fonda was a great artist. In its time Hollywood has discovered many stars but only a handful or so of truly fine actors and of those Fonda may well have been the best.

His was indeed the art that concealed art and, in the words of Sidney Lumet, led far too many people for far too long to come away from his plays and his films saying: "Oh well, another great performance from Hank Fonda. What else is new?"

David Niven

Just before David Niven was released from the clinic in Minneapolis where he had been undergoing tests, he phoned his younger son Jamie in New York.

"The good news," Niven said, "is that I haven't had a stroke. The bad news is that I've got motor neurone disease."

"Oh, my God," said Jamie. "What does that mean?"

"It means," said his father, "that I'm going to die and I'm going to die very soon."

He then boarded a plane for New York and found himself sitting next to Tom Brokaw, quite possibly the best of American TV journalists, who was at that time the main presenter of the breakfast show *Today* and who is now anchorman on the NBC News. Now Niven had been told in precise detail what effect motor neurone disease, which is incurable, would have upon him. He would lose the use of his voice, of his hands, of his legs; he would have the utmost difficulty in swallowing, even in breathing. Already his voice tended occasionally to become a little slurred, to such an extent indeed that when a few weeks earlier he had appeared on the *Michael Parkinson Show* on BBC television some people had thought he was drunk.

And yet, as Tom Brokaw recounted later to Jamie, "Your father was fabulous. He just made me laugh all the way back to New York." Well, not quite all the way perhaps because . . . "halfway across the country he turned to me and said, 'The most terrible thing has happened to me today . . .'" and then he told Brokaw what the doctors had told him. It was a most uncharacteristic act on Niven's part because he was never a man to share his troubles even with his friends, let alone strangers. But in the circumstances the desire to unburden himself to somebody must have been overwhelming, although to reveal what in journalistic terms would have been an amazing scoop to someone in Brokaw's position might have been, to put it mildly, unwise. It says a great deal for Tom Brokaw's innate decency that he chose to regard the information he had been given as confidential and told nobody about it except Jamie, a decision which, as Jamie pointed out, "gave Daddy an extra year in which the press and other people weren't hounding him".

On reflection, though, that anecdote also says a great deal about David Niven and the enormous affection in which he was held. Everybody liked him; nobody would have wished to hurt him or cause him distress. He was, in my experience, unique among actors in that it was impossible to find anyone who had a bad word to say about him. To one involved in a spot of investigative reporting – which is not to be confused with muck-raking or an act of iconoclasm, but which has nothing to do with eulogising either – it could have been most galling to find every interviewee's face light up with remembered pleasure at the mention of Niven's name and to hear them chuckling happily even before a single question had been asked.

I say it could have been but in fact it wasn't because I knew David Niven, too – not very well, alas, and not nearly as closely as I would have liked. But I knew him well enough to have noticed a most remarkable quality in him: he had the effect, while you were in his company and for some time after you had left it, of making you feel that life was a much more enjoyable and cheerful business than you had previously supposed. Sir Ralph Richardson had something of that quality, too, but not I think quite to the same extent as Niven.

"What were his faults?" I would ask of each of the interviewees, desirous of producing a rounded picture in which due prominence was given to the warts as well as the beauty spots. "Come on, put a bit of effort into it – he must have had faults, for God's sake. Nobody's perfect." And then articulate men like John Mortimer, barrister and playwright, and Peter Ustinov, actor, director, novelist, playwright and heaven knows what else, would flounder about, at a loss to find anything to say at all. Well, they would say, no, no, he wasn't perfect, certainly not – for they had no wish to malign the man – no doubt he did have all the faults and frailties that are common to the rest of us; it was just that they personally couldn't think of any, that was all.

Niven's elder son, David Jr., actually went away for five minutes to search his memory in an honest attempt to find something derogatory to say about his late father, while I tapped my foot impatiently and urged him to get on with it. But when he returned all he could say was that Niven could be verbally harsh and cutting when he had drunk too much gin and what kind of criticism is that, I ask you? I mean, everyone is unpleasant after drinking too much gin. What's more, when David Jr. and other interested parties pointed out this grievous fault, Niven stopped drinking gin and never touched the stuff again. He drank plenty of other things, it must be said in his defence, but he swore off gin.

The question is: how did this paragon – if that is not too harsh a description of an extremely lovable man – come about? Well, his great friend and perceptive journalist Roderick Mann believed that Niven had actually invented himself. "Everyone would say that he was the quintessential Englishman and he wasn't, really, because I never met another Englishman like him. I mean, he was the kind of Englishman that everyone thinks exists but doesn't. Perhaps there was an English type like that before the First World War but not now." The fact is that Niven did all the right things and showed all the right attributes to establish himself, whether intentionally or otherwise, in the public mind as the archetypal English gentleman. At the outbreak of

The "perfect English gentleman", to say nothing of officer.

219

World War Two he abandoned his Hollywood career, just as he stood on the brink of stardom, to return to Europe and fight; he was invariably charming, witty and erudite. He was, as Roderick Mann said, "like an extension of the most popular prefect at a public school. People used to say, 'Oh, he *can't* be like that; it's a mask.' But it wasn't a bloody mask – he really *was* like that. I've been out with him when we both got sloshed and that charm never slipped. In fact he got even more charming as he got drunker sometimes."

But if the Niven that everyone knew and whom, as far as I can tell, everyone loved was indeed self-invented one can only conclude that the invention was just about flawless. To have projected, as he did, a certain kind of persona for seventy-three years without ever being caught out in an uncharacteristic act of meanness or pettiness rather leads one to the belief that the mask, if there was one, was simply an identical replica of the face that lay underneath.

At this stage I should point out that what follows owes only a little to Niven's own two works of autobiography, *The Moon's a Balloon* and *Bring on the Empty Horses*. There are two reasons for this: in the first place I do not wish to be accused of plagiarism and in the second place his reminiscences (whether wholly true or not and I will return to that later) are so widely familiar that any repetition would be redundant. My object, in the TV documentary that spawned this chapter, was not simply to promote further Niven's own self-mocking, self-denigratory image of himself but to discover, as far as possible, what kind of image he presented to other people.

He was born on March 1st, 1910, in Belgravia, London, the perfect setting for one of his upper-class demeanour, the youngest of four children of William and Henrietta Niven. For the record he was christened James David Graham and was semi-orphaned in 1915 when his father was killed at Suvla Bay, Gallipoli. A year later, the widow Niven – who, incidentally, was French – married one Sir Thomas Comyn-Platt. Jamie Niven said: "I know he hated his stepfather," but apart from that Niven was never greatly inclined to reveal too much about his youthful likes and dislikes, although the actress Ann Todd, who knew him well as a young man, said: "He adored his mother. She was a lovely, lovely person."

It would appear (and here I must acknowledge a debt to Niven's own memoirs) that the antipathy he felt for his stepfather was mutual and the young Niven was sent off to a succession of boarding schools, good or bad depending on the family finances at the time. Eventually he went, as well-brought-up young gentlemen of his generation automatically did, to a public school – to Stowe – where he was extremely happy. This is worth mentioning because happiness appears to have been a comparatively rare commodity in his youth and such of it as there was seems to have been provided largely by his mother and his public school – unless one counts Nessie. Nessie, according to Niven, was the seventeen-year-old Soho tart whom he met when he was fourteen and who, he says, generously and without charge introduced him to the delights of sex. However, there are those among Niven's close friends who believe that Nessie was either another invention or, at best, a romanticised memory of a casual encounter.

But whatever part Nessie played in his life and whether or not she coached him to become an accomplished boudoir athlete, Niven developed into a more conventional kind of sportsman and gained his colours at Stowe as both a cricketer and a Rugby player as well as performing nobly in the boxing and fencing teams.

Friends who knew him about that time from the Isle of Wight, where the Comyn-Platts had a holiday home, remember Henrietta as both "a tall, fine-looking, very pretty person", and "a very formidable woman, very big. She had the most glorious great big eyes and I, for one, was terrified of her." She also, considering that we are talking now about the 1920s, must have been a rather tolerant, free-thinking woman because one of Niven's boyhood friends recalled: "David and his brother Max used to bring their girlfriends down for the weekend and they used to go out dancing at night and come back in the early hours of the morning and create absolute hell, waking up the entire household. So his mother, in her wisdom, built on a guest wing to the cottage, which had all the mod cons and various bedrooms for the guests and it was known, of course, as 'the Sin Wing'."

So, by the time Niven aged about seventeen went on to the Royal Military Academy at Sandhurst, there to prepare for a career in the regular army, it seems safe to assume that whether it was thanks to Nessie or whether he was self-taught, he was already sexually proficient. At Sandhurst he was a model cadet, played in the Rugby XV and appeared in a couple of college concerts, in which he wrote his own sketches, and even played the lead in a production of the play *It Pays to Advertise*. Such histrionic outings, however, were only diversions; at that time the idea of making a career as an actor would have seemed laughable. But nonetheless he was interested in the stage and certainly in young actresses and it was while he was at Sandhurst that he met Ann Todd.

She was in a play in Portsmouth – one of the first plays she ever appeared in – and Niven went to watch her every night. Miss Todd believed, as nice young women did in those days, that a gentleman and a lady should be formally introduced; Niven tried to find a shortcut past this system. So he got hold of a programme of the play and drew upon it two hearts, one at the top, one at the bottom. And from the bottom heart (Miss Todd's) he drew an arrow bearing love to the top heart (his). Miss Todd didn't like this approach and vowed to have nothing to do with him. But at the end of the week the play's author, Ian Hay, arrived in her dressing room and "behind him came a beaming Niven". Somehow he had managed to ingratiate himself with Hay and the introduction was effected; nor did Ann Todd ever regret it, for they became lifelong friends. And though her heart never did send up an arrow of love to his it would not have displeased Niven's mother if something of the sort could have been arranged.

Still, the Niven Ann Todd remembers from that first meeting was "very cocky. *Very* cocky. Very full of himself but now, thinking it over, I suspect very insecure inside, really." Nevertheless they became "very sort of brother and sister".

Ann Todd's role in the play was that of a schoolgirl in tunic and plaits and Niven had a photograph taken of her in this costume which he kept for years in his wallet, though not for such sentimental reasons as one might assume. "It was there," she said, "only for one reason, which was that when, now and again, he got into trouble with the ladies, he'd produce this photograph and say, 'Oh, by the way, I forgot to tell you – I'm engaged and here's my fiancée.' And he'd bring out this awful picture, sort of sepia-coloured, and show it to them."

But what was he like in those days, apart from being cocky, full of himself and insecure? "Well," she said, "he was just a lovely person. People adored him even when he was very young."

Up to this point Niven's career seemed assured: he was going to be a soldier and it's quite possible that if he had been accepted into the regiment of his choice, the Argyll and Sutherland Highlanders, he might have ended up as some respected but more or less obscure old general, pretty well unheard-of by the world at large. But he was not accepted by the Argyll and Sutherland Highlanders (which he had chosen partly because, despite his image as the quintessential Englishman, he was Scottish by descent) but was posted instead to the Highland Light Infantry in Malta.

His great army friend, Michael Trubshawe, said: "David *could* have been a good soldier; he had all the makings of a good soldier but the tragedy of the thing is that he didn't go to the regiment of his choice but to the HLI. Now in those days there were two battalions – one was called Home Service and the other was further afield. Our battalion in Malta really came under Home Service and there was absolutely nothing to do. Very quickly, I think, David became depressed by this situation. There were really only the four P's – parade (i.e. square-bashing), polo, piss-ups and poking. Now none of these four, enjoyable as they might be, is really guaranteed to help a keen soldier along the line. Whereas, if he'd gone to the 2nd Battalion, the 74th, who were in India, he might well have seen active service on the frontier and been able to apply the skills and training and dedication that he had learnt at Sandhurst. But it all faded. For instance, if one went into his room in barracks in Malta you wouldn't find him reading the manual of military law or the King's Regulations; you'd find him reading the *Tatler*. I've no doubt at all that he could have been a very good soldier because he had the love of the Jocks, the troops, and that's what all soldiering is about. It's not very difficult to be popular but to be respected is an entirely different matter and the makings of a good officer, and David always commanded respect."

Trubshawe, formerly of Cambridge University and a smart cavalry regiment, was as bored in Malta as Niven was and the pair of them combined happily in some most unmilitary activities.

Once they went to a fancy dress ball at the Opera House in Valletta, clad as goats. They wore goatskins over their heads and backs and had attached beneath them football bladders with gloves tied on – "to make the thing thoroughly realistic" – and as they crawled about on all fours their batmen followed behind, scattering black olives in their wake. "Well, that we hadn't realised." Trubshawe said, "was that the goat is virtually a sacred animal in Malta and there was absolute uproar, pandemonium and panic. So down the main street of Valletta disappeared two officers of the Highland Light Infantry dressed as goats, with everything dingling and dangling and waving in the wind . . . They nearly called out the fire brigade and the troops and everything, it was considered so serious."

This incident apart, Niven seems to have spent much of his time in Malta playing cricket and offering nocturnal solace to navy wives whose husbands were at sea. He and Trubshawe even invented the "husbandometer", a device that was placed on the harbour mole and was sounded (emitting a piercing shriek) whenever the Fleet was sighted puffing over the horizon towards port. As soon as the husband-ometer was heard "the brutal and licentious soldiery were to be observed whizzing out of various houses, doing up their fly buttons". And foremost among the brutal and licentious was young Lieutenant Niven leading his troops, as ever, from the front.

But even these diversions palled and Niven began to grow increasingly dissatisfied with this rather aimless military life, especially after Trubshawe left the regiment in January 1933. Before then, however, Henrietta had died of cancer and Niven, grief-stricken by her death, took four weeks' leave, raised such money as he could and embarked on the SS Georgic for New York.

One of the reasons for this trip was that he had earlier in London met Barbara Hutton, the Woolworth heiress, and she had invited him to visit her if ever he should go to America. Niven was never a man to turn down an invitation, being apparently confident that almost anyone would be glad to see him at almost any time and in this assumption he was certainly correct, especially on that first trip to New York. The wealthy Miss Hutton and her friends treated the penniless but engaging young army officer extremely well; Niven enjoyed himself so much that he had his leave extended and by the time he returned to his regiment he had developed a keen appetite for the kind of freedom that life outside the army could offer.

With Trubshawe gone and half the regiment – though not Niven's half – shipped to India he began to grow increasingly frustrated with his lot and it was while he was in such a mood that a young débutante named Priscilla Weigall implanted in his mind an idea which probably didn't seem too significant at the time but was to become so later. Miss Weigall came to the conclusion that Niven should become a film actor and to this end she introduced him to Douglas Fairbanks Jr., who did nothing for him at the time – largely because Niven was too shy to ask – but who later became one of his closest friends, and also to a producer at Sound City, one of many tiny film studios that proliferated during the 1930s. As a result of this Niven made his screen début as an extra in a racing film called *All the Winners*.

Nobody greeted his appearance with shouts of "Eureka!" or offers of lucrative contracts and Niven resumed an army career which was becoming more and more unsatisfying. And so, encouraged by an offer from a friend of a trip to Quebec in exchange for Niven's old Bentley, he sent in his now famous telegram – "Dear Colonel, Request permission resign commission. Love, Niven" – and set sail for Canada.

But idyllic though this visit turned out to be it hardly helped him solve his most urgent problem, namely what he should now do to earn a living. America, he felt, might provide the answer and in mid-October 1933 he returned to New York, although not, this time, to such a warm welcome. An amusing young soldier on leave was one thing; a slightly desperate young man in search of a job was something else again, and the people who had treated him so well on his earlier visit were rather less keen to see him the second time around.

Niven indeed could hardly have arrived in New York at a less auspicious time. With America still throttled by the Depression there were very few prospects for a penniless foreigner. But the good news was that Prohibition had finally been repealed and eventually he found a job as a salesman for a wine company, an outfit which later showed its appreciation of his services by displaying a photograph of him with the slogan, "Our first and worst salesman".

Actually, he can't have been that bad because he did manage to hold the job down while he looked around for something better. Niven was by no means content to remain in the liquor trade all his life and rapidly found contacts who might help ease his path to higher things. In his book *The Moon's a Balloon* he cheerfully presents a picture of himself at this stage in his life as a kind of happy scrounger, ever delighted to accept hospitality of any kind even though he was quite unable to repay it. His friends stoutly deny that he scrounged but are inclined to admit that he was the fastest draw in the east (and later in the west) when it came to accepting an invitation. But, they add, he amply repaid any hospitality he was given by being a totally delightful person to have around. Douglas Fairbanks, for instance, remembering the Niven of those earlier days, said: "He was just about like he always was – a wonderful raconteur, wonderful company, the best companion in the world. He never really changed from that."

The immediate effect of being everybody's favourite house guest was that he was introduced to the kind of people who could offer him social and professional betterment. For example, he was befriended by the society hostess, Elsa Maxwell, who thinking he might make some sort of film actor – a poor girl's Ronald Colman perhaps – presented him to the director Ernst Lubitsch, who was not exactly overwhelmed by what he saw and told him to forget it. Maxwell's next idea was to find her protégé a rich wife but potential rich wives were even less impressed than Lubitsch had been and so Niven reverted to Plan A, the idea of becoming a movie actor, which had begun to appeal to him quite strongly.

Indeed, the seed originally planted back in England by Priscilla Weigall had clearly taken root quite early because Ann Todd recalled that . . . "One day he said to me,

'I want to ask your advice. I don't think I want to stay on in the army; I've decided to be an actor.' I said, 'Oh, but you can't do that, Niven. You can't act, I mean don't be ridiculous – you can't *possibly* act. After all, if you had to go and begin acting you'd have to say something serious and I don't think you could even say "I love you" seriously. The audience would just pass away with laughing. No, no, you stay in the army . . .'"

So much for professional advice. Niven, no doubt having forgotten this, decided to listen instead to the words of Elsa Maxwell and, armed with an address book full of useful names, made his way by a roundabout route – via Cuba and Panama, in fact – to Hollywood, where he arrived in late summer of 1934.

The contact book proved helpful enough socially but did little for his professional aspirations, partly because he had no resident alien's visa and was therefore unable to work. He also, as an incidental embarrassment, had no money either.

Ever resourceful, however, he checked in at the Roosevelt Hotel on Hollywood Boulevard and introduced himself to the part-owner and general manager, one Al Weingand. "David said he had a problem," Weingand recalled. "He had no money. Well, he was a very engaging, attractive guy and we had plenty of spare rooms so I told him that I would stake him to a room for one month and I'll never forget the monthly rate then was sixty-five dollars. During that month he didn't have much to do and we would go out to lunch or he would have dinner with me and my wife." Weingand did not though believe Niven was a sponger – "The poor guy was just broke."

It says much for Niven's personality that he could enjoin a complete stranger to put him up for a month and even take him out for meals. But it is also greatly to his credit that eventually, Weingand said, "He paid me back in full. Every cent."

But before the debt could be repaid he had to overcome the problem of acquiring a work permit. His social peregrinations had brought him into contact with a number of prominent film directors and producers, some of whom showed interest in him but none of whom was able to employ him until he acquired some kind of official status. On Al Weingand's recommendation therefore he went to Mexico and – these things being more easily managed there apparently – set about getting his resident alien's visa, which duly arrived early in 1935.

Equipped with this he presented himself at the offices of Central Casting which, in those days, were to be found on Hollywood Boulevard. Central Casting was, and is, the agency which provides the studios with extras, people who stand in the background saying "Rhubarb, rhubarb" to each other while the stars get on with the action. Niven, being only twenty-five and full of optimism was undeterred by the sign outside which said: "Don't try to become an actor. For every one we employ we turn away a thousand." So he was taken on and registered as "Anglo-Saxon type No. 2008". Having thus pigeon-holed him to its own total satisfaction, the agency – or so he later claimed – promptly cast him as a Mexican. As a step up on the way to stardom it wasn't much but at least it was a start.

And in that he was luckier than most. There were literally thousands of registered extras in Hollywood and few of them averaged as much as three days work a week. So Niven, who reckoned he appeared anonymously in well over a score of Westerns, was already shooting better than par for the course. But still it was a long way from stardom or even from a humble speaking role in a movie.

Nevertheless, he continued to put himself about and was even given a screen test at MGM and perhaps it was because of this that a rumour came to be spread abroad that Irving Thalberg, MGM's immensely powerful head of production, was thinking of casting him in *Mutiny on the Bounty* (the Clark Gable – Charles Laughton version). This story was recounted to Sam Goldwyn, who was then running his own studio, and he – possibly wishing to spike MGM's guns; the G in MGM, after all, stood for Goldwyn, one of the studio's founders – promptly signed the virtually untried Niven to a seven-year contract.

Nowadays that seems a most implausible sequence of events but Hollywood in the mid-1930s was truly a land of opportunity. Production was high and so was the demand for new faces and so, with a bit of luck, a well-groomed, good-looking young man might reasonably hope for a chance in the movies. Never mind whether he had acting ability or not; if he had the right appearance acting ability wasn't necessarily considered essential – at least not to start with. It was something which, popular belief had it, could be acquired later. That this supposition was incorrect was proved by the number of good-looking young men (and women) who appeared briefly in films and were then rightly returned to the oblivion whence they had come.

Having signed Niven, however, Goldwyn could find no immediate use for him and not wishing to have him lolling about as an unemployed burden on the payroll, he lent him to Paramount. Thus it was with that studio that David Niven began a career which was to last for the best part of five decades: his first speaking role in a film was in a now generally forgotten drama called *Without Regret* in 1935. Niven's great moment came in a scene with the star, Elissa Landi, on a railway station. "Goodbye, my dear," he said. It's possible that audiences walked away choked with emotion at the poignant delivery of this line, though history fails to record any such response. But at least he must have done his tiny bit reasonably well because Goldwyn himself then employed him in *Barbary Coast*, wherein he was notable mostly for being thrown out of the window of a San Francisco brothel during a riot. (He did, actually, have a line of dialogue, too, but that was drowned in the background noise.) Still, he must have looked the part as he hurtled through the window because Columbia then borrowed him for another tiny role in *A Feather in her Hat*, and he finished 1935 back with Goldwyn again as a failed crook and all-round wastrel in *Splendour*.

Well, at least he was on his way. He had appeared in four films and earned 5,200 dollars and, what's more, better times were on the way. In 1936 he played his first starring role as Bertie Wooster in *Thank You, Jeeves*. Admittedly this was a B-picture made by Twentieth Century-Fox but it offered, at last, a real part and one that gave him an opportunity to show the inborn talent for light comedy that was to bring him such a lucrative career for the next forty-odd years. The Niven that most of us now remember was probably too sophisticated and worldly-wise to be acceptable as Bertie Wooster but the Niven

of 1936 may well have seemed tailor-made for the role. In any event it was an important landmark for him because, as a result, he was now regarded as an actor who could be entrusted with several lines of dialogue at a time. Thus 1936 brought him a total of five films, among them *The Charge of the Light Brigade*, a curious epic directed by Michael Curtiz in which the Light Brigade seemed to spend most of its time on the North-West Frontier of India and in which Niven played Errol Flynn's friend, a role he was destined to fill off-screen as well as on.

But life was not all work for Niven – indeed, he always ensured that it never was – and his social, to say nothing of his sexual activities, were also decidedly hectic. It was around this time that he became involved – according to his memoirs – with "a Great Big Star" who swept him off his feet, took him to New York, kept him away from his studio and his obligations thereto, got him into serious trouble with Sam Goldwyn and then, having all the clout of a Great Big Star, persuaded Goldwyn to forgive him.

Now there are cynical people who maintain that this lady never really existed and that Niven had invented the whole episode because it made a very good story. But others, more trusting perhaps in the author's veracity, have speculated ever since the book was published as to her identity. Niven himself, a gentleman to the end, refused ever to name her and it seemed that the secret may have gone with him to the grave. But my own investigations have perhaps cast a little light on her identity.

Since his early days in Hollywood Niven had remained a close friend of Al Weingand who was, in turn, a close friend of Ronald Colman. And with Colman Weingand had acquired San Ysidro, a ranch near Santa Barbara in southern California, which they had turned into a hotel-cum-weekend resort. It was, and still is, an extremely comfortable and respectable place but in the 1930s it was also used by the Hollywood movie colony as a kind of discreet fornicatorium, a quiet little spot in which they could conduct illicit, or anyway extra-marital, love affairs. And Niven, being among those who took advantage of this facility, was wont to go there with a lady who might, conceivably, have been the Great Big Star of his memoirs . . .

Weingand said: "There was quite a lot of frolicking at the ranch and David some-times came up with an attractive girl . . ." Yes – and no doubt he turned up with many an attractive girl but there was, surely, one attractive girl in particular . . .

"Well," said Weingand, "there was and they had quite a romance going on at the time. Merle Oberon was a very popular and new actress then and she and David would come up and spend a few days or a weekend at the ranch. I thought that would end up in a marriage. It was a serious affair, not just a shack-up deal – and we hotel men get to know the difference."

So then did he believe that Miss Oberon, the wife at the time of Sir Alexander Korda, was the "Great Big Star" of the memoirs? "I think so. I personally know of no other."

It's true that to describe Merle Oberon as a "Great Big Star" in 1936 would have been to stretch the point a little. But she was certainly a star – a much bigger star than Niven – and she became an even greater star later on.

Well, whether or not Miss Oberon was the Great Big Star of Niven's reminiscences she definitely shared his bed at San Ysidro – not, in truth, that this made her in any way unique, for by all accounts enough women must have shared his bed in those carefree bachelor days of the 1930s to have worn a groove in his mattress. By 1938, at which time he had appeared with some degree of noticeable effect in more than twenty films, he had set up home with the glorious but ill-fated Errol Flynn, who by then was separated from his wife, Lily Damita. The house they occupied was rented from Rosalind Russell who, knowing her tenants well, immediately dubbed it "Cirrhosis-by-the-Sea". In fact, it was in Beverly Hills and not really by the sea at all, unless you are prepared to concede the fact that the Pacific Ocean is only a fast twenty-minute drive away along Sunset Boulevard.

By Niven's own admission the house rapidly became "a hotbed of fun and bad behaviour". Booze and women flowed in equal abundance and if most of the women flowed towards Flynn, who was an acknowledged star, there were still enough leftovers and Flynn-discards to keep the more modest Niven ticking over quite happily. Miraculously, he even had enough strength left after the boozing and the bedding to make five films in 1939, among them *Wuthering Heights* with, significantly

In Paper Tiger *in 1975.*

or not, Merle Oberon and *Raffles*, another of his comparatively few top-starring pictures in which he portrayed the cricket-playing, upper-class burglar.

But before that year was out the drinking and the womanising had to be shelved, at least temporarily – as indeed did the film-making – because war had broken out in Europe and Niven had volunteered to take part in it.

At this point, in order to get some idea of the weight of the man, it's worth considering his position. He was twenty-nine years old, had appeared in twenty-two films and while by no means a star was surely quivering on the brink of stardom. He was leading a comfortable, even – by most people's standards – a luxurious life; there was no compulsion on him whatsoever to volunteer for active service; most of his British contemporaries in Hollywood signally failed to do so and his employer, Sam Goldwyn, strongly urged him against any such course of action. And yet, without hesitation, he immediately made plans to abandon his career and return to England to fight. Now why did he do that?

In his excellent book *Niven's Hollywood*, Tom Hutchinson provides as plausible an explanation as any: "There was a debt of honour to his own father killed during the first war and there was the irony of all those mock heroic roles in movies with stories from British history. His Englishness had been a passport to work and social success in Hollywood: now that debt, too, was called in."

What it boiled down to then was that old-fashioned thing, patriotism. As Michael Trubshawe said: "David knew

rightly that (a) as an Englishman and (b) as a regular officer there was only one thing he could do. And it was not an easy thing to do because he'd got farther than the bottom rung of the ladder by then: he was halfway up and the money was coming in and the parts were coming in. No, good God, he came back to rejoin the army and do what he conceived to be his job."

On his return to London, however, he was not exactly welcomed with open arms and hearts; indeed his reception was such that in his place even the Prodigal Son might have been tempted to say, "oh, sod it", and leave home again. The press greeted him with jeers on the lines of "Relax! The Dawn Patrol is Here." At first he even encountered great difficulty in finding an outfit that would accept him. He rather fancied the RAF but they turned him down and finally he had to pull a few strings before he could even be taken on as a second-lieutenant by the Rifle Brigade.

What Niven actually did during the war has never been made quite clear, mainly because he was always extremely reticent about it. Certainly he appeared in two propaganda films, *The First of the Few* in 1942 and *The Way Ahead* in 1944, but he had quite definitely not returned to his homeland to do that kind of work. "Far, far from it," said Michael Trubshawe. "Good God, no. He turned down so many requests through his commanding officer to make films that in the end the adjutant-general, who was a very big shot indeed in the War Office, sent for him and said, 'Now, Niven, I want you to make a film, you know. Will you do it?' And David said, 'Well, sir, if I'd wanted to make films I'd have stayed in Hollywood.' And the adjutant-general said, 'I thought you'd say that, Niven. Well, if you won't volunteer I'm afraid I shall have to give you a direct order. Is that understood?' And David said, 'Sir, that is understood,' and he went and did what they asked him to do."

Reluctantly. Because Niven was essentially a fighting soldier. Apart from his time with the Rifle Brigade he was also attached briefly, though mysteriously, to military intelligence, before volunteering for the Commandoes, an outfit not generally known for its willingness to take on recruits strictly on the strength of their photogenic profiles and twinkling blue eyes. And with the Commandoes he appears to have been involved both with the Dieppe raid of 1942 and the Normandy landings of 1944. Whatever he was doing in the army he was obviously doing it well because he ended the war as a colonel and was awarded the American Legion of Merit for his work in communications between the British and US invasion forces.

Afterwards he rarely spoke about the war, although he did admit to his son David that he was "scared to death for much of the time and just glad to get out alive and in one piece". And even Private Peter Ustinov who, in 1944, served in the curious dual capacity of Niven's batman and co-author with Eric Ambler of the script of *The Way Ahead* knew little of what else Niven had done between 1939 and 1945. He told Ustinov some tales of the army but "you could never quite believe them because they were such good stories."

But apart from ending the war as a colonel, Niven also ended it as a married man and a father. First at the Café de Paris then later at (a) a lunchtime concert at the National Gallery or (b) in a slit trench during an air raid at RAF Heston, depending on which of Niven's own conflicting accounts you choose to believe, he had met a WAAF officer named Primula (known as Primmie) Rollo, the daughter of Lady Kathleen and Bill Rollo. The slit-trench meeting makes the better story because, according to Niven, he jumped into it and landed on Primmie's dog which promptly and not surprisingly bit his backside. Ten days later he and the dog's owner were married with Trubshawe as their best man. The year was 1940. In December 1942 David Jr. was born and his godfather Noel Coward presented him with a silver cocktail shaker on which was inscribed: "Because, my Godson dear, I rather/Think you'll turn out like your father." It was not perhaps the kind of gift for which the average baby can find an immediate use but no doubt it came in handy later.

However, by August 1945 Niven was demobbed and the following morning at 5 a.m. was on the set at Denham studios to make what is still one of his most enchanting films, *A Matter of Life and Death*. It was another loan-out by Sam Goldwyn who had forgiven him for breaking his contract for such a frivolous reason as a war and had generously given him a new, five-year contract at a handsome figure.

Niven, aged thirty-five and worried about his future having made only two films in six years, was properly grateful for this continued faith. When the movie was completed (and it was chosen as the first Royal Command Film, as well as proving a success on both sides of the Atlantic) Niven, now a father for the second time – for Jamie had been born in November 1945 – set sail for America to fulfil his obligations to Goldwyn. Just as he had arrived to a cool reception in England in 1939, so he departed with an equally unfriendly send-off from the Inland Revenue, who neatly deprived him of virtually all his savings before he departed.

There now followed what, in retrospect, must have been very nearly the worst period in his life; perhaps the last few years when he was struggling against a most debilitating illness were harder but the year or so after his return to Hollywood had a vivid nightmare quality of its own. In the first place he had been warned by David Selznick that he would find changes – new directors and producers, new, ambitious young actors, new competition. In the second place the immediate films he was offered – and which he accepted gratefully – were *The Perfect Marriage* with Loretta Young and *Magnificent Doll* with Ginger Rogers, and what they had in common was that both were the purest tosh. Hardly a hero's welcome and depressing enough on their own but far worse was to come.

In May 1946, Niven and Primmie went to a party given by Tyrone Power. There was a barbecue and then Power and his

With Primmie, his first wife, at Jamie, their younger son's, christening.

guests, noted and presumably sophisticated movie stars, decided to play sardines. In the course of the game Primmie opened the door to what she thought was a cupboard, stepped through and fell down a flight of stairs into a cellar. She was taken, unconscious, to hospital where the next day, after an emergency brain operation, she died. She was twenty-five years old.

It could be argued that Niven never truly recovered from her death, a death which as Peter Ustinov said was "so absurd and so dreadful. The idea of dying when you're trying to find a place to play hide and seek is really so asinine that it makes one angry with fate. She was obviously very suited to him."

Michael Trubshawe, who perhaps knew her better than any of Niven's other friends, said of her: "She was an absolute darling. She was kind, she was fun and she was a wonderful mum. They were tremendously happy and her death absolutely shook the old boy to the core, all the stuffing was knocked out of him."

Niven's sons were obviously far too young at the time of their mother's death to have any real memory of her but David Jr. said: "Every time he spoke about her it was with tremendous love and affection." Jamie said: "He always spoke of her as a fabulous woman but he didn't really talk much about her, maybe because it was something that really bothered him a great deal. We all got the message that he loved her and we all got the message that it hurt him terribly when she died. But he didn't talk about her all the time. In fairness, you know, he was married for thirty-five years after that to another woman and I'm not sure that always talking about your first wife would have been terribly well received at home."

Niven's immediate response to the loss of Primmie was to turn to his friends. He rang Ann Todd, who was in New York, and asked her to fly out to stay with him and this she did. "It was extraordinary to see him. He became very bitter against life and fate and he was in a very, very bad state."

Ann Todd stayed with him for two or three weeks and after that it was Douglas Fairbanks and his wife who offered comfort and hospitality. Fairbanks was godfather to James Niven and of Primmie he said: "She was charming, absolutely charming.

Very pretty, typical English rose, very sweet – absolutely adorable." When Niven felt that he couldn't contemplate staying any longer in the house where he and Primmie had lived he left his sons with their nanny and took refuge with the Fairbankses. "He stayed for weeks and weeks and my wife actually answered all the letters of condolence that came to him because he couldn't face it. He was terribly distressed and remained so for a very, very long time."

Obviously in time the sharpest and most immediate distress passed but, in Roderick Mann's opinion, something of it remained even until the end of Niven's life. "He would talk to *me* about her, anyway. I think he fantasised about how it would have been if she'd lived."

But when, at last, Niven recovered from those first deep pains of grief there was work to return to – though he could have found little consolation in that. *The Other Love*, with Barbara Stanwyck, and *The Bishop's Wife*, with Cary Grant and Loretta Young, were both stinkers but even they seemed more than acceptable compared with *Bonny Prince Charlie*, which he made in 1948 on loan to Alexander Korda. Niven had no wish to be connected with this enterprise. In the first place a return to Britain presented him with tax problems and in the second place, being no fool, he could recognise a potential disaster when it loomed up before him and a disaster was what *Bonny Prince Charlie* turned out to be, taking up almost a year of his life and causing one of the less caustic critics to observe that the star looked about as comfortable as "a goldfish in a haggis". But despite his misgivings he had no choice in the matter since, by the terms of his contract, he was more or less obliged to go where Goldwyn sent him.

Still, the film could not be accounted a total loss because one day on the set he met Hjordis Tersmeden, a Swedish model and aspiring actress. Niven described this encounter as a "*coup de foudre*" or, to put it more simply, love at first sight, which is indeed what it must have been for ten days later – shades of his first marriage – on January 13th, 1948, they were married at Chelsea Registry Office, Michael Trubshawe again serving as best man.

"It must be admitted," said Trubshawe, "that Hjordis was very, very beautiful – an absolute knockout – and David succumbed." Nevertheless the speed of the marriage rather took the best man aback. "I think he was what you might call 'caught on the rebound' – you know what I mean?"

Douglas Fairbanks, on the other hand, said that he had been hoping that Niven would remarry. "He was a fish out of water; he was lonesome."

So with a new and beautiful wife to assuage his loneliness Niven returned to Hollywood – to "the Pink House", the home he had bought for Primmie but which she had never lived to occupy, and to more indifferent films. Worst of all, the ribald reception given to *Bonny Prince Charlie* notwithstanding, he was lent again to Korda to make *The Elusive Pimpernel*, which many perceptive critics believed to be even more dreadful than the previous Korda epic. *The Times* was so concerned about it as to say that "film audiences are in danger of forgetting what a really accomplished actor Mr. Niven is." Nor were things any better when he returned to Hollywood to find himself on loan again, this time to an American independent company, to make a frightful turkey called *A Kiss for Corliss* with Shirley Temple. The truest criticism of it came from Niven himself who described it as "a disastrous teenage potboiler".

By this time, however, he could take no more. Certainly he had been working regularly since his return from the war but to what end? His reputation seemed to grow increasingly tattered with each successive film and so he decided to rid himself of Samuel Goldwyn, a task which must have appeared unflatteringly easy. He went to see Goldwyn to say he wished to end the contract and Goldwyn said, "Okay". Now to some extent he had been egged on to do this by vague promises of employment from various hotshot producers but once he had done the deed he discovered, as many another actor had discovered in a similar position, that the hotshot producers suddenly remembered that, actually, they didn't really have any work for an unemployed freelance.

He was therefore firmly in the middle of the worst phase of his career, a time when some people even spoke darkly of him as "box-office poison", though it was not Niven, who always gave of his best no matter how dire the part, that was poisonous: it was the films which he had perforce to accept – films like *The Toast of New Orleans* and *Happy Go Lovely*, in both of which he was called upon to drift around looking elegant and quizzical, which isn't much of a contribution at any time. He was even so desperate to re-establish himself that he made a mildly disastrous venture on to Broadway, co-starring with Gloria Swanson in a flop called *Nina*. After that there were more films – *Soldiers Three* (from the story by Kipling – a long, long way from the story by Kipling), *The Lady Says No!* and *Appointment with Venus* – but all of them mediocre at best.

One explanation for the fact that he plunged desperately, if not happily, into a succession of movies which might quite easily have wrecked the career of a less resilient actor, was provided by his son, David Jr: "The first reason that would come to mind is the fact that maybe he needed the scratch. It helped pay the rent and keep food in all our mouths and clothes on our little tiny bodies. So I think, quite honestly, that a lot of it was work done just to make ends meet." Furthermore Niven had a pretty rich lifestyle to maintain. "I mean, he did everything first class; he didn't stint on anything. He always had lovely homes and plenty of people looking after those homes and plenty of people who were being entertained around those homes."

Jamie Niven said: "He always had that wonderful expression that he used about the films he made: first of all, who's in it? Second of all, where is it? Third of all, when is it? And last of all, how much?" But that came later, when he was back at or around the top again. In the late 1940s and the early 1950s, the first two questions were luxuries he couldn't afford – when and how much? were the only important factors.

Nevertheless, things began to improve considerably with *The Moon is Blue*, a most risqué comedy for the time (the mention of a girl's virginity caused the raised eyebrows of shock in the censor's viewing room), directed by Otto Preminger. Niven's performance as a suave seducer reminded cinema audiences (and no doubt readers of *The Times*) that he was indeed an accomplished actor. And the film's wide success enabled him to alternate between Hollywood and Europe (where, for instance, he made *The Love Lottery* and *Carrington VC*) not as a peripatetic mummer frantic for work but

In Separate Tables *with Deborah Kerr. He was not sure he could play the role – but it won him an Oscar anyway.*

as a star of some international renown. And in 1956 that renown became even greater when he appeared as Phineas Fogg in Mike Todd's truly mammoth production of *Around the World in Eighty Days*, certainly the most expensive film (when you take comparative costs into consideration) in which he had ever appeared and one of the remarkably few in which he was cast as the undoubted star.

It's one of the odder facts of Niven's career that although he was widely regarded as a star he was not, in fact, a star at all, if you accept the definition that a star is one whose name invariably appears at the head of the billing. If you look at a list of Niven's films you will find, far more often than not, that his name appears third or fourth. Even after *Around the World . . .*, which won the Oscar for the year's best film, he was next to be seen supporting Ava Gardner and Stewart Granger in *The Little Hut* and though he headed the cast in *The Silken Affair* he was soon back in a supporting role in *Oh Men! Oh Women!*, whose stars were Dan Dailey and Ginger Rogers.

I suppose the two actors with whom Niven is most often compared and with whom he is frequently bracketed are Ronald Colman (as whose successor Sam

Goldwyn originally saw him) and Cary Grant, an even greater master of light comedy than Niven himself. But Colman and Grant were stars by any definition while Niven, though certainly a star as far as the public was concerned, was actually regarded by the studios as a kind of prince of supporting players.

Still, by the mid-1950s Niven was, if not exactly at the top then well within hailing distance of it, a position he retained with the occasional upward and downward lurch for the rest of his career. By then, too, he had inserted his foot pretty firmly in television's doorway by forming, along with Dick Powell and Charles Boyer, Four Star Playhouse, which for a good many years was prolific in making films for TV.

In 1958 Niven achieved what was for him, and is for any Hollywood actor, the pinnacle of his career when he played the seedy Major Pollock in the screen version of Terence Rattigan's play, *Separate Tables*. Again it's worth noting that although he played one of the four equally important roles in the film, the main stars were Rita Hayworth and Burt Lancaster – or at least those were the names most widely used to sell the picture to cinema audiences.

The story, briefly, tells of two couples, Hayworth and Lancaster, and Niven and Deborah Kerr (with whom he had earlier appeared in *Bonjour Tristesse*). The chief link between the two pairings is that all of them are staying in the same private hotel in Bournemouth. Niven's was a very serious role, something he had not really essayed for some time and Deborah Kerr said: "I think he was a tiny bit scared. I remember him coming to me and saying, 'You know, chum, I don't know whether I can do this. I mean, this is serious stuff, isn't it?' But, of course, he did it superbly. Superbly."

Delbert Mann, who directed the film, recalled that originally all four parts were to be played by Laurence Olivier and Vivien Leigh, with Olivier also directing. But that fell through and Lancaster and Hayworth took over two of the roles, with Niven and Kerr taking the others. "I would think," said Mann, "that David's was the most untypical role he ever attempted. He was extremely nervous about it: it was a big challenge for him but whatever insecurities he might have had about the role he covered with the joviality and jollity that were so much a part of his character. I do know

230

that he worried about the part a great deal and would come to me and ask questions and we'd have to go off in a corner and have intimate discussions about the role and the background to it." But against that as an actor to work with he was . . . "Absolutely adorable, wonderful. He was a total, total professional. He came prepared; he had something to offer in rehearsal and on the set and he was a giving, loving, caring actor. He gave to the other actors, he was open to the director's suggestions. It was for me a kind of ideal working relationship, the likes of which I have had very few times in my career."

Delbert Mann believed that the winning of an Oscar would, nevertheless, have come as something of a shock to Niven. "I have no idea whether he expected to win it. I would seriously doubt it, knowing David and his habit of putting himself down. But for my taste it was certainly well deserved."

Deserved or not – and Niven's opposition in 1958 was Tony Curtis in *The Defiant Ones*, Paul Newman in *Cat on a Hot Tin Roof*, Sidney Poitier in *The Defiant Ones* and Spencer Tracy in *The Old Man and the Sea* – he carried off the Academy Award for best actor.

Speaking of Niven the man, Delbert Mann said: "I felt very relaxed with David. I felt I got to know him quite well. But I'm not really sure I knew what was going on in his mind."

That kind of comment was made by many others who also felt relaxed with Niven and believed they knew him well. There was always a part of him that was intensely private, that was masked even from the people closest to him. John Mortimer said that was one of the things he liked most about Niven and was what "made him such a good actor to play in *Separate Tables*, to play the sort of part in which you're always cheerful on the surface but underneath you're not. David certainly had terrific sadness in his life but he didn't burden others with it."

David Niven Jr. explained that part of his father's character by saying: "I think it was to do with the generation he belonged to. He felt that his problems were his own and why should he bore other people with them. Everybody has problems and his life was certainly not without them but he felt that he was best equipped to figure out how to solve them and he didn't see why he should cry on other people's shoulders."

But if Delbert Mann was unsure how well he really knew Niven the man he had no doubts at all about Niven the actor. "I would rate him absolutely the highest. I worked with a lot of very, very good actors and I would place David absolutely in the top category."

Delbert Mann's encomium is probably the highest Niven ever received. His own tendency was to disparage his acting ability with such rhetorical questions as "Can you imagine being wonderfully overpaid for dressing up and playing games?" He even told his sons to answer any criticisms of his ability that might be proffered by their schoolmates by retorting: "Well, he's a very, very bad actor but he absolutely loves doing it." In truth, he was a long way removed from being a bad actor. First of all, said Deborah Kerr, he took his acting "a great deal more seriously than he appeared to do". And beyond that . . . "He was very much better than he gave himself credit for and, of course, he was a superb comedian."

A comedian, yes – specifically a light comedian, which makes his Oscar for the essentially "straight" performance in *Separate Tables* something of a curiosity. To Douglas Fairbanks he was "an *excellent* light comedian"; to Bryan Forbes, who directed him in his penultimate film, he was "in many respects a very under-estimated actor"; to John Mortimer (who wrote the script for *The Guns of Darkness* in 1962) he was "wonderful. He learned the technique and the throwaway part of film acting perfectly"; and Peter Ustinov, a little less fulsomely, remarked: "I think he regarded the whole thing as a job but I think, too, he began to regard himself as an artist. He was very conscious of his limitations, he knew what he could do and what he couldn't do and within that he certainly was an artist. He knew when he would like to do a scene again because he wasn't satisfied and so on."

On that subject, the dispassionate (albeit affectionate) views of Jamie Niven are rather interesting: "I don't think he's going to go down as the world's greatest actor. I don't think he can be compared with Olivier and Burton and Richardson and people of that kind. I think he was a very competent professional and he enjoyed his work. But he didn't let it get blown out of proportion; he treated it very much as a nine to five kind of job and he didn't bring the work home with him. He thought he was a competent light comedian, which would probably be the general assessment, and he thought he was lucky because he did something that he enjoyed and that he was relatively good at. There were moments, I think, when he thought he was very good. He thought he was good when he made *Around the World in Eighty Days* and *Separate Tables* but he was very self-effacing; he wasn't an arrogant man. So therefore he probably felt that he wasn't as good as some of the great actors and I think that's right, I think that's a fair statement. I don't think he was – but he was very competent and he was a tremendous professional."

Strangely there is much to be said for all these somewhat disparate points of view. When the part was right for him, Niven *could* be wonderful; he *was* an excellent comedian and *was* a consummate professional. But, as an actor certainly, he did not have the stuff of greatness in him: what he sold, far more than technical virtuosity, was the personality of David Niven, an immensely attractive personality, and for most people that was enough.

But some time after he picked up the Oscar for *Separate Tables* and with success now dancing attendance on his career, Niven encountered a temporary setback in his private life. In July 1959 he and Hjordis decided to live apart. The fault, he acknowledged, was his: his new-found status as an Academy Award winner had drawn him temporarily into the familiar trap of putting his career above all else and when, later on, he said that at one stage he had become rather bigheaded it was probably this period that he was referring to.

The separation, however, lasted for only three months and a little while after the reconciliation – in fact in the spring of 1960 – the couple decided to move to Europe. One reason for this was that Niven was a little disenchanted with Hollywood, feeling that he had seen the best of it in the pre-war years. This, of course, may well have had much to do with the fact that he was now fifty and beginning to feel, as many people do, that the world was a better place when he was young. But the main reason for the move was financial. David Jr. said: "He was in the ninety per cent tax bracket and he really didn't have very much money. He'd done a lot of pictures but he had very little in the bank. As a matter of fact, as he explained it to us, the reason he decided to leave was that he didn't even have enough money to repaint the Pink House. So with the money he was going to have to raise to have the Pink House repainted he was able to buy a house in Switzerland where he was able to keep ninety per cent of his earnings instead of giving ninety per cent to the government."

Actually, it was Deborah Kerr who helped persuade him to choose Switzerland rather than some other European tax haven. She and her husband, Peter Viertel, lived at Klosters and one day on a visit to Hollywood they found Niven in a low mood bemoaning the fact that everything there seemed to be going down the drain, including his bank balance. "What does one do?" he asked. "Where does one go? You can't save a nickel here." And it was at this point that the Viertels planted the idea of Switzerland in his mind. Indeed, he rather took to Switzerland – he enjoyed the social life and he enjoyed ski-ing, at which he was not particularly adept, although he formed his own ski-ing club, its emblem a ham on skis, of which he was the sole member.

And speaking of members . . . John Mortimer's favourite Niven anecdote is of the time he was ski-ing downhill and discovered when it was too late to stop that he had forgotten to zip up his pants. "His vital organs became frozen," said Mortimer, "and he looked down and saw what he described as a very small, Eton-blue acorn. He was in terrible agony and arrived in the square at St Moritz doubled up in pain." With great presence of mind, however, Niven bundled himself into a taxi and asked to be taken to the nearest bar. Others in a similar predicament might have gone to a hospital but not Niven. Shuffling into the bar he demanded of the barman: "What do you do when your balls freeze?" The barman suggested a double brandy. Again others in like circumstances might have drunk the stuff but not Niven. He took the double brandy into the men's room and lowered his frozen parts into it and he was just beginning to thaw out when various other people came in to use the facilities and discovered the great actor apparently urinating into a brandy glass.

But the episode of the frozen balls came

later. Long before then he had made one of his better films of this period, *The Guns of Navarone*, in 1961 and he and Hjordis had adopted two daughters, Kristina and Fiona. According to Michael Trubshawe: "They wanted a family of their own but Hjordis was unable to have children." The result was that, since she didn't work herself, she had little to occupy her time, especially when Niven was busy on a film. "And then, it's the old story, David would come home tired and wanting to put his feet up – the old carpet-slipper treatment – and Hjordis would want to go out. In the end I think they decided for the sake of both of them, and especially for Hjordis, to adopt a couple of children to keep her happy and busy during the daytime. That's how it came about and it was highly successful."

Niven, by all accounts, was as loving and attentive a father to his two new daughters as he had been to his sons. But the two boys, though welcoming the girls into the family, were not unaffected by the change.

James Niven said: "I got on very well with Hjordis at the beginning but after the adoption our relationship changed a lot – not from my standpoint but from hers. I think from that moment on the relationship deteriorated enormously: she just wouldn't talk to you, she simply cut you dead all the time and that was a tricky thing to live with. I coped with it as best I could and we would try to make a joke of it. There were days that were good and days that were bad but there's no question – her relationship with me changed dramatically the day she adopted a child."

Perhaps that's understandable – a woman coping with two young children of her own (if not biologically her own then at least hers by choice) is likely to have less time and attention to spare for two teenage stepsons. Niven himself was unaware of the changed circumstances vis-à-vis Jamie and Hjordis, partly because nobody told him about it and partly because the situation was more or less resolved quite quickly when Jamie went away to boarding school and later to university. "So I really didn't have to see very much of her after that." As for the girls . . . "Dad was terrific with them, a fabulous father."

Meanwhile, Niven's career rolled on – a couple of Italian films were followed by the likes of *55 Days in Peking*, *The Pink Panther*

Niven's second family – with Hjordis and their adopted daughters, Kristina and Fiona.

and *Bedtime Story*, in which he appeared with Marlon Brando. None of them was particularly memorable, although Niven's own performances were as gilt-edged as ever. And so the next dramatic change in his career came in 1971 with the publication of the first volume of his memoirs, *The Moon's a Balloon*. It was Roderick Mann who started him on this enterprise after years of listening delightedly to his anecdotes. Niven was even more than a raconteur of near genius . . . "He was a great mental gymnast in that he would take some quite ordinary anecdote and spice it up and the stories were so good that I used to say 'You've *got* to write a book.' Well, he didn't for two or three years but finally he sat down and in longhand he began to write." When the book was finished and the working title, "Three Sides of a Square" had been changed to *The Moon's a Balloon*, Mann took it to his own agent and then to Hamish Hamilton the publishers, who were delighted with it. But then a rather considerable problem arose: it was suddenly remembered that some fifteen years earlier Niven had written a novel called *Round the Ragged Rocks* and was obliged to offer any new work first to the publishers of that book. Unfortunately, by the time this was discovered he had already signed a contract with Hamish Hamilton. What to do? Well, according to Roderick Mann, Niven wrote a letter to the publishers of the novel, a small American firm, purporting to come from his agent and saying, in effect: the actor David Niven

233

has sent us a heavy tome of theatrical reminiscences (in itself enough, as Roderick Mann, said "to strike terror in the flinty hearts of any publishers"). And the letter went on: we understand you have a two-book deal with Mr. Niven but we hesitate to send this tome to you without your express wishes, since it's very heavy indeed and we estimate it weighs about five pounds.

"And this went on and on," said Mann, "and in the end the Americans said, 'No way – we don't want to know.' So David was off the hook."

The Moon's a Balloon was immediately and immensely successful, much to Niven's own surprise, as indeed was its successor *Bring on the Empty Horses* and from then on he regarded himself as a writer as much as an actor. Both his sons say he found the act of writing "terribly, terribly difficult". He could neither type nor dictate so everything had to be written in longhand, a considerable task when, as David Jr. said, "the words didn't come easily and being the sort of perfectionist he was he rewrote and rewrote and edited and re-edited many times before he handed the manuscript to the publisher."

Nevertheless, it was his writing that gave him the greater satisfaction, possibly because he regarded it as work, unlike acting which he always declared was simply fun. David Jr. said: "The satisfaction he got from his acting came when he received his Academy Award: there at least he was acknowledged by his peers. The success he got from writing possibly gave him more pleasure because it was something that he did all by himself. Also it gave him a whole new lease of life and he was thrilled, absolutely thrilled, that people wanted to buy his books."

It's worth noting, too, that the success of his books owed more to the quality of the writing than to the name of the author, useful though that was in publicising and selling them. John Mortimer and Peter Ustinov, both excellent writers themselves, pay tribute to his talent and Ustinov believes that "he'll be remembered for his books almost more than his films because films always date, whether you like it or not. He had a very meticulous eye for the comic and the absurd."

These gifts were not quite so apparent in his novel, *Go Slowly, Come Back Quickly* but they were outstanding in the two volumes of reminiscences. Yes, but how true were the amazing stories he told therein? Roderick Mann believed, as I suspect most people do, that they were "slightly made better. I'd had adventures with David and then years later I would hear him telling the story and I'd think: Well, I know that, I was there, that wasn't the way it happened. But it was much better the way he told it. He was just incapable of being boring or allowing himself to be bored."

And so with his books being constantly reprinted, with film offers continuing to come along at the rate of at least one a year and with the producers of television chat shows eagerly seeking his services as a raconteur, Niven enjoyed perhaps the most fecund decade of his career. But it's one of the less agreeable characteristics of fate that there is always a price to be paid for success – or, as the Americans put it in a slightly different context, "There's no such thing as a free lunch." The bill for the apparently free lunch that Niven had been enjoying for most of the 1970s was presented in 1979 and it was a very stiff bill indeed.

He was in France playing his last important film role in *Better Late than Never*, directed by Bryan Forbes, when the illness which, eventually, was to kill him first became apparent. Bryan Forbes said: "I became aware of it when we were doing a scene on the beach and he suddenly said, 'Forbesy, I can't run. My legs won't work . . .'" And then his voice began to fail. "He couldn't articulate certain words . . . he found it very difficult to get his mouth round certain words, which is the most terrible thing for an actor."

About the same time he appeared on the *Michael Parkinson Show* when some people thought he was drunk and others, more charitably and knowing Niven was too professional ever to appear drunk in public, suggested to Jamie that something was wrong. Jamie phoned his father and said: "I saw a tape of the show and, I've got to be frank with you, aren't you concerned?" It was then that Niven admitted that he was indeed concerned and put forward the theory that he had suffered a stroke. Soon after that he underwent the tests that showed him to be a victim not of a stroke but of motor neurone disease.

Niven had never much liked the idea even of growing old. He accepted, of course, that it was inevitable but, according to Roderick Mann, he used to say: "I have a vision of myself as a young man of twenty-five and then I see this old poop prancing about on the screen and I can't bear it." The idea of being not simply old but infirm was almost intolerable to him. "I've always thought," he wrote in a letter to his publisher, "that was reserved for old farts but I sense now that young farts of seventy-two are coming into the firing line!"

That was in 1982 when he was close to the end; in the intervening years since 1979 he had fought with great courage against the debilitating effects of his illness. What affected him most of all was the inability to communicate. At one point he said to John Mortimer: "I think it's having talked too much all my life that's given me this voice."

Jamie Niven said: "He coped with it amazingly well and with a certain amount of humour. You've got to remember that this is a disease that is psychologically frightening because your mind is fine but your body is melting away and you know it and there's nothing you can do about it. And so you have to deal with the fact that you're dying slowly and that your ability to communicate with your fellow man is eroding."

Niven continued to write to his friends, first in his own hand until – in his own phrase – he was "fucked up gripwise, as they say on Madison Avenue", and then by dictating to a secretary.

In 1982 he even appeared, for the last time, in a film – *The Trail of the Pink Panther*, quite the worst of that lengthy series. When he was making this his voice was so far gone that his part was dubbed later by the American impressionist Rich Little. Had he been fit he would have strolled through the role; as it was it must have been unbearably arduous for him. So why did he do it? God knows, he didn't need the money. Perhaps he believed that if he was still able to work he could not be, no matter what the doctors said, as ill as he seemed. Or perhaps as Jamie Niven put it: "He'd committed to make the movie before he realised how ill he was. I don't think it was an ego thing – that he wanted to make his last movie. I think it was just typical that he'd made a commitment and the financing had been organised and he felt that he shouldn't let the producer down."

David Niven on his seventieth birthday in 1980.

When the filming was completed Niven retired to his second home in the south of France and, in effect, waited for death. Roderick Mann went to visit him two months before he died. "That was awful. I almost couldn't bear to go. Roger Moore had been to see him and said, 'You've got to go because he's asking to see you. Just bite the bullet and go,' so I went and it was horrendous because he couldn't speak. I literally couldn't understand what he was saying and he had shrivelled in his clothes. And we went and sat in the garden and I just looked at him and he looked at me and he smiled – he was twinkling away, you know, still, because the brain had stayed active. But it was very grim and very sad. And then when I left he stood in the drive and waved, right until the car was out of sight. He knew I wouldn't see him again and I knew it, too."

David Niven died on July 29th, 1983, in his home in Switzerland at the age of seventy-three. He had chosen to go to Switzerland, according to his son Jamie, "because he felt he could breathe better up in the mountains". Right to the end he refused to go on any kind of life-support system and when that end came, Jamie said, "I was happy for him because it was over and I was saddened because I had lost him. I felt that he was at peace and that was good because he had suffered so much."

Hjordis, his wife of thirty-five years, was not with him when he died. She was herself under considerable strain at the time and since his death she has lived almost as a recluse at their home in the south of France. To David Jr. she said that she would never again visit the house in Switzerland because it was there that Niven had died.

The funeral, held in Switzerland, was,

235

as Jamie put it, "a madhouse. It was a tiny little village and 350 photographers and most of the local people came. But it was a beautiful service and very touching. But it was a very hard thing to do – to bury your father in front of 350 photographers who don't let you alone. You felt like you were sharing it with the whole world. It was not a very private moment for any of us. I'd never realised how popular he was, I'd never realised that he was loved by everyone as much as he was."

Two stories which may help to explain why Niven enjoyed such universal popularity. The first was told by John Mortimer, who one day had invited him to lunch at the Mortimer house in the home counties. "We were having lunch at one o'clock and my son arrived at half-past twelve and said, 'I think I've seen David Niven about four miles away, walking down a country lane.' And what had happened was that he had arrived too early and was too shy to knock at the door and so he'd gone for a long walk to fill in the time, holding, as I remember it, a large pot of caviar that he had brought as a gift for us."

The second, and even more revealing, anecdote was told by Jamie Niven. "After he died we received some wonderful flowers from the porters at Terminal No. 1 at Heathrow Airport, with a card that said: 'To the finest gentleman who ever walked through these halls.' Some time after that I went to the terminal and thanked the head man there and asked him if there was anything particular that he remembered about my father. And he said, 'Absolutely. Your father had one man in particular who always used to take care of him here. One day there was a mad crowd of people in the place, just horrible, and your father jumped into his car and disappeared and didn't tip the man who looked after him. Well, the fellow thought that was a bit odd for Mr. Niven but he understood how it had happened and didn't worry about it. But forty-five minutes later your father walked back in to find the guy. He'd got halfway to London when he realised he hadn't tipped him and had come back to do so." Jamie added that this was "typical of the way he felt about people. He was humble. He wasn't a proud, arrogant, difficult man."

It was probably this kind of quality that made David Niven a star in the public mind and kept him a star even though he almost certainly appeared in more bad films than any other actor of similar stature. In nearly half a century he featured in eighty-nine pictures, in roles ranging from a cough and a spit to leading man, and very few of them made any noticeable contribution to the art of the cinema. He was indeed less an actor than a great screen personality; most of the time he simply played himself but that, granted his small but finely honed talent as a light comedian, was enough to save a multitude of mediocre films from total disaster.

John Mortimer felt that he had no illusions at all about himself as an actor. "I believe he thought it was all a huge joke – that he'd strayed into it from Central Casting because he hadn't anything better to do." Maybe. But there was undoubtedly more to him than that: he was the consummate professional, always on time, always word perfect. A man who truly believes that acting is a joke doesn't take that much trouble. Niven was proud of his craft but knew his limitations, although the ease and lightness of his touch on screen may have concealed a greater degree of talent than even he was aware of. At this stage, however, it hardly matters: what he left on screen was the indelible image of a hugely engaging character and I suspect that generations of movie-goers will continue to watch his films, bad though many of them are, simply because the very presence of Niven makes them feel better.

I believe that the truth about David Niven is simply this: no matter what he achieved as an actor or as a writer, his greatest success was as a man and that's probably the greatest success of all. Certainly it's the most difficult to achieve. To be spoken of, as he is, with universal affection is an extremely rare accomplishment. People who knew him remember him chiefly as a friend; they remember him laughing and causing laughter; they remember his loyalty and kindness, his modesty and his sensitivity to the needs of others. I could quote each of them at great length but perhaps the essence of what all of them said is best summed up in the words of John Mortimer: "He was a model of how people who are famous and who enjoy the terrific privilege of stardom or public acclaim should behave." As an epitaph it serves him well.

Index